THE
Unforgiving Minute

THE
Unforgiving Minute

A SOLDIER'S EDUCATION

Craig M. Mullaney

The Penguin Press
New York
2009

THE PENGUIN PRESS
Published by the Penguin Group
Penguin Group (USA) Inc., 375 Hudson Street, New York, New York 10014, U.S.A. • Penguin Group (Canada),
90 Eglinton Avenue East, Suite 700, Toronto, Ontario, Canada M4P 2Y3 (a division of Pearson Penguin
Canada Inc.) • Penguin Books Ltd, 80 Strand, London WC2R 0RL, England •
Penguin Ireland, 25 St Stephen's Green, Dublin 2, Ireland (a division of Penguin Books Ltd) •
Penguin Books Australia Ltd, 250 Camberwell Road, Camberwell, Victoria 3124, Australia (a division of
Pearson Australia Group Pty Ltd) • Penguin Books India Pvt Ltd, 11 Community Centre,
Panchsheel Park, New Delhi – 110 017, India • Penguin Group (NZ), 67 Apollo Drive, Rosedale,
North Shore 0632, New Zealand (a division of Pearson New Zealand Ltd) • Penguin Books
(South Africa) (Pty) Ltd, 24 Sturdee Avenue, Rosebank, Johannesburg 2196, South Africa

Penguin Books Ltd, Registered Offices: 80 Strand, London WC2R 0RL, England

First published in 2009 by The Penguin Press, a member of Penguin Group (USA) Inc.

Copyright © Craig M. Mullaney, 2009
All rights reserved

ISBN 978-1-59420-202-5

Printed in the United States of America
1   3   5   7   9   10   8   6   4   2

DESIGNED BY STEPHANIE HUNTWORK

For my brother, Gary, a warrior in every sense of the word

In memory of

CHAD FULLER

CHIEF

CHRIS

ROBERT OLSON

EVAN O'NEILL

ADAM THOMAS

AND

LUCAS WHITE

If you can fill the unforgiving minute
With sixty seconds' worth of distance run,
Yours is the Earth and everything that's in it,
And—which is more—you'll be a Man, my son!

—RUDYARD KIPLING, "If"

CONTENTS

I

Student

To someone who has never experienced danger, the idea is attractive rather than alarming. . . . Before you lies that golden prize, victory, the fruit that quenches the thirst of ambition. Can that be so difficult?

No, and it will seem even less difficult than it is.

CARL VON CLAUSEWITZ

1

Reception Day

In case of Sudden and Temporary Immersion, the Important
Thing is to keep the Head Above Water.

A. A. MILNE, *Winnie-the-Pooh*

"GET OFF MY BUS!" SCREAMED THE CADET IN CHARGE.
"You're not moving fast enough. Move it. Move it. *Move it!*" We stampeded
from the bus like a startled herd of wildebeest, clutching our small gym
bags with white-knuckled grips. As we poured into the hot July sunlight,
chiseled senior cadet cadre aligned our crooked ranks.

"Left, *face.*"

Forty eighteen-year-olds turned at different speeds toward another
white-starched cadet cadre. We must have looked ridiculous—a ragtag
collection of shorts, untucked T-shirts, and long hair.

"Drop your bags."

They landed on the pavement with a thud.

"You will now begin the administrative portion of your processing. Follow all instructions both quickly and quietly. During this process you will
pass water fountains. You are authorized and encouraged to use them. Do
you understand?"

I nodded my head with the others.

"Pick up your bags."

JULY 1, 1996, WAS STAMPED on my military record like a wine's vintage—
my "date of initial entry into military service." As my high school classmates

alternated between summer jobs, afternoons at the beach, and summer reading lists, I headed off to West Point, New York. R-Day, short for "Reception Day," was the first day of a six-week period of basic training. There was absolutely nothing hospitable about this first day of military indoctrination, beginning with an exercise in severing family bonds. After standing in a straggling line of twelve hundred would-be freshmen and their parents, I was herded into the basketball arena with another thirty "cadet candidates." I had ninety seconds to say good-bye to my parents.

After obeying my first military order, I marched up the stairs and through a set of double doors. Even before the door shut behind me, it became clear what my first year at West Point was going to be like.

"What are you looking at, candidate?" shouted a five-foot-five cadet. The volume of his voice was inconsistent with his height.

"Nothing."

"Aren't you going to call me sir?"

"Sir, yes, sir."

"Are you at the Naval Academy?"

"Sir, no, sir."

"Then stop making sir sandwiches, candidate. It's 'yes, sir' or 'no, sir.'" He lowered his voice to a vicious whisper. "What's your name, candidate?"

"Craig, sir."

"Is that your first name?" His eyes widened.

"Yes, sir."

"Do you think I care what your first name is? Do you think I want to be your friend?"

"No, sir."

"Just get out of my hallway. Move over to that table and fill out your tag."

"Yes, sir."

I hurried over and wrote my last name in big bold letters. The tag had a dozen boxes to check off as we were "processed" from civilians into military recruits. I hung it around my neck as instructed and boarded the school bus. I sat down on the plastic seat but was too cowed by my scolding to strike up any conversation. *What am I doing here?*

"STEP UP TO MY line. Do not step on my line. Do not step over my line. Step up to my line." A cadet glared at me under the black brim of a white service cap and swung his hand in front of his face, signaling that I should advance precisely to the line of demarcation pasted on the pavement in green tape. This was the first lesson in literal obedience.

He was the "Cadet in the Red Sash"—the first cadre member I needed to report to in order to join my company. I stood before him in a ludicrous uniform of newly issued cadet gym shorts, knee-high black socks, and Oxford low-quarter dress shoes. My head had been shorn of its five-inch locks, revealing a topography of old scars and virgin white scalp.

"Re-port," he bellowed at me from a distance of eighteen inches.

"New Cadet Mullaney reports to the . . . the . . ."

"Are you stuttering while you report?" His hot breath dried the sweat on my face.

"Yes, sir."

"Did I give you permission to stutter?"

"No, sir."

I began again: "New Cadet Mullaney . . ."

"Stop. What did you do wrong?" My newly bald scalp burned under the midday sun.

"Sir, I don't know."

"I don't know. I don't know," he repeated. "Is 'I don't know' one of your four responses?"

"No, sir."

"What are your four responses?" he asked, testing whether I remembered another cadet's instructions on answering questions.

"Yes, sir. No, sir. No excuse, sir. Sir, I do not understand."

"That's right, New Cadet. Why did you stutter? Did you not have sufficient time to practice?"

"I forgot, sir." I could almost see smoke billow out of his ears.

"'I forgot' is not one of your four responses. Try again."

"No excuse, sir," I responded correctly. I must have replied "No excuse, sir" a thousand times that first year, hammering into my head an acknowledgment of personal responsibility that eventually became second nature.

"Try again, New Cadet."

"Sir, New Cadet—"

"Aren't you going to ask to make a correction?"

"Yes, sir. Sir, may I make a correction?"

"Yes."

"Sir, New Cadet Mullaney reports to the Cadet in the Red Sash for the first time as ordered."

"Are you going to salute when you report?"

"Yes, sir. Sir, may I make a correction?"

"Make it."

I raised my fingertips to my eyebrow as I saluted and repeated my report.

"New Cadet, that is the sorriest salute I have seen today." I couldn't believe how many mistakes I was making. I am better than this, I told myself.

The red-sashed, barrel-chested cadet manipulated my arm into a better approximation of a West Point salute: fingers closed and extended in a straight line to my elbow, arm parallel to the ground, palm canted toward my eyes.

"Move out, New Cadet. I haven't got all day."

A line extended behind me, other sheep waiting for the slaughter. I picked up my laundry bag of new clothing items, ran up six flights of stairs, and walked briskly down the hall toward the room indicated on my tag. Inside the room were a coat closet, several dresser drawers, three bare desks and bookshelves, and three mattresses on metal frames. Other than the wooden gun rack, it could have been a dorm room anywhere. The linoleum floor, dull and drab, smelled of Lysol. For that matter, everything in the barracks smelled of Lysol. Outside the window a green parade field stretched to a copse of trees and a steep drop to the Hudson River, a half mile across. It wouldn't be such a long swim, I thought. Before I could introduce myself to my roommates, two knocks at the door preceded the entrance of a cadre member.

"Call the room to attention, dammit." I looked at his name tag. "You," he pointed at my chest, "the one eyeballing me."

"Room, atten-*hut*." We sprang to attention.

"You sound like a goddam Marine." He looked down at the tag still hanging around my neck. "Mullaney," he sneered, "do you think this is the goddam Marine Corps? There is no '*hut*' in the Army."

"Yes, sir."

"I'm Cadet Bellinger, as Mullaney here found out by investigation, and I am your squad leader. I am not your friend, your counselor, or your coach. Do you understand?"

"Yes, sir," we answered in unison.

"Say it like soldiers, goddam it."

"*Yes, sir.*"

"Much better," he said, satisfied for the moment. "I want you down there"—he pointed from the window down to the concrete pavement between our barracks and the parade field—"in five minutes. You will be wearing the uniform I am in right now. Do you see how I am wearing my uniform?"

"Yes, sir."

He strode out the door and slammed it behind him as we dove into our bags and assembled our uniforms in a flurry of brass buckles, black nylon socks, and gray trousers so abrasive that hair didn't grow on my thighs for the next four years.

WE STOOD IN A row under the shade of an elm tree in front of MacArthur Barracks. This was what the Army meant by a *formation*: any number of soldiers standing at attention and prepared for training, marching, or, more typically, waiting. We were being formed. The ten of us, sweating into new leather low-quarter shoes, would cohere over time into a more competent squad. I would soon learn the Rule of Four, a trick for remembering this strange new hierarchy. Sergeants with at least four years of experience lead squads in the Army. Four squads comprised a platoon, the smallest unit in the Army commanded by a commissioned officer. The focus of military training at West Point was to prepare the new lieutenants it graduated for just this role, to be platoon leaders. With seasoning, officers commanded at higher levels. Four platoons made a company, with around 150 soldiers and sergeants, which was led by a company commander, a captain. For most officers this was the highest level at which they would command before finishing their service. For officers who chose a career in the Army and earned promotions to colonel, they competed to command battalions (four companies) and brigades (four battalions). Only generals got the opportunity to lead entire divisions, such as the famed 82nd Airborne or 10th Mountain.

West Point was organized like a brigade. Cadets played the roles of sergeants and officers in order to give every cadet the opportunity to hone his or her leadership abilities. As new cadets, we were the privates. Our purpose was to follow, to obey, and to be *formed* in the image of our leaders. We had begun our transformation, reduced to a common denominator, at the barbershop. Now, dressed identically, it was time for us to learn how to walk again.

"I have two hours to teach you how to march like soldiers. Marching is what we do here. Every day. To breakfast. To lunch. After school. On Saturday mornings. Understood?"

"Yes, sir."

"Good," he continued. "Right, *face.*"

We turned to the right to form a column. Bellinger looked down at the ground in dismay. "We'll have to work on that. All right now, keeping your fists tight and your arms straight at your side, move your left arm forward and step forward with your right foot."

We moved forward with a lurch, frozen in midstride.

"Excellent. Now move your right arm and left foot."

Bellinger led us through twenty iterations of this choreographed awkward motion. I had always assumed marching was not much different from walking. I had never worried, for instance, about a bouncy step or gave much thought to swinging my arms exactly nine inches forward and six to the rear. I wondered how many cadre were laughing at us as we robo-walked across the Apron, looking like Monty Python's Ministry of Silly Walks.

"Not bad for starters. Let's add a beat." Bellinger began chanting: "Dum-dum-DUM-DUM-DUM, dum-dum-DUM-DUM-DUM."

Within fifty feet we were completely out of rhythm.

"Focus on the man in front of you. Do what he does."

This worked better, but I still walked like a marionette with no control over my own limbs. In the distance a bass drum beat a steady thump, perhaps alerted that over a thousand novices were trying to will their natural strides into an unfamiliar gait. The tallest had to walk at funeral pace and the shortest legs overreached comically. Around and around we marched—column left, *march*, column left, *march*, mark time, *march*, forward, *march*, dum-dum-DUM-DUM-DUM.

The sun began to sink behind the barracks as our newly constituted platoon streamed onto the parade field. Our families, having completed their own daylong indoctrination into military parenting, awaited us with cameras and binoculars. Our black shoes, peppered with fresh grass clippings, rooted us as firmly to the ground as the guidon flags planted in front of each company. We snapped to attention as the cadet commander introduced our class to the superintendent, Lieutenant General Daniel Christman, Class of 1965. In an address that was meant more for our families than us, he recounted the accomplishments of the nearly two hundred West Point classes that had preceded us. With hard work and perseverance, we, too, might join this Long Gray Line of distinguished alumni. The crowd applauded, and we raised our right hands at the command of our cadre. After swearing an oath to support the Constitution and obey the legal orders of superior officers, the band played the national anthem. A hum from our ranks grew louder as we sang along. In front of us, beyond the crowd, the American flag beat against the wind whipping between Storm King Mountain and Breakneck Ridge, down the Hudson River, and up the bluff where we stood—anxious, exhausted, and terrified. At the moment, joining the Long Gray Line seemed less important than surviving the first day.

With identical uniforms and shaved heads, we were virtually indistinguishable from one another. The transformation was a testament to the efficiency of military indoctrination. As the parade concluded, we marched past proud and nervous parents. At the command of eyes right, I searched for my own parents in vain. We turned our backs to the stands as the wind whistled past Trophy Point's cannons and drove us forward. We headed toward arched passageways marked with the names of hallowed battlefields. LEYTE GULF. CORREGIDOR. NORMANDY. Their chiseled letters faded into shadow. The ranks of white in front of me merged into gray stone, and a hail of terrifying commands grew louder with each perfectly measured step. The barracks, backlit by the setting sun, jutted out like boulders carved from the hill beyond. At its crest, two hundred feet above our uniforms of white and gray, stood the chapel—a mass of granite blocks soaring to a crenellated bell tower. It was impossible to imagine West Point built of anything other than granite and steel.

2

Beast

"Weren't you just ordered not to interrupt?" Major Metcalf inquired coldly.

"But I didn't interrupt, sir," Clevinger protested.

"No. And you didn't say 'sir,' either. Add that to the charges against him," Major Metcalf directed the corporal who could take shorthand. "Failure to say 'sir' to superior officers when not interrupting them."

JOSEPH HELLER, *Catch-22*

"WELCOME TO THE JUNGLE!" AT 5:30 A.M., SPEAKERS in the hallway blasted Guns N' Roses at concert volume. The door slammed open, and Bellinger flicked on our overhead lights. Temporarily blinded, I leaped out of bed. "Good morning! Outside. On the wall. Two minutes." Bellinger disappeared, and five seconds later another door slammed open. Crashes rippled down the hallway in beat with the bass line. It was appropriate to begin a military career in chaos, noise, and dumbstruck terror. This was the first full day of Beast Barracks, our six-week indoctrination into the Army. The three of us blinked and hoped we were all in the same bad dream. Throwing on T-shirts, gym shorts, and sneakers, we sprinted out into the hallway. Down the three-hundred-yard length of linoleum a whirlwind of new cadets scrambled to the bathroom urinals and dodged marauding cadre.

The other seven members of the squad joined us in the lineup. We pasted our backs to the wall as instructed and waited in complete silence.

Around the corner came Bellinger, wearing a bright yellow gym shirt and honing in on me like a shark that smelled chum.

"What is wrong with this picture?"

I looked down at my shirt. *Damn.* I had put it on backward.

"No excuse, sir."

"Goddam, Mullaney, it's called a uniform because you are all supposed to look the same." He continued slowly in order to emphasize each word, "You–are–not–an–individual."

"No, sir. I am not an individual," I parroted back at Bellinger. I had never considered that being an individual was a bad thing. *Was it?*

Bellinger turned to my roommate. "Did you check Mullaney before he left the room?"

"No, sir," he responded, unsure why he was being yelled at.

"So you're responsible for Mullaney walking out here with a case of uniform dyslexia."

"Yes, sir."

"This is a lesson for all of you. If there is something wrong with your uniform, if you don't so much as rinse off your toothbrush, I will know. You cannot fool me. Your only chance of surviving the next six weeks is to work together. The only way to fail is to fail one another. Do you understand?"

"*Yes, sir.*"

"Good. I want you outside with a full canteen of water in three minutes. And Mullaney, you'd better fix that shirt. Got it?"

"Yes, sir."

OUTSIDE, THE PLATOON SERGEANT addressed the platoon for the first time. "Raise your paw if you were the valedictorian of your high school."

A hand or two shot up.

"Come on. Raise 'em high. Don't be shy."

I raised my hand, and another five new cadets joined me.

"Raise your paw if you were class president."

Another four hands joined the eight that were up already.

"Varsity letter winners?"

Another twenty hands shot up.

"Look around, New Cadets. This is the last time I'll give you that privilege."

Nearly everyone's hand was in the air.

"Put your paws down." He continued, "If you came here thinking you were something special in high school, I have news—you're not special here. You are not God's gift to the United States Military Academy. West Point does not owe you anything. You have to earn it. Every single day. Remember that. By the end of this summer, five of you will wash out. The question is whether you will be one of those five."

WHAT AM I DOING HERE? I repeated to myself the well-rehearsed lines I had delivered to family, friends, and strangers. Are you sure you wouldn't be happier somewhere else? they'd ask. My happiness wasn't the point, I would respond; I wanted to serve my country. Are you sure you want to be an Army officer? Yes, I told them.

I hadn't come to that conclusion lightly. Like most of my high school classmates, I'd applied to a half-dozen universities. I'd gone with my parents to tour beautiful old colleges in New England. Admissions officers promised academic challenges and extracurricular fun. They promised well-paying jobs after graduation and powerful alumni networks. The hardest part, student tour guides confided to us, was getting in. I couldn't explain at first why I felt so out of place. Afterward, flipping through their glossy brochures at home, I realized what was missing. They'd asked nothing of me.

Growing up as the oldest of four kids in a working-class family, I'd been taught by my parents that responsibility preceded privilege. My father wore boots and a hard hat to his job at the gas company. Once a year he would bring me to work, and I'd watch him and his crew break up the sidewalk with jackhammers and backhoes. My mother's father, the Army veteran, had brought my father into the gas company he'd joined after the war. Like him, my father was a crew leader: the boss and the expert. "Hard work is the only measure of success," he would state conclusively. He was "on the line," on call, all the time. He and his crew repaired ruptured gas mains all over Rhode Island. Name a street anywhere from Olneyville to Wakefield and my father could get there without directions and rattle off the three closest diners and dive bars. When he met other fathers, he checked two things: their handshake and calluses. His own handshake was like the vice grips lining the enormous workshop in our basement. Marred with cuts from steel pipe, my father's hands were stubby and perpetually calloused. He earned every cent he brought home, and I had no reason to believe it wasn't a fortune. Every dollar went to give us what he didn't have growing up as the son of a part-time barber who made him work to buy his own toothbrushes.

We never lacked for any resource that my father thought would help us succeed in life, provided we were willing to work. He often labored around the clock, earning enough in overtime to have the satisfaction of outearning the managers, one of the few things I ever heard him brag about. When he wasn't at the gas company, he was busy at home: chopping wood, shoveling snow, building a deck, or trimming every one of a hundred shrubs around the yard. "Why pay someone else to do something I can do just as well myself?" One summer, using just that rationale, he decided to build a dry wall one hundred yards long and three feet thick. I lugged stones half my weight up and down that wall while he looked for just the right placement. "It ain't worth doing something if you aren't gonna do it right." He didn't believe in half measures. When I asked for a tree house, he built one with a deck, insulated windows, and a shingled roof. We had a television at home, but he never watched it. A relaxing night for him was a tall glass of vodka and orange juice, a printing calculator, and the dinner table covered with a month's accumulated bills. Hard drinking went with hard working. It took the edge off.

Going to West Point was one way to connect with my father. As I grew older my interests diverged from his. As a kid there was no doubt that I was a chip off the old block, as my father's friends told me. I tagged behind him everywhere he went. I had my own tiny work boots and gloves to match his. To the eyes of a child my father was Superman. He fried eggs without spilling the yolk. He split logs with an axe. He could swim across the bottom of the pool holding his breath the entire time. He parked eight-passenger vans in compact car spaces, always back end first. I was his "first-born," a carbon copy of his dark hair, dark eyes, and stubby hands. At four I was kicked out of preschool for getting in fights with the other four-year-olds. At five it was more bad marks at the public kindergarten. This was well-worn territory for the Mullaneys. My father had barely made it out of high school and, by his own admission, lucked out by marrying his more intelligent high school sweetheart, a pediatric nurse who could love unconditionally in a way his parents couldn't.

My mother's family had curiosity hardwired. My grandmother would enthrall me for hours with stories from any one of a dozen cross-country trips she had taken with my grandfather. The daughter of an Irish immigrant from County Cavan and a sailor from the Dutch Caribbean, my grandmother's stories kept me dreaming through the night and waiting for more. And whereas my father never showed any emotion, my mother and grandmother were Irish in the extreme, incapable of stemming a tear and the first to laugh at the slightest trigger. I have my mother's tear ducts.

Not surprisingly, my mother was in charge of our education. She read enough for the whole family and never left home without a book in her purse. As a small kid I was embarrassed when she laughed so hard reading in line at the grocery store. Later I would find the same look on my fellow soldiers' faces as I chuckled, nose in a book, waiting for helicopter flights in Afghanistan.

My love of books began in competition. In first grade Sue Ortelt became the first kid in the class to read. I was livid that someone had bested me, and I was even angrier that everyone else befriended her as a result. We had just moved to a new town, and I was the odd kid out in class. Don't let anyone ever tell you that they're better than you, my father intoned. I redoubled my efforts and eventually learned how to read. Later my mother told me that I had worried her with my intensity. The focus that had helped my father succeed against the odds also threatened to drive everyone else away; it seemed that I shared his ability to tune out everyone else while I was on one of my quests.

From the first time I picked out my own books at the library, I never stopped reading. I sensed early on that this wasn't what my father had in mind by hard work. He had a lifetime habit of reading the newspaper, usually at 5:30 a.m. with a thermos of black coffee from the percolator he cleaned with religious ceremony. But I never saw him read a book—there wasn't time to waste. Once when I went with him to his hometown barber, he woke up from his beard trimming to find me reading a calculus text-book. I was eleven.

Something had changed that my father couldn't grasp. I don't think he ever understood how I could pick schoolwork over yard work. How could I choose books over time with him? Didn't I want to work with him? He took out his frustration in his own way. No matter the success I had on report cards, I could always count on him to point out the one A−. When I did work outside, admittedly with reluctance, my work never passed his inspection. For five years I cut our two-acre lawn, and every single time my father would return home, take the lawn mower back out of the shed, and mow the lines straight where he had found mine bent. The absentmindedness transmitted from mother to son especially perturbed my father. Whether it was locking myself out of the car or flooding the house by leaving a faucet running, my father was constantly balling me out.

Although my father never touched a rifle, he was my definition of a soldier: hardworking, competent, and indestructible. West Point was the only school I visited where a bookworm couldn't possibly graduate. My father had convinced me that I possessed a deep-rooted, irreparable incompetence. How could I overcome my absentmindedness? What if I didn't have the stomach for hard work? My father always claimed he was a graduate of the University of Hard Knocks. If West Point wouldn't make him proud, I didn't know what would.

The adventures West Point promised attracted me like a moth to a flame. The glossy photos in the prospectus of helicopters, airborne parachutes, and rappelling captivated my attention. What was an Ivy League quad compared to a Ranger snaking through a swamp? A post in Europe or Asia was a world away from my home in North Kingstown, Rhode Island. We had a modest house outside of town where my childhood friends and I spent our days tramping through the woods and our nights racing under the giant sprinklers of local turf farms. The highlight of our year was the Quahog Festival, where Rhode Island's signature shellfish comes in 217 different varieties. On summer vacations, when my parents escaped work, they used to pack the camper with my siblings and me and tramp across New England as far as their small budget would take us. We drove to the top of Mount Cadillac, and the wind pushed us backward with the force of a hurricane. We spent hours hiking on paths that my father blazed in front of me, and when we came across a lake or a cave, I felt like the explorers I had read about. There were long days building elaborate sand castles and riding the waves at Matunuck Beach or scouring the forest for branches we could use to roast marshmallows. The two of us would wake up before dawn and row quietly onto the lake, snagging bullfrogs from the reeds with a long-handled net that he had to help me with. As I grew older and my horizons expanded from books and friends and school, my appetite for adventure expanded. I wanted more. I wanted to see a desert, to scuba-dive, to walk on the banks of the Seine. In short, I wanted to blaze my own trail. The Army's promise of overseas travel appealed to the wanderlust I had no outlet to satisfy in a small town in America's smallest state.

Perhaps the magnetic pull of West Point ultimately wasn't rational but emotional. The history-laden rhythm of a military parade reverberated like the incense-scented rituals of Catholic mass. Walking around West Point, I was swept up in its call to "Duty, Honor, Country." Self-sacrifice, integrity, and leadership echoed between the larger-than-life statues of Eisenhower and MacArthur. Cadets discussed courage and duty without a note of irony. They spoke without slouching, oozing confidence, projecting their chins, eyes fixed straight ahead. Around them my own spine stiffened with resolve. Whatever they had, I wanted. West Point offered more than an academic education. It offered an almost religious quest for perfection. I wanted to graduate a better man.

STANDING OUTSIDE IN OUR gym shorts that first morning at West Point, we didn't have to wait long to find out whether we would be one of those five in our platoon to drop out. Our cadre marched us to an exercise field, mounted an elevated wooden platform, and led the platoon through calisthenics. The squad leaders took turns on the stage, guaranteeing that they never got tired and that there were always a half-dozen eyes seeking out shirkers.

Even exercise, now dubbed PT for "physical training," had a purpose beyond fitness. PT is to the military what prayer is to a monastery—an opportunity to build cohesion and deepen obedience. West Point is a fitness cult, and every cult has its doctrine. Pain, we were told, is just weakness leaving the body. What doesn't kill you makes you stronger. The more you sweat in peace, the less you bleed in war. Every session began with commands better fit for marching than exercise. "At double interval, extend to the left, *march*. From front to rear, *count off*." Once arrayed in perfectly staggered ranks, we "executed" physical training. Most exercises were familiar: push-ups, sit-ups, bend and twists. Others were familiar but had strange names. For instance, a simple jumping jack was a "side straddle hop," announced with dramatic modulation and echoed back by us with equally false enthusiasm. Other exercises had to have been devised by seventeenth-century sadomasochists. The "swimmer" was the worst. Lying facedown in wet grass, we balanced on our bellies while lifting our arms and legs in a rhythmic alternation that made us look more like we were drowning than swimming.

After calisthenics we scattered into herds organized by running ability. My qualifying time had put me at the slow end of the fast group, guaranteeing that I would have to kill myself just to keep up. The pace was brutally fast, well under seven minutes a mile. The course hit every steep hill on campus, culminating in a mile-long climb from the Hudson River all the way up to the football stadium. Near the top my lungs verged on the edge of collapse. In the center of the formation, I had no choice but to push on. Had I stopped, a hundred feet would have stomped me into the asphalt mercilessly. Cadence calling replaced oxygen inhalation. We sang, over and over again, the same cadences—"A is for 'Airborne,' I is for 'In the sky,' R is for 'Rough and tough,' B is for 'Born to die,' O is for 'On the go,' R is for 'Ranger,' N is for 'Never quit,' E is for 'Every day.' I wanna be an Airborne Ranger. Live a life of guts and danger." The permutations were endless—wanting to be a paramedic "shooting funky anesthetic," a scuba diver "swimming in that murky water," and so on. By the end of the run, gasping for oxygen, I wanted to be an Airborne Ranger just so I could stop singing the damn cadence.

Later in the week our cadre released us to join new cadets in other companies for team sports. I followed several dozen classmates to the wrestling mats inside Arvin Gymnasium. Black and gold mats covered the floor and walls, and an odor of dried sweat permeated everything. It was a smell I loved. My one ambition apart from surviving Beast was to walk onto the wrestling team. The odds were long. Although I had been wrestling since age eight and had a respectable record in high school, my competition, Trent Moore, had swept his division in taking the Iowa state title. By September I would have to beat Trent to secure a spot.

Trent Moore was a mean son of a bitch. We had exactly the same build, but he had at least six visible scars and a bent nose that looked as if it had been broken and manually reset at a locker room mirror.

"Craig Mullaney." I held out my hand and introduced myself.

Trent just grunted and leaned over into his stance.

At the coach's whistle, five dozen cadets began sparring. Trent rattled my head as we locked up. His wrestling style clearly matched his personality. Before I knew it, he had popped my shoulder to knock me off balance, ducked under my hips, and lifted me off the mat with a textbook double-leg takedown. After smashing my body prone on the mat, he ground my head into the mat with his forearm so hard it bloodied my nose. The whistle blew again.

"Trent Moore. Nice to meet you."

We shook hands, beginning a friendship that endured bloody noses and eventually led to Trent's standing by my side as a groomsman at my wedding.

Between the wrestling bouts and sadistic runs, by the end of the summer we were running so fast that even the cadre stopped calling cadence, and we took one final graded PT test. The two-mile course ran straight along the railroad tracks and looped twice past an odious sewage treatment plant. I burned a blistering first mile split before turning and heading back past the smell of rotting waste. I closed on a cross-country recruit, and just as I pulled even with him, I sprayed vomit all over his shirt. He curled his lip in a scowl and surged ahead. I willed my legs to continue running despite the alternating dry heaves and goose bumps on my arms. This was the only chance I had to run for myself, not as part of a group. It was a chance to lengthen my strides and breathe at my own pace.

I crossed the finish line and collapsed in a lump by the road. A cadre member tapped me and handed me a sticky note with my time—11:36. It was the second-fastest time in the company, but on the cadet grading scale it was just fast enough for a B. I could still taste the bile in my mouth. Not fast enough.

MEALS DURING BEAST WERE an exercise in targeted torture. Eating at West Point was a purely functional enterprise, meant to be as efficient as calisthenics, marching, and shooting. This was industrial engineering. Food was the input; academic, physical, and military activities were the output.

The mess hall is a six-story secular cathedral. Inside the heavy oak doors that face the parade field, the entire four-thousand-person Corps of Cadets eats under the gaze of weathered flags and dead generals. Stained glass windows refract light through the outlines of armored knights and dough-boys kneeling in prayer. Where the hall's six cavernous wings converge, a stone tower bulges to the ceiling forty feet above. All commands emanate from this central pulpit, known bizarrely by naval terminology as the "Poop Deck."

On any given day in Beast, we marched in, splintered by squad, and racewalked to our assigned tables. Standing at attention was the last op-portunity to catch my breath.

"Take seats!" boomed a voice from the Poop Deck.

A thousand wooden chairs scratched across the floor, and our squad sprung into action. Even meals were leadership opportunities. Bellinger was the Table Commandant, responsible for good order and discipline. The rest of us rotated through the remaining duties in a cacophony of clattering plates, shouts, and the occasional clang of an overturned pitcher. One of us scurried to the head of the table and checked that eleven condiments had reported for duty and were prepared for action. A jar of "Beat Navy"–brand peanut butter retained its tinfoil seal. Conforming with protocol, the cadet unscrewed the cap and popped the seal by slamming the peanut butter jar into his forehead like a redneck crushing a can of beer. Another cadet skimmed gravy and announced it to the squad leader: "The scum-skimmed gravy is ready for inspection, sir."

The Cold Beverage Corporal and his sidekick by the ice bowl rapidly distributed ice water and sweet tea around the table. As new cadets we were obliged to know the specific tastes of everyone at the table, including the number of ice cubes Bellinger preferred in his cup (two). As waiters deliv-ered food to a hundred tables nearly simultaneously, they handed off their heaping platters of food at the foot of the table. After the mouth-watering tray (even mess hall food looks good to the famished) rotated around the table, a cadet held it up by his right ear at a 45-degree angle and an-nounced the remaining number of portions.

"Five and a butt servings of mashed potatoes remaining, sir." West Point refers to the incomplete portion of anything—food, beverage, and time—as a "butt," conjuring images of smoldering cigarette nubs.

Only after all the table duties were complete could we begin eating. Since every mistake during table duties cost precious time, we ate very little those first few weeks. A particularly egregious error, like the time I forgot to split the pile of salad bowls into two equally sized towers, could result in having to "touch the mural," a command that evoked as much dread as being told to reach one's hand into a python's nest. After gathering courage, I shot toward the southeast wing of the mess hall, eyes locked straight ahead on a one-thousand-square-foot mural celebrating military history. And just when I was close enough to touch George Washington, a cadre member snagged my shirt, held me hostage, and grilled me to discover whatever alleged offense had sent me into his lair. The next time, I split the salad bowls like a pro.

When we did eat, it was anything but natural. We sat through hour-long "blocks of instruction" on etiquette ("cadetiquette," as it is known at West Point) and practiced the nineteenth-century manners we were taught. We sat exactly one fist's distance from the table, plate one thumb joint away from the edge, eyes focused on the West Point crest at the plate's twelve o'clock. We never spoke unless addressed by the squad leader. Collective punishment was the law of the table; an error by one cadet stopped everyone else from eating. Even when there was a pause to eat, it took forever to get anything into my stomach. Eating required its own entry in the little book of cadet knowledge we carried with us everywhere like a passbook from Hell. The tone was set with the chapter's epigraph: "Tomorrow's battles are won during today's training." Then, point by point, were instructions for eating as detailed as a field manual. First, pick up your fork. Second, pick up your knife. Cut just one piece. Replace knife. Switch fork to the other hand. Stab, lift, and insert food in mouth. Replace fork. Chew no more than three times. Start again. Bellinger's well-trained eye looked for exactly three bobs of the jaw. Pity the new cadet who attempted four or five "big bites." It might cost the table the remainder of the meal. By the end of the first week we were starving.

In the rare event that we made it to dessert, an elaborate ritual ensued.

First, the designated pie cutter had to ask who was eating dessert. A number of eight or six was a relatively easy slicing job. More challenging were the missions requiring seven or nine perfectly equal portions. We kept pie-cutting templates in our gray service caps to aid our geometry, marking off the pie perimeter with guide marks. The slices had to be crisp; a muddled pie could mean a trip to the mural or suspended dessert privileges. The technique of choice involved dipping the knife in water and cutting the pie like a surgeon with a scalpel. Over time, we ate earlier and faster. It was us against them, and the only way to win was to "cooperate and graduate," the first principle of cadet life.

On the face of it, cutting a pie with a template was as ridiculous as calling a jumping jack a "side straddle hop" or having to memorize the number of gallons in Lusk Reservoir. In our room, after the lights were off and we were sure the cadre were gone, we laughed ourselves to sleep.

For my friends heading to normal colleges, the dorm room represented freedom from parents, a space to make their own, and a lair for dates. At West Point my barracks room was the last place I went for refuge. The obsessive-compulsive requirements of the mess hall extended to the barracks, where the standard of cleanliness exceeded that of an antiseptic operating room. Every morning involved a hundred cleaning tasks, from polishing the basin mirror and faucets with old newspaper to dusting every horizontal surface of the room, including the lip of the nameplate on the door and the upper surface of the fire alarm ten feet off the floor. My roommates and I specialized: I was the bed guy. Every morning I stretched the wool blankets over the mattress tight enough to bounce a quarter. The crease at the foot of the bed required an exact 45-degree angle. Over time we discovered that sleeping on top of the bed shaved a minute off the drill. Sometimes it was so hot in our sixth-floor room that I slept on top of my desk or on the floor. Whenever we had a question about organization, a three-inch-thick Barracks Arrangement Guide provided the answers. Even underwear had specified folding instructions: folded in three along the longitudinal axis, then once latitudinally. The only mark of personality in the room was a framed collage of high school friends and my family and two books: *Catch-22* and *The Brothers Karamazov*. I had somehow convinced myself there would be time to read during basic training. The two books were arranged, per regulation, in height order.

Only perfection was acceptable. Attention to detail was beat into my head with the regularity of a jackhammer. A loose belt buckle, an undone shoelace, dust on the brim of my service cap, all resulted in the same ominous rebuke: *You just killed your platoon.*

During those first few months, the connection between battlefield leadership and attention to detail was hard to make. Seven years later the link would be obvious. Military command, perhaps unlike any other profession, demands that its practitioners see with absolute clarity both the forest and the trees. Any number of missed details could compromise a mission, from forgetting to bring an extra battery for the tactical radio to skipping the maintenance for the one tiny piece of a machine gun that fails in a firefight. Miss a digit on a GPS coordinate, and an artillery round could land on friendly troops. One mistake really could kill your platoon.

THE FIRST THREE WEEKS of Beast focused almost entirely on teaching teamwork, building physical stamina, and adapting to West Point's peculiar traditions. The last three weeks of Beast, however, was about learning to soldier. We began by breaking in our combat boots.

"Outside in the hallway. Five minutes. Boots and swim trunks."

Our looks of incredulity only made Bellinger madder, and he repeated the uniform to make sure we understood.

"All right, New Cadets, lace up your boots. We're going marching."

He called cadence as he led us into an unoccupied wing of the barracks.

"Column left, *march.*"

He turned us into the men's latrine and then into the shower room.

"Prepare to shower."

I reached up and grabbed the shower handle.

"Shower."

On cue we doused ourselves with ice-cold water.

"Forward, *march.*"

We began to march around the shower in our sodden boots as Bellinger called out lefts and rights. As the showers warmed up, steam obscured the smile I had been trying in vain to restrain. Apart from submission, the only authorized emotional expression was false enthusiasm. Smiles were a sign of weakness.

"I can still see you, Mullaney. Smirk off."

"No excuse, sir."

The days blended into weeks as our shower-molded boots accumulated mileage tramping through West Point's wooded hills. At first Army field training was like an Outward Bound excursion. One day we got to rappel down a cliff and practice mountain climbing at a training area that was part of West Point but miles away from the barracks and classrooms. Near the top of the ridge the sun was bright, the morning air crisp, and the surrounding woods green and inviting. At the bottom of the valley, Route 6 snaked back toward West Point. I checked the knots in my Swiss seat for the fifth time and looked down to make sure the rope was routed through the carabiner clip. I tested my weight on the rope by leaning back, still yards from the precipice.

"Banish your inner weakness, New Cadet," encouraged a sergeant from the 10th Mountain Division sent to train cadets. He had both of the marks we had sung about in our repetitive running cadences: Airborne wings and the Ranger tab.

I walked backward slowly, a death grip on the rope. At the lip of the cliff I leaned back on the rope and stepped behind me. My boots were now perpendicular to the vertical rock face, toes pointed unnaturally toward the blue cloudless sky. There was nothing between my back and the ground except a vertical column of air. I turned my head, made ungainly by an oversized helmet, and saw my shadow fifty feet below.

"New Cadet, I'm not here to watch you philosophize." He stared down at my cantilevered body. "Get off my cliff."

And off I went. I pushed away with my eyes closed and bounced back onto the cliff face fifteen feet lower. This is cool, I thought, and bounded three more times until I was safely on a horizontal surface again.

Other training events were pure misery, such as the day we "built confidence" in the effectiveness of our gas masks. After a morning spent donning gas masks on command and sweating through charcoal chemical suits, our squad entered a concrete pillbox. Light entered through a small, dirty window near the low ceiling. We huddled together by necessity in the confined space. At the instructor's command of "gas, gas, gas!" I snatched my mask out of its case like John Wayne in a pistol draw. In less than eight seconds I had the mask over my head with straps tightened. A deep breath sucked the rubber into my cheeks, confirming that I had a good seal. Through my mask's eye portals, my squad mates looked like aliens from another planet. The door opened just long enough for someone to roll in a large can steaming from its side. The room quickly fogged up with a mysterious gas, and it became hard to see. Unconsciously, I held my breath. At last, with no alternative but suffocation, I breathed in through my filter. The tear gas, sucked through the mask, was harmless. Under the rubber mask, I relaxed. Our collective breaths rose and fell like hospital patients on life support.

"Take off your masks," the instructor commanded through his filter like Darth Vader.

Off came the mask and in came the gas. The first sensation was like someone pouring Tabasco sauce in my eyes. Then my nose began to run uncontrollably. Next to me, my roommate had a trail of snot stretching three feet from his oversized nose.

"Good drool, New Cadet. Keep it up."

Just as it became unbearable, the door opened wide, and we rushed for the exit. Outside in the bright light, a cadet corralled us and directed us to wave our arms at our sides like enthusiastic ostriches ignorant of the fact they can't fly.

"Under no circumstances," he added, "should you touch your eyes."

One of my classmates did, screaming bloody murder at a sensation equivalent to rubbing chili peppers on his cornea. My eyes clouded with tears, and my own trail of mucus dripped onto the dusty ground. Every inch of exposed skin was on fire. Eventually, the effects wore off, but not before our squad leader had snapped photos at this, our most vulnerable moment of Beast.

"You will never forget your first teargassing," he noted wistfully. "Anyone want to go again?"

THE MOST RELEVANT LESSON of basic training was how to kill, but it was seldom described so explicitly. I "engaged targets" and "provided suppressive fire." My rifle was "my new best friend." No matter where I went, to the latrine or the field mess, the rifle came with me. If abandoned, cadre members held the rifle hostage for a payment in push-ups. At night I slept with my rifle zipped inside my sleeping bag. The cadre encouraged us to pretend that the cold metal barrels were our girlfriends back home. Even in West Point's irony-free atmosphere, this was too much. I was still a virgin, but I knew enough about girls to know they didn't smell like gun oil. In silent protest I refused to name my rifle.

Target practice was difficult for those of us who hadn't grown up hunting. At first I missed even the fifty-yard "Ivan" targets that popped up from the brush wearing Soviet overcoats and furry hats. The recoil surprised me, and I scratched my cheek on the rifle sights. Yet after three days of sweltering bouts in the foxhole I could successfully "engage" three out of every four Ivans. In the event that green plastic dummies ever attacked my rifle platoon, I would be ready.

I kept my rifle obsessively clean by swabbing the barrel with cotton patches and oiling the springs of the ammunition magazines. I practiced the Army's time-tested techniques: yoga-inspired controlled breathing, balancing a dime on the barrel, and consistent aim. I learned better trigger control. "You don't pull a trigger, you *squeeze* it," emphasized the cadre. I enjoyed shooting. It was like a video game: clean, fun, and almost clinical. I knew, because I had to memorize it, that each bullet was

5.56 millimeters wide—not 5.55 or 5.57 but *precisely 5.56 millimeters.* I learned the muzzle velocity of the round, its maximum range, and how to strip and reassemble my rifle in ninety seconds. The detachment from reality was complete. Shooting at plastic targets gave me no sense of how a bullet might plow through an actual human torso. That would come later.

We also tossed live grenades, whose concussive explosions no one mistook for a video game. At the morning briefing they roused us like a crowd at a football stadium.

"Do you want to blow stuff up?"

"Hoooah!" we yelled.

Each of us took turns tossing grenades from behind the protection of a concrete wall. Afterward they brought out one of the Ivans to show us the damage from the grenade shrapnel. It looked like Swiss cheese. The purpose of shrapnel, they told us dryly, was to maximize damage to the target. As each fragment tumbles through a torso, bones splinter upon impact and send secondary projectiles into surrounding soft tissue. Everyone oohed and aahed. Ivan was just plastic.

The last vestige of the old Army remaining in Beast was the celebrated Bayonet Assault Course, designed for the sole purpose of instilling an aggressive warrior spirit. Standing in an empty field with our rifles, we chanted fierce infantry mottos. Apparently, there was no euphemism at bayonet distance.

"What is the spirit of the bayonet?"

"To *kill, kill, kill,* with *cold, blue steel!*"

"What makes the green grass grow?"

"Blood, blood, bright red blood!"

"There are two kinds of people in this world. What are you?"

"The quick!"

"What are they?"

"The dead!"

"I want to see your war face!"

One hundred and fifty cadets grimaced, *"Aaahhh!"*

"Butt stroke to the groin, *move!*

"Slash and hold, *move!*

"Whirl!" We spun around with our weapons and came back to the attack position.

"What do you want to be?"

"Infantry! Hoooah!"

Armed with giant pugil sticks shaped like oversized Q-tips, the instructors circled our ranks and pitted us against one another for bout after bout of concussions and bruised family jewels. "Honoré de Balzac," they'd joke when new cadets took shots to the groin. When we finished, we "fixed bayonets" on our rifles and charged through an obstacle course littered with straw dummies and rubber tires. We stabbed, slashed, and smashed accompanied by loud *"hoooahs"* and stern war faces. As we relaxed on the grass after running through the course, we looked like hell—mud smeared on faces, uniforms torn by barbed wire, and our heads matted with sweat and dust.

Running that course was pure exhilaration, an explosion of power and speed that unleashed an instinct for aggression. I liked the rush; I liked the mud and sweat; and I enjoyed pushing my body to the limit. In testing my endurance I also tested my spirit and the ability of my mind to transcend pain. Of the various career paths available in the Army, from logistics and intelligence on one end of the spectrum to infantry and armor on the other, the infantry hewed most closely to this raw display of physical aggression and mental fortitude. The cadences that accompanied our running were infantry cadences for a reason. Infantry, we were told, was where warriors were made.

I wasn't sure, though, that I wanted to be a warrior, a professional trained to kill. Screaming *"kill"* was a theatrical stunt, and none of us presumed it was anything other than false bravado. The bayonet course was a different matter. It disturbed me that I could plunge a bayonet into a straw dummy with ease (and even pleasure). Sitting on the grass, watching classmates emerge from the course in pairs, I did not question whether I had the will to get through Beast but whether I wanted to. I struggled to reconcile my moral code with what I had just done. The aggressive instinct channeled into a straw dummy was just as capable of putting a seven-inch steel blade into another soldier's stomach. Should I have found the exercise invigorating? What did that say about me?

My faith as a Catholic had formed my values in adolescence. At one point I had even considered becoming a priest. (Poverty and obedience, I understood. Chastity was a different matter.) Attending Mass every week taught me to love ritual and the rich symbolism of the Church. The Irish Christian Brothers who administered Bishop Hendricken, my all-male high school, ruled with clear standards, a code of honor as inviolable as the requirement to wear coats and ties. Although our classes were tough, the brothers were far tougher on our souls. "Be your best self," they must have told us a thousand times. Guilt was a constant companion and a concept that incorporated everything from missing a homework assignment to losing a wrestling match. Before confession every week I added those shortcomings to a bundle bursting from false witness, parental disrespect, and an adolescent's constant coveting of the fairer sex. The brothers admonished us to live lives of sacrifice, charity, and service. There were prayer vigils for disaster victims, fasts to remember the hungry, and requirements to serve in our communities without complaint. Above all we learned to sanctify others, seeing even in our enemies the image of God. After the bayonet course, when I doubted continuing at West Point, I made an appointment to see one of the Catholic chaplains.

His office was tucked between the mess hall and MacArthur barracks. After knocking on the door, I entered. Slashes of light from the window blinds cut across his desk and striped the dark wood paneling around me. An Army bible in camouflage was open on the desk. A silver-haired priest looked up at my uniform and spotted my name tag.

"Mullaney. Good Irish name."

"Thank you, Father," I said with a smile.

"Have a seat. How can I help you? Do you need a salvo of prayers to get through the week?"

"No, Father." I gulped. "I wanted to talk to you about whether I belong here."

"Why wouldn't you?"

"Father, I was at the bayonet course, and I got really confused. I liked the challenge, but I don't know how I feel about being an officer who has to inspire others to attack the enemy. I just can't see myself cheering while we kill. Can I serve in uniform without that enthusiasm?"

He leaned back and swiveled in his armchair. I was hoping for an answer but received a question instead: "It depends. Do you believe in a just war?"

"I think so, Father. Like World War II?"

"Sure, that's a good example. Do you think Hitler could have been stopped without war?"

"Of course not, Father."

"So you agree that war, although always horrible, is sometimes necessary to stop a greater evil?"

"Yes, Father."

"And those soldiers, were they killers in your mind?"

"No, Father. They had to kill, but I don't think they were killers. They had to kill in order to stop a greater evil."

"Did those soldiers deserve good lieutenants?"

"Yes, Father."

"Well, don't you think today's soldiers deserve good lieutenants?"

"Well, yes, I guess. But I'm still not sure that I'm the kind of officer they need. I'm not as gung ho as everyone else."

"Really?" He leaned forward and put his elbows on the desk. "Do you think they're any less conflicted than you? How many cadets do you think I see in the course of a week?" He arched his eyebrows. "Maybe the Army isn't for you, but I don't think you can make that determination without finishing the summer and spending time in the classroom. I think you'll be surprised to find your peers and your instructors are less 'gung ho' than you presume."

"Yes, Father."

"And you might also find that leading men in combat has more to do with duty than bravado."

"Yes, Father."

3

Falling Gracefully

The far object of a training system is to prepare the combat officer mentally so that he can cope with the unusual and unexpected as if it were the altogether normal and give him poise in a situation where all else is in disequilibrium.

s.l.a. marshall, *Men Against Fire*

"THE GOOD NEWS IS THAT YOU'VE SUCCESSFULLY COM-pleted Beast. The bad news is that you've just started Plebe year." We stood in formation with our summer platoon for the last time, and our cadre bid us farewell as we girded ourselves to join the companies we would stay with for the next four academic semesters. Behind them was a host of upper-classmen frothing at the mouth for fresh meat.

"On the command of 'fall out,' fall out and find your assigned company."

My lips mouthed the Lord's Prayer in silence: *"Deliver us Lord from every evil."*

"Fall out!"

For two months we had outnumbered cadre six to one. Now that the upperclassmen had returned from their summer training away from West Point, the ratio was reversed. Our new tormentors wanted nothing more than the satisfaction of watching Plebes stammer, stumble, and sweat for the next nine months. Officially, the rigors of Plebe year existed to inure us to stress and to teach us how to follow before we learned how to lead. In practice, however, Plebe year often seemed to be a nine-month spectacle of humiliation that afforded unhappy sadists an opportunity to project their misery onto us. There was also the cosmic law of Plebe karma, which demanded that upperclassmen revisit the trauma of their own Plebe year onto each new litter of freshmen. Each class believes that theirs was the last "real" Plebe year and is equally sure that they must reverse West Point's liberalizing slide. The sophomores ("Yearlings," like horses, or "Yuks," pejoratively), juniors ("Cows," so named because when they returned to campus from summer training, it was like cows coming home from pasture), and seniors ("Firsties," as in first class) in Company D-4 were no exception.

An hour after marching to our new barracks opposite Arvin Gym, the thirty Plebes assigned to my company packed into the tiny ground-floor room of another Plebe. We stank of sweat and fear. Outside on the front stoop were seventy-five fervent upperclassmen waiting impatiently for us to emerge from our impromptu headquarters. There was no way around them; the stoop they stood on formed the only connecting path between each of the twenty-room towers in Scott Barracks. Our task was to deliver over one hundred cellophane-wrapped laundry packs and an equal number of dry-cleaning bundles to every room in the company. As the thermometer spiked in the sauna we had created, it became clear how difficult this first mission was going to be. Problem one: We didn't have a roster of who lived in each room. Problem two: We were expected to know by sight the name of everyone in the company. Problem three: Any attempt to deliver a bundle had to be aborted if (a) you were stopped for a uniform infraction such as a smudged shoe, a misaligned belt buckle, or an imperfectly creased shirt tail; (b) you failed to recognize an upperclassman on sight; or (c) you were unable to instantaneously and correctly recite several dozen items of required knowledge.

Two knocks on the door preceded Cadet Aram Donigian's entrance into the room. A farm boy from rural Oregon, Donigian filled every square inch of his uniform with a wrestler's build. His nose was a hawk's beak, and his ears had the crumpled and puffy marks of cauliflower. He was the Company First Sergeant, the senior-ranking Cow in the company and the chief disciplinarian. Donigian was the bane of our Plebe existence.

"What is taking you Plebes so long?" He said *Plebes* as if it were a dirty word.

"No excuse, sir," I volunteered.

He lifted into the room a full-size cutout of John Wayne in *The Green Berets*. "This is 'the Duke,' Company D-4's mascot. Whenever you see the Duke, I want you to salute him. Understood?"

"Yes, sir."

He left the room with his cardboard cutout. Another two knocks rapped on the door, and a Plebe called the room to attention.

"Enter, sir."

An arm appeared and then the cutout of John Wayne.

"Are you saluting the Duke?"

Was he serious?

Thirty salutes snapped at our mascot. "Yes, sir."

Yes.

"Good." He entered the room. "Carry on, Plebes. The laundry isn't going to deliver itself." He looked at my name tag. "Mullaney, I want to see you out here with laundry in exactly one minute." He looked down at his stopwatch and began the timer.

Ten Plebes began tucking, buffing, and adjusting my uniform as another Plebe counted off the seconds remaining. *Cooperate and graduate.*

"Thirty seconds," he called out as my heart pumped faster.

"Someone tell me the days," I pleaded urgently.

"The Days" was one of our required knowledge items, an exact count of days remaining until the next football game, Christmas leave, graduation, and a half dozen other important dates on the cadet calendar. Given the newspaper headlines and mess hall menus we also had to memorize, every Plebe eventually gained the ability to "spec and dump," studying rote knowledge and clearing the memory bank as soon as the knowledge became irrelevant. It was a useful skill in some circumstances but intellectually problematic for most. Right now it was a skill in high demand. Another Plebe shouted the numbers. *Here goes nothing.*

Before I made three steps on the stoop, five cadets surrounded me and began yelling simultaneously, each infuriated by my inability to focus on their eyes. My brain began to shut down from sensory overload. Sweat dribbled down the inside of my shirt, the water I had been guzzling to stay vertical was about to burst through my bladder, and the blend of voices sounded to my ears as though someone were speaking in tongues. My lips mouthed my four possible responses in various combinations, but nothing satisfied the mob surrounding me. Then suddenly the door opened and a second Plebe emerged to draw fire from me. Then another and another— a swarm of Plebes trying to force safe passage for at least a couple of lucky ones. The strategy worked. One by one we built a multilayered picture of the company we had joined: names, rooms, favorite questions, and uniform pet peeves. During the four days we had before classes began that August, our company of Plebes persisted in a dozen similar missions, from surreptitiously delivering copies of the *New York Times* at dawn to running messages between Donigian and the battalion headquarters.

It is funny how some of the stupid things we did as Plebes would come in handy later. Our battalion would use the same intelligence-gathering techniques in Afghanistan to piece together a better picture of our enemy. Even the simultaneous hazing by upperclassmen would be useful in a firefight as a dozen different crises vied for my urgent attention. Most of the knowledge we memorized, on the other hand, was useless outside West Point's walls. Knowing the number of lightbulbs in Cullum Hall or the names of the four Army mules was less relevant than the things we should have committed to memory, such as the range of a howitzer or the number of minutes you could expect to shoot a machine gun before its barrel melted.

AS IF THE NORMAL trials of Plebe year weren't enough, there remained my attempt to make the wrestling team. After making the first cut at the end of the summer, only one opponent stood between me and my goal of walking onto a Division I team: Trent, the Iowa wrestler who had clobbered me at first sight. We started every day with morning conditioning practice.

Arriving just a few minutes early in the dark wrestling room, I would lie on the mat and close my eyes for the most peaceful moment of the entire day. At precisely 5:30 a.m. a pair of wrestling shoes creaked across the mat, flicked a dozen light switches, and turned on the stereo, always to the same song—Led Zeppelin's "Black Dog." And then the pain began. As Robert Plant belted his promise to make us sweat, to make us groove, to make it burn, and to make it sting, a six-foot, two-hundred-pound man we referred to as Satan followed through with our punishment. Trent was my partner. One morning we would run seven stories of stairs a dozen times. On another we would sprint on the indoor track, stopping to do pull-ups between laps. We would have to take turns running while carrying the other person's weight in a fireman's carry. After an hour and a half of hell, practice concluded with our bodies at total muscle failure. Eight hours later we returned to drill takedowns and thirty-second mini matches. I enjoyed this: Struggle for struggle's sake, a principle my father respected without ever stepping on a mat. I fight, therefore I am.

After a month the head coach held a wrestle-off to fix the final team. Trent destroyed me, 11–3. The only points I scored were the escapes he allowed in order to take me down again. I shook his hand at the center of the mat and walked off to the indoor track. My knees were raw with fresh mat burns and stung with sweat as I stumbled around the track. With the edge of my sweatshirt I wiped away from my mouth blood mixed with tears.

"Hey, you okay?" Trent draped his hand over my shoulder.

"Yeah, yeah, I'm fine. Just a little mat burn. Good match."

"No, seriously, are *you* okay?"

"I'm fine, man. I just need some time to myself."

"No hard feelings?"

"No hard feelings. The better man won."

"Wrong," said Trent, stopping to face me. "The better wrestler won."

I walked another lap or two and then headed back to the barracks for a shower. I closed my eyes and turned the faucet until it stopped. Under jets of scalding hot water, I made peace with my defeat. I had been wrestling for ten years, and although I hadn't won every match, none hurt so much as this, the final match. I let the steam clear my head and then, after toweling off, I called home and told my mother. We had a long talk, but mostly she just listened. My mother had a talent for making people feel better without saying a word. Focus on something else, she suggested at last. She was right—West Point had no shortage of challenges.

"Can you tell Dad?" I asked. "I don't want to tell him."

I hung up and was about to walk over to the mess hall when my door swung open. There was Trent and our wrestling buddies, Chris and Jim.

"We're going to order take-out. You in?"

The three of them smiled and punched my shoulder lightly in turn.

"Yeah," I said, "I'm in."

For the next four years I would eat most dinners, almost every Sunday brunch, and every tailgate burger with these three guys. Every Sunday after dinner Trent and I would go to Mass in the auditorium above the mess hall. When we had weekends off, my father would cart us back to Rhode Island in the big van. We would study together, carouse together, and suffer together through it all. I was the only guy not on the wrestling team, but it didn't matter to them.

CADETS REFERRED TO LIFE inside the granite castle as being "in the fishbowl." We swam around the bowl day after day with no change except the weather. We stood in formation two or three times a day, marched in squares between our barracks and the mess hall, and as Plebes "pinged" to class at exactly 120 steps per minute.

At first glance the movements of cadets through their daily activities would look as regular and synchronized as a well-tuned watch. By order of the cadet leadership, windows were open and aligned at exactly one clipboard's height. At a distance, in our gray trousers, black shirts, and short haircuts, we looked like an army of broad-shouldered clones. Every hour an announcement from the central PA system ordained the uniform by reference to a temperature chart. It boomed like the voice of God: "Attention all cadets. Attention all cadets. The uniform is: As-for-class under short overcoats. That is all. Out." Inside the barracks, off limits to non-cadets, the only difference between any two rooms selected at random were the name stickers pasted in fifteen different locations around the room: below the toothbrush, above the spit-polished boots and antique parade rifle by the door, and hanging on the inspection clipboard. Otherwise, each room was an eerie carbon copy of the next, from the books arranged in height order to the desk blotters whose X's through each day marched toward graduation.

Less obvious were the hundred ways we rebelled. The mess hall, far from the public eye, was one of the favorite venues for cadet humor. After the first few months of harassment, the upperclassmen at my table began to get creative. There were milk-drinking contests and white tornadoes (a concoction involving every condiment on the table) to induce vomiting. Then there were the first-aid drills we had to perform when one of us was "hit" on our shirts with a splash of spaghetti sauce. Later, one of the upperclassmen began bringing a gong to the table. At the sound of the gong, we had to ask sports and movie trivia or perform skits we had prepared during study breaks. I had no illusions about my status: I was a dancing bear.

The best meal of the year was the Christmas dinner in early December. Assisted by the other classmate at my table, that afternoon we delivered cigars and individually wrapped presents for each place setting. We dressed formally in full dress gray, a wool tunic studded with brass buttons, and marched to dinner in a jubilant wave of cadets. To the accompaniment of Christmas carols, our upperclassmen opened their gifts, and we dug into thick slabs of ham drizzled in maple syrup. As the waiters cleared our plates, and against the specific orders of the one-star general who served as Commandant of Cadets, we began singing the "Twelve Days of Christmas," simultaneously heaving our heavy oak table into the air in a competition to get our Table Commandant, standing precariously on a chair balanced on top of the table, higher than anyone else's. Across the six wings of the mess hall, four hundred tables soared in undulating waves as condiments spilled into the aisles and rattled off the floor. Captains and majors strained in vain to contain the mayhem. I heaved and heaved with the tune, nearly popping the brass buttons off my uniform and cracking a public smile a mile wide. It was a glorious riot. After dinner we moved outside under the stars, huddled against the cold wind whipping down the Hudson, and lit one another's cigars, enjoying one of the rare respites from "good order and discipline."

On any given night, a thousand amateur comics went to work distracting cadets from their studies. One night, two knocks on our door surprised my roommate and me. A Firstie walked in, possibly drunk, with a burning match and a can of hairspray.

"Ever see a flamethrower?" he asked us with a grin.

"No, sir."

Without warning he sprayed the aerosol and lit a fireball that nearly singed our eyebrows. He turned around and walked out of the room. Another night, he came by with a box of pizza and asked us if we wanted any. He opened the box at our affirmative response, and before us were a missing section of cardboard and his rather unappetizing slice of male anatomy. A smart Plebe quickly learns not to expect favors from upperclassmen. The first time I accepted a Firstie's offer to "hang out," I found myself suspended on two elbows from the doors of an open wardrobe.

Each exam week featured one of the more extreme rebellions against "the System." Trent, Chris, Jim, and I had covered Trent's walls in washable marker with the hundred names, places, and ideas we needed to connect in the ten hours remaining before our world history exam. Suddenly, what sounded like a thousand windows slammed open as cadets rushed to stare down at the floodlit cement quad.

"What is it?" I asked Trent.

"Naked Man," he replied.

And there he was—a cadet streaking across two hundred yards of open ground wearing nothing but a jock strap, with an officer and cadet on duty chasing him in vain. The quad roared with cheers as he evaded capture. Over the years "Naked Man" evolved into ever more creative exhibitions of flesh. There was "Naked Officer," involving a stolen officer uniform stripped off in dramatic fashion, "Naked Jedi Warrior," featuring a light saber made of a broomstick and tactical ChemLite glow sticks, and "Coed Naked Basketball" on the courts between Lee and Grant Barracks. According to legend, Cadet Edgar Allan Poe had found his way out of West Point by a similar prank: arriving at formation wearing nothing but a parade hat, starched belts, and a cartridge box. By day we were industrious models of obedient behavior. At night—well, it was a good thing no one was watching.

Even parades, in all their pomp and circumstance, masked controlled resistance. Assigned officers stood ready with clipboards poised to grade our performance. The suspense was palpable. Would our bayonets stay aligned at 45 degrees as we marched past the Commandant? Would we shift our eyes, *right!*, at just the appropriate moment? Drill and ceremony brought out every officer's latent Prussian. Meanwhile, whispers between cadets set the betting pool on the number of cadets who would pass out in the heat or lose their unwieldy tar bucket helmets in a gust of wind. One of the moments that confirmed my ineptitude at drill and ceremony took place during an afternoon parade practice. At the command of "Right shoulder, *arms!*" I lifted my rifle up to my right shoulder and accidentally stabbed with my bayonet a classmate standing in front of me. Frightened to say anything, both of us stayed quiet until we marched out onto the parade ground. It wasn't long before Donigian noticed the trail of blood streaming down my classmate's uniform.

Donigian stated the obvious, "You're bleeding."

"No excuse, sir," responded my punctured classmate with the tone of sangfroid we were all encouraged to adopt. What doesn't kill you makes you stronger.

Donigian escorted him to the hospital, where the medic sewed three stitches into the base of his neck. Back at the barracks that night, Donigian awarded my classmate a fake Purple Heart and ordered me to report to his room every morning for "additional instruction" in rifle drill. My incompetence at drill was more than a frustration. This was different from burning out a car battery by leaving the lights on. Then the only consequence was the silent treatment from my father, too disappointed to even tell me what I had done wrong. Now, armed incompetence had serious consequences.

MY INEPTITUDE ON THE parade field was compensated somewhat by success in the classroom. After a Catholic education, academic discipline at West Point was a relatively easy transition, but it did have its peculiar aspects. At Bishop Hendricken we had begun class with the Lord's Prayer. At West Point, class began with us standing at attention and delivering an accountability report to the professor: "All present and accounted for." Class was our place of duty; unexcused absences were punishable offenses. Nor was exhaustion a viable excuse. It was a four-year battle to stay conscious in class on less than five hours of sleep. Since attendance was mandatory, it was rare to sit in a classroom where there weren't a half-dozen cadets nodding their heads in a sleepy rhythm. There was an art to avoiding the whizzing hunks of chalk that exploded behind those whom instructors caught sleeping. Professors with combat arms backgrounds were the most creative with their punishments. If they caught you sleeping, they might "slit" your neck with a permanent marker. The message was clear: Stay alert, and stay alive.

My class took almost exactly the same sequence of courses for our first two years, and all of our homework, labs, and tests were uniformly synchronized. Every Plebe studied for exactly the same calculus or chemistry exam. The cooperative instinct to survive together was balanced by a sharp emphasis on individual achievement. It used to be the case that after each test, cadets' classroom seats were rearranged in order of class standing. That perversity died along with mandatory equestrian drills. Now cadets had to wait until the end of the semester to learn exactly where they stood in relation to their peers, ranked and ordered to three decimal points of precision.

Among our first classes was English 102, a.k.a. "Plebe Poetry," a course apparently designed to suck the soul out of Shakespeare. Literature had been a passion in high school; my wrestling coach used to shake his head in disbelief as I lay down between the stands at wrestling tournaments to read novels, oblivious to the matches, whistles, and screaming parents. If not for extracurricular reading, Plebe year might have extinguished my love of literature altogether. Twice a week I crammed in my room and delivered regurgitated recitations before the class. One by one we mouthed *Henry V's* Saint Crispin's Day Speech: "We few, we happy few, we band of brothers." *Happy few?* Didn't our instructor remember Plebe year? For a full eight points I needed to demonstrate an "informed reading with perfect accuracy and pronunciation; appropriate tone and attitude" of a rather odd assortment of poems. There was Othello's nostalgic farewell to "pride, pomp, and circumstance of glorious war!" followed by the morbid verses of Randall Jarrell's "The Death of the Ball Turret Gunner." On the one hand, we were exhorted to woo Andrew Marvell's "coy mistress," but on the other hand, we also had to repeat, like Macbeth, that life "is a tale / Told by an idiot, full of sound and fury, / Signifying nothing." And what was the value of mimicking Romeo when such a negligible fraction of us had our own Juliets. Comprehension, fortunately, wasn't graded.

Psychology, on the other hand, made perfect sense. Taking the course as a Plebe was an exercise in self-diagnosis. After we read about Ivan Pavlov's 1927 experiment with a dog and a bell, our workbook exercise was to identify the stimulus and response in a scenario involving a Plebe and a Firstie. Was Plebe year an experiment we were just being let in on? Pavlov hadn't figured out anything a cadet couldn't have told him: Every single time I heard two knocks on my door, my heart rate jumped. The double knock was the "neutral stimulus" associated with being flamed by an upperclassman. And it certainly seemed plausible that West Point was really just a large "Skinner Box," a device designed in the late 1930s to reward rats that performed a desired task with an associated incentive. Stanley Milgram's Yale experiments didn't sound far-fetched at all. Asked how far participants would go when asked to gradually electrocute students who answered incorrectly, our guess was close to Milgram's 60 percent, whereas the average American received Milgram's results with shock and disbelief. We had implicit faith, for better or worse, in the power of obedience. After class, reading the "Grand Inquisitor" scene in *The Brothers Karamazov*, I considered whether the fictitious Torquemada was correct in his skepticism of free will. To what degree had I asked for the authority to which I was increasingly bound?

History, unexpectedly, was my favorite class. In high school I had been so flummoxed by history that I dropped out of the advanced placement course with my head hung low. My West Point professor, a rare helicopter pilot armed with a Ph.D., took history in an entirely unfamiliar direction. High school history had been a sequence of dates and names to memorize. The most common questions began with what, who, or where. This was different. Now, every question began with why or how.

Difficult readings corresponded to our professor's high expectations. This was a course of ideas, ideas that had changed history. What did it mean for Albert Einstein to theorize that there was no fixed frame of reference for an observer? Was truth itself relative? He had us read a translation of Voltaire's *Candide*, prompting us to challenge Candide's assertion, repeated after each new calamity that strikes him, "Everything is for the best, in the best of all possible worlds." Was history predetermined? Was any other outcome besides this present possible? More philosophically, how could we explain suffering in an ordered world? Unlike calculus, history was nuanced and subtle. It was the hardest challenge I had ever faced as a student, an intellectual basic training. At the end of the course I decided to major in history.

FATIGUE MAKES COWARDS OF men. So said a prominent sign inside Arvin Gymnasium. West Point liked to remind us at every opportunity that we weren't just college students but also future officers. I doubted that any other college advertised its physical education courses as instrumental to developing "initiative, courage, and self-sacrifice." In order to imbue weakling eighteen-year-olds with the requisite "will to win," every Plebe took three grueling courses.

Gymnastics, affectionately dubbed "spaz-nastics," was the most bizarre of the three. For three months I tried in vain to perfect headstands, handsprings, and trampoline hip swivels. Scored on a scale of 0 to 5 by instructors who must have been trained in Romania, most of my attempts earned, encouragingly, a "high 2." According to the grading criteria, my performance was appropriately classified as "generally inconsistent," demonstrating "minimal control, poise, rhythm, and form." Not surprisingly for West Point, scores weren't rounded up. The finale of the course involved a combination floor routine and obstacle course that shook the dust out of the old wooden gymnasium, giving participants a telltale hacking cough that was a West Point rite of passage. If you don't vomit at the end of the obstacle course, they told us, then you didn't try hard enough. Hack, hack.

Plebe swimming was gentle by comparison, requiring only that I drop blindfolded from a ten-yard diving platform in full combat gear and swim across the pool in sodden camouflage. Outside the earshot of our instructors, we called it "Plebe drowning."

My career in boxing, the third course, had an ignominious start. Thrust into a class of varsity athletes, I was the runt. We drilled for weeks on combinations of jabs, hooks, and uppercuts before our instructor, a Special Forces major with triceps defined like the turns in a steel cable, opened a battle royal in the boxing ring. If someone hadn't made him equip us with gloves, he probably would have had us fight bare-fisted. The purpose of the course was less about technique than enduring acute pain. "No pain, no gain," he chanted as we stumbled into the ring and bludgeoned each other. By virtue of having started the semester on the wrestling team, I ended up in the same boxing section as Trent.

Despite the friendship we had begun to develop off the wrestling mat, he had no mercy in the ring. Technique I had in spades; the problem was my glass jaw. I went down like a sack of potatoes every single bout. Each time, Trent escorted me to the medic for smelling salts and an ice pack. I had a hard time trying to focus my anger at such a magnanimous opponent. Trent was that kind of friend: hard to like, harder to hate. Off I went to calculus with my head like cotton candy and a bruised chin that telegraphed to every classmate that I was another victim of morning Fight Club. In the end, I got a B in the class. I was surprised since I had gone 0–4 in graded bouts.

"Sir, why didn't you flunk me?"

"Because you kept coming back for more," he said, slapping me hard enough on the back to leave a palm imprint under my sweaty T-shirt. "That, and you fall gracefully."

Keeping in mind my boxing instructor's backhanded compliment, I attended a briefing for Plebes interested in joining the parachute team. Around the Corps of Cadets, the hand-selected team members strutted about like the supermen they probably imagined they were, unbound by gravity. I wanted to share that confidence and competence. They talked about performance under conditions of sustained danger, *in extremis*. I imagined I would need that in combat. Without telling my mother, I submitted a written application. After ten new teammates stormed into my room to welcome me, I was ecstatic. I should have been nervous.

"GO!" A FINGER POINTED menacingly at me as I crouched in the door of a helicopter. Tiny black specks, fifteen thousand feet below, scattered across the drop zone like ants on a cake crumb. At that height, reality approached the scale, and logic, of a map. I shivered under my jumpsuit.

"Go!" The finger wagged again and gestured toward the void.

I blinked hard and reached back one more time to touch the canvas pack on my back.

We spent two months just learning how to pack our own parachutes. "If the parachute fails," warned the coach, "you have no one to blame but yourself." There was no need for motivation with a margin of error so slim. I packed and repacked parachutes for hours, squeezing three hundred square feet of slippery nylon into a pack the size of a shoebox. I would return to my room with raw, bloody knuckles from wrestling with the lines. Now, after a dozen static-line jumps, I was ready to pull my own rip cord.

I leaped out and arched my back into the shape of a banana, as instructed. My eyes looked down toward the ground, and my body followed in a 120-mile-an-hour swan dive. I had never felt so alive—a million nerves dancing in the buffeting slipstream. Diving at the speed of a bullet train was the loudest silence imaginable, like a hurricane of emptiness. With every heartbeat I fell two hundred feet. The ground rushed toward me in a blur. One minute of free fall, sixty seconds alone to glide, to spin, to flip over and over and over, each rotation an insult to order. I smiled at the altimeter dial racing toward zero and pulled my rip cord. Imminent danger produces a bizarre clarity of purpose.

One one-thousand, two one-thousand, *whack*. Before I could count to three, my shoulders pulled taut and an invisible force snapped my body back to the vertical. A gigantic canopy billowed out in a sail of black and gold. A minute later my feet touched the ground again.

Plebe year was survival. Plebe year was endurance. Plebe year was obedience, discipline, and conformity. Every moment I spent above ground level was a refuge, a rebellion, a refutation. I needed to know I still owned part of who I was. Like Walt Whitman, I needed to "sound my barbaric yawp over the rooftops of the world." West Point deliberately trained my body and mind. Skydiving educated my soul.

4

Sleep Is for the Dead

An object at rest will remain at rest and an object in motion will remain in motion unless acted upon by an external and unbalanced force.

ISAAC NEWTON, *Principia Mathemetica*

"THE BEST SUMMER OF YOUR LIFE," SNICKERED THE upperclassmen describing the two-month block of field training we began a month after finishing Plebe year and starting Yearling year. At the end of June I returned to West Point for Camp Buckner—a surreal combination of a lakeside wilderness retreat and guerrilla training camp. At first sight it looked as bucolic as the lake where my father and I used to catch bullfrogs. Dozens of Quonset huts nestled in the pine-clad hills and sandy shores surrounding Lake Popolopen. Fishing docks and picnic tables fought for space between tennis courts and horseshoe pits. But cadets walked around in camouflage with rifles. Buckner was summer camp with automatic weapons.

Designed to expose us to the various branches of the Army—from military intelligence and aviation to infantry and artillery—Buckner packed a year's worth of military training into forty days and forty nights of rain, mud, and sweat. To make matters worse, I had snapped my wrist on a bad parachute landing earlier in the summer and was wearing a shoulder-to-wrist cast. Unless I wanted to repeat the "best summer," I needed to do everything my classmates did with 25 percent fewer limbs.

My personal demon at Camp Buckner was land navigation. Armed with an eight-digit GPS coordinate, a map, and a compass, the objective was to maneuver over hill and dale, through fetid swamps and up vertical cliffs in order to capture the code letters on small orange triangles mischievously hidden behind bushes and boulders. The first time I looked at a military map, I couldn't make heads or tails of the squiggly lines indicating altitude contours. Hence, the first few iterations saw me stumble through the woods as clueless as Hansel and Gretel without bread crumbs. Every tree looked the same. I returned to the course grader with an empty sheet of grid coordinates. The only comfort was comparing myself to the unfortunate cadets who wandered onto Interstate 87 by accident. Eventually I figured out how to read the contours and visualize hills and ridges without having to tramp to the top.

Navigating at night made day navigation look easy. Without the aid of night vision goggles, I crashed through briars and bushes with the grace of a sumo wrestler. We navigated in pairs, and my partner was just as hapless as I was. Every two minutes one of us fell to the ground as we tripped over a log or hidden gorge.

"Dammit!"

"What?"

"You snapped my face with another fucking branch." Wet boots made my language less poetic.

"I'm sorry," he replied sheepishly.

I could hear the cadre chuckling behind their night vision goggles. In order to protect my cast, I had to pirouette through the air in order to land safely on my left side. Fred Astaire meets Chuck Norris. We finished the course with half the points we needed and an hour over our time limit. "No-go" was the Army way of saying, "You failed. Try again." The fourth time was our charm. As the rest of our class played beach volleyball in the moonlight, we trucked out to the course for one last chance. An hour and fifty-nine minutes later, we crossed the finish line in sweat-drenched uniforms. We had passed.

Buckner's unstated agenda was to turn every cadet into an infantry officer. That message had more importance to me now than it had a year earlier. I had given a lot of thought to what I had discussed with the priest, and I was glad he had convinced me to stick it out. After Beast, the bombast had been more muted. There had been much more discussion of duty and honor than blood and guts. In fact, I had discovered how rare bayonet attacks actually were—just a fraction of 1 percent of all combat wounds, a reflection of Homo sapiens' natural aversion to intraspecies killing, especially at intimate distance. I might have to kill or order others to kill, but I was unlikely to find myself twisting a bayonet in someone else's liver.

Visceral concerns aside, there was still the matter of war's legitimacy in the first place. Studying history was a good antidote to idealistic pacifism. According to Plato, only the dead had seen the end of war. The Church concurred. I agreed with Saint Augustine that war should be a last resort, but I also recognized that warriors were needed when diplomacy failed. *Si vis pacem, para bellum.* Who seeks peace must prepare for war. I could either accept that responsibility or pass the buck. The brothers at Bishop Hendricken used to tell us: "To those to whom much is given, much is expected." It was a principle with deep personal resonance. During one of Buckner's lakeside Masses, we sang a refrain from Isaiah: "Here I am, Lord. . . . I have heard You calling in the night." I was conscious for the first time of what was expected.

As we spent nights marching through torrential thunderstorms, officers urged us on with motivational cheers. "Nothing but a little Ranger sunshine, cadets." "If it ain't raining, we ain't training." "You gotta love being cold, wet, and miserable. Love the Suck, men, love the Suck." On the face of it, their cheers were silly. Who could love being miserable? I had to admit, though, that their mantras worked. Brushing my teeth in the morning after a tough march really was a "10 percent morale boost." And it was hard to pity myself when I saw officers and other cadets smiling and laughing under the most adverse conditions. It wasn't so bad, I thought, just mud and rain. When I looked at the uniforms of the most heroic officers marching with us, cheering on languid cadets with little encouragements— "Come on, cadet, you've got it in you," "Keep pushing, we're almost there," "Don't quit on me"—their shoulders always seemed to bear the half-moon badge that marked a Ranger. I saw that leadership involved compassion in measure with conviction.

Their example pushed me through the last test of Buckner—Recondo, a full day of military skills tests, a grueling run under a heavy pack, a swim across the lake, and a series of scenarios designed to make us cooperate under the stress of time and fatigue. We gathered afterward by the lake at midnight, nearly twenty hours after our day had begun.

"I think you might need a new cast," offered a classmate, looking similarly ragged himself.

My cast was indeed in poor shape, caked in mud and soaked through with dirty lake water. My uniform was torn in a half-dozen places, and the camouflage paint on my face was smeared with sweat. My boots looked as if they had stomped through a swamp, and every muscle in my body ached. I was cold, wet, and miserable. And I loved it.

AFTER BUCKNER, LIFE AS a Yearling followed one of the laws we studied in physics: An object in motion stays in motion; an object at rest stays at rest. The cadets who stayed at rest, sleeping through long afternoons in their beds, had been liberated from the obligations and deprivations of Plebe year. If you slept half of every day, went their argument, West Point took only two years. Without the daily hazing, the only obstacle between Yearling year and graduation was maintaining a C average: "2.0 and go" was a frequent rejoinder to concerned instructors. Even the "Goat," the last-ranked graduate in the class, got promoted to Second Lieutenant, they liked to add.

For most of us, however, cadet life was a perpetual motion experiment. There wasn't enough time to consider where we were heading or whether we even wanted to arrive there. As Plebes we weren't allowed to look around in formation or while marching. Eyes front. The habit stuck. We each took as many as twenty credit hours a semester. Physics blurred into calculus in a mess of Greek letters. Morning workouts at the crack of dawn bookended the day with moonlit races to Thayer Gate and back. When I wasn't learning economics or history, I was practicing martial arts in gym class, tutoring the Plebes I was charged with developing, or leaping from helicopters. Trent and I stole a line from *Dr. Who* as our motto: Sleep is for the dead.

Yearling year was my first opportunity for upper-level electives. I registered for a two-semester sequence of French literature. If there wasn't time to read for pleasure, I could at least read for credit. My attraction to literature grew out of the same love of stories that drew me to history. Adventure, romance, courage: It was all there. My professor, a Swiss civilian Ph.D., was a pleasant change from the typical locked-and-loaded military professor. Although just as disciplined in her approach to academics as the officers, she was creative in her approach to what could have easily been a lifeless trudge through seventeenth-century France. She brought us off post to act out Corneille or Molière at her home. (She managed to get permission for the Firsties in the class. I tagged along, breaking at least seventeen cadet regulations.) At the end of the course, when discussing the development of surrealism, we made found-object sculptures and wrote nonsensical "Dada" poems. This was not what I had expected at West Point.

One author we read, Antoine de Saint-Exupéry, a daring pilot-intellectual, spoke of what I had been trying to articulate to my family about the draw of military service. Flying without instruments as a postal courier on the South American "Aéropostale," Saint-Exupéry wrote of the camaraderie that developed between men engaged in dangerous enterprise for the benefit of mankind: "The grandeur of a profession is . . . above all, uniting men: there is only one true luxury, that of human relationships." Danger was the great equalizer, the condition under which man was exposed, vulnerable, and ultimately heroic. I wondered at the time whether I would ever get the opportunity for danger and camaraderie, almost unique in the modern world to the profession of arms.

Apart from the rare, illicit champagne soirée at our professor's home, I didn't have many distractions from the monastic life of a cadet. Unlike the campuses where my high school friends partied five nights a week, West Point ranked dead last on a college survey of party schools. Dragging us down were fifty pages of draconian regulations dating to the Prohibition era. Alcohol in the barracks was strictly forbidden. So much as a single can of beer hidden in a footlocker could mean a hundred hours marching back and forth across the quad in full parade dress uniform. The Firsties could drink, but only at one location on the academy, watched over by humorless officers. Parties were so rare that the singular exceptions earned lasting fame. One urban legend told of a secret keg party on the top floor of our barracks the year before. They had allegedly lifted the keg from the woods behind the barracks with a pulley system designed according to plans from a required civil engineering course.

Besides beer, the other preoccupation of most college students is sex. The administration went out of its way to convince us that we were sexless initiates into a military monastery. We half-believed the rumor that the senior officers had placed an undetectable chemical in the "Beat Navy" milk cartons to hold down our libidos. Although there were nearly 150 women in my class of a thousand, they were never referred to as such by officers. The preferred language was biological, using "female" rather than "woman." Sexual liaisons between cadets happened, of course, but well out of sight of the officers. Cadet regulations stipulated that no two cadets of opposite sex could occupy a room without the door open at least 90 degrees. Even with three cadets in a room, male and female cadets were prohibited from sitting on the same piece of furniture. Cadets who insisted on dating each other were left with no other option but to exercise together. This led in due course to the well-worn joke about a cadet "date"—running in tandem around post. Public displays of affection, PDAs to the acronym-obsessed at West Point, were unconscionable. Holding hands would send an observant officer into a tailspin of outrage. In the event that one's hormones could not be restrained, there was only one outlet: "Flirty." Flirtation Walk's two square acres of wooded paths were roped off from the prying eyes of officers. At night they were free-fire zones of cadet fornication. Observing the lessons of Buckner, cadets were wise to bring flashlights, bug spray, and ponchos. Safely quarantined from forest romances, the rest of the campus carried on in celibate frustration.

Yearling year sped by bullet fast. Friendships forged at the drop zone and in marathon study sessions provided the only consolation to months of tedious lectures, physics problem sets, and military duties. The highlight of my year was the Brigade Wrestling Championships. The idea came from Aram Donigian, the same disciplinarian who had drilled military bearing into me over countless hours standing at attention outside his office.

"Mullaney, someone told me you were a state champion. Is that true?"

"Yes," I responded cautiously, "but in Rhode Island, not Iowa."

"Why don't you go for the Brigade title?" he asked, referring to the tournament open to any cadet who wasn't on the varsity team. "I'll coach you," he offered.

"Why not?" I said after thinking for a minute. I couldn't resist the opportunity to wrestle again. Beginning the next morning, we woke at 5:15 every day, then climbed the football stadium's stairs, power-lifted in the weight room, or drilled takedowns a hundred times in a row. After four months I was ready.

The tournament was intense, drawing several dozen state title winners who had just missed the varsity cut. Aram coached me from the corner of the mat as I advanced through the first few brackets. In the semifinals, I managed to eke out a victory. The final match took place on a single mat surrounded by cadets who knew nothing about wrestling but relished the gladiatorial drama nonetheless. In the second of two periods, the tendons in my shoulder ripped with a painful dislocation. I grunted and tried to shake it loose as my opponent felled me with a low-ankle takedown. He turned me from my stomach repeatedly, running up the points until the score was tied. Finally, I managed to force my shoulder back into its socket. I burned the clock, and we paused before a sudden death period. With my arms above my head, my chest moved like an accordion with deep breaths as I tried to regain my wind.

"Go for the headlock, Craig," Aram urged. "He's tired and hanging his head."

"It's too risky," I argued. "If I slip, it's done. He'll have two points."

"Don't slip."

I walked back out onto the mat a different person. A surge of energy flooded my muscles, and I focused on my opponent's neck. At the referee's whistle we butted heads in a wrestler's tie-up. I slipped my left arm under my opponent's armpit and behind his neck. Simultaneously, I shot my other hand behind his head, swiveled my hips beneath his, and lifted his body off the mat. His feet flew over his head as we landed with a thump on the mat. The impact knocked the wind out of him, and the referee slammed his palm onto the mat.

I leaped up, and the crowd erupted in applause as I lifted just one arm high in the air. My father smiled from the stands. From the corner of the mat, Aram ran to me and gave me a bear hug that my compressed lungs could hardly endure.

"You didn't slip," he whispered in my ear.

5

The Price of a Salute

It is as if a surgeon had to practice throughout his life on
dummies for one real operation.

SIR MICHAEL HOWARD

THE FIRST LIVING THING I KILLED WAS A RACCOON.
On a warm June night atop a Mississippi River bluff near Dubuque, Iowa,
the coonhound bayed incessantly, wagging its tail with the satisfaction of
having treed the raccoon we had been chasing for hours. I lifted the rifle
to my shoulder and squeezed the trigger just as I had on the firing range
with an M16. The raccoon fell to the ground, its fur a bloody mess. Entrails
leaked out in pink streams.

"It's a she coon." Trent punched me in the arm.

"Oh . . . damn," I said, looking down at the thing I had hunted so
fervently.

"Well, Daniel Boone, pick 'er up. She's yours now."

"How?"

Trent looked bewildered by my naïveté.

"By the tail, of course."

I lifted the mass of fur and blood by its bony tail and followed Trent
toward the pickup truck. The raccoon's blood smeared my jeans and left a
trail of red through the wheat. I had expected more of a Hemingway moment when I had accepted Trent's offer to fly home with him from West
Point on our first block of leave after Yearling year. I had hoped by hunting
to connect with a primeval tradition. Now I understood why hunting so-

cieties traditionally followed their hunts with ritualistic ablutions. *Maybe killing was just something you get used to?* We skinned the raccoon at Trent's farm, and I preserved the tail to bring back to my father. This was a tangible conquest he could understand. I pinned the tail to a large walking staff I crafted from a birch branch. I sanded it down and preserved it with linseed oil. Near the top I curled rawhide to make a handle. On its side, I carved ARMY DAD, burning each letter into the wood. When I returned home, my father replaced his Irish shillelagh with the staff I had carved. On his daily walks the raccoon tail drove our Labrador into a frothed frenzy.

AFTER A BRIEF THREE weeks of vacation, I returned to West Point for more summer training at Camp Buckner. Every cadet had to spend a month during his third or fourth cadet summer training underclassmen. It had been an illusion as a Plebe and Yearling to think the training was focused on us. In fact, West Point placed far more emphasis on the cadets leading the training. Can they build a team? Do they have what it takes to lead soldiers in the "real Army" beyond West Point's perimeter? My role, typical for a Cow, was to train a squad of twelve new Yearlings just one year younger than me. What limited authority I had stemmed from a combination of having gone through Buckner once myself and an enamel pin signifying my rank.

Leading was at once both simple and difficult. I made obvious rookie mistakes, taking shortcuts that I believed would preserve morale. One night after a long day shooting in the rain, I tried to get my squad some extra sleep by having them turn in their rifles to the arms room without cleaning them thoroughly. Predictably, the carbon left over from firing blank ammunition fossilized in the barrels, making the next day's cleaning five times more difficult. I had always criticized my leaders for being obsessed with details and tried the opposite tack with my squad. On one foot march, I failed to give them a packing list. The result: Half of them overpacked and struggled under the heavy load while the other half threw out items they didn't think they would need. One cadet glared at me as a thunderstorm drenched him.

"You didn't tell us to pack our ponchos."

"Here," I said, "take mine." I handed it over. "My mistake."

An officer marched up alongside me. Now, sans poncho, I was sopping wet.

"Another lesson for the kit bag," he said. "Trust, but verify."

In the military, I learned, details matter. I never failed to check my men before a mission again. Other lessons were subtler. For one, leading from the front was much harder than the slogan suggested. I had always thought my leaders had it easier than me. Being a leader changed my mind. General Eisenhower used to describe leadership as a piece of string. Push it, he would tell a young officer, and the string would bunch up in failure. Instead, he said, you had to pull. There is a chain of command, but there is also a chain of influence. To really get my squad to do anything, yelling was counterproductive. They might return to practicing knots, but as soon as I turned away, they would stop. Instead, I had to lead by example. If I wanted them to march faster, I had to march twice as fast with a smile on my face. If I wanted them to extend their threshold of pain, I had to push myself even harder, and under no circumstances could I afford to whine. I woke up earlier and went to sleep later than the squad every night. I said nothing, but they soon stopped complaining about fatigue.

The only way to gain my squad's loyalty was to show loyalty to them. I served them, not the other way around. They needed to know that I put their welfare above my own. In that sense, I imitated what I had seen my father do with his crews, making sure they had the equipment and training they needed, asking after their families, and covering for them during family emergencies. At the end of a long march along one of the ridges above Buckner, and before setting up my own tent, I first went around the squad and checked their feet one by one for blisters and swelling, doling out foot powder and moleskin as necessary. After sweating through thick socks, what their feet needed most was deodorant. Leadership smelled like blue cheese.

With fresh socks on our feet, and rucksacks comfortably off our shoulders and on the ground, we shot the bull, spit salty sunflower seeds into the tree line, and played hands of hearts as evening approached. A hum of crickets rose around us like an orchestra warming up, and mosquitoes began testing our bug spray defenses. Moments like these, in camp at the end of a hard day, were priceless. At the arrival of coffee and hot food trucked in by Humvee, a line formed in seconds. I was just as famished as my men, but the important principle—"Officers eat last"—placed me at the end of the line. A full stomach, a canteen cup of coffee, and the camaraderie of shared hardship—these were the tangible rewards of leadership.

I knew from my own struggles in Beast and Buckner that morale dropped quickest when I was alone. It was then that my focus shifted from completing a mission to escaping my own inner misery—a rock grinding inside my boot heel, a gnawing hunger in my gut, a shooting pain under the rucksack shoulder straps. The best antidote was a cohesive team. When someone else depended on me, I couldn't quit. As a Buckner squad leader, I spent much of my effort on building a strong team. I emphasized team successes over individual achievements and nudged the strong performers to help the weak. We developed nicknames, mascots, and inside jokes. I knew they had coalesced when they invited me along on a daring midnight raid to steal canoes from under the noses of the guards and paint our company logo on an enormous rock on the opposite side of Lake Popolopen. The squad no longer needed my motivation; they planned that whole midnight raid from the audacious beach launch to its ignominious finish standing at attention before the camp sergeant major.

But all the cohesion in the world was no substitute for tactical knowledge. Competence was the biggest morale booster. I drilled my squad every night after we returned from the field. While their classmates ate pizza by the lake, we reviewed procedures for calling in artillery fire.

"Why do we have to do this?" they moaned before setting to work.

"Because you want to win," I reminded them.

And win they did. At the end of the training block, they stood at the top of nearly a hundred squads at Buckner. After seeing their work pay off, my encouragement was superfluous.

This second summer at Buckner solidified my interest in becoming an officer. At the end of the summer, I had to commit to five years of service after graduation. Until that point, I had been free to walk away from West Point with no obligations whatsoever. A number of my classmates had, ensuring that West Point graduated only those who really wanted to be in the Army. The raw tests of physical mettle and blind obedience as a Plebe and Yearling had given me confidence but little inspiration. Up to then at West Point, I had only learned to follow. It was a necessary but insufficient preparation for leading soldiers. I couldn't have known either the challenges or the rewards of leadership without trying it first. After training my squad, I knew that I wanted to be a platoon leader. Making them succeed had given me a satisfaction far greater than any individual achievement. The very act of leading was motivating: I wanted to deserve the men I would one day lead.

"THE LAND THAT GOD forgot, where the mud is eighteen inches deep and the sun is blazing hot." All I knew about Fort Benning and Airborne School was what I had heard in a cadence. For once the cadence wasn't an exaggeration. It was easy to understand why the British had chosen Georgia as a penal colony. I arrived at Benning a few days after finishing my leadership tour at Camp Buckner in order to begin Airborne School. Every cadet was required to pass at least one military training course in order to graduate. Options included everything from combat scuba diving to mountaineering. For me the choice was obvious. After more than a hundred free-fall skydives with the jump team at West Point, I wanted to expand my parachuting repertoire of acrobatic sport to include skills more relevant to the infantry. Unlike the skydiving I had done already, Airborne School prepared its students to jump at low altitudes, ideal for penetrating behind enemy lines. After five successful jumps I could call myself a paratrooper.

As I stepped out of the air-conditioned van that delivered me from the airport, my skin immediately started to perspire. Uncontrollable sweat. The air at Fort Benning was so thick with humidity that my uniform soon looked as if I had worn it in a rainstorm. Water steamed off the sleeves. The sun had turned the lawn on the training fields into nasty brown stubble, and I feared I was going to wilt next.

Benning was more like an open-air museum than a twenty-first-century training center of the world's dominant military. This was a post built to train millions of infantrymen to kill Germans. Everywhere were vacant fields to train volunteers and conscripts. Old Sherman tanks stood poised at intersections as if awaiting a wand to bring them to life. Streets named after Pershing and MacArthur wound through neighborhoods of crisp red-brick officers' quarters. Huddled between shady trees were half a dozen statues dedicated to old battles and their heroes. At the center of it all was a handful of two-story barracks and training pavilions that made up Airborne School.

They say that Airborne School "crams five days of training into three weeks." It is really not that hard to jump out of an airplane and land on the ground. In fact, Leonardo da Vinci had anticipated the parachute concept five hundred years earlier. According to him, "If a man has a tent of linen, with all the openings sealed up, he will be able to throw himself down from a great height without injury." The Army's parachutes had one purpose: drop us fast enough that we would be a hard target to shoot and slow enough that we didn't break every bone in our bodies crumpling onto the drop zone.

The whole point of Airborne School, it seemed, was to frustrate us so much that we would do anything, even jump out of a perfectly good airplane, in order to graduate. After two long weeks on the ground, proving that we could shuffle out of a mock plane, count to four, and land feetfirst in sawdust, we advanced to the final week of five real jumps, four during the day and one at night. On our first jump day we ran in full gear down Cardiac Hill to the parachute sheds bordering the airfield. I picked up the main parachute and began putting it on. It was the most uncomfortable backpack ever manufactured. Around my waist I strapped a reserve parachute the size of a rolled-up beach towel. This reserve was supposed to give me confidence that "if my main don't open wide, I've got a reserve by my side." The next verse of the Airborne cadence was less comforting, warning that "if that one should fail me too, look out, ground, I'm comin' through." *From a height of twelve hundred feet, would I bounce or splatter?*

After an excruciatingly slow and meticulous inspection, the jumpmasters had us sit down and wait for the plane. The gear cut off the circulation to every part of my body, but we were forbidden to so much as scratch our noses lest we inadvertently screw up our gear. Unlike the jumps I had done at West Point with a parachute I packed myself, jumping with gear I hadn't prepared kept my hands firmly clasped on top of the reserve.

What made me even more nervous were the "motivational" videos they had us watch as the hours ticked by slowly and my bladder filled to the brim while I continued downing canteen after canteen of water. Each video showed the gruesome results of different parachute malfunctions. One by one, paratroopers crashed into the fuselage of C-130 cargo planes, severed their limbs on the static line that attaches each suspended jumper to the receding jump door, knocked themselves unconscious in inadvertent collisions, or tumbled unnervingly through the sky with misshapen parachutes doing little to slow their descent. The background music running through my head was "Blood Upon the Risers," an Airborne cadence sung to the tune of the "Battle Hymn of the Republic."

> *There was blood upon the risers; there were brains upon the chute*
> *Intestines were a'dangling from his Paratrooper suit.*
> *He was a mess; they picked him up, and poured him from his boots,*
> *And he ain't gonna jump no more!*
>
> *(Chorus)*
> *Gory, gory, what a hell of way to die,*
> *Gory, gory, what a hell of a way to die,*
> *Gory, gory, what a hell of a way to die,*
> *And he ain't gonna jump no more!*

Definitely splatter. One of my West Point classmates hadn't gotten the message about leaving his equipment alone after the jumpmaster inspection. He adjusted his chin strap and was immediately removed from the course. The last thing the instructors wanted was to drag a dead student off the drop zone because his loose helmet had blown off in the propeller blast. The trick about rules in the Army was knowing which ones were important. Precise details mattered more when making a parachute drop than when folding underwear for inspection.

By the time we waddled up the ramp into the belly of the cargo plane, all I wanted was to get out of the harness. And the only way out of the harness was to leap from a hundred stories high onto a sandy drop zone on the Alabama side of the Chattahoochee River. Five minutes after takeoff, the jumpmasters signaled for us to stand up. We hooked our static lines onto a guide wire running the length of the plane. At intervals the jump-master shouted the time remaining, and we echoed each report down the ungainly column. *"Thirty seconds!"* I counted down in my head while watching the jumpmaster lean out the open door and check for the right spot. He positioned the first jumper at the door, a five-foot-two student the instructors had nicknamed "Oompah."

"Go!"

Oompah did not go.

"Go!"

He stood frozen at the edge of the door.

The jumpmaster planted his size 12 boot on Oompah's ass, and out he went into the blue. Next in line, I heard Oompah's scream evaporate quickly. The drills had been so repetitive that I didn't have to think. After inhaling sawdust for two weeks and enduring Georgia's unrelenting heat, the blast of fresh cold air from the jump door was inviting. I stepped out into the breeze, counted to four, and watched my parachute unfurl like an oversized handkerchief above my head. "Airborne!" I shouted to no one and concentrated on the rapidly approaching ground. I did a pull-up with the risers by my head and slackened my speed just as my boots knifed into the soft sand of Fryar Drop Zone. I tumbled ass over head and completed a half-dozen revolutions before coming to a stop on my back. I tasted blood in my mouth where I had bitten my tongue. The sky above darkened with a hundred green parachutes dangling students. I made the sign of the cross and watched in awe.

The remaining four jumps followed a similar script of waiting hours for a minute of exhilaration. Almost everyone passed, including a student who broke his ankle on the fourth jump, wrapped it in duct tape, and finished the last jump before reporting to the medics. At the graduation ceremony a grizzly sergeant stood in front of me in a red beret. He took a set of silver wings from my hand, positioned them above my left breast pocket, and hammered them into my chest with his fist. "Congratulations, Airborne." Despite the welt he left, I smiled as he walked off. Minutes later our formation was running back to the barracks. "I wanna be an *Airborne Ranger*," the jumpmasters shouted. With unprecedented enthusiasm we echoed the cadence, most of us aware that we had completed only the Airborne half of that implicit challenge.

AFTER JUMPING FROM PLANES, I studied them. I had earned one of a handful of slots to spend the first semester of Cow year as an exchange cadet at the Air Force Academy, a jewel of glass and aluminum reflecting the purple Rockies in Colorado Springs. I spent most of my time there in a plane or in the classroom learning the physics and aerodynamics of flight. To give me a taste of life as a pilot, the academy sent me to the airfield to learn how to fly an engineless glider. Riding the thermal vents in nearly complete silence was both peaceful and exhilarating. I pasted a poem by a Canadian Spitfire pilot on the opposite side of my flight checklist. One verse in particular summarized the magic of flying: "Oh! I have slipped the surly bonds of earth / and danced the skies on laughter-silvered wings . . . . I've chased the shouting wind along, and flung / my eager craft through footless halls of air." I began to understand why cadets there walked to class with their eyes darting every few minutes to the clouds drifting above.

Despite the delight I took in flying or hurtling my body through clouds at skydiving practice, my future as an infantryman was at ground level. I took my first serious military history courses at the Air Force Academy, including an independent study with a distinguished historian of the Napoleonic Wars. Twice a week he and I argued the merits of Napoleon's battles throughout Europe. With giant maps spread on his desk, he taught me how to see terrain from a strategist's perspective.

"See how he concealed this division behind the fog?" he said, pointing to a map of Austerlitz. "Pure brilliance."

Military history's most quoted theorist, Carl von Clausewitz, was one of the Prussians captured at Austerlitz. My supervisor contended that this was the *fog of war* that Clausewitz alluded to in one of his most quoted passages: "War is the realm of uncertainty; three-quarters of the factors on which action in war is based are wrapped in a fog of greater or lesser uncertainty. A sensitive and discriminating judgment is called for; a skilled intelligence to scent out the truth." Reading Napoleon and Clausewitz, I began to appreciate the intellectual challenges of ground warfare and the vital importance that personal leadership held in wisely harnessing and directing military power.

I studied Napoleon's campaigns in Spain. Flush with victory in central Europe, Napoleon decided to engineer a coup in Madrid and replace the Bourbon monarch with his brother Joseph, an early example of "regime change." He expected to devote only a small fraction of his *Grande Armée* to the occupation of Spain. In fact, within two years more than half of French combat power was tied up on the peninsula. How, I wondered, had the best military mind of his age made such a disastrous mistake?

For one, Napoleon had drastically underestimated the degree to which the Spanish would resist foreign occupation. Small groups of irregular soldiers banded together and began the first insurgency in modern military history. It was Lord Wellington, the British commander who aided the Spanish resistance against their common foe, who coined the term "guerrilla" to describe them. Geography also conspired against the French: "The entire country was intersected by steep mountain ranges where roads were virtually nonexistent, much of the countryside was practically barren, and the whole terrain was more suited for guerrilla than regular warfare." Napoleon had failed to adapt to the guerrilla tactics, insisting on brutal reprisals against sympathetic villagers that only served to swell the insurgency with fresh volunteers. In a major reversal of Napoleon's fortunes, guerrillas managed to force the surrender of more than eighteen thousand French soldiers in a single day near the town of Bailen. Where organized Prussian corps had failed to stop Napoleon at Austerlitz, untrained irregulars succeeded in Spain. Five years later the French limped off the peninsula a quarter of a million soldiers weaker.

After the semester at the Air Force Academy, I returned to West Point. I took several history courses, including a required survey of modern military history. Our reading measured in the hundreds of pages per week, everything from the Pacific campaign in World War II to Mao's principles of revolutionary warfare. Oddly, in retrospect, I took just one paragraph of notes about the Russians in Afghanistan, whose experience with mountain guerrillas had been as unsuccessful as Napoleon's.

The most compelling assignments had little to do with tactics or strategy, however. Instead, I was drawn to the memoirs of other soldiers. My curiosity had become more and more amplified as my future came into greater clarity and proximity. I wanted to know what combat was like internally. Reading Erich Maria Remarque's *All Quiet on the Western Front*, I wanted to know where he found the resolve to keep fighting in the trenches. What did he think of his officers? Was there anything they could say or do to make his war less horrible? To understand the ferocity of fighting in the Pacific, we read E. B. Sledge's *With the Old Breed: At Peleliu and Okinawa*, recounting his experience as a Marine. According to Sledge, he "had gradually come to doubt that there was a place in the world where there were no explosions and people weren't bleeding, suffering, dying, or rotting in the mud." And yet he kept fighting. How? And why, after smelling the stench of rotting corpses that couldn't be buried, did he conclude that, all things considered, he would do it again?

For Vietnam we read James McDonough's *Platoon Leader*, the memoir of a West Point graduate guarding a strategic hamlet. Considering that everyone in our class would eventually lead our own platoons, this was the most relevant selection. What was war like for the leaders? Were the officers ever scared? At least according to McDonough they were. He wrote, "The absence of fear in the face of combat would be a suspicious abnormality of character." His biggest fear was of failing to protect his men, of making some mistake that might kill his platoon. And that concern, for McDonough, came in direct conflict with the imperative to repeatedly send his squads on dangerous missions. Reading a West Pointer's account of combat also raised the question of whether West Point had prepared him (and, by extension, us) for war. Was he ready? His answer, that he was better trained than most but still not ready, was unsatisfying. I couldn't accept his assertion that the line between skill and chance in combat was ill-defined. If he had killed his platoon, would he have considered it failure or bad luck?

Later in the semester I had my first opportunity to view a real battle-field, although its guns had been quiet for sixty years. The History Department offered history majors the chance to spend their spring break studying military history in Normandy, France. After nine years of French, I leaped at the chance.

I GAZED OVER THE lip of the cliff. Ten stories below, breakers smashed at the rocks like sledgehammers. The face of the cliff was almost vertical and wet shards of stone gleamed in the sunlight. The wind swept up and past me, whipping my coat and chapping my lips. I could taste the salt. No way, I thought. There was no way a group of soldiers could ascend a cliff like that under fire. I knew they had, of course, because the large monument behind me said so, but it was nevertheless a ridiculous and audacious proposition.

In the early morning of June 6, 1944, a force of just over two hundred commandoes from the U.S. Army's 2nd Ranger Battalion climbed the cliffs of Pointe du Hoc, precipitously poised between the D-Day assault forces at Omaha and Utah Beaches in Normandy, France. After defeating impossible odds to gain this strategic foothold, the Rangers repelled German counterattacks for over two days, reducing their numbers to fewer than fifty Rangers capable of continuing the fight.

Before our group of history majors and instructors left West Point, we had watched director Steven Spielberg's *Saving Private Ryan*, his portrayal of the invasion. The opening sequence of the film had left me nauseous. The Higgins boats ferrying troops ashore were bullet magnets. As soon as the ramp opened, vicious German machine-gun fire shredded the first ranks. Soldiers jumped over the sides of the boats to avoid the targeted funnel at the ramp, some drowning as bullets pierced their lungs in the water. On the beach, limbs flew through the air, severed by mortar and artillery rounds. The visceral horror that Spielberg managed to capture on film was so graphic that some viewers had protested airing the film on network television. This was what I was signing up for as an infantry officer. The historian in me wanted to examine the German bunkers and the exit ramps leading off the beach so that I could better understand the terrain that drove the strategy. The future platoon leader in me was less analytical. I wanted to be there, to imagine for myself what war was like.

When I had the chance at Omaha Beach, I waded out into the frigid water in my jeans and sneakers. The waves slapped at my knees. My toes turned numb in my wet socks. With the surf tugging me at my ankles, I turned around and looked at the five hundred yards of beach I would need to cross before assaulting German pillboxes on the bluffs. I imagined being pinned down by enemy fire and watching my company stumble through a nightmare. In the film, Captain Miller, Tom Hanks's character, is asked by a corporal, twice, "What do we do now, sir?" That's what all this boiled down to: What do we do—now—sir? *What would I say?*

I turned for answers to one of the officers leading our trip. Lieutenant Colonel Guy LoFaro was one of the smartest history professors in the department and also one of the toughest. He knew a thing or two about courage. A Ranger himself, LoFaro had fought at Grenada in 1983. Several years later, when he was a major with the 82nd Airborne, a crazed gunman had opened fire on a formation of soldiers exercising at Fort Bragg. Unarmed and wearing gym clothes, LoFaro had charged more than 150 yards to assault the sniper's position. When he was ten yards away, he took a 5.56-millimeter tracer round to his gut. Special Forces soldiers eventually wrestled the sniper to the ground. He pled guilty to premeditated murder and received the death sentence. After five major surgeries and a forty-five-day coma, LoFaro survived and was awarded the military's highest peacetime medal for valor.

"How do you know how you'll handle combat?" I asked.

"You don't," he responded. "You'll never know until you're there."

He paused and looked out over the cliff at the rollers drifting inexorably toward the shore. I nodded slowly as he discharged wisdom in measured, thoughtful bursts.

"What you know for certain is that it will be chaotic and loud, and you'll be ready to piss in your boots. You'll be more scared of letting down your men than anything the enemy's gonna do to you. And then you'll lead from instinct and judgment. *That's the price of a salute.*"

Later that week we had a tour of the American cemetery on the bluffs overlooking Omaha Beach. I separated from the group and wandered off by myself.

Eleven thousand white crosses were arranged in perfect rank and file. A cold mist crept through the pine trees, dampening the rustle of needles. Underfoot, my shoes crunched the gravel path as the surf crashed faintly below. The mist thickened, creeping slowly from the water and through the ranks of crosses, and for a moment it seemed that it wasn't the mist that was moving. The crosses themselves were marching again, toward me.

6

Class Dismissed

Ever tried. Ever failed. No matter.
Try again. Fail again. Fail better.

SAMUEL BECKETT, "Worstward Ho"

I KNEW ONE THING, I CONCLUDED: I DIDN'T KNOW enough. I hung my head and contemplated the disaster before me. I was in the middle of my last mandatory summer training period before beginning senior year as a Firstie at West Point. This last training evolution placed me as a so-called third lieutenant, leading a platoon in a real Army infantry battalion at Fort Lewis, a sprawling base southwest of Seattle. The exercise I was fumbling was my first opportunity to lead soldiers in a simulated infantry maneuver. It wasn't pretty.

Half of my platoon was dead or wounded during a simulated raid on a chemical weapons lab. Everything was going well as we spread out from the helicopters and rushed toward the buildings. When we began our final assault, the "enemy" released smoke canisters considered to be nerve gas. I gave the signal to don our gas masks, and we continued the assault. What I hadn't realized was how much the gas masks would slow us down. It was like running with half a lung. As my soldiers' body temperatures spiked, they began falling down with heat cramps. There was enough water in our canteens to survive, but I had overlooked one small critical detail. In order to drink from the canteen with a gas mask, we needed a special attachment on the canteen cap. The problem is that 99 percent of the time, when we weren't drinking from gas masks, the little attachment had a tendency to snap off. On a previous mission I had had the platoon dutifully tape down every single canteen cap, fixing one problem but creating another, much bigger problem. One by one as we dehydrated, we found it impossible to tear off the tape with our thick rubber gloves. I panicked as the situation deteriorated, making matters worse. It wasn't long before our numbers shrank to the technical definition of "combat ineffective." The real platoon leader, shaking his head in disbelief, blew his whistle and canceled the rest of the mission.

"Cadet, you damn near killed the whole platoon."

"No excuse, sir," escaped my mouth instinctively, and I stared at my boots for a second or two.

In a strange coincidence, I was training with the same unit whose audacity had won it fame on the cliffs of Pointe du Hoc in Normandy. The 2nd Ranger Battalion was one of the Army's premier infantry outfits, stocked with handpicked soldiers and officers. Their standard of physical fitness was almost superhuman. Every morning the real lieutenants took turns running me into the ground. The lieutenant who had unwisely allowed me to direct his platoon in the raid was the fastest of the bunch. A thirty-seven-year-old former sergeant, he ran half marathons every weekend "just for fun." When he took me out on "short" runs of eight miles or so, he pushed a six-minute-mile pace. My pride had to step in where my lungs gave out, usually at the sixth mile. The brains in the unit also surprised me. One officer had a Ph.D. in physics. Four of the soldiers in my platoon had Ivy League SAT scores. Every officer and nearly every soldier in the battalion wore a Ranger tab.

The unit's training regimen was intense. When we shot at the rifle range, soldiers burned through thousands of rounds until a perfect shot was instinctive. When that got easy, the lieutenant introduced new levels of complexity, from shooting at night at moving targets to obstacle courses designed to add heart stress to marksmanship. Convinced that he had the best marksmen in the company, he took it one step further with high-speed paintball matches. As we raided an airport hangar at Lewis, I took a round right to the nose. It knocked me to the ground, and blood gushed from the cut it left. Standing over me, my lieutenant rubbed salt in the wound.

"That'll teach you. Imagine what a real round would feel like if you forgot to look up a stairwell before charging up it like John Wayne."

"Yes, sir."

"You're going to be a platoon leader—the brains of the platoon. Think first."

What had amazed me at Pointe du Hoc was the courage demonstrated by the Rangers. Boldness seemed to be all that mattered. After a month with the 2nd Ranger Battalion, I realized I was only half right. Deliberate planning required smarts. Execution required practice. Details counted. Courage mattered only if you got those elements right. With that realization I returned for my last year at West Point with a new commitment. There was a lot to learn before I would be ready to take a platoon.

I BEGAN DRINKING COFFEE in my senior year at West Point. When I arrived from Fort Lewis, I learned that I had been appointed to the staff that served as the student government for the Corps of Cadets. My particular responsibility was to be the planner-in-chief, scheduling and designing everything from blood drives and team-building runs to parades and the festivities leading up to the Army-Navy football game. Right next door to my room lived Liz Young, a bubbly cadet from Connecticut I had first befriended in Plebe history. We worked around the clock. One month into the year I was so tired that I regularly collapsed at my desk before I could make it to the bed.

The only consolation for the sleepless nights was sharing them with a great roommate. In a lucky draw, I bunked with Bill Parsons. I had had a few classes with Bill and his twin brother, Huber, but I didn't know him well before we worked together on staff. His reputation preceded him. Bill was the number one cadet in the entire class, an academic star in international relations, fluent in French and Spanish, quick-footed, and hardworking. Bill had grown up in Miami but was the furthest thing from flashy. He had the quietness of sincere humility. Bill and I became close friends, burning the midnight oil as we wrote plans for the Corps of Cadets. It wasn't all work: When the stress level peaked, we joined forces in water gun battles in the hallway, charging into Liz's room and dousing her with two gallons of ice cold water. Before parades, we would play the soundtrack to *Braveheart* at top volume and pretend we were strapping on kilts, axes, and shields rather than heavy wool tunics and wooden rifles. Our obsession with *Braveheart*, *Gladiator*, and *Saving Private Ryan* reflected the decision we had both made to become infantry officers after graduation. We were eager to fast-forward through nine months of inspections, parades, and engineering classes. West Point's challenges were prosaic by comparison with the exposure we had each had to the Army beyond our isolated campus.

Occasionally, I joined Bill and Huber for Bible study. Growing up in Catholic Rhode Island, I had never known any Baptists. Bill was diligent about his faith, digging into the text, looking for the correct interpretation, memorizing passages. I couldn't imagine Bill without a concordance Bible tucked into his rucksack. His enthusiasm led to missions work, sharing his faith with potential college converts on spring break. My faith was much more private, a conversation between God and me that I wasn't eager to share. I preferred the solemnity of Mass and its reliable rituals. Singing praise was unnatural for me, as were the long prayers Bill said before meals. We had extended conversations in our room about religion, politics, and philosophy. After a trip we took to the Holocaust Museum, where we had stood inside one of the freight cars that had shipped Jews to Auschwitz, we argued about whether man was naturally good or evil. How, I asked, could you argue man's inherent goodness after seeing Nazi scientists dunk Jewish prisoners in ice water to test how long it would take downed pilots to become hypothermic? Back and forth we would go, citing verses and saints, until we both realized how late it was. Bill was the first close friend who pushed my assumptions, even though (or perhaps because) we hardly ever agreed.

A FEW MONTHS EARLIER, Major John Nagl, an instructor in the Social Sciences Department, had gathered Bill, Liz, me, and a couple dozen of my classmates into a room and encouraged us to apply for the Rhodes

Scholarship, a ticket to study at the oldest university in the English-speaking world: Oxford. Nagl's presentation was mesmerizing, with slide after slide of centuries-old quads, cobblestone streets, and portraits of former military scholars who had honed their wits in smoke-filled pubs over pints of warm beer. Given the harried pace of cadet life, the idea of an intellectual idyll in England, where I could spend an entire afternoon reading in a café or debating with scholars, could not have been more tantalizing.

"Only the best students in the country win," said Nagl at the end of his brief. "If you think you're one of the best, come back in the fall ready to work." The gauntlet had been thrown.

I had first run into Nagl at Camp Buckner the year before. After a brief discussion about graduate school, I asked him what I could do to prepare.

"First," he said, "relax.

"Second, buy a journal.

"Third, write in that journal every day. Observe. Analyze. Synthesize. The point is to write, ask questions, and, most important, to *think*."

"Yes, sir."

After I had returned from the Air Force Academy and produced two full journals for Nagl's inspection, he introduced me to Paul Yingling, a field artillery major who taught political philosophy at West Point. Arguing that a journal risked becoming an echo chamber, Yingling insisted that I test out my ideas over coffees with him. He cared less about the Rhodes Scholarship than he did about my personal development.

"Conversation," Yingling claimed, "is an end in itself." We talked endlessly about his favorite authors. I'd never engaged in a no-holds-barred discussion with a professor before. The questions were impossible. Did I agree with Machiavelli, must a prince be prepared to "enter into evil, when forced by necessity"? Was that applicable today, for an officer? Was it "safer to be feared than loved"?

"An interesting life," Yingling told me, "is one filled with controversial successes punctuated by occasional and spectacular failures." We picked apart T. S. Eliot's "Love Song of J. Alfred Prufrock," a poem about unrequited love that was one of a handful I'd copied into my journal. Don't be like the timid Prufrock, Yingling warned, asking yourself: "Do I dare? Do I dare disturb the universe?" Life wasn't meant to be lived from the sidelines. In one email exchange, Yingling drove home the sense of urgency I felt about preparing to lead outside West Point's gates. He suggested that I was "in the door," about to jump. "Very soon, the costs for making bad choices will rise exponentially. . . . Oxford may be your last chance to contemplate first principles in a systematic manner. . . . This process is like getting shot at: *It has the marvelous effect of focusing one's mind.*"

IN EARLY NOVEMBER, AFTER dozens of coffees with Yingling and an equal number of drafts of my Rhodes application, Bill, Liz, and I all received letters inviting us to interviews. Bill's interview was in Atlanta, but both Liz and I had interviews in the same Boston district. We spent the next two weeks grilling each other after hours about current events and policy nuance, thinking in vain that this was a test we could cram for. The invitation indicated that there would be a cocktail party the night before the interview. Like Cinderella before the ball, I realized I had nothing to wear. I was hesitant to arrive in my cadet uniform; my answers would be robotic enough without adding the larynx-choking wool tunic. I called up the best-dressed mentor I knew: Charles Hooker.

Charlie was a West Point graduate in his mid-forties who had opened his home and family to me and several other friends, including wrestlers Trent, Jim, and Chris. After a career in the Special Forces, he became a successful Wall Street banker and there learned the things they don't teach you in the jungle, such as picking the right Bordeaux vintage and distinguishing between hound's-tooth and herringbone. He was a natural mentor for a working-class kid who knew as little about the professional world as the real Army beyond West Point. Charlie's father had been a sergeant major, an enlisted man whose work ethic must have mirrored my own father's. In him I found the unconditional support of a parent and the experience of a soldier-financier.

Charlie and his wife, Lisa, put me through a high-intensity fashion exercise in the walk-in closet of their New Jersey home. Designer suits and footwear lined two levels stretching fifteen feet to the back.

"I think maybe the alligator-skin belt and wingtips. What do you think?" asked Charlie.

"Sure," I responded. *What were wingtips?*

"How do you like your cuffs?"

"Huh?"

"Regular or French?"

"French," I guessed, and Charlie pressed a pair of cuff links into my hand.

He began fitting a coat around my shoulders.

"How about that—it's a perfect fit." Charlie fixed a folded handkerchief in my pocket. "Craig, you are ready for cocktail combat."

Relieved of the burden of making a fashion faux pas, I packed my suit and drove to a set of interviews in New England. By the final round in Boston, I was able to relax at the cocktail party, despite the mahogany-paneled stuffiness of a Beacon Hill brownstone. Conversation hovered several levels above the typical mess hall banter I was used to. One gentleman asked me how I thought the Internet might transform the American economy. I sipped my chardonnay, garbled some nonsense, and got a nodding head that seemed to say, "You don't have a clue what you're talking about." I didn't. Only after the party did I learn from Liz, who was also interviewing in my district, that the gentleman I was unimpressing had been in President Clinton's cabinet. I hoped the interviews would go better. After the party, I called Nagl.

"What's your joke?" he asked.

"Huh?"

"You need a joke."

"Sir, you know me. I don't do jokes."

"Then I guess you won't be drinking warm beer. Fort Benning will be beautiful in August."

"Do you have a joke?" I was pretty sure this was what he had wanted me to ask from the get-go.

"You're interviewing right after Liz?"

"Yes, sir."

"When you walk in, ask the panel how you look in your uniform."

I woke up, went for a jog, snacked on a bagel, and read the newspaper. After finishing, I walked over to the St. Botolph Club. Before the cocktail party, the only private club I had ever entered was the country club where I had spent high school summers bussing tables and watching the wealthy kids lounge by the pool. I would have been intimidated even if the panel hadn't included a cabinet secretary. I hoped my uniform would make me look bigger than I felt.

"Good morning, Craig." An older lawyer in a pin-striped suit greeted me in the hallway. "Follow me."

I closed the heavy oak door behind me and paused as I took in the dark wood paneling, bookshelves of leather-bound volumes, and nine panelists arranged around a long table. I had learned their day jobs at the party. One presided over the Massachusetts Senate. Another younger Rhodes scholar ran a nonprofit that provided Internet access to low-income communities, while a third taught moral philosophy at Harvard. There was a surgeon who penned articles for the *New Yorker* and another full-time columnist who was syndicated in newspapers across the country. My seat was the empty one at the end, the one I had learned during Buckner ambushes to call "The Kill Zone." I gamely delivered Nagl's "joke" but heard only a couple of polite chuckles.

Yingling had encouraged me to approach the interview like a conversation rather than an interrogation. This was easier said than done. The actual interview was like getting cross-examined by a committee of Nobel laureates. Questions followed no logical path but instead jumped across fields in a way that made my brain hurt. Is the military a just instrument of power? Could you please outline the major works of French literature since the seventeenth century as they pertain to the development of the modern French novel? What is the second law of thermodynamics? Define a *good* war. Was Vietnam a good war? Would you expel a soldier who told you he was gay? When I gave a response I thought was good, they frowned. When I balked, they smiled. Fifteen minutes was an eternity. After thanking the panel for their time (like thanking a firing squad), I walked out in a daze. There was no way they were going to select me, especially considering the ridiculous résumés of the Ivy League candidates contending for just four slots. One guy spoke eleven languages fluently and had been an election observer in Kosovo. I was way out of my depth.

Liz had waited for me in the lobby, and the two of us walked down to a bar and watched our classmates cheering Army against Navy in the football season finale. Army was losing badly. I called my parents, who were at the game in Philadelphia, and told them my chances looked as poor as Army's. "That's okay, Craig," said my father. "You did your best." I wasn't sure. At halftime, we walked back to get the results in person. The nine scholarship candidates gathered in the waiting room, wringing hands and tapping feet. I twisted a piece of string in my pocket.

The interviewers filed into the room. I stood up next to Liz to receive the verdict. The pin-striped lawyer, acting as jury foreman, read each name slowly.

"Elizabeth Young."

Liz erupted with one of her patent smiles as the panelists continued with another three names.

"Oh, my God. Oh, my God. Oh, my God." Liz, her hair bobbing out of control, was practically jumping off the ground. She turned and gave me an enormous hug. As the guy next to me shot me a look full of daggers, I realized that the last name had been mine.

"I'm going to Oxford," I kept repeating under my breath as the panelists shook our hands one by one. I rushed off to the phone booth and called Nagl.

"I won, and so did Liz." I had to keep my voice down, knowing that the other students hadn't all left the building yet. Nagl's reply was unintelligible, something between "Hooah" and "Fucking A."

"Thank you, sir, for all your help. I couldn't have done it without you."

"Stop kissing my ass, Craig."

"How'd Bill do?" I asked.

"No dice."

"Oh." The news that Bill hadn't been selected deflated my excitement. I knew how disappointed Bill would be. Every step along the way we had been a team.

"Great job, Craig. Go celebrate."

My next order of business was to call my parents in Philadelphia. My father almost ruptured my eardrum as he announced the results to thirty thousand fans in Veterans Stadium.

"I'm proud of you, Craig. I'm really, really proud of you."

My mother told me afterward that when my parents returned home, my father took a trip to my hometown and found the preschool that, seventeen years earlier, had kicked me out. My father never forgot a slight. "Just thought you should know my son's a Rhodes scholar." He turned around before they even had a chance to figure out who he was talking about.

TRENT WASN'T GOING TO let me get a big head. As soon as I returned, we were back in the weight room at 5:25 a.m. I had been working one muscle, my brain, at the expense of the others. Trent quickly made that clear by breaking me set after set until my arms collapsed. The bench press was the great equalizer.

"Don't give me any of that 'Rhodes scholar' bullshit. An Oxford degree won't make you any stronger."

"Point taken," I gasped as Trent waited until the last possible second to lift the barbell I had let sink to my ribs. "It doesn't take a 'Rhodes scholar' to (fill in the blank)" became a frequent refrain in the Army whenever my ego inflated or I reverted to absentminded habits.

After winning the scholarship, my last six months at West Point were less frantic. I enrolled in one elective that acted as an antidote to academic grade grubbing. It was a contemporary poetry course taught by Marilyn Nelson, a visiting poet. I had debated signing up for another poetry class after Plebe poetry, but after hearing the Army Chief of Staff, General Eric Shinseki, refer to soldiering as an "affair of the heart," I decided to give it a try. I wasn't getting much "heart" training in the required steel design course I was taking with Bill and Huber Parsons. "Plug and chug," we called it, agonizing through mindless spreadsheets. Poetry, by contrast, was anything but a chug. We read Allen Ginsberg and James Dickey, William Meredith and Robert Lowell. Professor Nelson mixed it up with Yeats, Wordsworth, Frost, and Keats. Every class began with a five-minute meditation because, she said, poetry was the interior analogue of travel, an exploration of the mind and soul. We were also learning how to stand still. Poetry didn't happen to a mind crunching task lists. West Point was like looking at a newspaper photo at nose distance. You see the dots, but not the picture. Although combat would require us to see both the forest *and* the trees, West Point was a school for lumberjacks. I hoped to find some perspective in literature. It had been one of my compelling reasons for applying to Oxford.

In February I flew to England for a long weekend. I couldn't wait to see Oxford, even at the cost of two months' cadet salary. The weekend was a preview of my next two years. I bought last-minute tickets to an Irish play in London's West End and spent the next day walking around Oxford with no destination in particular. I attempted one of our poetry assignments, a Zen walking meditation: "Walk as if you are printing your footsteps on the ground." After nearly four years at West Point I was eager to walk with that sense of quiet deliberation, as if walking, like Yingling's conversations, was its own reward.

My last night had a full moon. The February night air was brisk, and the wind rattled the branches above the crushed gravel path. Magdalen College's deer herd huddled for warmth like gray ghosts in their enclosure. I stopped where a locked gate blocked my path. In the high stone wall to my left was a bronze plaque engraved with a poem by C. S. Lewis, the Magdalen professor who had written the Narnia books that turned me into a compulsive reader as a child. In the moonlight, I read the poem twice, the second time out loud. From my coat I took out my journal and scribbled a favorite line: "We shall escape the circle and undo the spell." That's what I wanted—to balance the education at West Point with its photo negative.

On the flight home I listed all the places I would travel: Prague, Istanbul, Moscow, Tokyo, Edinburgh, Cairo. I wanted to explore new academic fields, try new sports, and make new friends. On the other hand, I also had some delusional ambitions: sing in a chorus, write poetry, ski the Alps. The magic of Oxford on a moonlit night had gone to my head. I double-underlined, like a math answer, my number one priority: "fall in love." Approximately once every three months for the next two years I would revise my Oxford "objectives," adding requirements to gain a pilot's license, read all of Shakespeare, and pick up my father's ability to whistle for a cab with two fingers.

Romantic musings contrasted sharply with more immediate concerns. As a result of winning the Rhodes, and the peculiar logistics of officer training, I would have to finish Ranger School before the fall semester began at Oxford. My classmates, whose schedules weren't as convoluted, wouldn't start Ranger School, the Army's famously grueling leadership crucible, until the following January, after they had completed the Infantry Officer Basic Course. I would do that training, four months in length, only after I returned from England. If the basic course was like a bachelor's degree in infantry tactics, then Ranger School was a Ph.D. in physical toughness and mental endurance. Winning the Rhodes reversed the sequence for me, meaning that I would have, in West Point parlance, "a steep learning curve." More like vertical, I realized, as I spent my mornings in the gym with Trent and my afternoons running with Bill. I signed up for the Boston Marathon to give me an incentive to push harder.

Ranger School demanded that candidates understand how to write combat operations orders, the tactical plans written at a mind-numbing level of detail. I composed and briefed orders every week until I could rattle off plans without any note cards. "It's all about confidence," my mentor, Major William Ostlund, said repeatedly. A flawed order delivered on time and with confidence always beat an otherwise perfect but mumbled order. Ostlund told me I would rarely have time in combat to prepare ten-page orders. More often, he said, I would brief a plan conceived in fifteen minutes off a map spread out on the hood of a Humvee. The value of more detailed planning at Ranger School was in conditioning my mind to anticipate contingencies and instinctively take account of details.

A week after I completed the Boston Marathon, Ostlund surprised me with a mandatory physical fitness test. A high score was a prerequisite for Ranger School. At that point I could barely walk on my bruised feet. I met him at 5:30 a.m. by the train tracks. Lights were just coming on across the Hudson River in Garrison. As I stretched my cold muscles, Ostlund turned to me.

"Don't expect the Ranger instructors to cut you any slack for being a Rhodes scholar. If you're going to pass Ranger School, you'd better be able to get through a PT test with all the odds stacked against you."

It was a prophetic warning; I ran my two miles as fast as my sore feet could move and puked as I crossed the finish line.

"Just weakness leaving the body . . ." Ostlund smiled.

Training for Ranger School and preparing for Oxford occurred in parallel. I was just as unprepared to live by myself at a foreign university as I was to pass a guerrilla warfare course. For four years West Point had taken care of nearly every domestic chore, all in an effort to keep us focused on the serious business of academics, leadership training, and physical conditioning. I had no idea how to cook, had never done my own laundry, and my wardrobe consisted of two pairs of jeans and khakis and a few polo shirts. I had never balanced a checkbook or learned how to budget.

Major Nagl's wife, Susi, one of my history thesis advisors, took on my cooking deficiency. Twice a month I walked over to their apartment with three other cadets and took turns stuffing quail, distinguishing shallots from onions, and flambéing Bananas Foster. For months it looked as if I would starve in England. One night I made a mess of the pears I was supposed to peel before poaching.

"Craig, what did you do to those poor pears?"

Susi looked at the knife in my hands.

"Oh, dear," she exclaimed.

"What's wrong?" I asked.

"You're using the blunt edge of the knife."

"Right."

"That's okay. We'll just make a sauce. Good try, though," she added.

To my credit, I was adept at making coffee, and Susi taught me how to top it with homemade whipped cream laced with Kentucky bourbon. As valuable as the survival cooking lessons were the tips for choosing wine (Rule #1: Juice comes in boxes, not good wine). Susi had been on the Oxford varsity wine team. Back then she could tell the color, vintage, grape varietal, and year of six different wines—blindfolded. At this stage, distinguishing white from red was a challenge for my taste buds. I added wine tasting to my growing list of Oxford goals.

One Saturday I woke up at dawn and ran beside my company's team as they completed an all-day endurance course. After ten miles of running in jungle boots with a rucksack filled with eighty pounds of books, I collapsed facedown on my bed. My knees were flashing beacons of pain. I had broken the cardinal rule of military training: understanding the difference between hard and stupid. I awoke five hours later and drove with Trent, Jim, and Chris to New York City. We checked into our rooms at the University Club and changed into full dress gray, the most elaborate cadet uniform in our arsenal. This was Charlie Hooker's idea of a proper pregraduation send-off, the last big night for "his" cadets before we scattered to the four winds. Trent and Jim would head to Germany and Chris to Kansas.

The door to our private dining room opened, and Charlie's fellow West Point bankers greeted us in tuxedos. We began with vodka martinis and Beluga caviar, graduated to exquisite veal scallops and 1985 Bordeaux, and retired to the billiards room with Cuban cigars and vintage port. As the night grew late, the old grads sent us to Greenwich Village with a driver and town car. Driving through Manhattan with the windows open, surrounded by friends, and buoyed with spirits, I was on top of the world.

Twelve hours before I had been marching with an eighty-pound rucksack on my back. Five weeks later I would be facedown in mud.

GRADUATION WEEK ARRIVED AS the boxes I packed for Oxford steadily climbed to the ceiling. Next to the crates of books were duffel bags stuffed with gear I would need for Ranger School. The two destinations couldn't have been any more different. Fortunately, my father had arrived with his eight-passenger van to help me move. Even after four years of military training, I still wasn't allowed to pack the van. Like lawn mowing, egg frying, and car washing, this was a skill over which my father believed he had a monopoly. The rest of the family tagged along for several days' worth of award ceremonies and parades. My mother and father couldn't stop smiling, despite the unsparing heat. My sisters, Bridget and Kelsey, swiveled their heads at every well-built cadet who jogged past. I was so consumed with packing, however, that I nearly missed my brother's curiosity.

Although he was the third of four kids and already a freshman at Bishop Hendricken, we all saw Gary as the baby of the family. The rest of us shared my parents' dark eyes and dark hair. Gary, on the other hand, was a Swede like my grandfather. With dimples, blond hair, and blue eyes, he looked nothing like us. As a cruel joke I told him as a toddler that he was an adopted son. He believed me until my mother provided his birth certificate as evidence of his lineage. Gary and I did share one passion in common: wrestling. He had started at age five and developed a peculiar style characterized by insane flexibility, earning him the nickname "Gumby." That winter I had watched him wrestle in the freshman state championships. He slipped out of his opponent's cradle like Houdini and then pinned him. Now that he was older, he no longer smiled incessantly during his matches; instead, he scowled. He had developed a wrestler's intensity. *Maybe we weren't so different.* As I packed, Gary tried on my uniforms and swashbuckled against Bill's younger brother with my parade saber.

The first award ceremony we attended was for history majors. My family looked on from the front row of the auditorium as the chair of the History Department called me to the podium. I was the recipient, he read, of the John Alexander Hottell Award for excellence in history. He handed me a beautifully engraved cavalry saber and posed for a photograph. I looked into the audience for Colonel LoFaro, the officer who had taken me to Normandy. He smiled back as I caught his eye. Earlier in the year, LoFaro had taken a group of us on a tour of West Point's cemetery. "I come here whenever I need to refill my tank of motivation," he said. It was somewhat morbid, I thought at the time. How could dead West Pointers be motivating? Then he led us to a simple gravestone belonging to a 1964 graduate, John Alexander Hottell III, the namesake of the history award. Hottell had studied as a Rhodes scholar before earning two Silver Stars for gallantry in Vietnam. He died in a helicopter crash while flying to visit wounded soldiers in a hospital. Before he died he had sent his wife an obituary that he wanted published in case he was killed. LoFaro read from the obituary:

> We all have but one death to spend, and insofar as it can have any meaning, it finds it in the service of comrades in arms. And yet, I deny that I died FOR anything—not my country, not my Army, not my fellow man, none of these things. I LIVED for these things, and the manner in which I chose to do it involved the very real chance that I would die in the execution of my duties. I knew this, and accepted it, but my love for West Point and the Army was great enough—and the promise that I would someday be able to serve all the ideals that meant anything to me through it was great enough—for me to accept this possibility as a part of a price which must be paid for all things of great value. If there is nothing worth dying for—in this sense—there is nothing worth living for. . . . I lived a full life in the Army, and it has exacted the price. It is only just.

We all have but one death to spend. On stage I turned the silver scabbard in my hands and curled my fingers around the ebony hilt.

"THE FIRSTIES ARE SO SHORT . . ." began Liz Young from the Poop Deck at the center of the mess hall.

"How short are they?" shouted three thousand underclass cadets at our last breakfast at West Point.

"The Firsties are so short that they have fewer minutes to graduation than the Plebes have weeks."

Just a few hours after the taunting announcement in the mess hall, we lined up in order of class rank to receive our diplomas. Bill Parsons and I stood at opposite ends of the graduation podium, our classmates at attention in long lines behind us. Vice President Al Gore stood between Bill and me. He had just delivered our commencement address, warning about the challenges of joining a peacetime military. It was less than two years before the disasters on 9/11 validated his injunction not to be complacent with our conventional military strength.

An officer read *William Parsons* off his diploma. I winked at Bill as he took the first diploma in our class as the valedictorian. His class standing meant he was shipping off to his first-choice assignment with the 173rd Airborne in Vicenza, Italy. His was the path I would have taken had I not won the Rhodes. We looked forward to meeting up in Europe and continuing our conversations.

At the first syllable of *Mullaney,* I walked up the ramp and shook the vice president's hand. As I moved off the podium, I pumped my diploma over my head and returned to my seat. Nearly a thousand names followed mine. The sole moment of excitement was the announcement of "the Goat," the guy in our class who managed to finish last in the order of merit. As the announcer called his name, the entire class erupted in applause. The reward for his accomplishment was the same second lieutenant bars we received and a bag of 935 silver dollars—one from every member of our graduating class. As the last member of the class sat down with his diploma, the brigade commander called us to attention. We sang the alma mater and swore a commissioning oath to "support and defend the Constitution against all enemies, foreign or domestic." We took the obligation "freely, without any mental reservation or purpose of evasion." The brigade commander turned to face the class and gave the command we had been waiting four years to hear.

"Class dismissed!"

I bent over and flung my cap as high as I could. It joined nine hundred other white caps above our heads like a flock of doves. I leaped across the aisle and gave Bill an enormous bear hug, lifting him off the ground. The white folding chairs toppled like dominoes as cadets bulldozed paths to embrace friends. I found Liz bouncing like a SuperBall. Trent was unusually happy. I think he was even smiling. He bear-hugged me, just to remind me that he was the stronger wrestler. It wasn't long before families intercepted cadets. Charlie Hooker, impeccably suited in West Point colors, found me first. I reached out to shake his hand, and he pulled me in to wrinkle his suit.

"Craig Michael!"

I heard my mother's distinctly accented voice, employing the first and middle name combination that was always sure to get my attention. This was the only way she ever got my head out of a book as a kid. With a purse in one hand and a camera in the other, it was unclear whether she wanted to take a picture, cry, or give me a hug. She tried to do all three at once. As we hugged, I saw my father behind her. He was crying. His face was beet red, and tears were drenching his beard. He didn't even try to wipe them away. I had never seen my father cry before, not once.

7

Black and Gold

The first quality of a soldier is constancy in enduring fatigue and hardship. Courage is only the second. Poverty, privation, and want are the school of the good soldier.

NAPOLEON

NOT FOR THE WEAK OR FAINTHEARTED. THE BLACK and gold sign at the entrance to Ranger School read like an insurance waiver. One more step with my bald head and stuffed duffel bags was like a signature confirming I understood the risks. A few dozen of us huddled by a nondescript chain-link fence in the pitch-dark. Finding Camp Rogers had been its own reconnaissance exercise. It lay hidden in a dismal corner of Fort Benning's tangled forests, well beyond view of Airborne School's 250-foot towers. A friend dropped me off at 4:30 a.m.

"I hope I don't hear from you," he said as he waved me off. "If I do, that means you either got kicked out, died, or quit."

Of the three hundred students gathering in the dark, fewer than half would pass the course. The investment advice that Charlie Hooker gave me a few months before became particularly relevant. Past performance was no predictor of future success. West Point graduation was barely eight days behind me, and the starch, shine, and polish were already quaint artifacts. Failure was a distinct possibility, perhaps even a probability.

The duffel bag on my back carried more than boots and batteries. It also strained under the weight of expectations—my own and also those of West Point instructors whom I knew I couldn't face in failure. The image in my head of LoFaro shaking his head in disgust was as scary as the barrel-chested Ranger instructors staring at us from the other side of the fence. Returning was as dim a prospect as moving forward.

RANGER SCHOOL WAS ESTABLISHED during the Korean War. Every year nearly three thousand officers and enlisted soldiers, screened and trained in advance by their units, churned through Ranger School's meat grinder. The Army designed the course to build combat leaders, mimicking the stresses of combat through severe food and sleep deprivation. Between mock ambushes and raids testing tactical knowledge, students marched insane distances under heavy rucksacks in order to test their stamina and will. By one student's count, we would march as many miles as the distance between Boston and Philadelphia.

Ranger School consisted of three successive phases—Darby, Mountain, and Swamp—each building on the foundation set in the previous phase. Those who weren't successful in a particular phase were either dropped from the course or allowed to repeat the phase as "recycles." For the small minority who passed straight through without recycling, the course took nearly nine weeks. In the end, fewer than half the class typically earned the right to wear a two-inch black and gold Ranger tab on their left shoulder. Napoleon had boasted that he could get a soldier to risk his life for "a bit of colored ribbon." With sixty-one days of pain staring me in the face, I had to admit Napoleon was on to something. For an infantry officer, the Ranger tab was an unspoken prerequisite for respect and promotion. For all practical purposes, Ranger School was mandatory. Many commanders refused lieutenants who arrived at their first units without one, telling them in the fashion of the Spartans to return with a tab or not at all.

"FORTY-FOUR. FORTY-FIVE. FORTY-FIVE. FORTY-FIVE. Let's go, Ranger. Keep pushing."

My triceps shook uncontrollably as they approached muscle failure. Forty-nine was the magic number I needed to hear from the Ranger Instructor (RI) grading my push-ups.

"Forty-six. Forty-six. Keep your back straight, Ranger. Forty-six. Is that how you do push-ups at West Point?"

It was a rhetorical question. The ache from my muscles matched the desire I had to reach out and punch this RI. He seemed to be intentionally discounting my push-ups.

"Ten seconds, Ranger. You'd better move that ground. Forty-seven. Two more, Ranger. That one was no good. Forty-seven. Forty-seven. Five seconds."

I heaved my body up with the last reserve of strength in my chest.

"Forty-eight. Good, Ranger. Three-two-one-time."

I collapsed onto the ground.

"Ranger, you are a 'no-go' at this station. Do you understand?"

I nodded from the dewy grass where I lay exhausted. Yes, I understood. He had just failed me on push-ups, a nonnegotiable prerequisite for joining this Ranger class. I hadn't done fewer than one hundred push-ups on a fitness test since Plebe year. By not counting half my push-ups, this RI now had me in a precarious position. Pushing forty-nine more repetitions on exhausted arms was going to be twice as hard.

"You have ten minutes until your retest, Ranger. Wait over there with the other rejects. Look at it this way"— he grinned—"you'll be back at the main camp in time for breakfast."

I sat down and stretched my arms across my chest. My watch ticked off the minutes. I absolutely could not return to West Point and tell people I had failed Ranger School before making it through the first hour. Maybe it was the anger and fear welling inside me that gave my chest an adrenaline rush as another RI pointed at me and said, "Take two, Ranger. Let's go."

I positioned my arms shoulder-width apart and awaited his command.

"Go."

I pushed slowly and concentrated on form.

"Twenty . . . thirty . . . forty. One minute, Ranger. Nine more. Forty-seven. Forty-eight. Forty-nine."

I smiled as he called out "forty-nine." I looked up, asking with my eyes whether I needed to keep going.

"Don't eye-fuck me, Ranger. Just keep pushing. This is Ranger School. We don't do minimums. I want you to push until your arms fall off."

I reached eighty before the two-minute clock ran out.

"You passed, Ranger." He checked a mark on his clipboard. "Go stretch out for the run."

The humidity was a shock to my lungs on the two-mile run, but I still crossed the finish line in the middle of the pack. Marathon training had made my legs much tougher than my arms. At an RI's command, I sprinted to change into camouflage and boots for the next event—the Combat Water Survival Test. We boarded a bus as the sun broke the horizon and began to add heat to the humid air. Fifty of us ran off the bus and formed up on a grassy patch next to the pool. For an hour the RIs had us on our backs doing flutter kicks until our abdominal muscles cramped. Then they turned us over to exhaust our legs with mountain climbers. Then back to flutter kicks. Then over to mountain climbers. The point was to exhaust us before we even dipped a boot in the water.

"Move, move, move!"

We rushed into the fenced-off pool area swarming with RIs. We lined the edges of the pool and observed an RI demonstrating several aquatic skills we needed to imitate successfully. The first event was a fifteen-yard swim in full combat gear.

"Rangers demonstrating undue fear will receive a no-go."

What about "due" fear?

When it was my turn, I jumped in and began paddling with one arm while suspending a rifle above the water with the other. At the tenth yard I began to look like a candidate for a lifeguard rescue. My boots were like concrete blocks, and my uniform dragged through the water like a parachute.

"Ranger, you are not authorized to drown," shouted the instructor who escorted me from poolside with a giant hook poised to snatch me from the bottom.

"No excuse, Sergeant," I gurgled between bobs.

The next event was a perverse twist on Peter Pan. A bear of an RI, playing the part of Captain Hook, marched Rangers off the ten-yard diving platform. Freezing on the platform meant an instant no-go. I ascended the ladder after requesting permission. Captain Hook pulled my wet patrol cap down over my eyes and walked me to the edge. I took a deep breath, stepped into the void, and crashed the surface with a loud splash. As I swam toward the light, my shoulder was loose, and I knew I had to be careful of dislocating it again. After the wrestling tournament with Aram, it had never fully healed. A trip to the medical clinic was the shortest route out of Ranger School.

The temperature peaked in the nineties as our bus returned to Camp Rogers. We rushed into the barracks to change into dry uniforms and formed up by the dining hall. A half-dozen pull-up bars signified the dining ritual we would perform as an ablution before every meal at Ranger School. Just like a Catholic with rosary beads, the Ranger student recites the six verses of the Ranger Creed in a strangely rhythmic intonation before performing pull-ups at the dining hall entrance. By the time I finished Ranger School in mid-September, I would recite the Creed a thousand times; enough repetitions to forever tattoo its tenets on my memory. In an all-male bass chorus, we vowed to uphold the prestige and honor of the Rangers, to never fail our comrades or leave them behind on the battlefield, to demonstrate intestinal fortitude, and to complete whatever mission we were given. Mounting the pull-up bars, each Ranger knocked out ten pull-ups and an extra one for the "Airborne Ranger in the Sky," a prayer that attached an almost mystical reverence to the mission we had embarked on.

As expected, dinner was rushed and chaotic. Twenty-one-hour days in the Georgia heat sweated off reserves of fat faster than a sauna. Ranger School was probably the only place outside a dietician's clinic where calories were counted so obsessively. We could expect enough to keep us alive, but not enough to compensate for what we burned. The object was to consume as much food as quickly as possible—period. Talking was a waste of calories that we needed to survive. Before entering the mess hall, they warned us in the gravest terms not to sneak food out of the chow hall. The fact that they mentioned smuggled sugar packets gave some indication of the desperate measures Rangers had resorted to in the past.

Three hours of supervised pain immediately followed dinner. We sprinted on full stomachs to retrieve our duffel bags and lined up "on the rocks," a formation area lined with jagged gravel. We spread our bags twenty yards away from our positions, dumped the contents, and began a "layout," a time-tested haze that served the purpose of screening our luggage for "contraband," the actual term used to describe an unauthorized item that might give a Ranger student an unfair advantage. Punishable items included Tylenol and civilian long underwear. The layout was like an extended shuttle run. As the RI called off an item from the list, I ran to my pile, grabbed a pair of "boots, hot weather," ran back, and placed them on a poncho at my position. When we were too slow or lacked appropriate "motivation," the RIs motivated us with rounds of flutter kicks or push-ups. As we pushed, rocks dug into our palms, eventually puncturing the skin and leaving recognizable Ranger stigmata. The packing list was nearly three single-spaced pages long, encompassing everything from lip balm to fingernail clippers. By the time we finished, it was nearly midnight. I fell asleep on my plastic mattress before the filaments cooled in the lightbulbs.

Sleep was a precious commodity. We counted and savored minutes of rest like calories of food. Three hours was a gift. Most nights we counted less, and some nights no sleep at all. This first week at Ranger School at Camp Rogers was no exception. The RIs referred to it as "RAP Week," short for "Ranger Assessment Phase," a week's worth of gut checks that whittled our numbers by a third. Each event was an opportunity to avoid wasting taxpayer dollars on someone who lacked the "intestinal fortitude" demanded by the last verse of the Ranger Creed.

The second day began three hours after the first ended. The lights banged on, and minutes later we were running. The five-mile predawn run was at a slow eight-minute-mile pace, but even that pace cast some students from our ranks, especially when the out-and-back route carried us back over the start line without slowing. This was a frequent tactic in Ranger School. We were never done when we thought we were. "One hundred percent and then some," they'd echo the Creed. "You're not going to give up just because the finish line moved a few yards." After breakfast a medic jabbed our arms with a dozen inoculations and sent us to a giant sawdust pit to reinforce the soreness with close-quarters combat skills. Paired off, we threw headlocks and hip tosses, jabbed and ducked, and learned how to block knife attacks. In between kung fu kicks and bayonet thrusts (*"Blood, blood, bright red blood! Whirl! Kill!"*), we ran lap after lap around the perimeter, echoing "Ran-ger" with every step. The heat was unbearable. Even the sawdust couldn't absorb the sweat soaking my uniform. Medics and RIs circled like vultures, the former seeking out Rangers they could boot out as "heat casualties," and the latter making sure we weren't pulling punches on our boxing partners. I skirted both adversaries as best I could, but not everyone was as lucky. Five dehydrated Rangers were pulled out and removed from the course in the first twenty-four hours. Nearly seventy more joined them by the end of the week. Each victim reinforced the RIs' message to "hydrate or die." I paid heed and swilled water by the gallon, downing ten to twenty one-quart canteens a day.

The third morning tested our land navigation skills and followed up with a water confidence course. Falling into water was apparently something Rangers were expected to do a lot of in combat because our next event was the "Suspension Traverse," a.k.a. the "Slide for Life." I climbed an eighty-foot tower and looked down the length of a guide wire sloping at an angle above the lake to a mass of tires intended to bounce malfunctioning Ranger students who failed to release from the wire at the appropriate command. Like an aircraft carrier crewman signaling F-18s, an RI on shore waved a pair of signal flags. I held on to the pulley with an iron grip and tried in vain to ignore the raw wounds where my blisters had popped.

I flew down the wire and dropped at the next signal, adopting an L shape so that I wouldn't "break myself," to use the words of the RI.

MALVESTI. EVEN THE NAME of the obstacle course we attempted on day four sounded nasty, like a poisonous snake or an incurable skin disease. The torture began with a climb up a ramp of cargo netting. I watched in shock as a student began convulsing on the net. Heatstroke, said the RI nonchalantly. An ambulance arrived and carted him away. Business as usual. On the other side of the netting, RIs turned fire hoses on a fifty-yard length of mud—the dreaded Worm Pit—ensuring that the water was frigid and miserable. A rat scrambled out of the muck moments before I dove in. Gooey mud and cold rancid water seeped into my ears and nostrils. I emerged and faced a climbing obstacle built with logs as thick as telephone poles. There were ropes to climb and descend and then a horizontal ladder of monkey bars. The mud of every Ranger that had gone before me coated the bars. It was worse than lard. Every time I slipped and fell into the mud, I had to begin again from the start. After a dozen attempts, I made it across. I dove into the last pool of mud, deeper and nastier than the previous cesspool. Inches above my back were strands of barbed wire emplaced to keep our heads and butts down in the mud. I turned my head sideways and was plowing a furrow through the slime with my helmet when my shoulder overextended and then dislocated from its socket with ripping pain. I stopped moving.

"Get out of my mud, Ranger!"

My mind flashed to a jump I had made the year before. My shoulder had dislocated in freefall, rendering me unable to pull my parachute. I had to pop it back into its socket at 120 miles an hour. It was the first time I had ever been mortally afraid. This pressure was less compelling, but the pain was greater. My arm was limp and screaming even louder than the RI.

"Move, Ranger!"

I started crawling with my other arm, dragging the disabled arm through the mud like a useless appendage. I moved at half the speed of the other students but made it to the end. When the instructors weren't watching, I popped the shoulder back into place.

That afternoon, the RIs corralled us into twelve-foot squares for boxing matches. It was only a fifteen-second bout, and all I needed to do was jab enough with my left to keep my opponent at arm's length. I jabbed and jabbed, but some instinct kicked in when I saw his left side open up. I went for the kill with a right cross and threw my shoulder out again. Thirty seconds later I woke up lying on my back.

"Ranger, you're going to the clinic." An RI stood over me like the Eiffel Tower.

I struggled in vain to dissuade the RI. Fortunately, I had better luck convincing the medic that I could continue with the course. For a moment, sitting on the examining table, I considered quitting. Dozens had already quit. In Ranger parlance, they had LOM'd: dropped out for "lack of motivation." At West Point I had always risen to the challenges. The challenges of Ranger School, however, were on a different scale, and I wondered whether I could take two more months of punishment at this voltage. At the moment, motivation was scarce. A medical "drop" was an honorable reason to leave Ranger School, I rationalized to myself. No one would call me a coward or a failure if I had a legitimate medical excuse. It was the easy way out. I could be on a plane home to Rhode Island in twelve hours, sitting by the pool with a margarita. Covered in mud and sweat, the prospect was especially appealing. Ranger School could wait a couple of years, I told myself. Maybe after Oxford?

Another voice, however, urged me to stay. This sort of decision had an audience of one. Forget what my father would say as he picked me up at the airport. Forget LoFaro, Ostlund, and Charlie. Would I be able to look at myself in the mirror again if I quit? So I stayed in the course, a decision I would curse during every painful march or sleepless night staring out at the dark from a cold patrol base. There were no good days in Ranger School, just variations of bad. It demanded an almost inhuman level of endurance.

I mounted the pull-up bars that night and strained with one good arm to knock out my eleven repetitions. As we stood outside and shouted the six verses of the Ranger Creed, I shouted six words louder than the rest. And for the rest of the course I repeated those words to myself whenever the temptation to quit resurfaced.

"Surrender is not a Ranger word."

8

Movement to Dawn

Do your duty—and never mind whether you are shivering or warm, sleeping on your feet or in your bed.

MARCUS AURELIUS

IF CAMP ROGERS WAS TOO DISMAL A PLACE FOR FORT Benning to recognize with road signs, Camp Darby must have been Hell's furnace. Getting there from Camp Rogers was an all-night sixteen-mile march along sandy firebreaks in Georgian pine forests. I carried sixty pounds inside my rucksack and a squad machine gun in my hands. Every ounce of its 16.41 pounds strained my exhausted biceps. I had already lost ten pounds in Ranger School; at this rate I would disappear before finishing. My boots were still damp from the mud, and my socks bunched up into folds and rubbed the soles of my feet raw. As my eyes followed the luminescent cat's-eyes sewn on the helmet of the Ranger in front of me I bobbed in rhythm with him. Rhythm was good, taking my mind off the blisters and variegated pains spiking my lower back, shoulders, and hips. Our class stretched out nearly a mile, but not nearly as far as it would have if everyone who had started Ranger School was still with us. Fewer than two hundred remained of the three hundred who had begun RAP Week five days earlier. In case this fact renewed our confidence, the RIs made sure to remind us every time they crept up on a marching silhouette that RAP Week was the easy part of Ranger School. We had only reached the start line.

What remained were fifty-six days of small-unit patrolling through the

Darby, Mountain, and Swamp phases. Our instruction in the lost art of patrolling began at Camp Darby, an outpost in the woods consisting of just a few open-air classrooms covered in corrugated tin. An outside observer would probably have mistaken it for a guerrilla camp in Central America. In a way it was. The scenario was simple. A group of drug-crazed rebels on the fictitious island of Cortinia threatened the central government. Our mission was to shut them down using the two most basic tactics in the infantry textbook: ambushes and raids.

Firepower and air support would help us in the field, but the RIs insisted that the true keys to success were subtler. Only with careful planning, thorough reconnaissance, and stealth could we hope to beat the Cortinian Liberation Front. Our movement through the terrain had to confound the enemy's expectations. If we took the roads and well-beaten paths, we would soon find our roles reversed, with our columns ambushed and our patrol bases raided.

RIs focused on teaching us how to win a guerrilla war in professional but painstaking detail. Classes under the tin roofs were long and hot, lasting until midnight on some occasions. We learned how to build our own booby traps, how to disguise our uniforms with twigs and leaves, and how to pick up the spark of a sentry's cigarette from a quarter mile's distance. A class on an L-shaped ambush could last four or five hours. If we could have gotten away with it, we would have rolled our eyes in boredom. Vietnam was our parents' war. We thought guerrilla warfare had gone out of style with the Contras. Even our instructors admitted that the tactics were antiquated. They told us that the ambushes and raids were merely vehicles for testing leadership under stressful conditions. "You won't actually need to know how to conduct an ambush in Kosovo," quipped one instructor. Ranger School had eliminated its desert phase in 1995. Back then, no one had expected we would lead platoons in Afghanistan and Iraq. This was still a year before 9/11.

In order to assess our comprehension, the RIs devised three-day field exercises hunting a trained opposition force dressed in Cortinian uniforms.

Every day we rotated through leadership positions in our squad, taking turns planning, leading treks through the bush, conducting attacks, and finally establishing new patrol bases under cover of night. It seemed like one long march through vines and briars. Our fumbled raids and noisy ambushes would have scared off any enemy long before they entered the kill zone. We were careless and sloppy because careless and sloppy couldn't get us killed, not in Ranger School. I never believed I would ever conduct a real ambush. And I never believed I would ever *be* ambushed.

The longer we stayed in the bush, the dumber and clumsier we became, by compromising our reconnaissance missions, leaving weapons on prisoners, or losing one another as we crashed through the woods following fireflies rather than the luminescent cat's-eyes on our buddies' helmets. We weren't going to convince anyone that we were an elite force. Sustaining the ability to talk in complete sentences was difficult enough after a couple of weeks without adequate sleep. As we inevitably became more careless with equipment, the instructors made us tie everything to our vests with "dummy cords." As a result, we lost fewer weapons, batteries, and radios, but became a lot slower exchanging items between rotating squad leaders. Two Rangers trading radios looked like a game of cat's cradle. Without much juice to power one's brain, disentangling wires and nylon cord was like computational physics.

Moving through the woods at night was comical. Our silhouettes bulged with ungainly buglike rucksacks. They weighed in excess of a hundred pounds at times, especially when wet. We were supposed to watch our flanks for an enemy attack, but the only thing we really cared about was finishing the night without breaking a leg. Our helmets tilted down toward the ground as we looked for deadfall and the wait-a-minute vines that lived up to their name. We smelled god-awful—a combination of dried sweat, bad breath, oily, matted hair, coffee, and tobacco spit. Stealth was impossible. Inevitably, one of us would crash through a bush after falling asleep standing up, poke a stick up his nostril, and curse the fucking Airborne Ranger in the Sky. Herds of elephants are quieter than a squad of Ranger students on a night patrol. Ranger School, in essence, was one long, miserable, loud, and uncoordinated movement to dawn.

On one of these all-night suckfests, we pulled into our patrol base a few hours before dawn and spread out in a circle facing the night. We exchanged the coordinates of a rally point in case we were overrun, and a handful of Rangers took first watch while the rest of us passed out in impromptu fighting positions, so-called Ranger graves hacked out of the dirt to hide half our torsos from imaginary bullets. I fell asleep confident that I would get an hour of shut-eye.

I awoke to machine-gun fire. Muzzle flashes sparked around the patrol base as sleeping Rangers lurched awake and fended off the attack. No one fired back. I couldn't figure out why. When the dust settled, I realized what had happened. Our watch had fallen asleep, leaving no security against an enemy attack. The RI had made a point of our lapse by depressing the trigger of our machine gun. Our failure to stay awake was understandable; we had been operating continuously for well over forty hours without sleep.

"Wake up, Rangers. If you can't stay awake, I'm going to help you." He had the authority of God issuing Moses the Ten Commandments.

"Get on the road. Now. *Move it*, Rangers!" We lined up on a sandy road somewhere in Cortinia and awaited our punishment.

"We're going walking." He bounded ahead at speed-walking pace, and we strained to keep up. "Let's go, Rangers. We have a long walk."

We followed behind for miles. The moon cast our shadows along the road. We walked long enough to see the moon shadows lengthen. Eventually, he slowed down and faced our squad. He moved down the rank slowly, examining each face like a witness checking out a police lineup. He asked each of us one simple question: "Why are you here?" The answers were predictable, ranging from "For the challenge" to "My platoon sergeant made me." I admitted with the other infantry officers that I hadn't had a choice.

"Wrong answer, Ranger," he said to each person before addressing the group. "You are here for one reason." He paused for effect. "You are here for the troops you are going to lead. You are responsible for keeping them alive and accomplishing whatever mission you're given. I don't care if you're tired, hurt, or lonely. This is for them. And they deserve better. You *owe* them your Ranger tab.

"Fuck self-pity," he added with a hiss. *"This isn't about you."*

9

Mountain Men

This is another type of war, new in its intensity, ancient in its origins—war by guerrillas, subversives, insurgents, assassins; war by ambush instead of by combat; by infiltration instead of aggression, seeking victory by eroding and exhausting the enemy instead of engaging him. . . . It requires . . . a new and wholly different kind of military training.

JOHN F. KENNEDY,
Graduation Address, West Point Class of 1962

I USED TO LOVE MOUNTAINS. WHEN OUR BUS PULLED past the quiet college town of Dahlonega, Georgia, I looked out the windows and saw a virginal wilderness of astounding beauty. We were done with the first third of Ranger School. Nearly half the class we began with had washed out entirely or remained behind as "recycles" to repeat RAP Week and Darby with the next class. Ranger School was more of a marathon than a sprint. We had finished our warm-up and would start hitting the hills. Nevertheless, I was excited to have traded the sweltering plains of southwestern Georgia for the cool winds north of Atlanta. If God had forgotten Benning, it was in order to spend more time in this beautiful section of the Appalachian Mountains. As we stepped off the bus, turkey vultures wheeled in the sky above our heads. I would soon understand why they lingered.

After a short "phase break" to consume as much junk food as we could find, shave our heads, and throw our nasty uniforms in the wash, we reassembled for inspection. We dumped our bags, and the RIs began combing through them for contraband. The RIs caught one Ranger who had attempted to subvert the tobacco quota by stuffing extra smokeless tobacco into several tins of Skoal. It was a clear violation of the orders we had received before the phase break. He was booted from the course on the spot. None of us thought the punishment out of proportion. Sneaking extra tobacco was almost as egregious an offense as stealing another Ranger's food. Tobacco was the fifth food group—as important to survival as sugar and protein. On every patrol we left behind trails of tobacco spit. The nicotine was the only thing that could keep a man awake after two or three days without sleep.

"Any more blue falcons in the class?" questioned an RI. Being called a "blue falcon" was one of the worst insults in the Ranger vocabulary. The phrase stood for "buddy fucker," a Ranger who sought an unfair advantage over his peers.

"No, Sergeant!" we belted out in unison.

"Good," he said. "Then we can get on with training. If any of you try any more games, you'll be out of here faster than a bear with its ass on fire."

Training began with a short briefing on environmental hazards. The more I heard these, the more convinced I became that the Army had chosen the most inhospitable locations on the planet to put their training bases. Dahlonega, for example, hosted several varieties of poisonous snakes and spiders. On almost every patrol an RI would parade down the column with a copperhead he had killed by smashing it with his hiking staff. Each kill earned a notch on the staff. Later in the course, one of my classmates had the misfortune of being bitten by a brown recluse, a poisonous spider. He said nothing until the phase finished. As a result, the medics were forced to excise a softball-sized abscess from his ass. At every opportunity afterward he would moon the rest of us while showing off his cross-shaped scar.

The flora was nearly as bad as the fauna. Poison ivy layered the ground everywhere, always at the precise coordinates where we planted our ambushes and patrol bases. Invasive kudzu vines hung in green curtains like giant topiary structures, and enormous clumps of mountain laurel formed dense, prickly barriers to movement. The mountains themselves were the last environmental hazard. Beware of unmarked cliffs, the RIs told us. A dozen Rangers every year fractured limbs falling off precipices, awakening from their catatonic states to wincing pain and the laughter of RIs.

We spent the first week of the phase learning how to knot ropes, climb cliffs, and rappel back down. It was the only week in Ranger School when we slept and ate well. Long after Ranger School, most Rangers still reminisce about Dahlonega's famous blueberry pancakes, fluffy pillows studded with fresh mountain blueberries. At night, falling asleep to a symphony of crickets and owls, I dreamed of pancakes dancing through showers of maple syrup.

The reason for letting us rest had nothing to do with pity. We slept for the same reason airline pilots did: because climbing was a technical sport that required concentration in order to avoid disastrous errors. We spent days mastering knots because a bad knot could kill a climber. At the end of the week we had the opportunity to put our lessons to the test. The RIs bused us to the foot of Georgia's tallest mountain, Mount Yonah, and marched us to the summit in less than an hour. The burn in my quadriceps gave me some inkling of the pain to come during the patrol segment of Mountain phase. Climbing the bald summit was nerve-racking but easier than sitting at the top belaying my partner. I was like a construction worker at the top floor of a skyscraper's scaffolding. The only thing keeping me from tumbling to my death was a small snap link connected to a screw in the rock. After I got used to the vertigo, I appreciated the stunning view across north Georgia and the hawks wheeling through the sky at eye level.

The second day at Yonah was less serene. I was climbing an eighty-foot cliff when halfway up the incline my shoulder dislocated. My belay man caught my fall before I did more than bang my knees on the rock. I bit my lip to avoid screaming in agony.

"Get up my rock, Ranger. I haven't got all day," yelled an RI peering at me from above.

I stared up the cliff face. Dear God, just get me up this rock. I reached up with my injured arm but couldn't even get it over my head. I hung for an eternity on the fingers of my good left hand.

"Ranger, get off your knees and start climbing. The only way off this cliff is from the top."

"Yes, Sergeant," I replied.

"Don't 'Yes, Sergeant' me, just get up the damn mountain."

I planted my right toe a foot higher and reached for the next handhold with my left hand.

"Good, Ranger. Keep going."

I pulled my left leg up and found another good toehold.

"Excellent."

I repeated the three motions with my good limbs and faked the motion with my right arm. It worked. I got up to the top, and the RI slapped me on the back, a rare gesture of goodwill.

"Just one more climb, Ranger." I moved off and rested my arm before a last painful and, fortunately, successful climb. My arm was sore marching down Yonah, but still attached. So far the Mountain phase had lived up to its billing—getting to the fight really was half the battle.

A FEW DAYS LATER it became apparent that the relative pampering of the first week had been an anomaly. They had just fattened us up for the slaughter. A fresh set of RIs began to train us in platoon tactics, optimized for mountainous terrain. The most memorable of the bunch was Gunnery Sergeant Oakes, a hard-nosed Marine who never raised his voice. I would learn more from him than any other instructor at Ranger School. When it was my time to lead a real combat patrol, it would be his advice I heard in the back of my head.

"Rangers," he intoned, almost at a whisper, "outwit their enemies."

Careful analysis of the terrain was critical, and the smart commander understood that the straight line between two coordinates was rarely the fastest. Oakes taught us how to avoid being silhouetted on ridgelines by traversing along the slopes.

"Use the mountains," he said, "or they will use you."

We spent hours in the planning bays before conducting practice missions. Oakes believed that deliberate planning saved lives. Before picking ambush sites, we pored over our maps. Oakes taught us to attack from the high ground along roads. He drew out the ambush kill zone like a geometry exercise, teaching us how to position and aim our various weapons in order to maximize their effects. And yet, he emphasized, we had to show the flexibility to deviate from the plan when conditions changed.

"Sixty percent of command is anticipation. The rest is innovation." Real roads would never look as they did on a map. "Expect it," he warned. "Recon the objective and move the ambush as necessary."

Oakes also believed in drills. Like a football team running plays, an infantry platoon could practice combat. The platoon leader was the coach and quarterback, training, writing the game plan, and calling the plays. There were important differences, Oakes pointed out: Football teams didn't bring body bags to games, and infantry platoons could practice a lifetime without playing a game. Fundamentally, though, winning a fight meant building the same discipline. False bravado wasn't enough to prevail; competence and teamwork were the keys. Many Rangers talked a big game, said Oakes, but we would learn how to "walk the talk." He emphasized calm amid chaos. Riffing on Clausewitz, Oakes noted that in the fog of war, the most basic actions had to be instinctive.

"You need to be able to win with your eyes closed."

He was being literal. The next day we did our drills blindfolded. At first our platoon bumbled around like kids striking a piñata. After two days of practice, we could set a platoon of forty Rangers in a midnight patrol base in under thirty minutes.

Most important, Oakes had us evacuate casualties. One afternoon we shuttled fake casualties up and down an abandoned airfield for hours. It was exhausting work, it was morbid, and it was invaluable. Every mission we planned in Ranger School had to include a plan for getting casualties triaged, bandaged, and moved. We couldn't always expect to land a medevac helicopter on a "hot" landing zone. We might need to carry a comrade for miles to safety. Just a few casualties could consume the platoon's effectiveness by requiring three or four men to carry each body. Oakes was teaching a lesson I didn't understand until later—that bloodless battles were exceptional. Rangers expected casualties on both sides. To plan for less was irresponsible.

The training fell short. No notional casualty evacuation could mimic real wounds. We didn't learn how a stretcher got slippery with blood. We didn't learn how to move at a crouch for fear of becoming casualties ourselves. We didn't learn how to plug punctured lungs or how to clean viscera off gear after a fight. And we never carried dead weight because Cortinians only fired blanks.

MOUNTAIN FIELD EXERCISES WERE twice as long as the ones in Darby and three times as complicated. On the first day the excitement of a helicopter air assault kept our adrenaline flowing through the first marches up and down the Tennessee Valley Divide. The thrill wore off quickly as day ran into night and back into day without rest or food. Longer patrols meant heavier packs stuffed with enough food and water to last several days. Carrying one hundred pounds or more up 60-degree inclines broke down whatever muscles remained on us. One of the RIs laughed as we stood panting on the slope. "We don't need to kill you; the mountains will." That explained the vultures.

Ernest Hemingway claimed hunger was a discipline you learned from. Although we ate military "Meals, Ready-to-Eat" (MREs) twice a day, the calories were too few for backbreaking mountain treks. At West Point we had joked about MREs, calling them "Meals Rejected by the Enemy" and "Meals Rarely Enjoyed." Back then if I had received the insalubrious ham slice or slimy beef frankfurters, I gave away the main entrée and subsisted on the packet of dry crackers. In the mountains, by contrast, we worshipped MREs. Soldiers would bury blank ammunition to lighten their packs, but no Ranger ever buried so much as a sugar packet from his MRE. If I could discipline my appetite or make strategic trades with a classmate, gourmet preparations were possible. Ranger pudding, for instance, combined the cocoa beverage powder with creamer and sugar. Mixing coffee with imagination turned the substance into a mochaccino.

We slowly starved. Without a proper mirror, it was easiest to observe the changes in my classmates. The metamorphosis from healthy twenty-one-year-olds to gaunt POWs was dramatic. By the middle of the course, many had lost twenty or thirty pounds. Baby fat was the first to go. Stomachs tightened, muscles sharpened, and cheeks sank beneath the dark caves that used to be eyes. Then came ketoacidosis, a medical condition normally associated with acute starvation. The chemical by-products of metabolism under severe stress made us stink. I learned from the discipline of hunger that starving bodies smelled like paint thinner. Had Hemingway reached the same conclusion?

Hunger and fatigue made a mockery of our best plans. On the first ambush we conducted, we waited in the dark patiently. There was no moonlight at all, and the stars were totally obscured by the thick canopy above us. The hum of cicadas muffled the small sounds we made shifting on our stomachs and bobbing our heads in a struggle to stay awake. Below us, a strip of gravel road curled around the mountain.

A split second after the patrol leader's signal shot, we opened up in an arpeggio of machine-gun fire, grenade simulators, and M16s. The flurry of flashing muzzles was the most exciting thing we had done in a day spent in a beleaguered march up nearly vertical mountain slopes. After a mad minute of firing, we assaulted down the hill, tripping over our own boots in the brush, and stopped, breathless, on the other side of the road. I turned to look back at the kill zone. There was something wrong: There were no vehicles or dead Cortinians on the road.

"For fuck's sake, Rangers!" Our RI stood in the center of the road, took off his patrol cap, and flung it on the ground. "That was the wrong truck. You just scared the daylight out of a bunch of fucking civilians on their way to drinking beer and getting laid. At this rate you'll be in Ranger School so long you'll forget how."

He fired the entire chain of command on the spot and marched us until daylight. A few sleepless days later I got my chance. On my first patrol as the platoon leader, I took over after the RI fired my predecessor for being too slow in the planning process. I made the best of a bad plan and moved the platoon toward the objective. During our movement I lost radio contact with my platoon sergeant at the rear of our column. He drifted on a different course that cost me precious minutes as I struggled to reconsolidate. Just as we did, the RI grinned at me, pulled an artillery simulator out of his pocket, and triggered it.

"Incoming!" I screamed and heard it echoed through the column.

Sssssssss—*boom!*

"Twelve o'clock, three hundred yards!" I commanded, ordering the platoon to continue in the direction we were going toward a rally point three hundred yards away.

I crashed through a tangle of mountain laurel, cursing every step as my stress factor doubled by the minute.

Sssssssss—*boom!*

We ran again.

Sssssssss—*boom!*

And again.

The RI kept us moving for over a mile up a mountain through briars, bushes, and vines. By the time the artillery stopped bombarding us, I was thoroughly lost. I called my squad leaders to the center of our perimeter and asked their opinion. I triangulated from their guesses and hoped for the best.

"Where are we, Ranger?"

I gulped and pointed to the map with my thickest finger, hoping our true location fit somewhere under its shadow.

"Ranger, are you *sure?*"

Getting this wrong meant failing the patrol. I had no choice but to guess at our position.

"Not quite, Ranger. Artillery is no excuse for getting lost." He pointed to our correct location, about two inches and a mile away. I dropped my head, certain I had failed the patrol.

"If you can still pull off the ambush on time, this won't matter."

"Yes, Sergeant." I crossed myself in silent prayer as he turned away, and then hammered out a plan with my squad leaders. The ambush we set up was nearly perfect, the best we had done yet. Unfortunately, we were two hours late. It might as well have been two days. All that mattered was that we missed our quarry. *Step up to my line. Do not step on my line. Do not step over my line.*

It was a hard way to learn a lesson. I failed again during my second patrol and was "recycled" along with half my platoon. It meant repeating the entire Mountain phase: the rock climbing, the one-hundred-pound rucksacks, and those damned ridges. We sat cleaning our weapons by the barracks while the rest of the class boarded buses for the Swamp phase in Florida. I turned the same piece over and over in my hands, scratching against the carbon with a toothbrush and cleaning solution. It took my mind off failure.

A few days later I snapped out of the funk. I had picked up a book to read, *Gates of Fire* by Steven Pressfield. I zoomed through it in between the odd maintenance jobs they had us perform while we waited two weeks for the next cycle of Ranger students to arrive. In the book a Greek warrior recounts his brutal training with the Spartans and the Spartans' heroic, outnumbered stand against the Persians at the Battle of Thermopylae in 480 B.C. I copied a passage from the book and stuck it in my Ranger handbook. "The hardship of the exercises is intended less to strengthen the back than to toughen the mind. The Spartans say that any army may win while it still has its legs under it; the real test comes when all strength has fled and the men must produce victory on will alone." I had one last chance to advance to the final phase in Florida. All I had left was willpower. They could kill me, but I wasn't going to quit.

Friends from West Point sent notes of encouragement after news spread through the grapevine that I had been recycled. Bill Parsons, predictably, sent biblical verses. Aram, my former wrestling partner, was already a Ranger. He put my predicament in familiar terms. "Wrestle hard and give it your all. And, win or lose, KEEP YOUR HEAD HELD HIGH. Beat them and stand firm!" Aram was destined to become either a general or a motivational speaker. I wrote back and signed off with our personal salutation, "No Regrets." Liz Young, the classmate going to Oxford with me, didn't know what to write a Ranger student, but I appreciated the effort. "I hope your spirits are high." I could hear her voice writing it, inflecting the last word in a verbal question mark and bobbing her hair. My spirits weren't high, but knowing friends were pulling for me lifted them considerably.

IT WAS I A.M., cold, raining, and as dark as ink. Ten days earlier, all the Mountain recycles were incorporated with the next class of Ranger students who had arrived at Dahlonega. After training together, we headed up the ridges. We had just finished a successful ambush and recovered our rucksacks when the RI called my name. "Your patrol," he said.

Finally, I had an opportunity to get the "Go" I needed to pass the Mountain phase and advance to the Swamp phase. The mission was to march the platoon to a grid coordinate several miles away, set up a patrol base before dawn, and avoid being overrun before the next platoon leader took over. Under most conditions it would have been an easy mission. Not that night. It was our fourth night in the field, and adrenaline was the only thing keeping me awake.

My peers were little better than zombies. Most had passed the brink of consciousness and entered a state RIs called "droning." It began the night before when one Ranger became so confused with sleep deprivation that he wandered into another platoon's patrol base and failed to remember even his own name. ("Ranger, it's on your name tag.") Hallucinations were common for droning Rangers. Urban legends of students ordering pizza deliveries to grid coordinates or mistaking trees for soda machines abound. The closest I had ever been to this state of mental dysfunction was in a hypobaric chamber at the Air Force Academy. At a simulated altitude of thirty thousand feet, I couldn't even write my telephone number backward. Ranger School was worse than that. One night I nearly wandered off a cliff following a firefly. Simple calculations were nearly impossible after even three days without sleep. Adding distances between checkpoints was futile. I began to chew Redman tobacco, but even that buzz wore off under the droning spell. There was simply no cure for droning other than sleep. The rest—tobacco, push-ups—were only palliatives.

When I took over, my men were walking dead. After moving out, the column stopped abruptly. I marched to the stop and found a Ranger staring at a tree.

"What's up?" I asked. "Why'd you stop?"

Pointing to the tree, he replied, "The man in front of me stopped."

The actual Ranger in front of him, however, was already fifty yards down the trail. I coaxed, cajoled, and herded the platoon for the remainder of that miserable night, but we were moving too slowly to reach the planned base before dawn. After consulting with my squad leaders, I decided to adopt a new location for our patrol base. It was a gamble. I doubted the RI would approve the deviation (patrol bases were planned and monitored by higher headquarters). The base we set up was a mess of positions zigzagging around laurel bushes, but it was adequate. The alternative—forty droning Rangers still marching through daylight—would have left us easy targets for a Cortinian ambush. As the adrenaline wore off, it was a struggle to keep my eyes open when I checked on the machine-gun positions.

The sun rose, and the RI who had stayed silent throughout our meandering trek approached me to debrief the patrol.

"How do you think you did?" he asked with the standard Socratic opener.

"I'm not sure, Sergeant."

"Good move, changing the patrol base. I'm impressed you managed to even get off the mountain with this group. You all were droning pretty hard."

"Yes, Sergeant." I suppressed a smile as it dawned on me that I might have passed.

"Keep this to yourself, Ranger. You're a Go."

"Yes, Sergeant. Thank you, Sergeant." After nearly three months I had finally earned my ticket to the last and toughest phase of Ranger School: Swamp phase. I said a prayer and threw another plug of tobacco in my cheek. I suddenly felt wide awake.

10

Tab Check

I woke up in my foxhole in a cold sweat. I had a nightmare
that I was still in Ranger School. Thank God that I was in
Vietnam. Compared to Ranger School, combat was easy.

COLONEL ROBERT A. "TEX" TURNER,
former Ranger Department Commander

"AN ALLIGATOR CAN OUTRUN A MAN," SAID AN RI AT
the front of the auditorium. He had an ugly snout that bore an uncanny
resemblance to the baby alligator he led with a leash. No, he responded to
a Ranger's question, no Ranger had ever been killed by a gator. Then again,
he added, there's a first time for everything. If we found ourselves being
chased through the swamps, the best tactic was to run at right angles. Apparently gators have difficulty making turns. Just don't zigzag, he warned,
or the alligator will cut you off, literally.

After dropping onto Auxiliary Airfield #6 of Eglin Air Force Base in
northern Florida for the final phase of Ranger School, the first thing I
noticed was that it was as flat as a Dahlonega pancake. Not even a small
hill broke the level horizon. It was late August on the Gulf Coast, and heat
rippled off the tarmac in waves. As I ran off the drop zone with my parachute, I stopped to down a canteen of water. I hadn't forgotten the Ranger
who convulsed with heatstroke on Malvesti. The bleached bones of rodents
poked out of the grass ominously. Camp Rudder (named after the Ranger
commander who had led the assault on Pointe du Hoc in Normandy) was
intentionally isolated. The farther we were from civilization, the less likely
someone would hear us scream.

RIs shouted, Rangers hustled, and bags emptied. Standard protocol at Ranger School. The second event was more dramatic—a reptile class taught by specially trained Army snake handlers. We got a sneak peek at the cottonmouths that slithered through the swamps along the Yellow River.

"You will know they're in your swamp when you smell 'em," concluded the instruction.

What does a poisonous snake smell like?

Swamp training was brief but intense. We altered our navigation techniques for flat land, practiced paddling Zodiac rafts, and drilled ambushes and raids. What we lacked in practice we made up during the field exercise—a ten-day mission to defeat the Cortinian Liberation Front. Dropped behind enemy lines, our mission was to seize their planning bases, disrupt their logistics routes, and disguise our own movements by winding through the worst terrain in all of Ranger School.

The exercise began inauspiciously. One of my squad mates was rushed from the drop zone with a sprained neck. No sooner was he evacuated than a thunderstorm clapped above our heads. The RIs had told us that Eglin Air Force Base has the highest density of lightning strikes in the United States. As a precaution against electrocution, every time the RIs saw lightning they stopped us. Obediently, we dispersed to the four winds in small groups of three or four, huddled under our ponchos, and enjoyed fifteen minutes of precious sleep before the storm passed and we continued the mission. It was the only way to cool down in the heat, although our uniforms promptly dried after we started marching again.

Hunger and fatigue were the real enemies in Florida. Apart from the lightning drills, we didn't sleep for the first four days. The last six were only a moderate improvement, and even then our sleep deficit reduced us to drooling idiots. It got so bad that the RIs had us stand up on the perimeter of our patrol bases like emaciated shooting targets. They knew that the minute we reached the horizontal, our helmets would topple off our heads as we fell asleep.

After seizing our objectives, we marched mile after mile on sandy roads that doubled the effective distance. Some nights the only thing that kept me going was holding the straps on the rucksack in front of me. Other nights I hummed Don McLean's "American Pie." Three times through made a mile. Thirty times completed a march.

THE BOILING WAS A mission I'd heard about even before arriving at Ranger School. It began with the sort of image that recruiters hang on their office walls—four squads of camouflaged Rangers floating down a slow, murky jungle river. At the coxswain's command, our paddles dipped into the putrid water and propelled us past mangrove forests. All eyes concentrated on the shores, looking for alligators. It was almost too clichéd to take seriously, and we didn't. The RI enjoyed himself (he wasn't paddling) by whistling tunes and cracking dirty jokes about our mothers. At a designated mark on the map, we paddled to shore, disembarked the Zodiacs, and moved toward the objective, a Cortinian base camp. A long rain shower delayed our attack and worried the instructors. Tragically, six years earlier four Ranger students had died due to a combination of rising water, falling temperatures, and fog. Our attack wasn't tragic, but it was ugly. No one anticipated a barbed-wire obstacle, and a few Rangers, including me, shredded their uniforms in the dark. Ragtag, indeed.

At midnight we set off in a single file to cross through the Boiling Swamp. Mud swallowed my legs to mid-calf. As I lifted my boots, they popped out of the sludge with a sucking gasp of foul air. Within minutes we were chest-deep in fetid water. My rucksack floated up to the surface with a layer of swamp scum as thick as gravy. Gnarly mangrove roots hid underwater. At each step, roots whacked my legs, each time at a different spot, leaving welts under my sodden uniform. We moved through the swamp as fast as possible; no one wanted to test the diligence of the RI who had screened the lane earlier for alligators. We stopped when it became clear the point man was lost. It was 2 a.m. by now, and the temperature plummeted quickly after we stopped moving. When we began again, I picked up an unusual smell of musk.

"Do you smell that?" I asked another student.

"Yeah," he said, "that's a cottonmouth."

"Oh," I replied as nonchalantly as I could under the circumstances. So, *that's* what a poisonous snake smells like.

The platoon's situation deteriorated rapidly. We stopped again to swim across a wide river, but then the RIs canceled our crossing. The water was rising too quickly, and the current was too strong. They radioed headquarters for motorboats to be dispatched to pick us up and bring us downstream. During the hour it took the boats to arrive, we stood in place in chest-deep water as the temperature dropped. The cottonmouth rumor spread quickly, and nearly all of us were shaking from early-stage hypothermia, fear, or both. Eventually, the boats arrived and brought us to drier ground. We hiked into a patrol base, and the RIs attempted to dry us out by making us build fires. We stood by the fires in shivering clusters. "Ranger TV" was what the RIs called it. That night I fell asleep standing up and stumbled into the fire, twice.

When we woke in the morning, the new RIs handed out mail. I opened a letter filled with wise advice from Bill Parsons, my old roommate. "Persevere, persevere, persevere," he wrote, "and remember that this training could one day save your life." He left a verse from Saint Paul's letter to the Philippians. I penned it into my notebook where I would see it every day, "I have learned the secret of being content in any and every situation, whether well fed or hungry, whether living in plenty or in want." Saint Paul would have made a good Ranger.

Our attack on Santa Rosa Island, the culminating exercise of Ranger School, was only a few days later. Santa Rosa lay a few miles off the Florida coast near the entrance to Pensacola Bay. In the late afternoon, trucks deposited our platoon on Fort Walton Beach. Driving through the town was part of the torture. I was torn between directing my attention at the Kentucky Fried Chicken or the bikinis. I hadn't seen either in nearly four months. After sunset we pushed off from the beach in our Zodiacs and crossed the sound, choppy from wind and bulging with the wakes of merchant tankers. The moon rose over our heads as we paddled, casting everything in a silvery light. My shoulders ached with each of a thousand strokes.

On the opposite shore we disembarked and then headed into the moonlit dunes. I carried one of the platoon's machine guns that night—twenty-three pounds of cold steel. Crawling into place through saw grass, we set up on top of a sand dune. Below us were a handful of tents, stacked crates, and a half-dozen Cortinians. The ammo bearer next to me linked his belt of ammunition to the starter belt, and we looked for a signal from the platoon sergeant. The moment before a raid commenced was always the quietest. No scratching, no sneezing, no wiggling, only every so often a deeper breath above the wind like a whale breaching the sea.

His hand dropped in a karate chop, cutting the humid air. A half second later, tracers illuminated the objective and three dozen Rangers blasted through their ammunition. The barrel of my machine gun began to glow as I fired off eight-second bursts at the enemy soldiers running between tents. The rhythmic burps from the machine gun thrust the gun stock back into my shoulder. The muzzle sparked like a magic wand releasing bolts of lightning. At a signal from the patrol leader, I unlatched the gun from its tripod and rushed down the dune. My boots were barely in the sand long enough to leave an impression. Moments later I was on the opposite side of the objective. Under my sweat-soaked shirt, my heart raced and my lungs heaved. Back on the ground, I lay next to my ammo bearer. We didn't need to say a thing. It was over. The last major mission was complete. In less than a day we would walk across the finish line.

We both turned our heads and stared out at the Gulf of Mexico. Oil tankers plowed through the water, stretching away in deep midnight blue. A yellow moon beat a path across the waves like a spotlight shining on our position. The air was salty and humid. I recovered my breath slowly and picked up the whirr of helicopter rotors announcing our departure. I lifted the machine gun, suddenly much lighter, and joined the other silhouettes kneeling in a circle by an abandoned gravel road. Black Hawk helicopters approached like steel dragonflies. As they hovered above the road, static electricity charged the rotor blades with spectral sparks.

Twenty hours later we stumbled back into Camp Rudder. It was 2 a.m. on September 11, 2000—ninety-nine days after I had begun Ranger School and exactly one year before our guerrilla training gained newfound relevance.

FOUR DAYS LATER WE graduated. Only 150 remained from the over 300 who had started at Camp Rogers on Day 1. Our wrinkled uniforms hung on us like rags on scarecrows. Bill Parsons stood in the stands with a couple of our West Point classmates. They had gotten permission to break away from their basic course training down the road to attend the graduation. Bill's letters throughout the course had been among the few reminders that the world continued to turn outside Ranger School. I caught his eye and winked.

In the graduation speaker's remarks, he emphasized the responsibility that came with wearing a Ranger tab. "When the nation calls, you must deliver. You will spend the rest of your lives living up to the reputation of being a U.S. Army Ranger. Remember the Creed and strive always to meet that standard."

Six Ranger students posted to the front of the formation. One by one they bellowed their assigned verse of the Ranger Creed. Finally, the honor graduate of the course sucked in a gulp of oxygen and belted out the last line, pausing for emphasis after each clause.

"Readily will I display."

"The intestinal fortitude required."

"To fight on to the Ranger objective."

"And complete the mission."

"Though I be the lone survivor."

The commander addressed the crowd: "Friends and family who would like to pin their Ranger's tab should step forward at this time."

Out of the mass of proud commanders, sergeants, and veterans, my parents found me in my now oversized camouflage. I was thirty pounds lighter than when they had last seen me. I reached into my pocket and handed a crumpled black and gold Ranger tab to my father; for nearly four months I had carried that tab in my shirt pocket as motivation. I resolved to add a carving of the Ranger tab to the wooden staff I had given my father three years before.

My hands, nicked and bruised from months in the field, now had the calluses to match his. My father squeezed my hand as if he were trying to break it and wiped away his tears before the other Rangers could see him. He took the tab, unlatched the safety pin with his knobby fingers, and pinned it through my sleeve, careful not to stab my shoulder. Two inches of black and gold thread—a bit of colored ribbon.

11

Lost in Translation

Mistrust all enterprises that require new clothes.

E. M. FORSTER, *A Room with a View*

SUNKEN CHEEKS, A SUNBURN, AND A SHAVED HEAD. Just a week after finishing Ranger School, I arrived in Washington, D.C., to meet my Rhodes classmates. The letter my mother had opened for me while I trudged through Florida's swamps called it "Sailing Weekend." When the first American Rhodes scholars had traveled to England a hundred years earlier, they sailed there, hence the name. In late September, thirty-four of us showed up in Washington wearing the same wide-eyed expressions and mismatched suits.

By the time I met my classmates in Washington, I was sure my selection committee had made a mistake. I should never have read the pamphlet of biographies that the Rhodes secretary had sent in advance. My classmates carried academic distinctions I didn't even think possible for twenty-two-year-olds. Two weren't even that old; they had graduated from college at eighteen with mathematics specialties that sounded complicated—combinatorial topology and epidemiological urns—but perhaps also vaguely related to gardening. We included in our ranks an Orthodox Syrian who spoke Aramaic and an African American who spoke Swahili. There were two neuroscientists, several self-proclaimed foreign policy experts, and a half-dozen AIDS researchers. Cecil Rhodes, a colorful nineteenth-century British tycoon who never claimed to be an intellectual himself, had been eager to avoid insular bookworms. Our class certainly fit his bill. Among our number were a figure skater statistician, a licensed pilot and physicist, and an economist film producer. Rhodes had placed a particular premium on those who demonstrated a passion for "fighting the world's fight." I must have been selected on that criterion: to provide security for the rest of the group while they opened orphanages, cured diseases, and spun poems for prison inmates.

I had begun to wonder what my classmates did when they weren't saving the world or deciphering it. One, said the pamphlet, organized ultimate Frisbee tournaments. A second golfed at Saint Andrews. Another math whiz could compute his own minuscule body fat after he finished triathlons. Others professed more strenuous hobbies such as juggling and sand sculpture. And lest our ballroom dancer be without music, our class could form half an orchestra with cellists, horn players, and vocalists. All we were missing was a guy to hit the little triangle. That would be my contribution.

The week in Washington was designed to bond our class before we arrived in England and to impress upon us the lofty expectations of our selectors. Former scholars lunched with us at the Senate and lectured us in the Supreme Court. The British ambassador, Sir Christopher Meyer, invited us to the embassy for a black tie dinner. Wearing my uniform, I was nearly mistaken for one of the guards by Sir Christopher. Our last event before boarding the bus to Dulles Airport was lunch at the Cosmos Club. I sat at a table with generals who had a dozen stars between them. An announcer read each of our biographies as we stood one at a time to receive the applause of our predecessors. The unspoken message was transmitted loud and clear. There would be no more applause until we had really done something worthwhile. By comparison with their records, we had only just begun to "fight the world's fight."

THE NEXT DAY, AS our bus drove into Oxford on the "wrong" side of the road, it occurred to me that I had traded one old, gray campus for another. When I said as much to my West Point classmate Liz Young, our

English escort overheard us and chuckled, less at my comparison than at my conception of "old."

The bus deposited me on Turl Street, a cobblestone lane barely fifteen feet wide. The Turl dated to the original tenth-century Anglo-Saxon settlement. Old, indeed. A gateway arching above my head supported an enormous wooden door. A smaller door set into the same oak was ajar beside a bicycle laden with books in its front basket. I stepped through and caught my first glimpse of Lincoln College: a square of perfect emerald nestled in the center of four ivy-clad walls turned a bright red by their autumn leaves. I ran my hand along the stone, warm in the sunlight and smooth from age.

With the exception of a break in studies for the English Civil War, Oxford University had been graduating scholars for more than seven hundred years. Currently, Oxford's eighteen thousand students, a mix of British undergraduates and international graduate students, were split among forty plus colleges. The colleges served as the hubs of academic tutorials and social life under the degree-granting umbrella of Oxford University. Colleges varied in age, size, and traditions. At older colleges like Merton, one could imagine Latin and Greek reverberating across cobblestone quads. Some newer colleges eschewed tradition altogether and attracted students who placed a higher premium on functional plumbing than crenellated battlements. There were tiny colleges smaller than my elementary school and behemoths whose wine cellars supposedly rivaled the Queen's. Unlike most British menus, there was a college for every taste and persuasion. My choice, encouraged by Major Nagl, was Lincoln College.

When Lincoln was founded in 1427 (more than sixty years before Columbus sailed across the Atlantic), seven colleges had already taken the largest chunks of prime real estate in Oxford. Richard Fleming, Bishop of Lincolnshire, had intended for Lincoln College to teach young priests how to combat heresies against the Catholic Church. And although Lincoln retained the clerical title of Rector for its senior administrator, Fleming hadn't had much success against the heretical. The postcard-perfect "church" at Lincoln's southern boundary, for instance, had been converted by the college into a sanctuary for books rather than souls. At least its fate was better than another outmoded church in Oxford. One witty entrepreneur had turned the latter into a nightclub called Freud's.

For a small college of fewer than three hundred undergraduates and two hundred graduate students, Lincoln could boast a proud roster of "heretical" alumni. The most senior, John Wesley, founder of the Methodist Church, had held his first religious services at Lincoln while he was a Fellow there in the eighteenth century. Another Fellow, Lord Howard Florey, had earned the gratitude of sailors worldwide after his Nobel-worthy discovery of penicillin. Last but not least were the two authors who had found their inspiration at Lincoln: John le Carré, the spy novelist, and Theodore Geisel, better known as Dr. Seuss. His description of green eggs and ham perhaps owed more to Lincoln's breakfasts than Geisel's imagination.

Another American scholar named Katie Larson stood with me inside Lincoln's gates. Like Dr. Seuss, Katie intended to study literature at Oxford. Not only was she fluent in French, but she was also a professionally trained opera singer. The musical training infected her Minnesota accent with an additional lilting cadence that was immediately endearing. With dark hair and eyes that matched my sister Bridget's, Katie was similarly inclined to wide smiles and easy laughter. We became fast friends.

At the moment, however, as we stood bags in hand on Lincoln College's threshold, our eyes followed the windows' stone tracery and the rush of spectacled undergrads darting by. The cockney welcome of Sue, the college porter, broke our trance. She greeted us from a perch inside the gate positioned to waylay curious tourists and drunken students.

"Can I 'elp you, luv?"

"We're the two new American grad students," said Katie.

"That much is obvious."

"We're trying to find our rooms," I added.

"Just a minute, luv, while I fetch your keys."

As she searched, I whispered to Katie, "I thought the British were supposed to be reserved. Why does she keep calling us 'love'?"

Katie shrugged.

After Sue gave us our keys, we headed across Oxford's main thorough-fare, High Street, and down another narrow path to Bear Lane, our suit-cases clickety-clacking down the cobblestone streets. The portcullis that opened to our quad was only twenty steps away from the "fine traditional ales and wines" offered at the Bear Pub. I suspected the proximity might prove to be a distraction. It would.

At Oxford my room was considered luxury digs. In the United States my room would have been classified as a closet. I shared the apartment with a Norwegian named Marius. He was diligent and blond. He ate whole-grain crackers and Jarlsberg cheese. Given his intense work habits, that was nearly all I learned about him in the nine months we shared our closet condominium. After briefly exploring the kitchen, I stopped to use the bathroom. It took me several minutes to figure out how to operate the toilet. There was no flushing lever. Luckily, my Nordic roommate came to my rescue.

"Pull the chain."

"Right."

He disappeared, and I yanked the chain hanging from the ceiling. Eu-reka. I went to wash my hands in a sink with two faucets. The choice was binary: cold or hot. I turned both faucets on and waved my hands like an epileptic magician, first scalding them and then freezing them. I had even worse luck with the "shower," which consisted of a bathtub, a shower wand, and no curtain. I filled up the bathtub and took my first bath since grade school, with barely enough water pressure to wand the shampoo from my head. Had the Industrial Revolution skipped Oxford? I dried off and re-minded myself that the "challenges" of Oxford had nothing on the ameni-ties of Ranger School.

TWO KNOCKS WOKE ME the next morning as I burrowed for warmth beneath paper-thin sheets. An elderly woman walked in.

"Excuse me," I said as politely as I could for 7 a.m.

"Just 'ere to hoover yer room and empty the dustbin, luv. I'll be by-the-by ev'ry morning except weekends."

The dull roar of a vacuum cleaner solved the first riddle. So this was hoovering. The dustbin, apparently, was my trash. And the woman who'd nearly seen me naked was my "scout," a vestige from the "old" Oxford when aristocratic students had servants to make them tea and prepare their wardrobes. As late as 1962, Oxford's official handbook noted, "The scout will make the bed, wash up, and if there is the sort of fire that needs laying, lay it." They didn't make fires anymore (fortunately, since I didn't have a fireplace), but they still tidied up after students.

In the kitchen my cupboards were empty. Given that I had no schedule and no food, I resolved to hunt and gather. I ordered a breakfast "bap" at a sandwich shop and chewed through soft bacon I had anticipated being crunchy. The next agenda item was finding a gown. Yes, a gown. Academic gowns were required for evening meals at the college and length mattered. Worn over jeans and a sweater, my gown reached my knees, not nearly as long or as sophisticated as those for professors. Oxford called its professors "dons," lending the weathered scholars an aura of Latin authority. In full regalia they wore mink-lined hoods and hats one would expect to find on Elizabethan apothecaries. I hadn't expected to wear a uniform at Oxford, but as I diligently made my way through Oxford's eleven-hundred-page Examination Regulations, I read that on special occasions, such as an exam or graduation, I would need to wear *subfusc*: a white-tie tuxedo worn with a black gown and a carnation boutonniere. Failure to comply could get me booted by the *Invigilator*, a title appropriate for an academic superhero. It occurred to me that I might be the only person to have ever read Oxford's regulations.

Buying a mobile phone and opening a bank account later that day were exercises in bureaucratic jujitsu. The one required the other. I couldn't open a bank account without seventeen pieces of evidence to support my residence claim, including a verifiable phone number. And no matter how much I asserted my financial solvency, I couldn't get any of the four mobile phone companies to recognize my American credit card. One of my friends laid the blame on a fictitious "Ministry of Revenue Prevention," the same ministry she claimed caused the pubs to close at 11 p.m. and made "never complain" an exhortation for customers rather than store clerks.

Walking around Oxford made me something of an anomaly. Bikes flew by with unnerving speed and a complete disregard for pedestrians. I hesitated to buy a bike until I had had more time to explore. After four years of rushing through life, I wanted nothing more than a quiet walk. I ambled back to Lincoln and got the same tingle as the day before when I stepped over the threshold, and into another encounter with Sue the porter.

"There's a note for you in the pidge."

"The what?"

"The pidge. You know, the pigeon post."

I blinked.

"Anything you want mailed around Oxford, just give to me, and it'll get to another college just like a pigeon had dropped it off. Your pigeonhole is that cubbyhole over there with the rest."

"Cheers, Sue."

I was trying to use the lingo in my phrase book. Reading it was the only way I survived my first week in Oxford. Britishisms confounded even the simplest tasks. Directions were perilous before I learned that the British first floor was an American second floor, that pedestrians walked across "zebra" crossings, and that Magdalen College was pronounced "Mawd-lin." I also found a pocket-size book that the War Department had issued to every American service member heading to England in 1942. Its first observation: "British reserved, not unfriendly." Other illuminations of the obvious included these: "The British don't know how to make a good cup of coffee," and "At first, you will probably not like the almost continual rains and mists." The weather forecast was, to use the British phrase, "spot on." When making small talk about the weather (a British obsession), there were actually two schools of thought. Optimists chose to highlight "sunny spells." Realists, more accurately, forecast "dull and damp." In either case, both schools agreed that one should not leave the "flat" (apartment) without a wooly "jumper" (sweater) and a "brolly" (umbrella). I vowed to try my optimist attack on the next awkward encounter.

In my pigeonhole was a copy of the Middle Common Room access key. The MCR was the college's graduate lounge. The key came with a note from the graduate treasurer, Meena Seshamani. I had never seen a name like that before. I guessed from the script that it was a woman but wasn't sure. I wandered past the Front Quad and through a tunnel cut in the wall to Grove Quad, cool in the shade of a three-hundred-year-old London plane tree. A sign staked in the lawn read CROQUET ONLY.

Ducking through a door to my left, I climbed a spiral staircase of worn stone. My shoulders barely fit in the narrow passageway. A few steps up, I bumped into another student.

"I'm looking for the MCR," I said.

"New here?" she asked.

"Yeah, I got a note and a key to the MCR from . . ." I paused. "Meena 'Shay-sha-manny.'"

"That's 'Say-sha-money.'" She smiled. "Don't worry. Everyone screws up my name. Just call me Meena."

Meena led me up to the landing and showed me the MCR. Dappled light from the quad entered through a large bay window. We sat down on a futon and chatted. I assumed from Meena's striking complexion and unusual name that she was Indian. As we traded small talk, I learned that she had grown up in suburban New Jersey. When we stood to leave, Meena swung her book bag over her shoulder. It was the size of a Ranger School rucksack, but bright blue, with a large reflective strip and her initials. I had last seen a bag like that in high school. She pulled her hair back from her eyes and smiled. What an incongruous combination of beauty and bad fashion.

LATER THAT SAME DAY I arrayed my new gown over a crisply ironed shirt and walked with Katie to dinner at Lincoln, my first taste of Oxford's nightly ritual of formal sit-down meals. Three long wooden tables stretched the length of the hall toward an elevated dais reserved like an altar for the silver-haired dons. Above my head was a peaked ceiling thirty feet high, sewn together with dark beams of timber and iron tie-rods. Candles lit the room from sconces braced between gilded portrait frames of Lincoln's founders.

I sat down on the bench and introduced myself to the other Americans Katie had found in the hall. Although Americans made up a significant percentage of the graduate students at Oxford, most weren't there on Rhodes Scholarships. Some paid their own way; others had small stipends from their departments or colleges; and many held other prestigious fellowships such as the Marshall, Rotary, or Fulbright. Meena, I had learned that afternoon, was a Marshall scholar. Matt and Hayden, sitting across the table from Katie and me, were Rotary scholars.

Matt Humbaugh was a Harvard statistician studying Russian economic reforms. At six feet six inches, Matt was perhaps the tallest person I had ever met. He spoke in a string of mathematically conditioned superlatives. "On a scale of one to ten, one being a guy who just won a hotdog-eating competition and ten being a starving refugee"—dramatic pause—"my hunger is at a twelve." Matt also ended up being the best dancer at any Oxford party, using his wingspan to power improbable twists, bends, and gesticulations.

Hayden Hamilton was nearly as tall as Matt and dangerously prone to exaggerated finger snapping, especially after downing several of his trademark cocktails. Between college and starting Oxford's MBA program, Hayden had spent a year "researching the effects of tourism on indigenous mountain communities in Nepal." I had no idea what "indigenous" meant. Over the course of the year, Matt, Hayden, and I would become inseparable—listening to guest speakers, drinking at the pub, traveling— and usually engulfed in an argument on anything from politics to art to one of Hayden's clever business schemes.

As the bells outside clanged the seventh hour, the doors swung open, and students scrambled for their seats as gowned dons marched to their elevated positions of academic grace. Next, a nod triggered a student's recitation of a Latin prayer. The only words I could decipher from the gibberish were *Dominum nostrum*—our Lord. After the prayer, dinner began. Waiters delivered plates of peas, mystery meat, and boiled potatoes. I plowed through my meal out of habit.

"Craig," Katie said, staring at my nearly empty plate, "slow down."

"Yeah, man. You're not in Ranger School anymore," said Hayden.

Eating slower made the taste linger longer, though. To swallow, I had to tell myself that the food was better than an MRE. I should have counted myself lucky; Lincoln at least had an endowed chef. Before I had time to spear my last mushy pea, dessert arrived. It was an unidentifiable pastry. Was this treacle? Or Yorkshire pudding? Why didn't the phrase book come with pictures?

"Mmmm," Matt murmured, smothering his in thick, gooey custard.

"Want some?" he asked, stretching three feet across the table with the custard pitcher.

"I'll pass, thanks."

The other adjustment from a military mess hall was the caliber of conversation. It was as if I had landed on the planet Scrabble. Matt used words like "defenestrate" and "lachrymose." Hayden was even stranger. He combined a Ranger's command of curse words with Matt's triple word scores. Dinners with them were verbal obstacle courses, but a complex vocabulary helped unlock complex ideas.

Katie headed back after dinner, and Hayden, Matt, and I walked down into the cellar beneath the dining hall. This was the crypt bar known as Deep Hall. At one point in its history, Lincoln had even operated its own brewery. That tradition ended centuries before, but one interesting vestige remained. Every year on Ascension Day, Deep Hall served free beer to students from Brasenose College. This was no gesture of charity. It was repayment of a blood debt. In the Middle Ages, during one of the many riots between "town" and "gown," a mob of townsmen chased a group of students to the front gate of Lincoln. The porter opened the sanctuary to only the Lincoln students he recognized. The Brasenose man who remained behind, pounding on the oak with his fists, was stoned to death by the mob. Every year since, Lincoln has attempted to expiate its sin with pints of beer flavored with medieval ground ivy.

Three six-foot-wide stone pillars held up the hall above, and the low ceiling just barely accommodated Matt and Hayden's height. The smell of spilled lager and salt-and-vinegar potato chips infused the cold and dim room. I slid into a vaulted booth with Hayden while Matt stooped over to the bar and ordered three imperial pints from the bartender. Before I knew it, there were nine empty glasses on the table, and we were locked in debate.

"Who do you think has done more to change the world for the better," asked Hayden, "Mother Teresa or Bill Gates?"

"Mother Teresa," I said. "She's a saint."

"Is sainthood our yardstick for achievement?" asked Matt. "I completely disagree."

"Yeah," Hayden chimed in, "Mother Teresa is probably a saint, but she's only helped a few thousand people in one city. Look at Gates. Microsoft changed the way billions of people interact with one another through the computer."

"You don't have to invent a new technology to have impact," I said. "What about caring for the sick and destitute? Isn't that worthwhile service?"

"Of course it is," said Hayden, "but that's not the point. The point is scale. Who's done more?"

"If it's just scale, then of course it's Gates," I conceded, "but you're not saying making a billion dollars is service, are you?"

"That's exactly what Hayden is saying," answered Matt.

"If I make a billion dollars, that's because millions of people value a product I've developed. I will have demonstrably improved their lives," said Hayden.

"Well, yeah, I guess. But millions of people value cigarettes, and I wouldn't say Marlboro is a virtuous company."

"Okay, but Windows isn't fucking tobacco," replied Hayden.

"Yeah," joked Matt, "the government doesn't make Microsoft put warning labels on Office."

"Maybe they should," I said, thinking of the awful PowerPoint presentations I had sat through at West Point.

Hayden had the last word.

"If I'm Bill Gates, and I take that billion dollars and invest it in society, I could fund a thousand schools. I could do more to reform education than the federal government has done in fifty years. I could build a hundred hospitals in Africa." He emptied his fourth beer. "I could fund ten Mother Teresas for the next century." He snapped his fingers and slammed the glass back on the table.

Over the months to come, Oxford's best instruction would occur in dining halls and pubs. Perhaps that was the real reason Cecil Rhodes was so hesitant to choose bookworms. In any case, I would agree with the author Graham Greene by the end of two years: "Oxford had at least taught me to drink pint by pint with any man."

12

The Gift of an Interval

Be very careful not to underestimate the complexity involved in moving a boat with a pole between point A & B. Invariably, you will also visit points D, E, and Y, but you will have learned something along the way. . . .

Look confident and don't slouch.

DAVID BRAMWELL, *The Cheeky Guide to Oxford*

IN SOME WAYS, WEST POINT WAS THE PERFECT PREParation for Oxford. After four years with almost no freedom, Oxford's was intoxicating. It was exactly what I needed after West Point, a chance to catch my breath. I heard other students express a different sentiment, that they were living in a cliché, that Oxford was antiquated and overrated. For them Oxford was a name on a degree. Period. It opened doors. I couldn't understand that perspective. For me Oxford *was* the door Rhodes had opened. The gowns and gargoyles, the pubs and the spires, afternoons "punting" in an English gondola with strawberries and champagne: These weren't clichés to me. Duncan Bush, a Welsh poet, called Oxford a place that believed in its own myth. So did I.

ROWING WAS THE CLOSEST Oxford ever got to the militant obedience I was accustomed to. Every morning at 6:30 I joined seven undergraduate men and one small coxswain shivering together in a narrow rowing shell perched precipitously at Lincoln's dock. If I rubbed the sleep from my eyes and leaned forward on my tiny wooden seat, it was just possible to see the crew on the next dock through the morning fog. Moving their shell from shoulders to hips to water, they looked like lumberjacks felling a redwood and floating it downstream.

"From bow to stroke, count off!

"On three, shove off."

My head snapped back to the center line of the boat as we pushed off from shore and glided down the Thames. Here in Oxford they called it the Isis, conferring upon it an almost mythological reverence. It was at its most beautiful in the moments before dawn, as the wooly mist absorbed the first light and hovered just above the glassy belt of obsidian winding its way along the banks. Our cast was less majestic than the setting. We ranged in height, weight (measured in "stones," each equal to roughly fourteen pounds), and skill. Even our accents varied dramatically, from snooty Etonian to indecipherable Scottish to quirky Rhode Island-ese. Our outfits screamed amateur to anyone who had watched a proper crew before. There were striped woolen scarves, pom-pom hats, and button-down shirts. Unused to exercise outside a fenced enclosure, I wore Army exercise gear. A year before 9/11, this was less daring than it would become later. As the season progressed, the undergrads asked me to call cadence when we attempted to drop our oars in time with one another. The cadences helped our rhythm, and they sang along heartily, but I sincerely doubted any of them really wanted to be Airborne Rangers.

They surprised me. One morning lightning cracked above us, and we turned at Folly Bridge to head back in. The rain slashed at us, and the cox ordered us into a choppy full sprint. We heaved like Roman slaves in a galley, grunting in unison while getting drenched. It was miserable. And yet I didn't hear a single complaint as we left the boathouse. My pocket-size 1942 service members' guide was correct; the Brits were tough: "The English language didn't spread across the oceans and over the mountains and swamps of the world because these people were pantywaists."

The cultural transmission worked both ways. I began calling my sneakers "trainers," which I had to concede was both accurate and motivational. I also learned that sport at Oxford was little more than a cover for postpractice drinking. An 11 a.m. Saturday row was usually followed by a couple of pints of English bitter in Deep Hall. This was carb-loading. It wasn't just the rowers, either. With every student above the drinking age, nearly every event—athletic, academic, or extracurricular—featured at least a half-dozen cocktails. My knowledge of these concoctions was limited; I had spent my prime drinking years guzzling canteens of water.

ALTHOUGH OXFORD'S FORMAL DEBATES, held in a building consciously modeled after Parliament, were as vociferous as any boxing match, my first year at Oxford was less contest than conversation. Like the crooked streets that took the least efficient paths between destinations, learning wandered like a playful discussion, with no predetermined course and no hint of a destination. Back at West Point, Major Yingling had said that conversation was an end in itself. At Oxford that was certainly true. Education there could hardly have been more different from West Point's structured curriculum. Where the military academy had taught me how to answer questions, Oxford taught me what to ask.

The first term was a shock to every academic instinct I had honed. I had no required classes, no syllabus of readings to complete, and no examinations to sit. This didn't square with my expectations of Oxford. The way Nagl had described it, Oxford was like *Survivor* for smart people— the weakest minds got kicked off the island. Instead, students seemed to divide their time between sports, travel, and the pub. Studying was a distant fourth priority. I hadn't discovered yet that a third of the student body, those within a year of their final examinations, practically lived in the library. Undergrads adhered to the British cult of the amateur. The ultimate success was to gain a first-class degree without anyone knowing you had studied. You were all the more brilliant for never being seen to have sweated.

It took me five weeks to track down the supervisor notionally tasked with directing my research. When we finally met in his room at Brasenose

College, I found his books before I found him. They were stacked like ammunition crates around a desk littered with notes and an antique typewriter.

"Hullo. You must be Mullaney."

"Yes, sir."

"Quite." He cleared his throat and adjusted his bifocals. "Interested in the Congo, are you?" I had emailed my intention to examine American involvement in a secessionist insurgency there in the 1960s.

"Yes, sir."

"Why don't you write something up before next term, and we'll have another chat in February."

"In February?" It was three months away.

"Seems about right."

"What should I write about? How long should it be? Where do I start?"

"Let me think." He rattled off a dozen books from memory, and I quickly wrote them in my notebook. He must have picked up my distress signals. "It's easy, really."

"It is?"

"Yes. Just find a question and then answer it." This sounded like a bad college application essay. "Read and think." He paused and swirled his tea. "Simultaneously if possible."

Quite. I walked out with my notebook, more confused than before. I returned to my flat and stared at the academic planner I had brought from home. There was more white space on it than I had ever seen on a calendar, and I wondered how I would fill my days. Unscheduled time did not happen in the Army. My roommate, Bill Parsons, had joked that if West Point had wanted spontaneity, someone would have scheduled it. I had excelled at the academy by figuring out how to juggle the demands of fifteen masters all vying for undivided attention. I had studied history notes during math class and done math homework during history. I had rehearsed French skits during runs and, in one absurd attempt at marathon training, worn calf weights to class. At the end of every week, every semester, and every year, there had been a grade point average calculated to the hundredths to measure one's productivity: 3.98 was a 5 percent gain on a 3.79. At West Point education had been a matter of numeric calibration.

At Oxford I reverted to habit. I filled in blocks of time for rowing, sleep, and exercise. Next, I downloaded the lecture schedules of every subject I was even remotely interested in, and I plugged lectures into my schedule—everything from nineteenth-century European diplomacy to twenty-first-century bioethics. I calculated milestones for each chapter of the dissertation I planned to write and blocked off hunks of time for research and outlining. After all that, I realized most of my days were still blank slates. Even assuming thirty-seven minutes a day for personal hygiene and seventy-eight minutes a day for meals, I counted something on the order of six hundred minutes unaccounted for.

At West Point the challenge had been meeting the instructor's expectations. At Oxford the challenge was to meet my own. There were no grades to measure success, against either an instructor's standard or my peers. During that first term at Oxford, this ambiguity was completely disorienting. In essence I was handed a library card and told to make the most of two years. In retrospect, this was an important lesson to learn before commanding in Afghanistan, when I would almost always operate independently. Only in training did I get a distance and direction. In combat the mission would seldom be so clear.

Curiosity overcame my dilemma. No sooner had the term begun than dozens of notices began filling my pigeonhole. There were lectures and guest speakers for all comers, and Matt, Hayden, and I made the rounds nearly every night after dinner. We heard Gary Hart speak about poverty and Charlton Heston about gun control. We met the director of UNESCO and attended panels on the Congo, HIV/AIDS, and patent law. One night Liz Young invited me to a security seminar with her international relations classmates.

"It's amazing how many lectures you go to when they're optional, isn't it?" said Liz.

MOST OF THE TIME the Rhodes scholar label meant nothing at Oxford. With nearly two hundred of us from around the world, all hailing from former British colonies, we were a dime a dozen. In contrast with the mystique associated with the scholarship at home, admitting to the designation at Oxford was rarely advantageous. One too many Rhodes scholars had puked on a pristine lawn, snoozed through a lecture, or failed his exams. As at West Point, perception and reality were two different things.

On occasion being a Rhodes scholar did open up some unique experiences at Oxford. When President Clinton came to speak at Oxford, I stood five feet away as he recounted to my Rhodes classmates the famous handshake he engineered between Yasir Arafat and Yitzhak Rabin. At a conference a number of us were invited to, Mikhail Gorbachev shared a podium with Henry Kissinger. During lunch, at a table that also included General Wesley Clark, I asked Roger Bannister, the man who broke the four-minute mile on the same track where I decided to take my annual Army fitness test, how I could improve my time. (His advice: Drink less, run more.) Bono made an appearance in designer sunglasses, Chuck Berry played "Johnny B. Goode," and James Earl Jones echoed the voice of Darth Vader. I took lots of pictures because I had no expectation of ever hobnobbing with the famous again, and certainly not after I traded my gown and fountain pen for camouflage and a rifle.

Some of my most memorable evenings were spent at the Oxford Union. Barred by great iron gates, the Union looked like a haunted mansion. Its fame stemmed from its vaulted debating chamber and the dispatch boxes where five former prime ministers had cut their teeth.

Hayden, Matt, and I waited in line outside for a much-heralded debate. In contention was the proposition: "This house believes in the right to hunt."

"Only at Oxford could you see a debate on fox hunting," said Hayden.

As we walked into the chamber, a tuxedoed student handed us the house rules.

"Hayden, you're going to have a hard time," said Matt.

"Why?"

"Booing and hissing a speaker is both a *grave* and *pointless* discourtesy."

READING WAS A SERIOUS matter at Oxford. Students didn't take majors; they "read for a degree." It was up to us to figure out what was worth reading and how much. Founded in the early seventeenth century, the Bodleian Library held a copy of nearly every book published in the United Kingdom over the last four hundred years. There were so many books (more than eight million) that browsing more than 120 miles of shelves would have been inefficient, even for the uncommonly patient English. Instead, a veritable army of librarians fetched books for students from the caves extending beneath and beyond the original library foundation. Before being granted access to the library, I had to sign an oath:

> I hereby undertake not to remove from the Library, nor to mark, deface, or injure in any way, any volume, document or other object belonging to it or in its custody; not to bring into the Library, or kindle therein, any fire or flame, and not to smoke in the Library; and I promise to obey all rules of the Library.

After seeing the collection, I understood the damage an errant match could cause.

With the advice of better-read colleagues, I made a prioritized list of all the books I wanted to read at Oxford. (Making lists was a habit I inherited from my mother. At Oxford I just changed the material from operational tasks to books to read, countries to visit, languages to learn, and beers to taste.) I spent my mornings reading for my ambiguous history assignment. In the afternoons I made my way to one of a half-dozen cafés to read the stuff that really captivated me. My book list kept lengthening, contrary to my nicely organized plan of attack. One book would prompt another, throwing the whole schedule out of whack. Much of my reading grappled with the role of the individual in society. I wanted to tackle the tension I first discovered when Bellinger, my Beast squad leader, made me repeat after him that I was not an individual. I had long ago dismissed this as an exaggeration designed to make a point about cooperation, but the larger question remained. What obligations did an individual owe his community? Where did *I* end and *we* begin?

As a second-year cadet at Camp Buckner, I had had my copy of *Nineteen Eighty-Four* confiscated. Now I had a chance to finish where I'd left off. Reading Foucault's *Madness and Civilization* alongside *One Flew Over the Cuckoo's Nest* had me convinced for a period of weeks that West Point had much in common with an insane asylum (and not just because cadets routinely streaked nude during full moons). Oxford, in general, made me much more skeptical of authority. But then I would have a conversation with Liz, and she would point out that we had *volunteered* for the Army. She also reminded me that we would soon *be* the authority. She had a point.

When my Rhodes class left Washington, not one us felt worthy of the opportunity we had been granted. Who could? Yet Oxford was such a unique environment that the self-consciousness soon evaporated. We momentarily stepped off the treadmill. The most important accomplishments at Oxford would never fit on our résumés. The list of goals I wrote in my journal when I first visited Oxford the year before changed. I added new objectives: "Make best friends for life. Slow down. Figure out how I will fight the world's fight. Put people first. Read and think deeply." At West Point I befriended a wrestler who had knocked me off the team and a Baptist who had beaten me out for valedictorian. At Oxford, for the first time, I befriended those with whom I was not competing.

A group of my Rhodes classmates began meeting every Tuesday to chat over warm Guinness. We met in the back room of the Eagle and Child, and named ourselves the "Inklings" after the group J.R.R. Tolkien and C. S. Lewis had congregated with in the same pub fifty years before. Our discussions were all over the place. One week the topic would be the Holocaust. The next, we would talk about stem cell research or health care reform. Paul, the triathlete mathematician; Susanna, the sailing neuroscientist; Newman, the Syrian Orthodox theologian; and Jason, a future doctor studying *Beowulf* were among the regulars. The two I became closest with were Rob Yablon and Brandon Dammerman.

A Wisconsinite, Rob was working on a Ph.D. in inheritance taxation. Rob was also an amateur comedian and an ultimate Frisbee champion. At the Rhodes talent show, Rob had us all falling off our seats as he parodied an English grocery store.

"I never thought I'd have to make a choice between *regular* and *mushy* peas.

"Digestive biscuits. How is it possible for a cookie that weighs fifteen grams to have eighteen grams of fiber?

"Let's play a game: English dessert or venereal disease. Treacle? Spotted dick?"

Brandon was a math scholar and squash fanatic from Columbia University who most closely resembled Matt Damon in *Good Will Hunting*. For weeks Brandon would make an appearance at every party, a total socialite. Then he would disappear for a month to work on Fermat's last theorem. I imagined him scribbling Greek in wax pencil on his mirror. For the Inklings, Brandon was the designated devil's advocate. He could always be counted on to say something apparently ridiculous and then follow up with an insightful explanation. During one discussion, Brandon exclaimed that the death penalty was "a celebration of life."

"What are you talking about?"

"Executing murderers shows how much we value the lives of innocent victims."

Between lectures, debates, and the pub, there was rarely a night at Oxford without some learning opportunity. Our group took advantage of our close proximity to London to expand our cultural horizons. We saw *Copenhagen* on stage in the West End, watched the Royal Ballet at Covent Garden, and stopped in London's many museums. Brandon and I spent one long day in the Tate Modern Art Gallery. I didn't know what to make of the abstract pieces but enjoyed trying to puzzle through them with Brandon.

"What's this supposed to mean?" I asked.

"I have no idea."

We stared for another five minutes but remained unenlightened. On the bus ride home, Brandon read with a pen, continually scribbling in his book. When he finished, he branded the book with the date. Imitating his example proved to be a great way to track my own reading interests over time. As soon as I returned to my flat, I plotted where I would hang a half-dozen Rousseau and Van Gogh prints I had bought in London. In my cadet room there had been a prohibition against posters. At Oxford, without a "knickknack" quota, I could plaster posters on every vertical surface.

Not every night was a cerebral experience. As a result of joining Bacchus, one of two Oxford wine societies, I spent at least a few nights every term quaffing Bordeaux and Riesling with Matt and Hayden. My tasting notes were always clear until the fifth glass in the flight. Susi, my West Point wine coach, would have been disappointed. One tasting was so exceptional that, as we left Magdalen College, Matt brought with him one of the lawn signs. As we walked back toward my flat for a nightcap, Matt sauntered with a five-foot wooden STAY OFF THE LAWN poised on his shoulder as if it were a baseball bat.

A policeman stopped us two hundred yards from the gate.

Matt turned and greeted him with an entirely innocent smile. "Good evening."

"What are you doing with that sign?"

"What sign?"

"The one over your shoulder, mate. That's private property of Magdalen College."

"Right," said Matt, examining the sign. "I see."

"Yes."

"I'll just return it then."

"Please."

We stayed put while Matt obediently returned his souvenir. Nights like that reminded me of a scene I liked in Jack Kerouac's *On the Road*. When an older man approaches the narrator and his buddy in their car, the two assume he is a sheriff. "You boys going to get somewhere," the sheriff asked, "or just going?" As Kerouac followed up, "It was a damned good question." Most of my life up until Oxford I had been "going to get somewhere." Now, with friends like Matt, Hayden, Rob, and Brandon, I was discovering that Oxford was about "just going," with no particular destination in mind. Unlike a Ranger School patrol, getting lost *was* the objective.

"CRAIG, HOW DOES THIS thing work?" asked my father, standing help-lessly in front of a ticket machine at Oxford's train station. "Is 'return' the same as 'round-trip'?"

"Dad, let me do it." I stepped in and ordered our "return" fare to Chesterfield, a few hours north of Oxford. I had already spent a week intervening in similar crises of confidence for my father: showing him how to use the bizarre British washing machine, translating menus, and explaining to him how to convert prices to dollars in his head.

The trip to England was my Father's Day present. I had already visited a half-dozen countries, and my father, at twice my age, had never taken a transatlantic flight. His trip was the talk of the gas company before he left. His buddies took trips to Florida, not to Europe.

"Craig," he told me, "I can buy my own ticket. You don't have to."

"No, Dad. It's on me. I'm a lieutenant now. I can afford it."

"If you insist."

"I do."

As he nodded off to sleep on the train, snoring lightly with his head against the window, I opened my journal and began writing. My father's visit was a strange role reversal. Normally, he had what John Updike attributed to Red Sox legend Ted Williams—an "intensity of competence." This trip was the first time I saw him baffled by anything.

Showing him around Oxford was like a shot of confidence in my arm. I pointed out the Oxford curiosities I thought he would find most interesting, such as the stuffed dodo and shrunken heads at the Pitt Rivers Museum and the private deer herd at Magdalen College. I found an extra gown for him to wear and took him to the dining hall for dinner. Like me, he didn't know what to make of the food, but he enjoyed going down to Deep Hall after dinner and buying pints for Matt, Hayden, and me.

"This is warm," my father said, wrinkling his face. He never drank beer, let alone at room temperature.

"That's how they drink beer here, Dad."

"Hmmm."

"It's an acquired taste." He had told me the same thing when he bought me my first beer after high school graduation.

West Point had been a halfway house to independence. There, I had still relied on my father to ferry Trent and me back to Rhode Island for holidays. While we slept twelve hours at a stretch, he would go right back to work shoveling snow or heading to the gas company for overtime. He had endless reserves of energy. On Saturdays in football season, I could count on him being at every game, grilling burgers for my friends. He didn't even like football. When I was tight on cash, he would slip me a couple of fifties, no questions asked. Without my father I had had to make my own way in England, navigating a foreign culture, learning how to cook, and managing my own finances. I didn't need him anymore, not in the same way I had before.

Much of what I wanted to show my father at Oxford he couldn't see. When I took him to Blackwell's Bookstore, where I bought a month's salary's worth of used books, he remained at the door looking out at the bikes rattling past on Broad Street. When conversations at the pub with my friends shifted from small talk to philosophy, he would get up to bring the next round of beer.

My father woke up as we arrived at our destination. There, an English family whom Bill Parsons had introduced me to during graduation week picked us up. June in the Peak District was stunning—stone walls, grazing cattle, and heather moors. We put our bags down in our hosts' remodeled sixteenth-century barn. The tension evaporated from my father's thick neck. He threw on a warm sweater and disappeared for an hour. Before we left three days later, my father had compared notes on building dry stone wall, fertilizing flower beds, and trimming hedges. He was in his element. I, on the other hand, opened a book, curled up by the Aga stove, and fixed myself a pot of tea. Outside the window, my father played fetch with the cocker spaniel.

I HAD PLANNED MY father's visit to coincide with the most exciting week of the Oxford calendar: Eights Week. For four days in May the Isis hosted a circuit of rowing races involving nearly 160 boats and as many as eighteen hundred rowers. The banks overflowed with crowds of drunken spectators cheering their college's boats. Since the Isis was too narrow for head-to-head races down its sinuous course, the format was a "bumps" race.

Our heat of thirteen boats lined up on the banks with a length and a half between crews. Eight of us wore identical polo shirts, giving us a professional appearance that our rowing didn't merit. The ninth, our pace-making "stroke," was a last-minute replacement for a chronically absent teammate. He wore the singlet of an Oxford Blue, the long-legged specimens that crewed Oxford's varsity boats. He was our ringer. We sat in the boat coiled at the "catch," ready at a command to call forth the strength of gods. The sun was bright, and a light breeze rippled the water around us.

A pistol fired. Oar blades churned the Isis into thick foam as we bolted from the start position toward the boat in front of us. Winning a "bump" meant passing their bow and knocking them out of the race. If we did, we would start the next day's heat with our order reversed. If we accomplished the rare feat of bumping four days in a row, advancing in the heat order each day, our boat would earn "blades," entitling each of us to an antique oar with our names and the names of our victims gilded on the oar blade's face.

We weren't able to pass the boat. Instead, our coxswain steered us right into it at ramming speed. No matter, it counted as a bump. We cheered from our seats and splashed water on the unlucky crew. We did the same on the next two days, ramping our excitement to fever pitch. In a show of solidarity, none of us washed our shirts or underwear. We smelled awful. I worked up the team with a locker room speech I stole from Vince Lombardi (not as big a legend in England, I found out). If we succeeded, the cox promised we could throw her in the Isis. Thousands crowded the docks and stood ten deep on boathouse roofs as we pushed off to our starting position a mile upstream. My father waved, and a smile broke white from the center of his beard.

As we fidgeted in our seats, the crew in front of us, wearing Viking helmets with horns sticking out the sides, taunted us with a soccer chant to the tune of Handel's Hallelujah chorus.

"You're all wankers. You're all wankers. You're all wankers, all wankers, all WA-AN-KERS."

I tightened the wing nuts on my footplate and gripped the oar. The smoke had barely cleared the pistol barrel before we lurched forward out of sync. It took several strokes before we were in tune again, and the Vikings were already a couple of lengths ahead. We settled into a rhythm and closed the gap slowly. We were still a half length back when we turned the corner and headed down the stretch past the first boathouse.

"Give me a Power Ten!" shouted the cox, urging us to invest all our strength in ten superhuman pulls.

"On three-two-one, let's go!"

We counted together on the exhalation, reaching farther back for the catch and putting extra relish on the finish. Lactic acid rushed through my legs and arms. My vision blurred as it became impossible to suck in enough oxygen to fuel my strokes. Cheers from the crowd kept me conscious, and then there was a louder cheer as we passed their bow. We won the race.

"Give us a cadence, Mullaney," shouted our ringer.

"I wanna be an Airborne Ranger!" I boomed with what little air remained in my lungs.

The crowd drowned out the crew's response. Adrenaline kept our arms and legs moving mechanically, thrusting us past banks thronged with onlookers. As we pulled even with the Lincoln boathouse, our oars churned the water, moving us faster and faster. Passing the boathouse at full throttle,

I looked up at my father standing on the roof and pumping his fist in the air. I shouted the cadence again, louder, but we no longer had the strength in our quaking legs to keep the pace or the rhythm. The boat lunged in darting spurts, and our blades chopped the water out of tune. Momentum carried us downstream, past the boathouses. My father's fist blurred in the crowd and disappeared.

"To half-slide, on three-two-one," yelled the cox. Our speed bled as our strokes shortened through the water. "And quarter-slide, on three-two-one. Easy there."

Our oars lay flat like spoons on the surface of the river, and we drifted with the current. I leaned over my oar and steadied my heaving chest. We splashed water on one another, victorious but spent. Water dripped off our oars and back into the river. In the distance, a faint roar rose from the crowd as another boat swept past its prey. I dipped my hand in the river, letting the cool water slip through my open fingers. We slowed to a halt, and I caught my breath.

13

Oxford Standard Time

They wandered at random, choosing the narrower ways and coming suddenly on colleges and long old walls. Nothing seemed modern now. The past had them by the throat.

JOHN GALSWORTHY, *The End of the Chapter*

OXFORD IS ONE OF THE MOST ROMANTIC PLACES ON the planet. After passing through on a trip to London, William Wordsworth exclaimed the power of Oxford's domes and towers to overcome "the soberness of reason." Two hundred years later the modern world had barely intruded on Oxford's magical spell. It looked best on cloudy days, with students scattered underneath umbrellas. The misty rain that never disappeared for long gave Oxford the look of a faded black-and-white postcard. Its giant portals conspired with antique lanterns and marbled walls to give it an aspect of timelessness. The shops lining its streets were in on the ruse, sporting names that beckoned to a different era: Ede and Ravenscroft, Duckers, Shephard and Woodward, Walters on the Turl. Bicycles rattling on cobblestones provided the rhythm and whistling birds the melody. Walking along the river, watching students float by on wobbly wooden punts wearing straw hats and toasting champagne flutes, I found it easy to forget the world rushing past Oxford's eddy.

Rowing helped open the doors to English dating culture, a topic of more interest to me than the African colonial history I was ostensibly studying. Joining my teammates on "crew dates" with ladies' boats taught me valuable lingo I would have been lost without. If I spotted an attractive woman, I should call her "fit." For reasons unknown to me, a woman on the other extreme was a "minger." Whether fit or minger, most women wore skirts little wider than tea towels, and the colder the weather, the farther the skirts receded north above the knees.

Matters of intergender recreation were another mystery. "Snogging," for instance, had nothing to do with the flu. It was the equivalent of teenagers "making out." "Shagging" occurred several beers later. Having a "rubber" was scant precaution; in England, that was a pencil eraser. A British woman had spoken with our class before we left for England. She made it clear that the British approached sex with much less reservation than Americans.

"Are there differences in the dating cultures?" I asked.

"Oh, you'll have *no* problem." She winked. "English women *love* American men."

"That wasn't quite what I was getting at."

"Do you mean, should you kiss a girl on the first date?"

I raised my eyebrows.

"Yes." She smiled.

I scribbled along in my notebook as she continued. *OK to kiss on 1st date.*

"Britain is a 'post-Christian' society. You won't find the same American concept of guilt."

After eight years of monastic celibacy at nearly all-male institutions and a lifetime of Catholic guilt, I was more intimidated than encouraged. Once I had arrived at Oxford and gone prowling with Matt and Hayden, it became clear my Yankee accent worked no wonders with British women. I began to wonder why Nagl had called Oxford a "target-rich environment." "Take my advice," he had said. "Find a wife."

I TOOK HIS ADVICE seriously and focused like a laser-aiming device. I attended "stoplight" parties in bright green, signaling my availability, with no luck. I chased undergraduate rowers who made fun of my accent and hit on American graduate students who knew better than to get involved with an overzealous soldier. So much for "you'll have *no* problem." A couple of weeks after arriving, I attended our college's semiannual house party. Hayden had by this time plied me with several drinks.

"This is *good*. What is it?" I asked.

"A lemon drop."

"What's in it?"

"About a cup of sugar and two of vodka."

"Really? Can't taste the vodka at all."

"That's the point." Hayden grinned.

Inebriated and completely uninhibited, I found Meena, the Indian fashion disaster I had met my first day at Lincoln, in the corner of the room. British pop music shook the walls and the beer in my cup. With the other hand I reached across and touched the crystal pendant hanging around Meena's neck.

"I like your necklace." Without realizing it, the rest of a bad pickup line tumbled out of my mouth before I could stop it. "Do you have a man?"

Do you have a man? Did I just say that? I tottered and reached for a lamp to stabilize.

Meena arched her eyes. "No, my parents gave it to me," she replied before walking off and leaving me with the lamp.

TWO MONTHS LATER I was at another party at Freud's, the church-turned-nightclub, with Matt and Hayden. I was smart enough this time to pass on the third round of Brandy Alexanders. As I scanned the crowd, I saw Meena sitting with a group of Lincoln grad students.

"Guys, I'll catch up with you later."

Hayden finger-snapped his assent. Matt bobbled his head with the drumbeat.

I slid in next to Meena. She was wearing a slinky dress that marked a distinct upgrade from the oversized sweaters she normally wore.

"Hey."

"Aren't you going to compliment my necklace?"

"About that . . ."

"Forget it. You were drunk."

Meena turned her head abruptly. An Indian in a tux and thick-rimmed glasses had tapped her shoulder from behind.

"Can I buy you a drink?" he asked.

"No," she replied coolly, "that's okay."

"No, really. I'd like to buy you a drink."

"I'm fine. Thanks."

"I'll be back in a minute then."

As soon as he departed for the bar, Meena turned back toward me.

"Do you want to dance?"

"Really?" I asked.

"Yeah."

Meena led me to the dance floor. I attempted in vain to close the middle school distance between our hips. As I looked past Meena at the bar, the Indian emerged from the crowd holding two cocktail glasses. He soon discovered us on the dance floor and made a beeline toward us. *He wouldn't, would he?*

He would.

"Can I get your phone number?" he asked Meena as we continued dancing.

"No," Meena replied, rotating away from him.

"You know, you should really get to know me. I'm the most interesting man you'll meet in Oxford." He tried to slip her a business card, turned, and walked out the door. By the time the door shut, the song had ended.

"Want to dance again?" I asked.

"No, that's all right. Thanks."

Meena walked off toward the door, her hips swaying slightly with each long stride.

THE NEXT DAY I played Elton John's "Tiny Dancer" on repeat in my room. The Norwegian stared me down in the kitchen and then left the flat, slamming the door behind him. Alone and incapable of scholastic concentration, I plotted what I would later refer to as my "wooing offensive." Unfortunately, the school term was at its end and I left a few days later for seven weeks of travel, so it wasn't until I returned to Oxford in late January that I carried out my plan. I left emails and notes in Meena's pigeonhole nearly every day. I asked her to the movies, invited her on walks, and even offered to cook her dinner. Each time I struck out. One night I ran into Meena as she was walking back from Lincoln with Jan, the German scientist who had become her protective male housemate.

"Are you going to the Super Bowl party?" I asked.

"Yeah. Are you?"

"I think so. Do you want to grab a drink beforehand at the Turf?"

"Sure."

"That sounds like a good idea. I'll come, too," said Jan, swathed in black and wearing rectangular glasses. That doesn't sound like a good idea, I thought.

The three of us had an awkward drink at the Turf Tavern—the pub where Bill Clinton hadn't inhaled—watched over by Jan and an extant section of Oxford's fourteenth-century city wall. Fortunately, Jan stayed behind when Meena and I departed for the party. We walked through Magdalen College's old cloister and up a narrow stairwell to the MCR. I knocked, and an American friend opened the door.

"Are you guys together?" he asked.

"No," said Meena, slicing my hopes with the blunt edge of a knife. I walked home by myself.

Finally, I resorted to covert ops. I learned that the Oxford Union was arranging a trip to Paris for Valentine's Day. Dozens were likely to go. The price was right, and I had nothing on my schedule. I sent Meena an email asking for her number. I need to talk to you, I said. When she called, she started by asking if something was wrong. Clearly, I hadn't learned subtlety at Ranger School. I proceeded to ask her, as nonchalantly as I could, whether she was interested in a student trip to the Louvre. I was going, I said, and Brandon, the mathematical contrarian, was going as well.

"Where do I get a ticket?" she asked.

"Well, I'm a member of the Union. I'll pick it up."

"Oh." I wasn't sure whether she got that I was asking her on a Valentine's date to Paris. "It sounds interesting. Let me think about it."

She took a couple of weeks to get back to me, enough time to indicate what parachutists call "a soft landing." I was surprised and elated when she finally agreed. She would insist later that she had no idea the trip had co-incided with the most romantic holiday of the year. "It was just a cheap way to see Paris."

BRANDON HAD NEVER BEEN to Paris, and he was eager to see *every-thing* in the twenty-four hours we had on the ground. We tried. Notre Dame, the Champs-Elysées, the Arc de Triomphe, and Les Invalides. This was not a tour for the weak or fainthearted. We spent two hours in the Louvre, enough time to sprint from the *Venus de Milo* to Géricault's *Raft of the Medusa* and then to the *Mona Lisa*. Meena was nearly as inscrutable as Da Vinci's subject. Was she smiling? Was she impressed with the art notes I had cribbed the week before ("This is the *sfumato* technique")? The last time I was in the Louvre, at the end of my Normandy visit, I had been a lot more focused on the art. On this visit my focus was on Meena.

A cold winter light hung in the brisk February air as we walked past carts selling paperbacks along the banks of the Seine. Brisk gusts shook tiny whitecaps from the gray water. We made our way slowly to the Latin Quar-ter, stopping every hundred yards for a photograph. Brandon played his role well, manipulating our photo poses so that I got my arm around Meena as often as possible. It took us two hours to find a restaurant suitably authentic for Brandon's tastes. White tablecloths draped a half-dozen cozy tables inside a small café. We warmed up with crocks of onion soup, the bubbling Gruyère cheese melting over the fresh croutons. Our garçon brought out the first bottle of Côte de Rhône, and we clinked our glasses.

"To Paris," offered Brandon.

"To Paris."

Brandon and I shared a chateaubriand steak larger than a textbook, but Meena, a vegetarian, munched a salad that looked much less appetizing.

"Why didn't you order something else?" I asked.

"Everything has meat in it."

"I hadn't noticed," I said. *Damn.*

The garçon twisted open a second bottle of wine and refilled our glasses. Meena, having polished off the salad, made steady progress through the bread basket.

"Dessert, monsieur?" asked the garçon. *"Mousse au chocolat? Crème brulée?"* We wagged our heads no.

"Peut-être un digestif? Un whiskey ou un calvados?" My ears perked at the calvados, a strong liquor I had tasted first in Normandy. It was a wicked combination of apple and fire.

"Pour trois!" I smiled and hoped Meena wouldn't mind my ordering for her and Brandon.

Five glasses later we were the only ones left in the restaurant. Brandon and I chatted in bad French with the staff, and Meena looked as if she was about to keel over from exhaustion.

"Allons-y!" I said, and the three of us walked outside and through the Quarter like contestants in a three-legged race. We had been walking for thirty minutes when Meena stopped and patted down her ski jacket.

"Oh, no," she exclaimed.

"What?"

"I left my camera behind. I need to get it."

"I have no idea how to get back to that restaurant," said Brandon. Meena turned to look at me.

"I do," I said. "Follow me."

Ranger School had at least prepared me for this. I could maneuver in almost any setting now without getting lost—even drunk. We returned to the restaurant, had another round of calvados on the house, and claimed Meena's camera. The next morning the three of us walked to Montmartre and climbed the stairs to Sacré Coeur basilica. A choir practiced in the background, and I took a seat in a pew to pray, hoping that I had won some points with Meena by saving her camera. I sat next to her on the long bus ride back to Oxford, and we talked the entire time, about our families, our disappointments, our ambitions. I didn't want the conversation to end. When I said good night to her at Lincoln, I did what T. S. Eliot's Prufrock couldn't—I "squeezed the universe into a ball" and I kissed her. Meena kissed back, short and sweet.

MEENA DISAPPEARED FOR TWO weeks. I eventually pinned her down to a dinner date. Remembering our dinner in Paris, I thought strategically. Pizza would be perfect. Even I could enjoy a well-made vegetarian pizza. We picked up our conversation as if there had never been a pause. When I returned to my room that night, I wrote in my journal: "I have the lingering thought that I just might be dating a future spouse (long shot)."

After the mushroom pizza, we started seeing each other daily, one of the benefits of Oxford's loose rhythm. In the middle of the day we would buy groceries at Sainsbury's and head to the river for a picnic and a long walk around the meadow. On one rainy afternoon she joined me for tea in my flat. While I was in the kitchen boiling water, I heard Meena burst out laughing from my room. I poked my head around the door, where Meena stood reading a spreadsheet posting on the back of my door.

"What's this?" Meena asked.

"Nothing, really."

"Number of push-ups completed? Number of study hours?"

"Well, you see . . ."

"You're crazy. *Tum pagal ho*," she repeated in Hindi, laughing. Her whole body shook when she laughed, like a volcano erupting.

"How can someone so goofy be this intense?" Meena asked, pointing to exhibit A. Next to it was further indictment: my list of countries to visit and skills to acquire. I was glad she didn't read far enough to see "Find a wife" on my list of things to do, a few entries after learning how to throw a boomerang and tie a bow tie.

Since I had no vegetarian recipes in my arsenal, she coached me through several burned iterations of Indian cooking. Every dish began by popping mustard seeds and sautéing dry lentils and hot red chilies. I hadn't expected to like curried cauliflower or radish *sambar*, but I did. For dessert she made rice pudding with almonds. It was even better than Ranger pudding. I was in charge of coffee. Earlier, I had bought an old-fashioned grinder with a hand crank. I ground just enough fresh beans for two cups and set to work on the bourbon whipped cream recipe that Susi had given me at West Point. I whipped and whipped and whipped some more. As my right arm got tired, I shifted the whisk to my left hand. More whipping. Crests of amber cream started to form, and my whisk beat on. Then, complete collapse. My overzealous whipping had been too much. As the crested cream reversed into liquid, Meena bent over laughing. I smiled meekly and poured the cream into the coffee.

We began that stage of an Oxford relationship some called "intellidating," a probing of IQs every bit as romantic as it sounded. I gave her books to read about West Point and the Army, and she didn't recoil. In fact, Meena gave me my own reading list: a primer on Hinduism, a history book about Indian independence, and a novel set in Mumbai. I wasn't sure whose culture was more foreign, but it didn't matter.

I dove into Indian culture headfirst (or heartfirst, to be more accurate). We started at the movies. "Bollywood," Bombay's ambitiously nicknamed film industry, produces far more "fil-ums" than the United States. Given the epic length (three hours or longer) and enormous casts of these films, this was impressive, especially considering the elaborate choreography of the ten song and dance routines sprinkled through a typical Bollywood film. Suddenly, the hero would start dancing on a moving train or the scene would cut to the Alps where a couple danced in fields of edelweiss. It was like watching *The Sound of Music* mashed up with *Saturday Night Fever*. The key difference, at least to a twenty-two-year-old like me, was the absence of any display of affection. Every time two characters moved toward an embrace, the scene cut to a sweeping Himalayan panorama, a Victorian prudishness that rivaled West Point's.

Meena taught me my first Hindi lessons. Hindi was no joke; it had its own unrecognizable alphabet, including four different sounds for "T." I spent weeks like a grade school student tracing the letters in my notebook. Meena would patiently point out where I had joined two letters inappropriately. For practice, I wrote the lyrics to Bollywood songs. My favorite, from a love story set in the turbulent period of India's independence struggle, described a young man falling in love.

When I saw this girl, she seemed to me like . . .
a blooming rose
a poet's dream
a candle burning in the temple
a dancing feather
like a slowly growing feeling of intoxication.

Language also gave me a window into Indian habits. There were three ways to say "thank you," but *kal* could mean either "yesterday" or "tomorrow." Apparently, excessive gratitude went hand in hand with a flexible concept of time. Communicating in Hindi was more than translation; it also involved body language. Shaking one's head could mean either yes or no. It depended on the angle of the head shake.

Meena watched me row, and I went to see her practice martial arts. I knew I had met my match. She was smart enough to earn a Ph.D. in economics by age twenty-four, yet humble enough to entertain my questions. She could break boards with a fist in the afternoon and wear a ball gown with grace in the evening. She was as intense as any Ranger but could disarm me with just one slightly crooked smile. Romantic poetry I couldn't understand as a Plebe now made sense.

Susi, the gourmet British chef, wine connoisseur, and wife of Major Nagl, visited Oxford in April. Meena joined us for afternoon tea at the Grand Café, a small refuge of baroque glass and gold leaf elegance along High Street. As Susi recounted my encounter with the dessert pears during our cooking lessons, Meena laughed and I shrank in embarrassment. When

Meena shared my failed attempt to whip cream, the two laughed together at my expense. After Meena left to go back to work, Susi put down her tea and smiled coyly.

"Oh, I *like* Meena. She's perfectly *wonderful*."

"Really?"

"Yes, Craig. She's a keeper."

"I think so, too."

"I can't wait to tell John. Bravo!"

Soon after, I invited Meena to the Rhodes Ball, confident in Susi's seal of approval. My jaw dropped when I saw Meena gliding toward me in a long red dress with spaghetti straps, trailing a red silk scarf behind her. Under the scarf was a gold necklace filigreed in an Indian design.

"I like your necklace."

"Very funny."

"You look beautiful."

The cocktail hour was on the lawn outside Rhodes House, an imposing mansion of windows and stone. A saxophonist set the mood while waiters passed out champagne. The setting sun cast everyone in warm gold as they floated by in gowns and tuxes, drifting back into the nineteenth century. Inside, we entered a dark library set with fine silver and linen. Tiny flames flickered from candelabras. As we ate our meal, a harpist played in the background. After dinner we were ushered onto the lawn for dessert under the stars. A fire juggler, stilt performer, and unicyclist entertained while we ate ice cream and sipped cordials. Later, as we swayed to jazz in the ballroom, I held Meena close and moved my hand to the curve above her hip. My hand fit perfectly. As the night ended and we gathered outside to walk home, I told Meena I loved her.

"You don't mean that," she said, averting her eyes.

"I do."

"You're drunk."

"I'm not."

The next day I found Meena outside Lincoln's gate and told her again, this time in Hindi.

"Main tumse pyaar karta huun."

"How'd you learn that?" she asked, sounding more interested in my Hindi than its translation.

THE BELLS ON CHRIST Church's Tom Tower ring every night at exactly 9:05. Up until the nineteenth century, English cities had set their clocks according to their distance from the Royal Observatory at Greenwich. Oxford, one degree west of Greenwich, had set its clocks five minutes slow. I had also come to adopt Oxford Standard Time. Time had become a currency to spend, not, as it had been at West Point, a resource to hoard. Some nights I dispensed with my watch altogether and allowed my course to be guided by the chiming bells echoing from Tom Tower like a chorus of brass bullfrogs. An evening spent wandering through Oxford's cobblestone lanes, accompanied only by the whispers of stone gargoyles, was never wasted time. Walking arm in arm with Meena, it seemed at times as if my heart beat as loudly as the bells. But although every rational argument strained against a relationship with an ambitious, peace-loving Indian who had never seen a rifle or combat boots, reason had little defense against Oxford's charms.

On my twenty-third birthday, Meena gave me a book. At nearly fifteen hundred pages, *A Suitable Boy* was an intimidating gift. Its length suggested that we would be together long enough to discuss my reaction. Inside the cover Meena left a cryptic inscription:

> *I can think of no better book to entertain you with insight into the*
> *world of arranged marriages, family politics, and religious conflict that*
> *comprises Indian culture. Suffice it to say, it won't answer the question*
> *of whether you are a suitable boy. Sorry.*
> *Love, Meena*

14

Beyond the Cloister

For years and years I have dreamed of the wonders of the Turkish bath; for years and years I have promised myself that I would yet enjoy one. Many and many a time, in fancy, I have . . . passed through a weird and complicated system of pulling and hauling, and drenching and scrubbing . . . and, finally, swathed in soft fabrics, been . . . lulled by sensuous odors from unseen censers, by the gentle influence of the narghili's Persian tobacco, and by the music of fountains that counterfeited the pattering of summer rain.

MARK TWAIN, *Innocents Abroad*

TRAVEL IS THE GREATEST TEACHER. WHILE AT OXFORD I was eager to visit as many of the world's classrooms as I could, stopping only when I had filled my passport or emptied my bank account. Unlike West Point, when six days of leave was generous, Oxford breaks up a year-long vacation with just three eight-week terms. By my calculation, I had roughly forty weeks of available time to hop around the globe before my return to the Army. With a lieutenant's salary and a host of willing travel partners, I traveled as far as I could away from Oxford, especially after I lost faith in any "sunny spell" breaking through the "dull and damp."

My classmate Rob, the tax expert comedian, planned our first trip outside Europe, a three-week journey through Malaysia and Thailand with Dave Adesnik, another Rhodes classmate. Southeast Asia introduced me to chaos. No sooner had we cleared customs at the airport outside Kuala Lumpur, Malaysia, than a crush of tourist touts assaulted us, hawking tours and hotels. We parted the throng and headed outside with touts following in our wake. The taxi we chose at random from a honking horde outside the terminal charged a small fortune to dodge through traffic at perilous speeds, all the while blasting bad pop music. As we alighted in Chinatown, I nearly hacked up a lung trying to breathe. It was like sucking on an exhaust pipe. I considered returning to the airport and flying to a nice beach somewhere, but the taxi had already picked up new prey.

Kuala Lumpur, the capital of Malaysia, offered me my first glimpse of Islam. On the ceiling of our hotel room was an arrow pointing to Mecca. Everywhere we walked, we were within earshot of the Muslim call to prayer. Within minutes of the muezzin's call, the streets emptied as the faithful said their prayers. Faith interacted with globalization in unanticipated ways. Take the "Ramadan Special" offered at Dunkin' Donuts. For the equivalent of $1.30, they offered six doughnuts and a cup of coffee (but only before sunrise and after sunset). While we wandered past Gucci handbags and Sony electronics for sale at the mall, every television broadcast the Friday prayer services.

Rob suggested a visit to the Masjid Negara, Malaysia's national mosque. We were soon following the faithful through a warren of alleys. Merchants sang the praises of their particular prayer mats. Eager salesmen sold audiocassettes of popular sermons out of open suitcases. It was like the parking lot at a concert. We took off our sneakers, buried them in our backpacks, and followed the crowd into a mosque larger than any cathedral I had visited before. The guidebook told us it had the capacity for fifteen thousand people, big enough to hold half the population of my hometown. The three of us, two Jews and a Catholic, wandered into the main prayer hall, an expanse of prostrated supplicants broken only by vertical columns. I had never been in a mosque before. I looked around at what must have been a thousand men in the room. There wasn't a single piece of furniture, just row after row of men kneeling and touching their foreheads to the floor. The air inside was cool and clean, a contrast with the choking pollution outside. This was refuge. Over our heads, the roof soared above the congregation in a fantastic shape like the inside of an open umbrella. Later, in

Afghanistan, I would observe the same geometrical precision in religious art. Somehow, the interlocking triangles and stars helped the process of spiritual deliberation. We stood transfixed and drew our own inspiration from the architecture.

Unfortunately, a vocal Malaysian in a white tunic and crocheted hat interrupted our contemplation. He frowned, gesticulated wildly with his arms, and shook his head. In response, we smiled contritely, bowed, and then struggled against the current of prayer-goers in order to leave the alleys surrounding the mosque.

After a week in Malaysia we worked our way north toward Thailand. On the resort island of Pulau Penang, we stayed in a cheap hotel recommended by the guidebook. When we woke up to catch a five o'clock bus to the border, we found the front doors locked, bolted, chained, and blocked by a couch. The manager, a sidearm tucked into his pants, let us through. A second later the bolt slid back in the door.

"So much for trusting a guidebook," I said as we looked more closely at our neighborhood. Motor scooters and cars occasionally stopped at the building across the street. Sometimes money and packages were exchanged. Sometimes a woman would get out. Sometimes a woman would get in.

"Drugs and prostitution?" offered Rob.

Considering that Malaysia had the death penalty for drug trafficking, this realization left us eager to leave, and quickly. An SUV pulled up and asked if "we needed anything."

"Just waiting for a bus." Rob smiled.

He must have decided we were too stupid to cause any problems and drove off. Ten drug deals later, the "bus" arrived. In point of fact, it was an antique Volkswagen van that compressed fifteen people, three sacks of rice, and several crates of dried beans. There were no seatbelts and no air-conditioning. As we pulled away with a lurch, the driver took a swig from his hip flask. I hoped it was cough medicine and not whiskey. I have had more comfortable journeys walking through swamps.

After a week learning to scuba-dive in the islands, we caught a flight to Chiang Mai, a city in northern Thailand known for its Buddhist temples.

After the severe formality of Malaysia's mosques, Thailand's temples were almost playful. Giant stupas stood like golden ice cream cones turned upside down. The roof eaves fluted at the end into fanciful curves, silhouettes of temple dancers, and dragon wings. Small signs, poorly translated into English, offered pilgrims practical advice such as OUT OF DEBT, OUT OF SAD. One temple in Bangkok left a more cryptic notice at the gate: IT IS FORBIDDEN TO ENTER A WOMAN EVEN A FOREIGNER IF DRESSED AS A MAN. Nearly every other temple welcomed tourists eagerly, a distinct difference from our experience in Kuala Lumpur. After forgetting to wear long pants to one temple, a saffron-robed monk smiled and handed me a pair of bright blue pants. They seemed tailored for a fat midget, and I doubted I looked any more sanctified than I had in my khaki shorts.

When a teenage monk approached, I anticipated being ejected from the grounds. Instead, he told us he wanted to practice his English. Soon the rest of his friends surrounded us. Their English was as good as our Thai, mostly stock greetings and questions such as "Where are you from?" But after we got them talking about their training and lives at the temple, they opened up.

"We like basketball and American football."

"My favorite team is the San Antonio Spurs."

"I like Hulk Hogan."

They had also watched a fair number of American films. That explained why so many of their questions were about girls.

"Do you have girlfriends?" they asked.

"No," we replied sadly. At this point I had only just begun my wooing offensive.

"That is okay," they assured us.

When a blond woman walked past, one monk leaned over and asked, "Do you think she is beautiful?" I nodded. He wanted to learn good English pickup lines, and we obliged him. The monks scribbled one of Dave's favorites in their notebooks, something like "Heaven just called and told me they're missing an angel." I didn't divulge my necklace tactic, though.

"What do you call a man who dresses like a lady?" another monk asked.

"Drag queen," we replied.

"Dry clean?"

"No, *drag queen*," we said again, guessing that volume correlated with comprehension.

They repeated it over and over again to make sure they had it right. We spent more than an hour with them, enough time to ensure several headaches for their English teacher. A few days later we flew south to Bangkok.

Bangkok combined Chiang Mai's temple culture with the soul of an Asian metropolis. The clash of civilizations was even more apparent here than in Kuala Lumpur. Slums, temples, and gleaming skyscrapers competed for a skyline obscured by such heavy smog that taxi drivers wore surgical masks. This was the fault line of globalization. One night while we toured a ritzy part of town, an elephant walked past sporting a blinking taillight suspended from its tail. Monks browsed pop music albums. Stalls selling shredded papaya and wonton soup competed against Baskin-Robbins, Pizza Hut, and Schlotzky's Deli. One woman who had parked her ox-driven cart on the street came back with a bucket of chicken from KFC. Televisions beamed American sitcoms and a Thai replication of *Who Wants to Be a Millionaire*. My favorite was an original Superman cartoon with a slightly altered introduction. Instead of fighting for "truth, justice, and the American way," the Thai Superman fought for "truth, justice," and a second of muted silence. Little did I know that negotiating this collision of East and West would soon become both a professional and a personal imperative.

OVER THE FOLLOWING MONTHS I would take a dozen such trips with other friends, searching for the rich texture no history book could deliver. Unfortunately, Meena's research kept her tied to Oxford except for occasional weekend excursions to London and Edinburgh. Each time I returned with a journal filled with new adventures and a small present for Meena. My first gift, predictably, was a crystal necklace from Prague.

When I flew out of Heathrow on these trips, I left looking for a sepia-toned past. With Brandon I watched Giza's pyramids in the moonlight, climbed into Petra's crescent canyon, and listened to the Friday prayers at Jerusalem's Wailing Wall. With Matt and Hayden in Istanbul, I explored the magnificent Hagia Sophia. For a thousand years it had stood as the largest edifice in Christianity before being converted to the principal mosque for the Ottoman Empire. I craned my neck for nearly an hour examining its mosaics. A million squares of color, an entire kaleidoscope of devotion, shone brilliantly, even in afternoon shadow. An icon of Mary seemed to hover in the dome. Enormous black pendants hung down, embossed with Koranic calligraphy in shimmering gold.

During our travels, Hayden introduced me to photography. Handing me his bulky camera in Prague, he pointed at one of the spires on St. Vitus Cathedral.

"What do you see when you look at that spire?" asked Hayden.

"What do you mean?"

"Look through the camera. Shut everything out of your field of view except your one small frame. What do you see that you didn't before?"

I put my eye to the viewfinder and panned across.

"The clouds are stacked in the same horizontal pattern as the stones," I said.

"Good," he continued. "What about texture? How do you think the stone would feel to touch? Use the zoom. Get closer."

I twisted the zoom with my right hand. With my eye pressed to the camera, I had the sensation of flying toward the cathedral.

"It looks smooth, like the wind has worn down the rough edges."

"Okay. Where would you place the spire in your picture?"

"In the center," I said.

"Why?"

"I don't know. Doesn't the subject always go in the center?"

"Not necessarily. What if you put the spire on the right side?"

He was right. It was an entirely different picture. Now my eye was drawn toward one gargoyle, strutting out from the spire toward the clouds. It was a winged lion, and at the center of the photograph, I imagined it lifting off the spire and soaring into the clouds.

"Take the shot."

I paused at the end of my exhalation and squeezed, just as I had learned to do with an M16. The shutter opened and closed, but there was no recoil.

After that photograph I saw everything differently. It was like turning up the volume on my eyes. From the one gargoyle I never would have noticed, I began observing a hundred details for every one I had before: the curve of rice terraces, swirling clouds at sunset, a man selling baklava from the trunk of a car. Photography was an act of possession, claiming a moment as uniquely mine, as only my eyes had seen it. Before, my guidebook had told me what to look for. Now, at Oxford and abroad, I was my own guide. I lingered. I zoomed. I focused and panned at my discretion. In short, I learned to see with my own eyes.

AT TIMES, THE WORLD Mark Twain had described in *Innocents Abroad*, a record of his nineteenth-century "Grand Voyage," seemed to be disappearing overnight. Where were the spice-laden caravans and eager carpet merchants? My journey featured a world in flux, struggling to preserve local tradition while the future unfolded at the speed of the Internet. No matter how rural the village, we were almost always able to find an Internet café. Every kid we met, from an eight-year-old Jordanian nomad to those Thai monks, wanted to trade email addresses with us. Satellite dishes were more common than water tanks on the roofs of Cairo slums. Will Smith was a bigger star in Turkey than in America. Other global brands were as ubiquitous as English signage. I could have circled the world without ever eating in a place other than a McDonald's or Starbucks.

It was certainly harder now to find one of Twain's Turkish baths, but Matt, Hayden, and I looked for one just the same during our trip to Istanbul. It was hidden in a narrow alley skipping down the hill toward the Sea of Marmara. We walked in through its creaky door, paid two dollars each, and moved to rickety wooden stalls to change. I emerged wearing a thin towel loincloth-style.

"You guys look ridiculous," I said. With Matt and Hayden's height, the towels looked smaller than saucer doilies.

"On a scale of . . ." Matt began to calibrate how small the towels were but was interrupted by a three-hunded-pound masseur who grabbed his forearm. He had a long handlebar mustache and a bald scalp. Hayden and I followed through a tunnel of sweating marble. Inside the caldarium, daylight pierced a hundred star-shaped holes in the roof, and a raised marble octagon stood in the center of the room, bathed in dim, speckled light. Around the perimeter were a half-dozen faucets and benches. The masseur took us each in turn. I watched with a wince as he scrubbed Matt's back with a glove that looked as if it was made from Brillo pads. When I stepped up to bat, it was as painful as I had imagined. My skin rolled off in clumps. He body-slammed me onto the central marble slab and twisted my left arm behind my back to touch the sole of my right foot.

I paid money for this, I said to myself while my body was bent like a human pretzel. I winced as the masseur yanked my bad right shoulder out of its socket. "What doesn't kill you makes you stronger" now had new meaning. I was being stretched, both literally and figuratively. Like others before, a full passport gave me self-reliance of a different sort than what I had developed at West Point. Travel was a continual confrontation with the unknown, each journey the mental equivalent of leaping out of a helicopter. Later, my intuition would prove correct. Comfort in ambiguity would be as essential to leading in combat as the ability to plan. West Point, an institution with instructions on folding underwear, was poor preparation for chaos. Bangkok and Istanbul were perfect.

The masseur's knee dug into the small of my back and cracked my spine. When the torture ended five minutes and three dislocations later, I slowly regained motor control. We returned to our rickety cabanas, swallowed aspirin, and lay down for a nap, satisfied that vestiges of Twain's world still lingered. Twain had found the bath as odious, the masseur as satanic, and the whole experience as much a "malignant swindle" as we did. Lying down, swaddled in thick towels, I thought of what I would tell my grandchildren—like the stories my grandmother had told me—about the umbrella-shaped mosque in Malaysia, the teenage monks, and the smell of a three-hundred-pound Turkish masseur.

15

Balanced

Surprise: to strike the enemy at a time or place or in a manner
for which he is unprepared.

U.S. ARMY OPERATIONS FIELD MANUAL (FM 100-5)

"HAVE YOU SEEN THE NEWS?" ASKED AN ELDERLY CLERK
in a rural New Zealand convenience store as I approached the counter with
a carton of eggs. "No," I said. I hadn't watched the news in the month it
had taken me to reach New Zealand via South Africa and Australia. It was
September, and I was near the end of an around-the-world summer vacation between my first and second years at Oxford.

"Are you American?" he asked, tipped off by my accent.

"Yes. Why?"

He looked down at the floor and then back up at me.

"What happened?" I asked.

"Someone flew a plane into the World Trade Center." He motioned
with his eyes toward a small television on the wall behind me. "I'm
so sorry."

The towers crumpled to the ground in a cloud of dust and debris.
My God.

I walked out of the store, returned to the hostel, and gave the eggs to
someone else. Another student helped me find the TV room, already
thronged at 9 a.m. with dozens of bedraggled backpackers. I was the only
American. On the screen, the planes crashed again and again and again.

I spent the rest of the day on the tour I had already paid for, an afternoon "zorbing." We drove to a large hill and walked up to the top where a

white inflatable ball twenty feet across sat. The ball was hollow on the inside. I crawled in, and the operator poured a bucket of soapy warm water over my head. He released the rope holding the ball in place, and I began rolling down the hill. I flipped inside the plastic orb as the suds sloshed around me, as if I were inside a washing machine. When my zorb slowed and stopped, my internal gyroscope was still spinning.

When we returned to the hostel, the manager asked whether I wanted to use his phone to call home. I dialed Meena's number.

"How are you?" I asked.

"Okay. How are you?"

"I'm not sure."

"I know what you mean."

Did she? Did she realize everything had changed for me? For *us*? Although I knew I wouldn't be recalled from Oxford before completing my degree, 9/11 directly impacted the path my career would take after I finished my studies. A week later, while I camped on a small island near Fiji, the tribal elders invited me into their thatched hut to watch CNN with them.

"What will America do?" they asked.

I had been asked about the military before on my travels, but my answers had always been academic. Now it was personal. It was apparent the moment President Bush promised to hunt down the perpetrators. I knew in my gut that this wasn't going to mean a cruise missile strike. There would be boots on the ground—one day, my boots.

THREE MONTHS BEFORE, MEENA and I had begun a conversation about our future. We were sitting in my flat. Meena was reading a book, and I was on the phone with Major Nagl talking about where I should go after Oxford. After our call finished, I reached to my desk and grabbed a yellow legal pad. I turned it on its side and drew two parallel lines, one for each of us. Next, I made hash marks for each year for the next five years.

"Here's where I go to Benning for training. Here's where I arrive at my first unit. I'll be there for a year and a half, and then I'll go back to Benning for more training."

Meena's face was blank.

"Now, on your line, this is the last two years of medical school, and then"—I looked up at Meena—"I need your help. What are your next—"

"What?" Meena interrupted. "Why do you need to know?"

"So that we can coordinate our careers."

"What the hell do you think you're doing? We just started dating."

Her expletive caught me off guard. Meena never swore. I meekly replied, "It's been five months."

"Who knows where we're going to be?"

"It's just that—"

"No. We're not having this talk. Not now."

At that point, with a year left at Oxford, I was already thinking about how to make our relationship work after leaving England. I had already decided that I wanted a life with Meena. And, as I had learned at West Point, I was attempting to fill in the details. I wanted to know where the parallel lines would cross. Meena, on the other hand, was more tentative.

I had first introduced Meena to my West Point world at a friend's wedding in Germany. We were driving back from the reception with Trent, the snub-nosed Iowan. We were lost, Trent was at the wheel, and I cringed in the backseat as Trent described the tempo of his training. How, I wondered, would I find the time to make a long-distance relationship work?

Trent turned abruptly to Meena and threw his compass at her. "Give me the cardinals."

"The what?"

"You know, the cardinal directions," Trent barked. "North, south, east, west."

Meena laughed at Trent and his scowl evaporated. "I have no idea."

"North is off to the right," I said from the backseat. Meena and I clearly had a different sense of direction.

I met Meena's family for the first time a month later in New Jersey. Meena picked me up from Charlie Hooker's house nearby and told me the ground rules as we drove to her house.

"When we arrive, call my mother 'auntie' and my father 'uncle.'"

"But—"

"It's an Indian thing. Trust me," she said. "And don't forget to take off your shoes."

"I know." Meena had already instructed me in this custom when I visited her house in Oxford.

"I'm just reminding you." She continued, "My mother has cooked lunch for us. Eat whatever it is and smile. You'll have to stop her from refilling your plate at least two refills in advance."

"Got it."

"And under no circumstances can you reach for my hand, put your arm around me, or hug me."

"How about a peck on the cheek? Can I do that?"

Meena stared back. "Very funny. No, you may not kiss me. Remember— no public displays of affection."

"Right."

We pulled into a cul-de-sac and parked in front of the house.

"Ready?" asked Meena.

"It's go time."

We entered through the garage, and Meena's mother opened the door.

"Hi, *kannama*. Come in." Her smile was broad and inviting.

I walked in and took off my shoes. Check.

"Mom, this is my friend Craig."

Meena's mother offered her hand.

"It's nice to meet you, Auntie." She smiled when I said "auntie." Check.

From the background, Meena's father greeted us. He was the tallest Indian I had ever seen, like an El Greco figure with lanky limbs. Meena had his hooked nose.

"C-raig"—he pronounced my name as though it had two syllables—

"I've been reading Tom Clancy in preparation for your visit. Watch out. I might ambush you while you're sleeping." He smiled mischievously, a goofy glint of teeth.

"I sleep with one eye open," I deadpanned. Meena's father laughed.

"Lunch is ready," said Meena's mother from the kitchen. "I made lima bean sambar, spinach, and okra curry." She couldn't have chosen three vegetables that I disliked more.

I was directed to a seat next to Meena's grandfather. A former tax administrator in India, he wore an all-white *lungi* and had his hair perfectly combed and waxed in a 1920s side part. Ladle after ladle appeared above my plate as Meena's mother arranged rice, spinach, and okra, and covered the rice with the souplike sambar. She placed a spoon and fork next to my plate. I dug in with dramatic gusto. For love, I would eat okra.

Meena's grandfather said something in Tamil to her mother that I couldn't understand. He glanced at my plate and Meena laughed.

"What?" I asked.

"My grandfather is surprised that you are eating like us, with your hand."

"Craig," Meena's mother said, smiling from ear to ear, "we'll turn you into a South Indian in no time."

RETURNING TO OXFORD IN October 2001 to start my second year, I knew things were going to be different. Hayden and Matt had left for new jobs after their one-year programs concluded. Meena would go into hibernation to write her doctoral dissertation on British health care, and Oxford's damp attractions would be dull after the initial excitement of being a freshman. Being in England that autumn often felt like an alternate reality. How else to explain, in the wake of 9/11, how the Oxford Union could debate the legalization of marijuana and whether "Englishmen are funnier than Americans." The guest speaker who drew the most excitement was Jenna Jameson, a porn star.

In my own life, a note of seriousness intruded on my days where before they had been carefree. My military identity set me apart from both my peers and British society more generally. At one event I made the mistake of wearing my uniform. A British undergrad mistook it for a costume. Corrected, he rudely asked whether I had ever killed a man. "I'm about to," I responded, and he scurried back to his gin and tonic.

By now there were a number of military academy graduates at Oxford besides Liz and me, and we became military ambassadors to American civilians. Eventually, we would all go to war. We met to cook elaborate dinners at my apartment, giving us a space to ask one another questions that our civilian peers might recoil at. How do you feel about killing? Would you call an air strike on a village if you were taking fire from it? The new military scholars wanted to know where I was going after Oxford. I was the test balloon; how would I transition to a military at war from a university locked in the fourteenth century?

Our American classmates were more understanding than the Brits. They approached the officers in our class with questions about military strategy and the ethics of war. They wanted to know how I felt about Kabul being bombed and whether the video footage of children's severed limbs made me doubt my service choice. The short answer was no. The longer answer I would give after a pint or two was that I, too, found the civilian casualties revolting. Who wouldn't? But until we found a more humane way to kill or capture their leaders, what choice did we have? After watching those planes crash again and again, I had no doubts about this war's legitimacy. These men, who had killed thousands of innocent Americans, who had beheaded prisoners in public spectacles and stoned adulterous women, were no martyrs. Lastly, I had taken an oath at graduation to serve when called—"without any mental reservations or purpose of evasion."

While the questions of just means in war were abstract for classmates holding law school acceptance letters, they were concrete for me. I reread Michael Walzer's *Just and Unjust Wars* and tried to work out how I would respond to a sniper in a mosque or a kid holding a rocket-propelled grenade. Was I allowed to shoot? Did I need to shoot? *Would I be able to shoot?* Walzer's answers weren't always clear, and in that sense I was grateful for the interval Oxford provided to think deeply without the pressure of actual combat. Soon enough I would need my own answers.

I heard more thank-you's for my service than I had the first year, but I wasn't sure what to make of the gratitude. For one, I hadn't earned it. While I sipped chardonnay at college garden parties, my classmates were gearing up to deploy to Afghanistan, the "graveyard of empires" that the BBC kept emphasizing. Thinking of Bill and Trent, training their men for war, I wondered again whether I belonged at Oxford. Was this experience relevant to the responsibilities I would soon have?

MY SISTER BRIDGET JOINED me during my second year at Oxford to study history as part of a study-abroad program. On a Christmas trip we took to Rome, I had many long conversations with her about Meena. My father, eager for us to enjoy our sibling trip, put us in touch beforehand with Matt Glover, a coworker's son in seminary at the Vatican. My sister swooned when we met Father Matt, a tall, dark-haired Romeo. "How could a guy like that take himself off the market?" she asked. Father Matt took us to Mass with the other seminarians. I had never been to a church before with so many clerical collars. We had a personal tour of Saint Peter's and Father Matt shared his favorite restaurant with us, a small nook hidden away in an alley near the Pantheon. In the back of my head I was already contemplating having Father Matt officiate at my wedding. If Meena had known that I was asking a priest about hypothetical interfaith ceremonies, she would have killed me.

On the train ride from Rome to Vicenza, where we would spend Christmas with Bill Parsons, I read a book that Meena had given me before the trip.

"What are you reading?" Bridget asked, curious at the notes I was making in the book.

"The *Ramayana*."

"The what?"

"It's a key Hindu scripture. Meena gave it to me." It was actually an engrossing story, although I needed an index to keep track of the names.

"Uh-huh," she said. "Can I make an observation?"

"Sure."

"You, my brother, are hooked."

"I am." I smiled. Whether stepping on her toes in a Viennese waltz or channeling Matt Humbaugh's exaggerated dance moves at a club, I had no inhibitions around Meena. I gave her my journal, and she read it from cover to cover. Handing it back to me, all she said was "I love you."

Bill had bulked up in the year since I had seen him. He was already in command of an infantry platoon. Our roles might just as easily have been reversed. Making dinner on Christmas Eve illustrated what each of us had learned since leaving West Point. Bill answered the hundred questions I had about being a platoon leader. How did you decide what to train? How is your role different from your platoon sergeant's? What's your relationship with your company commander? His answers were thorough, but I didn't have the sense to take notes. On the other hand, Bill was of little use making dinner. After buying groceries and laying them out on the kitchen table, I asked Bill for a cutting board and knife. All he had was a pocket-knife. I even had to show him how to turn on the stove. Over a bottle of wine, our discussion turned to religion.

"Is Meena Christian?" asked Bill.

"No. She's Hindu."

"Isn't that a problem?"

"We haven't really talked about it yet."

"Maybe you should."

The subject came up when Meena and I rendezvoused in Slovenia over New Year's. Our dinner conversation wandered from my impressions of the Vatican to a discussion Bill and I had had about whether Jesus represented the only path to salvation.

"What do you think?" Meena asked.

"I think so," I began, but my translation of what I had discussed with

Bill came out all wrong. Meena's eyes bored straight through me. For me it had been a theological debate. For Meena it was personal.

"But if Jesus is the only path to salvation, then all non-Christians would go to hell, right?"

"No, that's not what I mean. . . ." It was too late, though. Meena left the table and returned to the room.

"If that's what you believe," she announced when I entered, "fine. But we shouldn't be together if you think our religions are incompatible. I don't make judgments about you. Don't judge me."

I tried to wrap her in a hug, but she squirmed away.

"Just think about it," she said.

Nothing was clear anymore—neither the faith I had grown up in nor the career I had trained for. I stayed awake all night thinking. There were only two things I knew for certain: I wanted to serve my country and I wanted to spend my life with Meena. How could I do both? I walked downstairs to the hotel lobby, weary but sleepless, and slumped in a over-stuffed armchair by the fire. All that remained were a few dying embers. I asked the receptionist for stationery and set my thoughts to paper. I wrote and crumpled a dozen sheets of paper, tossing each at the fireplace where they flared up and turned to ash. By morning I had composed a four-page letter. What I wrote is between Meena, God, and me.

WITH SIX MONTHS REMAINING at Oxford, I lived in two worlds: Oxford's circuit of costume balls and drunken revelry and the Army's implied pressure to prepare for war. My men wouldn't give a damn whether I was a Rhodes scholar. All that mattered was whether they could trust me not to get them killed. I did my best to prepare for that responsibility while savoring Oxford's charms.

I enrolled in a course on South Asian history. Meena had given me a book about the Indian fight for independence that had sparked my interest. How, I wanted to know, had religious differences escalated to the point where neighbors hacked one another to pieces in massive communal riots?

Nearly half a million people were killed as British India was partitioned into Muslim-majority Pakistan and Hindu-majority India. I read as much as I could, drawn to the region for both personal and professional reasons. When I could get Meena away from her research, she began teaching me more advanced Hindi. Its linguistic cousin, Urdu, was spoken along the border area between Afghanistan and Pakistan, where I would find myself two years later. There, the language training would pay unexpected dividends.

Finally, I tested my progress by taking a trip to India, hoping that my capacity for chaos had increased since my journey to Southeast Asia. Meena was in the final stage of writing her thesis and couldn't join me. After I offered to buy her flight, my sister Bridget, ever ready for an adventure, agreed to go, as did another American couple, Tim and Jada. I had known Tim at West Point, where he had been an exchange midshipman in my cadet company.

Tim Strabbing was more normal than normal. He had a flat Michigan accent and a flat crew cut. As a Marine, Tim was a walking, talking recruitment poster: intensely patriotic, tough, and smart. Tim and Jada arrived in India a week before us. Tim, however, hadn't yet learned what I had during my trip to Asia with Rob and Dave: What you see isn't always what you get. Within hours of arriving in Delhi, Tim fell into a classic tourist scam and bought a one-way flight to Kashmir from an "official tourist officer." When Tim and Jada joined Bridget and me in Jaipur, Tim still wouldn't acknowledge how precarious their situation had been. After Colombia, the disputed territory of Kashmir had the second-highest kidnapping rate in the world.

"Oh, come on, guys. Who would kidnap a Marine?"

Mark Twain had been entranced by India when he visited in 1897, calling India "the one land *all* men desire to see, and having seen once, by even a glimpse, would not give that glimpse for the shows of all the rest of the globe combined." Three weeks wasn't enough time to see even a sliver of India's riches, but we made it as far as our small budget allowed. I forced the group to sit through a Bollywood film that was more entertaining for the active crowd participation than the movie itself. Against Meena's advice, we ate street food and lived to tell about it. We dodged a salesman who tried to sell us American quarters for a dollar each and feared for our lives driving through the mountains on one-lane roads.

By coincidence, we were able to see the Dalai Lama drive by in the small Himalayan town that served as the Tibetan capital-in-exile. Combined with visits to the Sikh Golden Temple, the Taj Mahal, and the holy city of Rishikesh, our Indian travels gave us glimpses of four major faith traditions. I could have read a dozen books without learning as much. There was no substitute for watching prayer lamps float down the Ganges at sunset, spinning Dharamsala's Buddhist prayer wheels, or joining Sikh pilgrims in a communal lunch. I began to understand how cultures could accommodate one another, how it was possible for a country with thirty-five official languages and twenty-two thousand dialects to function. I returned to Meena with a suitcase of saris and a new appreciation for her heritage.

Time moved more quickly as our return to the United States approached. By now our paths were more certain. We had chosen our next steps with the objective of minimizing the distance between us. Before beginning her economics Ph.D. at Oxford, Meena had already completed part of medical school. Now, with the Ph.D. nearly done, she still had three more years of medical school to complete at the University of Pennsylvania in Philadelphia. After four months of infantry training in Benning, I would go to the 10th Mountain Division in upstate New York. Meena liked that it was only a half day's drive from Philadelphia. She didn't like that in the 1990s the 10th Mountain had deployed more than any other unit in the Army. That spring the battalion I hoped to join was engaged in a vicious battle along a ten-thousand-foot mountain range in eastern Afghanistan. I wasn't sure how it would all work out.

Katie Larson, the woman who had stood with me at Lincoln's gate on the first day, sent me a long note to lift my spirits. She had spent two years apart from her fiancé. "Long distance is hard. You have to trust that as you each change on your own, your relationship will also change along with

The U.S. Military Academy at West Point provides future Army officers with a four-year undergraduate education and extensive leadership training in preparation for five years of active duty service.

With my roommate Bill Parsons (*right*) after a parade. A devout Baptist, Bill would later graduate first in the class and serve as a Ranger in Iraq and Afghanistan.

My younger brother, Gary, then fourteen, trying on my cadet uniform.

Aram Donigian (*left*), my nemesis during Plebe year, standing with me after coaching me in a West Point wrestling tournament.

John Nagl and his wife, Susi, mentored cadets applying to study at Oxford, their alma mater. They also gave me my first lessons in cooking, wine, and relationships. "Take my advice," John told me before I left for England. "Find a wife."

Vice President Al Gore presents me with my West Point graduation diploma.

My father pins my Ranger tab on my shoulder after I'd completed three months of training in swamps and mountains and dropped over twenty pounds.

The Malvesti Obstacle Course, day four of Ranger School. Ranger students must crawl the last fifty yards of the course through mud and cold water with barbed wire only inches above their heads.

Celebrating with Meena after completing my last Oxford exam. Oxford students are required to wear traditional *subfusc* to exams—dark suit, white bow tie, and academic gown.

With Oxford classmates Matt (*left*) and Hayden (*center*) at an Istanbul restaurant. One of the benefits of Oxford's flexible academic schedule was the opportunity to travel widely.

Our platoon, posing before a morning patrol along the Afghanistan-Pakistan border.
(*Credit: Robert Nickelsberg*)

Captain Ryan Worthan, my company commander and boss. A rugby fanatic from Iowa, Worthan would earn a Silver Star in Afghanistan, the Army's third highest award for heroism in combat.

Sergeant First Class Vern Story, the platoon sergeant. My second-in-command, Story was a tough but soft-spoken former Marine from Arkansas. A humble professional, Story refused to wear his Ranger tab or Airborne wings on his uniform.

The "Ghetto Sled," a Humvee stripped for parts that picked me up in Gardez after a helicopter flight above the infamous Shah-i-Kot Valley.

Children asking for food and water followed us wherever we patrolled in Gardez. Although these kids hammed it up for the camera, others reportedly set the landmines that threatened our Humvees.

Connecticut native Specialist Mitchell Markam provided comic relief when he wasn't firing his .50-caliber machine gun.

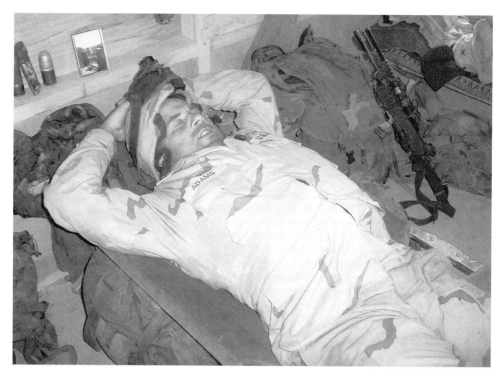

Sergeant "Chuck" Adams, sleeping in his uniform. A former Marine, Chuck refused orders to shower for the first six weeks of the deployment, fearing it would diminish his fighting spirit.

During a mission to vaccinate livestock, I posed for photos with a camel, only to have it gallop away at full speed with me still hanging onto its hump.

"0 KM TO HELL." Our firebase at Shkin was only five miles from Pakistan. In the weeks before our arrival, insurgents had begun flooding across the porous border, targeting the base with rockets and killing two soldiers.

Staff Sergeant Chris McGurk on Losano Ridge. His squad, patrolling on foot, triggered a violent enemy ambush when they surprised three hidden enemy fighters poised to detonate five landmines under our Humvees. *(Credit: Robert Nickelsberg)*

Kneeling next to my radio operator Joshuah Howe (*right*) on Losano Ridge, just ten feet from where an enemy mortar had exploded harmlessly into the dirt. The Pakistani border post that had fired the mortar stands halfway up the mountain behind us.

Our makeshift shrine to Private First Class Evan O'Neill, killed by an enemy sniper while we patrolled near Losano Ridge. *(Credit: Robert Nickelsberg)*

Major Paul Wille, the battalion operations officer, challenged me to box in front of the company at Shkin. After West Point and Ranger School, this was the only boxing match I didn't lose; I'd finally learned to take a punch.

The battalion commander, Lieutenant Colonel Mike Howard, presents Specialist "Red" White with two medals for combat valor. Red's sixth sense kept us safe; his wisecracks kept us sane.

Captain Andrew Gallo, my West Point classmate and bunk mate in Afghanistan, was a die-hard Yankees fan and body builder. Here he poses with an insurgent snowman at Orgun.

Our Humvee after a roadside bomb explosion on Losano Ridge. With nothing but sandbags to deflect the blast, one soldier lost a leg and several others were scarred by shrapnel.

Being blessed by Meena's grandmother during the Hindu portion of our two-day wedding. Around our necks we wore traditional rose garlands.

Charlie Hooker, a former Green Beret and Wall Street banker, holds his West Point ring out with three of his former cadet mentees at my wedding reception: me, Iowa wrestler Trent Moore, and Andrew Gallo.

Dancing to Indian music with my best man, Oxford classmate Bryan Leach, during the wedding reception.

Fr. Matt Glover blesses Meena and me at our Catholic wedding. My mother, in a purple sari, stands to my right.

With my siblings, Gary, Bridget, and Kelsey, on Bridget's wedding day.

My parents, during a visit to Oxford in 2002.

Relief-in-place. Gary graduated Ranger School nearly eight years after me. Soon after, I left the Army and he deployed to Iraq.

you. It takes hope, good humor, and idealism. It takes a massive dose of courage to protect the relationship at all odds. It is hard, but worth it. You'll both be stronger as a result." I kept Katie's note and thought of it often when my courage flagged.

JUST BEFORE LEAVING OXFORD, I took one last morning row down the Isis. I borrowed the boathouse keys from Sue the porter and jogged past Christ Church meadow and its herd of cattle munching dew-glazed grass. At the boathouse I grabbed two oars and placed them by the dock outside. I dipped my hand in the river and sifted the current with my fingers. The water was cool velvet. I returned to the boathouse, lifted a one-seat scull out of the rack, walked back with it to the dock, and lowered it into the water. After securing the oars in their locks, I slipped into the scull. A duck from the opposite shore sent the only ripples across the water. As I glided toward dawn, the rhythm of my arms and legs pulsed with my heart. I pulled at the oars, and they swept past my sides like a swan's wings. As I moved, the cool air dried the sweat on my neck.

Every once in a while I turned an eye to check that I wasn't heading for the bank. Most of the time I stared past my feet, down the long length of the stern, watching the tiny ripples of new strokes join my wake. Kierke–gaard said that life could only be understood by looking backward but that it had to be lived forward. Balanced between water and sky, I skimmed past the drooping willows and into the fog.

16

From Athens to Sparta

"He's an Oggsford man."

"Oh."

"He went to Oggsford College in England. You know Oggsford College?"

"I've heard of it."

F. SCOTT FITZGERALD, *The Great Gatsby*

WALKING WITHOUT AN UMBRELLA WAS A PLEASANT change. I had been back in the United States for a week, and it hadn't rained once. It was good to be home, I thought to myself, even as enormous civilian Hummers whistled past me on Route 95 and made me wonder what else had changed in the year since I had last been home.

Meena and I were in the process of a convoluted road trip to Fort Benning, Georgia, where I was due to begin a final bout of infantry training before reporting to the 10th Mountain Division. Beginning in Rhode Island, I picked up the new car my father had chosen for me and bought with the money I wired him. He left it in the driveway, washed and topped up with fuel. In the trunk were jumper cables and an extra battery, "in case you leave the lights on by accident—again."

We drove north from Rhode Island to the lake cabin in Maine where my family stayed for a week every summer. My brother, Gary, and I grappled for hours until I ended up thrown off the dock into the lake.

"Oxford made you soft," he taunted from the dock.

"You just got lucky," I shouted back from the water.

Gary was much stronger now, and taller. I first noticed how much taller when he visited Oxford that spring. I bought him a Guinness at the pub, his first beer. When we stood up to leave, it was as if he had sprouted an extra six inches. He now had me by three inches. I couldn't believe he was already a senior in high school. He would soon be the same age I was when I dropped my bags in front of Arvin Gymnasium.

I woke up early in the morning so I could join my father reading the paper and drinking coffee.

"When was the last time you saw this side of sunrise?" my father asked me. The flecks of gray in his beard matched the pattern on his flannel pajamas. He had more wrinkles now.

He handed me a mug of high-octane coffee and sank into the nearest camp chair, reading glasses perched on his nose, red from the cold. I missed the routine we had shared before I left for West Point. Every day I would leave the house with him at 5:30 a.m. so that he could drop me off at high school on his way to work. He wore the same thing every day—work boots, dark blue jeans, and an orange gas company sweatshirt. Driving in, my father never said much. We would listen to 98.1 WCTK, the only country station in Rhode Island. He never sang along or tapped his boot with the music, but I did. Sitting in the passenger seat, I must have looked ridiculous to him with my nose in an algebra book humming along to Alan Jackson. Looking at him now, I wondered whether the early morning schedule was finally wearing him down.

With a full trunk that made the back of the car sag visibly, Meena and I headed south from Maine to New York City. Like most visitors to Ground Zero, I gasped at the size of the hole. A chain-link fence separated tourists from the workers bulldozing earth and twisted steel below. Friends and relatives had pinned laminated photos to the fence. Their edges were curled and frayed from time and weather. It had been almost a year. Until that moment the collapsed towers had been an abstraction. I had been on the other side of the planet on 9/11, and even in England there had been a gaping distance between my life and the tectonic shifts taking place in the United States. We exited the opposite end of the walkway and pushed past impromptu souvenir stands. Whatever had changed in the United States didn't include its entrepreneurial spirit. But, my God, who would buy a World Trade Center snow globe? Eleven months wasn't enough to turn tragedy into comedy. A customer picked one up and shook it. Debris swirled around the miniature buildings. Just as it settled, he shook it again.

The war in Afghanistan had begun to drift further and further from the front page. The first units had barely returned from Afghanistan before a new war loomed on the horizon. The United States was pushing for weapons inspectors to reenter Iraq. Debates at the United Nations dominated the news, and for the first time in my life I was intimately connected to foreign affairs. The drum roll for war had begun, and I stood a good chance of deploying if those negotiations failed.

Meena and I stopped in New Jersey to spend a week with her family. There was a distinct difference from the summer before when I had first met them. The lighthearted banter was gone, replaced by politeness. I doubted now whether Meena's mother was still intent on turning me into a South Indian. They knew that Meena and I weren't just "friends," although we still avoided even the slightest hint of affection for each other. Their questions were pointed.

"Craig, will you deploy to Iraq?"

"Tough question," I responded. "I don't think so. I doubt Saddam Hussein will evade another ultimatum."

"But, Craig, if we went to war, would you go?"

I ducked the question. "Depends on what units are used. I think it will probably be armored units, but I'm going to an infantry division."

I was conscious that Meena's mother would remember exactly what I said. I had never met anyone with such perfect recall, although Meena was a close second.

"How much time do you owe the Army after Oxford?"

"Roughly five years," I said.

"What will you do then?"

I blanked, wondering how I could get out of answering the million-dollar question.

"Well," Meena's mother said, abruptly changing the subject, "how about lunch? I made masala dosa and pearl onion sambar."

I decided that I needed a wooing offensive for Meena's parents. In the kitchen, while Meena's mother stirred the sambar simmering over the stove, I tried out my Hindi by singing to her the song Meena told me was her mother's favorite, *"Tujhe Dekha To Yeh Janaa Sanam."*

"Oh, my stars," she exclaimed, smiling. "You know that song?"

"Yes, Auntie."

"I love that song," she said and began singing it herself. Her voice was light and beautiful.

Meena's father was more difficult, however. The two of us sat on the couch, and he clicked through television channels in total silence. I read the same edition of *Time* three times, cover to cover.

Later in the week I took Meena's family on a tour of West Point. I thought this would be a great way to highlight the ideals and principles that drew me to the military. Meena's father had applied to the Indian Military Academy when he was younger. He read Tom Clancy compulsively. How could he not love the Army after seeing West Point? Instead, as Plebes marched past us with rucksacks and rifles, the trip only reinforced his fear that I would leave his daughter behind while I risked my life. That night I cooked a three-course meal featuring recipes from different regions of India. They complimented me on my cooking, but the loudest noise around the table was the cracking sound of papadum crackers.

Meena had never been south of the Mason-Dixon line before our drive to Georgia. We sipped sweet tea in South Carolina and shared a plate of Waffle House grits outside Atlanta. During the drive, she told me the concerns her parents had relayed to her about our relationship.

"Don't worry, Craig," she told me. "I still want to make this work, even if it takes five years to be together."

"What doesn't kill you makes you stronger, right?" I said.

While Meena slept in the passenger seat, I questioned how long her commitment would endure. The books she had given me when we first started dating had increased relevance now. Hadn't the young woman in *A*

Suitable Boy married the suitor her parents chose for her? The *Ramayana*, the Hindu epic Meena had given me to read in Italy, was all about filial duty. Rama, the hero, suffered exile rather than disobey his father. "As long as our parents are alive," he said, "it is our duty to obey them. If I fail in this primary duty, I can gain no satisfaction or good name through any amount of wealth or power." In all those films we had watched, almost every Bollywood heroine had chosen duty when pulled between duty and love.

In India I had read the "matrimonial" advertisements, a section of the newspaper some twelve pages long. It was like a classified section for spouse shopping: "Hindu parents invite correspondence for their cultured, beautiful, slim medical student daughter, 25/5'2"; from a suitable, cultured MD/ professional boy with a similar background. Please send recent photo and bio-data." I hadn't seen any advertisements asking for an alliance with "Caucasian, 5'9", Catholic, military officer, prospects unclear."

Eventually, we reached Fort Benning, and I moved into the barracks that housed all the new officers. I drove Meena around Airborne School and out to the Ranger School compound at Camp Rogers. Stepping out of the car for a photo, I immediately began sweating. Four months of Benning's heat was going to be unbearable. We stopped at Ranger Joe's, and Meena watched with shock as I shed my floppy mop of long hair for an infantry high-and-tight (also known, with good reason, as a high-and-stupid). With a newly air-conditioned scalp, I tried on the camouflage uniform that the seamstress had upgraded with first lieutenant rank. Meena looked at me as if I were from Mars.

As we drove toward the airport, I wanted to know what would become of our relationship. I was as determined to keep her as I had been to get her to accept a date in the first place. Surrender, after all, is not a Ranger word. What I lacked in hairstyle, I would make up for in persistence. Meena was worth every effort. Before she boarded the plane for Philadelphia, I waved an airline itinerary at her.

"See you in three weeks," I said. Later I began crossing off the dates on my desk blotter like a Plebe counting the days until Christmas.

THE INFANTRY OFFICER BASIC COURSE was the one Bill Parsons and my other classmates had attended while I had been in Ranger School. Sixteen weeks long, it was a time-consuming box to check before reporting to Fort Drum to take command of a rifle platoon. The basic course couldn't have been more different from Oxford. The aimless days wandering through cafés and bookstores were a distant memory within a week. Oxford had been like a chairlift station, where the chair came off the high-speed gear and moved at a glacial pace so that the skiers could board. At Benning my life was back in high gear, moving uphill. A busy week at Oxford might include two classes, usually optional. Here the word "optional" didn't exist. My self-sovereignty was replaced with the dictates of a training schedule that began at 5:30 a.m. and finished at 7:00 p.m. Three months before at a Rhodes dinner, I had eaten next to English lords. Now I was a lowly lieutenant again, eating spoonfuls of MRE #7. My first night I spent two hours with a black magic marker conforming my backpack to Benning's all-black standard. Although I wore lieutenant rank, it was as if I were back at Camp Buckner.

Two years in England had made me soft. When we took the first PT test, at 4:15 a.m., I flopped. I hoped I wasn't going to prove the old joke that a Rhodes scholar was someone with a great future behind him. It took two months before I could match my old scores and hang with the front-runners in the company. Marksmanship was even worse. I hit barely half of the targets when I made my first return to the range. "Too much reading at 'Oggs-ford,' Mullaney?" taunted the course commander. If there was one thing I had to do well, it was shoot. No infantry commander worth his salt could command a platoon's respect without an expert marksman rating. With the help of classmates who had spent more time hunting than studying, I eventually scored high enough to earn the grudging respect of the commander.

Adjusting to the infantry mentality from Oxford was a harder target. The thick field manual we studied minced no words. The primary role of the infantry was close combat, "characterized by extreme violence and physiological shock." It would be "callous and unforgiving." And unlike anything at Oxford, "its consequences are final." Reading this on page one of the manual, my new "Bible," made me wonder how much Oxford had prepared me for anything involving violence or shock. I had to revert to a vocabulary I had intentionally suppressed at Oxford. Deadlines were "suspenses," classes were "blocks of instruction," and "accountability" replaced attendance. There was a long list of acronyms to memorize, ones I hadn't used since Ranger School. It was a language designed for efficient commands over a radio, but there was another, more serious reason for stripping sentences. The real purpose was to reduce the sensations of panic and fear, to transform confusion into procedural formulas. Reporting "three Friendly KIAs" was meant to be less visceral than detailing that Jones, Smith, and Reed were dead and beyond help. Casualties were triaged at the CCP, a "Casualty Collection Point," a designation suggesting a tidy hospital ward. In training, when I radioed for a helicopter to pick up the dead or wounded, I followed a laminated "9-Line Medevac" card in my pocket, supposedly making it harder to forget a logistics detail and easier to work past the horror of a soldier hemorrhaging blood by the pint. I wondered whether this would work in practice. Since none of our instructors had combat experience, there was no one to ask.

Meena described how doctors followed a similar logic in the hospital. When a patient nose-dived toward death, the preferred term was "decompensating," not dying. In the operating room, every surface of the body was covered except the "field" where the surgeon operated. High-risk surgeries went awry all the time, but the best surgeons barely raised their voices or paused when their efforts failed. Where people confront chaos and death as situation normal, the ability to constrain panic by procedure and sanitized language was critical to survival and success. For the military it was just more pronounced. Unlike surgeons, our own lives were at risk while we operated.

During our nightly phone calls, I must have learned as much from Meena's descriptions of medicine as she did about plastic explosives.

"How was your day?" I asked Meena one night.

"It was awesome! I removed a bullet from a guy's neck."

"Wow."

"What did you learn today?"

"We had two classes. The first was on how to conduct a drug test. They showed us what a fake penis looked like."

"Do people really use those?"

"If they know their urine's going to be hot, they might."

"What else?"

"We had a lecture, 'A Short History of the American Rifle: 1600 to Present.' It was engrossing."

Then there was the day that began with presentations from two Afghanistan veterans. They had fought in Operation Anaconda, the large mountain battle against al-Qaeda in 2002, and recounted the fight for our class. It was the only moment in the course where reality intruded on Fort Benning's isolation. A gaggle of students remained after class to ask the questions we were dying to know. What was it like? Were you ready? How would you have prepared differently? We could have asked questions all day but for the fact that our next class shared the same auditorium. The two veteran officers (a precious and rare commodity in the Army of 2002) were replaced by a pudgy Army historian who spent the remainder of the afternoon instructing us on the close order drill practiced by units in the Civil War. He brought us outside to practice the formations and commands, as if we would fix bayonets and charge al-Qaeda like Joshua Chamberlain at Gettysburg.

Although a year had passed since combat operations began in Afghanistan and less than six months remained before American forces invaded Iraq, nothing in the course specifically addressed those challenges. Benning was a training center caught between the Cold War and the new Global War on Terror. Instructors and students alike wanted to prepare for the latter, but resources and doctrine remained rooted firmly in the former. The oversized parade fields were as antiquated for the fight we faced as horse cavalry was at the start of World War II. The entire experience was a time-consuming diversion from the platoon I was anxious to lead at Fort Drum.

Before I knew it, my class was graduating. Some students had already been pulled from their Ranger School slots and sent immediately to units deploying to Kuwait. The rest girded themselves for a winter debut at Ranger School, one of the least pleasant ways to spend January. Despite my rusty start, I had been named the platoon honor graduate, an unexpected confidence boost before reporting to the 10th Mountain Division. I hopped in my car and drove as fast as I could north from Fort Benning. After Airborne School, Ranger School, and the basic course, I was eager never to return.

I KNEW FORT DRUM would be cold, but this was ridiculous. A few weeks after graduating from the basic course, I drove north from Philadelphia on I-81 past Wilkes-Barre, Binghamton, and Syracuse, and finally through a whirling blizzard before arriving at the home of the 10th Mountain Division. Four steps outside were all it took before I began shivering, despite wearing long underwear, a wool sweater, and a ski jacket. My lips instantly chapped in the frigid air, and five minutes of exposing an ungloved hand was enough to open up bleeding cracks on my knuckles. Driving was treacherous; snowdrifts fifteen feet high had turned the roads on post into icy tunnels.

When the weatherman reported a high of 20 degrees Fahrenheit, I didn't realize that he meant *negative* 20. That day, Watertown, New York, an old mill town thirty miles south of the Canadian border and just east of Lake Ontario, was the coldest place in the continental United States. Only later would I realize that −20 degrees was relatively balmy. Temperatures that winter routinely dropped below −40 degrees with the wind chill. It quickly became apparent why the 10th Mountain Division led the fighting in Afghanistan. Compared to Fort Drum, Afghanistan's climate was temperate.

Driving around Fort Drum was a lesson in the 10th Mountain Division's storied history, with each road bearing the name of a different battle fought or hero remembered. The division's story began with the successful assault by Norwegians equipped with cross-country skis against a much larger German force. The head of the National Ski Patrol proposed to General George Marshall that the United States create its own ski-borne mountain division for the anticipated fight in the Alps. Marshall agreed, and the 10th Mountain Division coalesced at Camp Hale, Colorado, around a nucleus of New England skiers.

The 10th Mountain saw its first combat in Italy in 1945 against Hitler's defensive Gothic Line south of the Po River valley. In a daring night assault, two battalions climbed fifteen hundred vertical feet and dislodged a much-surprised German force at the Battle of Riva Ridge. Shortly thereafter, they managed to capture Mount Belvedere with a bayonet attack. The division fought several other important battles in Italy, but it was the assaults on Riva Ridge and Belvedere that defined the 10th Mountain's character. If a mission demanded a mobile force ready to assault impossible odds in the toughest terrain, the 10th Mountain Division stood ready.

I made a careful study of the division's recent history before reporting to the 1st Battalion, 87th Infantry Regiment. The battalion had been busy. One company had been in the rescue force at Mogadishu in 1993. Another had occupied Port-au-Prince airport during 1994's Operation Uphold Democracy in Haiti. Then there was Bosnia, Kosovo, and, most recently, Afghanistan. Just about every soldier at battalion headquarters who passed by me wore a combat patch on his right shoulder. Nearly three-quarters of the soldiers remaining in the battalion had fought in Operation Anaconda, the marquee battle of the Afghanistan campaign. The trophy case was filled to capacity with ski poles, captured weapons, black-and-white photographs, and maps of the mountainous terrain. Its Latin motto, *Vires Montesque Vincimus*, was apt. We conquer men and mountains.

The battalion adjutant announced my arrival to the battalion commander. I stood patiently outside the office of Lieutenant Colonel Paul LaCamera, a name I knew well from the reports I had read about Anaconda. He was a West Point graduate, a Ranger Regiment alumnus, and the recipient of a Silver Star, the military's third highest award for heroism.

When he called me in, I stepped up to his desk and snapped the sharpest salute I had given anyone since Plebe year. Behind him were framed guidon flags, engraved bayonets, and a dozen other mementos from a career commanding warriors. LaCamera had the look of a grizzled football coach: prematurely gray, rugged, and gruff. He ordered me to sit down, asked a few questions about my background, and then dove into what I imagined was a stock speech delivered to every new lieutenant showing up to command one of his platoons. LaCamera spoke in cryptic one-liners like Yoda in camouflage.

"Skill and will," he told me, "win battles." I wrote it down dutifully in my green notebook.

"Any knucklehead with sufficient practice can shoot a rifle straight," he said. "Will, on the other hand, is different. Will takes character."

"In our profession," he continued, "mustering will in bad conditions is every bit as important as knowing how to kill."

Unlike some of the senior officers I had interacted with at Benning, LaCamera congratulated me on graduating near the top of my class at West Point and earning a scholarship to Oxford. He saw no contradiction between intellectual ability and the iron will that he suggested was necessary for warriors.

"Officers are paid to *think*," he emphasized. "Your educational pedigree matters only to the degree that it helps you train your men and make better decisions under fire. Stupid platoon leaders," he added with a preemptive scowl, "get my soldiers killed."

As if to underline the importance of his advice, he told me that he expected the battalion to deploy in less than six months, back to Afghanistan, or perhaps, if the diplomats failed, to Iraq. I saluted and moved out smartly.

The most important person I met that first day was my platoon sergeant. Platoon sergeants run the Army. As the senior enlisted man in a platoon, a platoon sergeant is technically subordinate to the platoon leader, always a junior lieutenant like me. The literal translation of *lieutenant*, a French word, gives a sense of the position I found myself in—"place holder." I had half a day of experience in the real Army. My platoon sergeant had eleven years. Without a doubt, platoon sergeants make or break platoon leaders. A good one—experienced, competent, and patient—can teach a lieutenant everything he needs to know to train and deploy a platoon to fight in combat. A bad platoon sergeant, on the other hand, can wreck a lieutenant, land him on the commander's carpet at the position of attention, and impress bad habits resistant to change. For months I had said the same prayer every night before sleeping: "Please, God, give me a good platoon sergeant."

I lucked out. My platoon sergeant was one of the most talented noncommissioned officers in the company, perhaps even the battalion. I had expected a cold reception from a sergeant ten years older than me, who had already become a sergeant by the time I graduated high school. I had imagined being eaten for lunch. Fortunately, he wasn't that type of platoon sergeant. It wasn't that he cared two bits about me. His only concern was his men. He had brought them through combat in Afghanistan without any casualties. He wasn't about to let some rookie lieutenant hurt his men on the next deployment. To him, my success meant the platoon's success.

There were a thousand things about being a platoon leader that no one had taught me at West Point. My platoon sergeant helped make up much of the difference. Planning any training at Fort Drum involved a maze of agencies like something out of a Kafka novel. He taught me how to grease the wheels like a pro, repeatedly urging me to "find the guy who will say yes." Whether it was making small talk about bass fishing with the sergeant at Range Control or promising marksmanship time to the cooks in order to secure more field rations, my platoon sergeant had the golden touch. With his help the training plans I submitted to the company commander survived intense scrutiny, earning the all-important mark of approval: "squared away."

The platoon sergeant's acceptance was easier than the rest of the platoon's. The testing began the first morning after I arrived at Drum, before

I had assumed official command of the platoon from my predecessor, a feisty Italian. I was lifting weights with him and the other lieutenants from the company, and he asked me if I wanted to observe one of the squads doing PT. I followed him to a corridor outside the gym's racquetball courts. Inside one was a squad cheering two soldiers boxing each other.

No sooner was I in the room than a soldier asked if I wanted to box. I took his invitation as a sign of goodwill (my first mistake) and agreed to fight (my second mistake).

"Sergeant, you want the new lieutenant?"

A cross between Rocky Balboa and a linebacker walked out to the center of the court and held his hands out for gloves. What was I thinking? I asked myself as another soldier taped gloves around my wrists.

"Helmet, sir?" another soldier asked.

"Of course not," I replied, hoping my bravado would intimidate my much larger opponent. I was also hoping my boxing skills were less rusty than my rifle aim.

We pounded gloves and began the fight. Given my uninspiring record, I would have been happy to survive two rounds of pounding without getting knocked out. My future soldiers clearly had a favorite, and it wasn't me. To their raucous applause, the sergeant planted his third punch underneath my chin and lifted me a foot off the ground. I landed on my ass. Above me stood two opponents. A voice spoke to me, but it sounded like someone shouting underwater in a pool. "Two-three-four." I stood up on "five" to face my opponent, who by now had resumed a single silhouette. I threw a few weak jabs that he easily dodged before planting a cross square on my mouth. Down I went again, this time for a full ten count. I came to as three soldiers lifted me to my feet and took me to find an ice pack for my swollen lips.

"That was the platoon boxing champion," said the lieutenant.

"Oh," I mumbled.

"It could have been worse."

"Uh-huh." I had been told sergeants taught lieutenants the ropes, but I hadn't expected such a literal demonstration. Being knocked out wasn't exactly the way I had imagined introducing myself to the platoon. The ringing in my head was the starkest indication of how far I had traveled from Oxford's delicate refinements. As Charlie Hooker, the Green Beret banker, had warned me, returning to Sparta from Athens was much tougher than the other way around.

"Look at the bright side," one soldier smiled. "You lasted longer than most."

I hoped I had at least fallen gracefully.

17

Murphy's Law

Infantry platoons and squads rely on two truths:

1. In combat, infantrymen who are moving are attacking.
2. Infantrymen who are not attacking are preparing to attack.

INFANTRY FIELD MANUAL (FM 3-21.8)

I PLUNGED THROUGH SNOW UP TO MY CHEST, TRY-ing to follow a straight magnetic heading through a blizzard to my first land navigation coordinate. I could barely see twenty yards ahead through the swirl of snow. Training at Drum was not going to be easy, but getting lost in a blizzard was nothing compared to the confusion of leading a new platoon.

The supply depot issued me the same gear worn by scientists in Antarctica. I filled two duffel bags with "extreme cold weather" gear. Included in my new kit were giant lobster claw gloves and similarly oversized rubber boots guaranteed to keep my toes functional at −40 degrees. They gave me several sets of quarter-inch-thick long underwear and a balaclava, a warm hood that I mistook for a Greek dessert when I read it off my gear list.

When my platoon sergeant advised me to dress warmly for PT, I threw on a sweatshirt under my jogging suit and added a wool beanie for my scalp. A few minutes outside made it clear that I should have worn the Greek dessert. At 6 a.m. we stepped off along with fifteen thousand other 10th Mountain soldiers starting their day in the most painful way possible. The pace I had planned was far too fast for the ice covering the roads, and my lungs soon ached from the superchilled air. It was like inhaling dry ice. Somewhere around mile three of the five-mile run, I realized that the thermometer at Drum was as far below 32 degrees as August temperatures in Fort Benning were above the freezing mark. When we returned to the office, my platoon sergeant couldn't stop laughing. I immediately plunged my hands into my crotch to warm them up; my beanie was covered in a crust of salt crystals, and snot descended from my nose in fragile icicles. He unzipped his jogging suit and revealed two layers of long underwear beneath his sweatshirt.

"Toasty, huh?" he smiled. "Next time, follow my lead."

My platoon sergeant taught me how to exercise my ears again, listening to a career's worth of hard-won wisdom. His eleven years at Fort Drum made him something of an anomaly—like a Nepalese Sherpa volunteering to climb Mount Everest repeatedly. His tenure coincided with the 10th Mountain's busiest decade and included tours in Somalia, Haiti, Bosnia, and, most recently, Uzbekistan and Afghanistan. As he joked, there weren't many more blank pages left in his passport.

The rest of "Spearhead" Platoon was a motley crew. The thirty-seven soldiers I inherited ranged in age from eighteen to thirty-four and hailed from every corner of the United States. I was most surprised at the number of soldiers with families of their own. Nearly half were married, and many were engaged. There were as many toddlers in the extended Spearhead family as there were soldiers in the platoon. As we deployed later that year, those families would weigh heavily on my shoulders. General Colin Powell had told my class at West Point to safeguard the lives of America's "sons and daughters." He had understated the responsibility demanded of twenty-three-year-old lieutenants; we also needed to protect America's fathers and mothers, husbands and wives. Before we left, I wrote letters to spouses and parents promising to do everything I could to bring home their soldiers.

The soldiers in the platoon were a cross section of America that most of my ivory tower peers would never have the privilege of meeting, let alone joining under arms. Their blue-collar pedigrees matched my father's, and I felt immediately comfortable around them. And although I didn't make a point of telling them that I had watched both of my parents join union picket lines, I did let on that I loved stock car races and grew up listening to country bands like Alabama and the Oak Ridge Boys. Recalling what my father taught me, I didn't want my soldiers to assume from my diplomas that I thought I was any better than them. I wasn't.

At least six of my soldiers had joined the Army in the first weeks after 9/11, but most had joined for reasons ranging from college money to steady employment. They included a zero-handicap golfer, a graffiti artist from El Paso, and a pimpled rapper from Queens, New York. Kids from Kentucky, Tennessee, and Arkansas debated the merits of NASCAR drivers, bourbon brands, and *Playboy* playmates. They smoked by the carton, dipped tobacco when the cigarettes ran out, and greased their arteries with an endless supply of junk food. Their language was as profane as their diet was myopic. Much like the George Carlin routine, they employed "fuck" with surprising dexterity: "this fucking sucks" or "the fucking Army," and often, just before morning formation, "Fuck . . ." The most articulate could string six or seven "fucks" in one sentence and still be understood.

Such a cast came with the sorts of problems that consumed 90 percent of my attention in "garrison," the time when we weren't training or deployed overseas. Many of the problems were of the financial variety that one would expect from eighteen-to-twenty-one-year-olds. Every month I would receive notices for unwieldy credit card balances, delinquent child support payments, and bounced checks. Every bank was happy to lend money to soldiers—at high interest rates, of course—and they could count on Army units to do the collecting for them. I sat down with several soldiers to work out basic financial plans to dig them out of debt or to teach them how to balance a checkbook. Living on my own for two years in England had given me some experience managing limited finances. Other issues were less easy to map solutions to: the occasional soldier who tested positive for drugs in his urine, one who went AWOL for two months, two suffering recurring nightmares from their first deployment to Afghanistan, and another who needed legal advice in order to divorce the stripper he had married on an impulse.

On top of monitoring their body fat, allergies, and run times, it was enough to make me long for the simplicity of leading a Ranger School platoon. Leading a real platoon was far more complex than I had imagined, and it involved much more than the tactics, endurance, and analysis I had learned at West Point. It demanded the tact of a marriage counselor, the ear of a priest, and the skills of a social worker—and all this before anyone fired a shot in combat.

UNCERTAIN WHETHER WE WOULD deploy to Iraq or Afghanistan, we trained for both. We began with basic rifle marksmanship. (LaCamera: "Soldier, you are either a marksman or a target.") In temperatures well below zero, we dug in the snow and shot tens of thousands of rounds at targets. LaCamera was also insistent that we make the training as realistic as possible: "Men, Afghanistan is not a rifle range." We practiced shooting moving targets and then began moving ourselves, firing at silhouettes from our knees, feet, and even squatting cross-legged. The subzero temperatures brought us closer together, quite literally, in order to stay warm as we huddled at the range. Fortunately, no one became a "cold casualty," Army code for hypothermia, and I never had to test the approved response of zipping two naked soldiers into a sleeping bag together.

I got a new boss in March. Captain Ryan Worthan took over command of the company and immediately made his presence felt. Worthan was shaped like a Humvee and was nearly as indestructible. He had a bald head as large as a bowling ball. At West Point a few years ahead of me, he had captained the rugby team, a collection of crazed athletes whose tenacity, grit, and hard-drinking reputation stood out even at a school that claimed no shortage of would-be Vikings. Like LaCamera, Worthan had also served in the Ranger Regiment.

Within days of assuming command, Worthan took us to the field to practice maneuvers with live rounds. It was part of his planned "stress inoculation"—building up our tolerance for the effects of altitude, noise, and dark so that we would be ready for combat. As I rotated my squads through the lane he had designed to test a basic maneuver, Worthan followed along with a notebook. As soon as a squad looked as if they had mastered the drill, Worthan would pronounce a squad leader or team leader wounded or dead. Predictably, the attacks quickly foundered. In the postmortems that followed every exercise, Worthan pointed out to us that everyone needed to be able to do their boss's job, and I needed to train my subordinates to do mine.

"You have to assume you will be killed," noted Worthan without skipping a beat, "or be ready to take over the company when I am. Make yourself dispensable."

As if he had cued a soldier to prove his point, both of us were nearly killed later that night during a warm-up run with blank ammunition. We were standing on the objective watching one of my fire teams arc around a bunker. All of a sudden, a light much brighter than a standard muzzle flash lit up his face, and a dull explosion erupted nearby.

"Cease fire! Cease fire!" yelled Worthan.

We began investigating what had happened. It turned out that one of my machine gunners had blown the small blank firing adapter off his gun. The only plausible explanation was that the ammunition was mixed up. He was firing live rounds. If he had managed another burst of fire in our direction, there would have been two practical examples to support a dead commander's last lecture.

After Worthan's temper cooled (about three days later), he offered some "advice."

"One of the hardest things I had to learn as a lieutenant," he told me, "was knowing the difference between things I'd never perfect, and things I had to. I'd never get my platoon to perfect even the simplest battle drill. No matter what," he said, "some real-world condition would interfere with the X's and O's I chalked up on the board.

"On the other hand," he said, "there is zero margin of error with live rounds."

"Yes, sir," I said in apology.

"Do you know Murphy's Law?" he asked.

"Yes, sir."

"Well, there's a Murphy's Law for combat, too. Rule number eleven: Friendly fire isn't."

I laughed, but not too much.

"I don't have many rules of my own." He counted them on his hand. "Never lie. Never eat before your men. Never leave a man behind. Understood?"

"Yes, sir." I saluted and returned to my men.

WHILE WE MARCHED IN the snow, another group of soldiers marched across the Iraqi border. Our deployment schedule immediately accelerated. Although the date swung like a pendulum between October and May, it eventually settled on a mid-July deployment. We would relieve the 82nd Airborne in eastern Afghanistan and remain there for a six-month tour. As the 3rd Infantry Division made its famous "Thunder Run" to Baghdad in morning installments on the mess hall televisions, there was a subtle change in seriousness among my fellow officers and the men we led. Life accelerated as we compressed our training schedules and squeezed more hours into already busy weeks.

Our platoon spent more and more days shooting at the range. Over time, I became increasingly assertive as a platoon leader and added my own twists to the standard training events. With a nod to Gunnery Sergeant Oakes's training in Ranger School, I had my men practice changing ammunition magazines with their eyes closed. If they couldn't do it blindfolded, then they weren't ready to do it under pressure in a firefight. I ramped up the physical training routine, adding endurance marches, trail runs, and uphill sprints.

Everywhere we ran, we carried a portable stretcher for casualty drills. One morning I tagged along with Sergeant Reggie Huber's squad. Huber was a grizzly bear. He towered over the platoon at six feet two and a hefty 230 pounds. When his temper flared, soldiers scattered as far as they could from his curdling rage. But when Huber talked about his three kids, his face brightened, and he seemed as cuddly as a teddy bear. Huber was also one of my smartest soldiers and frequently reminded the platoon of that fact. Huber once told me that he planned to return to St. Louis and become mayor. After a few months with him, I had no doubt he would.

I pointed at Huber, "You've been shot in the gut." Curses echoed from his squad as I made them tug Huber up a 45-degree slope. They huffed and puffed for ten minutes, two steps forward and one step back, lugging Huber as he moaned in artificial agony. His men knew not to complain; Huber and the other Anaconda vets had been reminding the privates for months that everything would be twice as hard with bullets snapping around them.

Before LaCamera relinquished command to his replacement, he made a concerted effort to train the officers and sergeants in the finer points of "violence management." He began with a series of weekly conferences to analyze and learn from relevant historical battles. One afternoon, a lieutenant presented the 1993 battle in Mogadishu, made famous by Mark Bowden's book *Black Hawk Down*. As that discussion proceeded, Sergeant Major Sean Watson, the battalion command sergeant major (the senior enlisted man in the battalion), became increasingly agitated. When the unlucky lieutenant briefing us botched his description of one of the Rangers' landing teams, Sergeant Major Watson interrupted.

"Excuse me, Lieutenant. Let me take it from there."

It turned out that Sergeant Major Watson had been there, in Somalia. He was the senior sergeant on one of the four helicopters that had surrounded the Olympic Hotel in Mogadishu. Watson's hard-won wisdom would be invaluable once we got on the ground in Afghanistan. On an ambush, for example, he told us it was best to shoot for the enemy's knees.

"Why?" asked another lieutenant.

"Because your enemy's more likely to crouch in the kill zone than jump."

LaCamera then moved from the past to the present—the assortment of modern technologies that would be at our disposal in Afghanistan. In the back of the auditorium he used for these briefings, someone had painted a quote from a Cormac McCarthy novel: "Before man was, war waited for him. The ultimate trade awaiting its ultimate practitioner." LaCamera stood in front of the quote and introduced the Air Force liaisons we had to work with on the ground in Afghanistan.

"You are the musicians of Mars," LaCamera said. Heads nodded as lieutenants figured out the mythological reference to the Greek god of war. Like a conductor managing an orchestra of woodwinds and brass, he expected us to know when and how to use a payload of Air Force bombs, a volley of artillery rounds, and an Apache helicopter's chain gun. Each had its advantages and disadvantages. I had to know which type of munition to use for each target and how to synchronize multiple weapons in order to win. I had to know that a mortar's high trajectory made it a better weapon than a howitzer for firing over a high ridge and how to balance that advantage against its comparatively smaller burst radius. Combat for all infantrymen is a test of will, endurance, and courage. For a leader, combat is also cognitive—the challenge of managing extraordinary complexity under extraordinary pressure.

"Every profession has its tools," said LaCamera. "Ours are just more expensive and deadly."

Worthan quizzed us on these finer points of tactics at every morning meeting. The facts we memorized were dry but critically important, covering everything from the maximum ranges of different weapons to the minimum safe distance you could safely stand without absorbing shrapnel. He had us read and report back on military histories compiled by Russian soldiers writing about their fights with Afghan mujahideen, the generic name for the many bands of rebels fighting the Russians, often with American-supplied weapons. Whenever possible, they "hugged" the Soviets by attacking from distances so close that it negated the Russians' overwhelming air superiority. We could assume they would know our bombs' specifications as well. Afghan fighters were masters of their terrain and used the mountain folds to hide their ambushes and retreats. They particularly enjoyed blitzing Soviets when their tanks drove through narrow gorges so steep that the tankers were unable to elevate their barrels. The mujahideen had also displayed impressive creativity, such as mounting decoys on ridges to draw errant fire and planting secondary ambushes to attack reinforcements. More than anything else, the Afghans capitalized on consistent patterns that made the Soviets predictable.

"Habits kill," warned Worthan.

I called an old professor of mine from West Point to try to get some language materials for Afghanistan. The best he could do was a dozen Visual Language Translators. The name sounded fancier than the product, a laminated card with cartoon figures and phonetically spelled phrases. The idea was that a soldier could point at a cartoon and his interlocutor would understand from the picture to "get down on the ground." There were two problems. Problem one was that the cards were designed for Iraq, not Afghanistan, and the phrases were in classical Arabic, not Pashto. Problem two was that the cards were great for identifying Iraqi missile launchers but not so great for finding out who the tribal chief was and where his allegiances lay. Try miming that to an angry Afghan.

The last days before we left involved more pencil sharpening than chest bumping. We packed boxes and crates and loaded them on freight cars destined for a port in New Jersey. There were rosters of wives' phone numbers to compile, computers to back up, and last-minute supplies to distribute. I took a dozen vaccine injections in my arm and signed several legal documents. It didn't occur to me that it was unusual for a twenty-four-year-old to have a notarized will and a life insurance policy. I checked the box for maximum coverage.

18

Mission Accomplished

When I see your face, the stones start spinning!
You appear; all studying wanders.
I lose my place. . . .
In your presence I don't want what I thought I wanted.

JELALUDDIN RUMI

DEPLOYING CONDENSED MORE THAN TRAINING SCHE-
dules. It also compressed our personal lives. Between Benning and Drum,
early that winter, I had taken a couple of weeks of vacation with Meena.
In two weeks we attempted to make up for six months of infrequent weekend visits. Returning to Oxford, we had dinner with Katie Larson and her
husband at Lincoln. After two years of distance, they had finally made it
work. Seeing them together made tangible what Meena and I hoped to
achieve with, as Katie had told me in her note, a potion two parts tenacity,
one part hope, and three parts courage.

From England we flew to Rome with Marine First Lieutenant Tim
Strabbing, his girlfriend Jada, and my sister Bridget. Father Matt gave us
all another tour of the Vatican.

"It's nice to meet you, Meena," he greeted her. "Craig's told me a lot
about you."

Meena laughed nervously, as she usually did when being introduced.
"It's nice to meet you, too."

The three of us sat down for afternoon espressos near the Via Veneto.
Meena and Father Matt engaged in a spirited conversation on the common
threads of divinity, morality, and mutual respect underlying world religions.

Grace, Father Matt said, worked in mysterious ways. I had my own question, though.

"Father Matt, how would a Catholic-Hindu marriage work?"

Meena's glare told me I had overreached.

"Maybe you two should talk about that first?"

WE TALKED IN CIRCLES. Meena wanted to get married, but she was in no rush. She was entrenched in her own medical training. Yet despite our harried schedules, we continued to make time for each other, driving 334 miles each way to preserve and nurture our relationship. Between five and eight hours after leaving, depending on how bad the snow was, I arrived in Philadelphia. All week I looked forward to those visits with Meena. Together we explored the city, stopped in Little Italy to buy cheese at Di Bruno's, spent an afternoon in the Philadelphia museum, and ate sushi near Rittenhouse Square. It was a world away from the Army life I lived from 0600 on Monday until 1700 on Friday. Phone calls no longer sufficed. I wanted more than the sound of her voice. I ached to be *with* Meena, to bury my head in her hair, to smell the chilies frying when she cooked, to see that crooked smile break across her lips.

Every other week I had to submit a request to drive outside the hundred-mile radius surrounding Fort Drum. Under "Reason for Request" I would write "Girlfriend." At work it was uncomfortable referring to Meena as my girlfriend when my commitment to her was of a different order of magnitude. The upcoming deployment was pressing the issue. It came up during a visit to close friends in New Haven.

I had first met Bryan Leach at Oxford where we both studied history. A champion debater in high school and a distinguished actor at Harvard, he had since enrolled at Yale Law School. At Oxford our friendship developed through weekly poker games. With a couple of scotches under his belt, Bryan's profanity quotient tripled, although his bets were always well placed. After twenty weeks of poker against a statistician, an economist, and a physicist, Bryan was the big money winner. He was also training his advocacy skills. I needed his help convincing Meena to bet her chips on me.

As a first-year law student, Bryan developed some experience in arbitration. Sitting Meena and me down at his kitchen table, he broke out a yellow legal pad (a familiar prop for us) and walked us through a mediated negotiation. Each of us took turns making our case while Bryan squiggled notes. When we finished our arguments, Bryan summarized:

"Party A claims that an engagement would secure the necessary leverage for him to request an assignment after Fort Drum someplace closer to Party B. Practically speaking, Party A envisions this engagement happening before a deployment this spring or summer. Is that right?"

"Yes," I replied.

"Party B contends that such a contractual agreement, antecedent to a dangerous deployment, would leave Party B exposed to the risk of said danger. Is this correct?"

"Yes," Meena replied, laughing at Bryan's tongue-in-cheek formalism.

"If my analysis is correct, engagement is an eventual certainty for both parties, although the timing is the source of dispute. Do you agree?"

We nodded.

"Party B, would you not also benefit, in terms of support, from elevating your status from *girlfriend* to *fiancée*?"

"You have a point," said Meena.

Bryan tapped the yellow legal pad with the pencil and reached his conclusion. He folded his hands, looked at us, and said, "My recommendation is that you get engaged sooner rather than later. Either way I'd urge you to discuss this with your parents."

"Party A concurs," I said.

"Let me think about it," said Meena.

A month later she agreed that we should talk to her parents. The next Saturday we drove together from Philadelphia to meet with them in New Jersey. Meena's father led us to the formal sitting room. Her parents sat on one couch. We sat opposite them. Two dozen trophies Meena and her younger sister had earned fifteen years ago were stacked on the adjacent piano.

I desperately wanted them to offer their daughter's hand. Instead, Meena's father offered tea.

WHEN I FIRST TOLD Charlie Hooker about Meena, six months after we had started dating, he made me sign a cocktail napkin promising I wouldn't get engaged until after I left Oxford. A year and a half later, I convinced him Meena was "the one." He took me to his private jeweler, an Indian man occupying a windowless office in Manhattan's diamond district. I specified exactly what I wanted the ring to look like—a band of Indian 22-karat gold with three pristine diamonds and four rubies. I shook the jeweler's hand to seal the agreement. The price was left unspoken.

I proposed to Meena a day after the ring arrived. As we walked along a Newport cliff, the sun was brilliant on the Sakonnet River. I stopped to take a photo and reached into my pocket for the ring. I turned to Meena and pointed at the crystal pendant I had given her at Oxford.

"I like your necklace. Do you have a man?"

Before she could respond, I kneeled and asked her to marry me.

The next day I dialed every number in my phone book. When I called Bryan, he insisted on taking credit for the "contractual agreement."

"Does that mean I need to pay your contingency fee?" I asked.

"This one's on me."

19

Line of Departure

A son should never be a judge of his father.

IVAN TURGENEV, *Fathers and Sons*

I CAN STILL REMEMBER MY SISTER'S VOICE ON THE telephone: stunned, wounded, and flat. It was her twenty-third birthday. Meena and I were about to drive the final leg of our trip from New Haven, where we had visited Bryan and his wife, to Rhode Island when Bridget's call interrupted dessert.

"Dad's not coming home for dinner."

"Working overtime again?" I asked.

"No. He's just not coming home."

"Huh? What do you mean he's not coming home? Is he okay?"

"I don't know . . ." Her confusion spilled out. She sobbed now in heaving waves. "He said he was moving in with a friend from work."

"That's it? That's all he said?"

"That's it."

"I'll be home as soon as I can." I handed Meena the keys and sat silently in the passenger seat as we sped home. Meena drove with one hand and held mine with the other.

Back in high school our wrestling coach used to have us form a wide circle at the end of practice. Bull in the Ring, he called it. The exercise was meant to quicken our reactions and to make us tougher. Everyone got a number. When it was my turn, I would step into the circle, the coach would call out a number at random, and I would turn as quickly as possible to defend myself. You got to stay in the ring as long as you could win the point. The hardest challenge was always the one you didn't see coming.

My parents had been married for twenty-eight years, and yet for reasons I couldn't begin to fathom, my father suddenly threw all of that away—a beautiful home, four kids, and a loving wife. I couldn't believe that the father who had always emphasized commitment was walking away from his. There must be some mistake.

Three days later it was Easter. My father returned home for the holiday, but he still didn't speak to me. We sat around the dining room table, and my mother brought in a platter of ham slices and then the twice-baked potatoes (her specialty), glazed carrots, and creamed corn. She sat at the foot of the table, opposite my father. Dinner was quiet, with just the scraping of knives and forks on the nice plates my mother took out three times a year. I had just sunk my fork into a piece of apple pie when my father stood up from the table and walked into the kitchen.

I heard him open the door to the basement. I folded my napkin neatly and placed it on the table.

"Excuse me, please." I pushed my chair in and left the table.

I opened the door and walked down to the basement. The old wooden stairs creaked under my weight as a hundred thoughts collided in my head. I thought I could say something to repair everything. What that something was, I had no idea. I had counseled soldiers on their broken marriages. How do you do that for your own father?

The basement was my father's territory—workbenches with vices, a drill press, shelves he had built and stacked with little pull-out bins for screws and nails. Saws hung from nails in the wall, arranged by type and length. Next to the door was a calendar of pinup models holding power tools. February was still up, two months too late. An old black radio lay on the counter with a film of dust on top. I think I was the one who had broken off the antenna years before. I had never bothered to ask my father how to use his tools, and he had never bothered to show me.

"Dad," I said, standing on the bottom step and blocking the stairs. "What's wrong?"

My father stood for a minute without saying a word. Under his eyes were heavy red bags. "Craig"—he paused as if he were revealing a profound truth—"people grow apart. Your mother and me . . ." He trailed off and looked down. When he turned his face back to mine, it was as if he had aged a hundred years. "This doesn't change anything, Craig. I still love you."

What had I expected to hear—that this was just a short break? That he needed time? That there was someone else? That he wanted my help? *People grow apart*—that's what you hear when a girlfriend has figured out that things won't work out. How do you stay together for twenty-eight years, raise a family, build a home—and then say you've grown apart? When, precisely, had that happened? Before or after he had visited me in England? Had he already made this decision while we drank coffee and read the paper together in Maine? Over Christmas while we opened presents? Was it a well-crafted plan to leave on Bridget's birthday? I wanted answers I could challenge. I wanted a knock-down, drag-out argument. I wanted to take his answers and refute each one. I wanted to pummel him until he surrendered. Then I wanted him to ask me for forgiveness.

My father drew close to give me a hug, but I turned my back to him. As he stepped up the stairs, I stayed with my back to him and leaned on the stair rail. As my father walked past me, his jeans brushed against mine, making the hair stand on the back of my neck. I stood in place, leaning on the stair rail. A minute later the front door closed. I remained on the bottom step and cried.

HE ASKED MY MOTHER for a divorce three weeks later, refusing to go with her to marital counseling. "Mullaneys don't quit"—that's what he had always said. What did he think he was doing now? When I was younger and got too cold shoveling snow, he would send me right back out. "You're not done," he would say. I was *never* done. That was what he had beaten into my head every year until I left for West Point. That is what had gone through my head when I thought about quitting after getting cut from the wrestling team, when I had run the last mile of the Boston Marathon to see him watch me from the stands, and when I had wanted to leave Ranger School after dislocating my shoulder.

Visiting my mother later that spring, I couldn't help but judge my father. Now *he* was done. My father hadn't been there after Meena accepted my proposal. He hadn't been there when Bridget graduated from Providence College, summa cum laude. He wouldn't be there for Gary's graduation from high school or to grill burgers for Gary's cadet friends when he went to West Point. He wouldn't be there for Kelsey in high school, nickel-and-diming every expense her older siblings took for granted: a calculator, a textbook, a prom dress. And, most important, he wouldn't be there for my mother. He had walked away, quit, surrendered.

As I sat drinking coffee with my mother, his SUV pulled up in the driveway. My father walked around behind the house and took something out of the pool house. He got back in the SUV and drove away. I was leaving for a combat tour any day, but my father didn't have the courage to come in the house and say good-bye to me. My mother reached across the table for my hand. I pulled my hand away and stood up. I walked to the living room and grabbed the wooden staff I had topped with a raccoon tail and carved for my father. I slammed it crosswise over my knee and cracked it in half.

That was the last time I saw my father.

I DID A POOR job of stepping into the role he left vacant, and I had almost no opportunity given my imminent deployment. I made one last trip home before I deployed to Afghanistan in order to wish my brother good luck as he began at West Point. The lawn was overgrown and the house was a mess. No one had trimmed the hedges. Gary approached me the morning he was about to leave for West Point.

"Craig, will you show me how to shave?" he asked. Gary had barely three whiskers on his chin, but after my stories, he was petrified of anything that might draw fire from the Beast cadre.

"Hold it like this," I said and helped Gary hold the razor at the correct angle to his face. We stood together in the tiny first-floor bathroom, barely enough room for the two of us to fit.

"Start at your sideburns."

Gary swiped down along his cheek and then rinsed the razor under the hot water.

"Good. Now the jawline. I always do the right side first," I said.

I leaned in closer for this critical step. His jaw, at eye level to me, had an extra thick crest of shaving cream, looking like a fake Santa beard. His large hand dwarfed the small razor.

"No, no, no," I interrupted, grabbing his wrist. "You want to go in the opposite direction, against the grain."

"Huh?"

"Like this." I flipped his wrist around and corrected his technique. "Go slow and keep your skin taut with your other hand."

"Ow." He nicked his chin. "Sorry."

"I nick myself all the time. Don't worry about it." I passed him the aftershave. "Slap this on."

"It stings."

"That's the point," I said. "It puts hair on your chest."

"Hey, that's what Dad says." Gary frowned.

"I know. Sorry."

"It's okay," said Gary as he rinsed the razor under the hot water. I reached over, shut off the faucet, and watched as the milky water swirled in the drain.

I turned and gave him a bear hug, thumping his back with my fist. "I love you, Gary."

II

Soldier

The nation that will insist on drawing a broad line of demarcation between the fighting man and the thinking man is liable to find its fighting done by fools and its thinking done by cowards.

SIR WILLIAM FRANCIS BUTLER

20

Master the Transitions

Small wars are conceived in uncertainty, are conducted often with precarious responsibility and doubtful authority, under indeterminate orders lacking specific instructions.

SMALL WARS MANUAL,
U.S. Marine Corps, 1940

DEPLOYING TO AFGHANISTAN WAS A SLOW IMMERSION, like Dante's descent into the Inferno. The journey began at Fort Drum's rapid deployment facility—an airport terminal with X-ray scanners, uncomfortable seats, and television sets tuned to Major League Baseball games. Apart from the boots and body armor, we could have been at the Syracuse airport.

The wait was interminable. Soldiers did what soldiers do when any delay passes the fifteen-minute mark: They fell asleep. Six-foot-tall Mitchell Markam curled into the fetal position with an unloaded pistol firmly in his grip. Markam's Connecticut upbringing clashed with the gangster persona he tried to project to the rest of the platoon. A digital photo of this pose set his cause back several months. After perhaps four hours, Markam awoke to the sound of a dozen soldiers carrying large insulated vats of food. Thoroughly embarrassed, he joked with a hint of gallows humor that this was our "Last Supper." Servers gave us each a rubbery T-bone, spicy Mexican rice, and three brownies. After dinner an Air Force sergeant ushered us into a holding area behind a big blue curtain decorated with the 10th Mountain Division crest and its motto, "Climb to Glory."

The platoon folded into seats before the projector screen. The much-awaited intelligence briefing began with a list of the dangers awaiting us in Afghanistan: camel spiders running faster than thirty miles an hour, cobras, ticks. I gave a half-comical, half-serious look at Markam and another soldier snickering in the back row about giving each other tick checks. Our next briefing curiously interposed the threat of dehydration with the perils of flash flooding.

We knew more about Afghanistan's flora and fauna than the tribes inhabiting the districts we patrolled. We could identify the Hindu Kush Mountains and the Helmand River on a map of Afghanistan, but knew little about the dry riverbeds surrounding our bases. We knew politics at a national level, but not at the local level where it mattered. We had Arabic phrase books that were useless in Pashto-speaking provinces. Success in Afghanistan wouldn't hinge on our ability to thwart camel spiders.

We walked out of the terminal and stretched in a long line across the shimmering hot tarmac toward an enormous cargo plane. Its cavernous fuselage slowly swallowed our small profiles. The departure for Afghanistan lacked the Hollywood drama I had expected. There was no flourish of trumpets and drums to send us off, no cheering crowds. Whatever nervousness I had had about the deployment dissipated during the countless delays, briefings, and speeches we were subjected to for weeks. Even the youngest privates approached the journey overseas as a novelty rather than a life-changing embarkation. If they were nervous, they hid it well, perhaps eager not to show their butterflies before the nonchalance of the veteran sergeants.

Two long columns of webbed seats stretched toward the cargo pallets loaded high against the rear ramp of the plane. Fort Drum's summer humidity baked us as we waited to taxi. I fought the impulse to undress, remembering from previous flights how cold an unheated cargo plane gets as it reaches altitude. Before long we were airborne to Frankfurt, Germany. Soldiers splayed out in the aisles and on the web seats, wearing earphones and earplugs to dull the roar of the jet engines. As the temperature dropped, soldiers unpacked poncho liners and wrapped themselves in the soft quilted camouflage. I drifted off to sleep, thinking of the last thing Meena had told me before we said good-bye: "Keep me in your heart and know that however great the distance, I am with you always."

TWO FLIGHTS AND SEVEN thousand miles later, we walked off the back ramp of the cargo plane and into Afghanistan. The heat nearly knocked us over, sucking the oxygen out of the air and leaving us breathless. It was like walking into a furnace. My boots felt as if they were melting into the black tarmac. The sky was a red canvas of dust obscuring the setting sun. As we deplaned, soldiers standing guard at posts scattered around the airfield scanned the horizon. Beyond them, barely visible through the choking haze, a ring of barren mountains stuck up out of the flat plain like shards of glass embedded in concrete.

As if on cue, a soldier materialized out of the dust and introduced himself. I asked him the temperature.

"One hundred twenty-eight in the shade, sir."

KANDAHAR AIRFIELD HAD A confused appearance. Built in the early 1960s by American contractors, the terminal's scalloped bays arced in a wide semicircle. Peeling paint and vacant gates made it resemble a disheveled version of Dulles Airport. Along the airfield bomb-blasted hangars bulged with American helicopters.

Beyond the hangars we followed a grid of dirt roads lacing together rows and columns of tents. Industrial air-conditioning units hummed as they pumped cold air through bright yellow ducts into the tents. Above, a spider's web of electrical wires powered video games and DVD players inside. Banks of dust hovered everywhere in an ochre fog. Porta-Johns hosted long lines of soldiers with rifles slung over their backs. The soldiers' desert uniforms made them nearly impossible to see. We stood out with our fresh uniforms, body armor, helmets, and rucksacks. The soldiers at Kandahar had disposed of those impediments months before.

After dropping our rucksacks at our designated tent and replacing our heavy Kevlar helmets with the floppy "boonie caps" everyone else was wearing, we headed toward the smell of hot food. We were soon lost among the tents, passing the same volleyball and basketball courts for a second and third time. Eventually, we reached a complex of large tents with a line extending fifty yards outside the door. Before we could enter the chow hall, we decontaminated our hands at portable hand-washing stations. The scene inside was more Ponderosa than Beetle Bailey. A civilian contractor checked ID cards and marked a sheet for each hungry mouth. Before us was a spread of unimaginable variety. Mountains of mashed potatoes surrounded slabs of pork and chicken bathed in barbecue sauce. Inside the refrigerator were ice-cold Cokes, Snapples, and Gatorades. We ate on real plates with real forks and knives. By the bulging bellies of some infantrymen in the room, it was clear that tonight's meal was no exception. Markam rushed up to me with a mile-wide smile and a super-sized cup of soft-serve ice cream.

"Sir, you can eat here four times a day!" He waited for a reaction. "They even have a midnight meal. Can you believe it?" Markam rushed off to tell the other men in the platoon.

I walked back by myself and collapsed facedown onto a dusty cot with my boots still on.

"WAKE UP, MULLANEY." I turned on my side and recognized Captain Worthan, my company commander, standing over me. I sat up and dug the dust out of my eyes.

"Yes, sir."

"We're going on the next bird to Gardez. Get your ruck and let's go."

"Roger, sir." I glanced at my watch. I had been asleep for only twenty minutes. "Sir . . ."

"Yeah?"

"The whole platoon?"

"No. Just you. Your guys will meet you there."

"Yes, sir." I fumbled in the dark and put my body armor on over my uniform. I hoisted my rucksack on my shoulders and grabbed my weapon. On the way to the airfield I exchanged my empty magazines with seven fully loaded ones. Real bullets weighed more than blanks. My blood began to pump faster. Here we go, I said to myself. The adventure begins.

In the dark I tried to match Worthan's long strides toward the airfield. A crew chief ushered us aboard one of two Vietnam-vintage Chinook transport helicopters creating a hurricane on the tarmac. The Chinook lurched off the ground in the pinkish hue of a dusty dawn, and we surged toward the ring of mountains I had observed earlier. Apache attack helicopters buzzed like mosquitoes protecting our flanks, scanning for threats as the parched desert floor slid beneath us.

Our flying flotilla sped just two hundred feet above the highest peaks, emerging on the far side at a dizzying height over broad valleys and steep gorges. The landscape was almost devoid of vegetation. In places, the ground cracked like old parchment. Between infertile plots stood the iso-square shapes of Afghan family compounds with high walls and guard rs. An occasional grain silo stood silent sentry between hulks of old ian tanks visible even from our altitude. Long lines of dots like giant ills extended from the mountains toward the valley floors. These were vertical ventilation shafts of a medieval system of underground irriga- tunnels. As we flew farther and farther from Kandahar, it seemed as if were rolling the clock back from the twenty-first century. The view from height probably hadn't changed much in six hundred years.

21

Dust

In a few years hence, when the present generation of turbulent intriguers shall have been swept away, the task will be comparatively easy. As it is, the progress we have made towards pacifying . . . is perfectly wonderful.

SIR WILLIAM MACNAGHTEN, *Kabul, 1841*

OUR CHINOOK SCREAMED ABOVE RIPPLES OF ROCK jutting out from scorched earth. The midday sun banished every shadow except our own silhouette, like a flying carpet beneath us. We were only minutes away from Gardez, but at the time I knew almost nothing about the place where I was about to spend the first months of my combat tour.

Gardez is the capital city of Paktia Province, an area roughly the size of Vermont. It sits astride two important and ancient trade routes. From north to south, Gardez connects Kabul with the city of Khost. From east to west, Gardez lies between the Tora Bora mountain complex on the Pakistan border and the ancient city of Ghazni. The dominant Pashtun tribe in Paktia had fought every conquering force from Alexander the Great's army to the motorized regiments of the Soviet Union. Eventually, all foreign forces had been routed in battle or quit in frustration.

Above the roar of the rotors, Captain Worthan yelled into my ear as he pointed out the Shahi-Kot Valley beneath us. I picked out the familiar shapes I had stared at on maps during that veterans' guest lecture at Fort Benning. The Whale. Roberts Ridge. The Finger. Against a thousand al-Qaeda and Taliban fighters dug into caves on these steep ridges and fearsome peaks, coalition forces had suffered more than eighty casualties.

Seeing the peaks and ridges with my own eyes, the battlefield looked even harsher than I had imagined back in Benning's air-conditioned auditorium.

As a cadet, my visits to Normandy and Bastogne had helped me decide to join the infantry. There had never been any risk of a German sniper picking me off while I wandered among old foxholes, debating tactical decisions with academic detachment. The battlefield below me now was no historical artifact. This war was still a work in progress, and these ridges still harbored enemies intent on killing my men and me. My gaze narrowed on the rifle barrel between my legs, and the helicopter banked into its final approach to Gardez.

"HOP IN OUR GHETTO sled," joked a blond lieutenant wearing shades. I shook the lieutenant's hand, and he tossed my rucksack into the backseat of a cannibalized Humvee. The ghetto sled had no hood over the dust-crusted engine block and was missing its doors. Most notably, there were no windows or roof. Markam later proposed that we send a picture to General Motors as a concept design for a Hummer convertible.

The "airfield" we had landed on was a straight stretch of Paktia Province's only asphalt road, blocked off on both ends by two Humvees in only slightly better condition than our improvised airfield shuttle. We kicked up a whirl of dust as we rumbled along the dirt road from the landing zone toward our new home. Along the perimeter of the base were Hesco barriers stacked like giant five-foot-tall Lego blocks. These dirt-filled mesh and wire cages were topped with triple-standard concertina barbed wire. A sandbagged guard post concealed a machine gun and a pair of soldiers.

Inside the perimeter loomed an impressive compound. Leased from a local farmer by American Special Forces at the beginning of the war, the firebase was a traditional Afghan home. Twenty-foot-high dirt walls connected medieval watchtowers at each corner of the rectangular compound. The entrance was a pair of steel gates eight feet high and painted with an assortment of Technicolor flowers. A smaller door was inset in the left gate, and soldiers passed in and out like petitioners entering a cathedral.

The curtain wall was several feet thick, insulating the perimeter rooms from dramatic temperature shifts and making the building nearly invulnerable to rockets and mortars. The inner courtyard held a small orchard of fruit trees surrounded by a path of crushed stones neatly corralled between painted rocks. (Someday an anthropologist will marvel at painted rock artifacts and wonder what totemic power they held for the military. It was the military custom: If it moves, shoot it. If it doesn't, paint it.) A long, open-air tent in the middle of the orchard hosted 82nd Airborne soldiers who were grunting as they pulled and pushed barbells and spun recycled gym exercise bikes. The Texas state flag fluttered above one of the watch-towers, and a songbird lilted from a hidden nest.

After dropping our bags in a tent, Worthan and I hurried to the mess hall for a series of introductory briefs. An officer turned on the projector and began with a rapid-fire overview of our mission. Since neither of us had known exactly where we would be located upon arrival in Afghanistan, this brief was the first we learned of our specific mission. We had two responsibilities. Our first priority was to protect the Gardez Provincial Re-construction Team. The team comprised a dozen or so Army reservists from Texas, one itinerant government aid worker, and a single State De-partment political officer. In theory, this small team managed the recon-struction contracts for the entire province. They needed my infantry platoon to guard the base and escort them on their routine inspections of school and clinic construction projects. Our second mission was to "show presence" in the city of Gardez. This meant patrolling the city a few times every day to intimidate the "bad guys." The next slide was a map of Gardez with checkpoints and routes superimposed in bright reds and greens. It looked straightforward, logical, and simple. Patrolling this area was not going to be so hard, I thought. Only later would I learn the first rule of Afghanistan: The closer you look, the less you understand.

Our intelligence briefing followed. The white board was a scribbled maze of dotted lines that looked like the board game Chutes and Ladders.

Stick figures represented local thugs, rival police chiefs, and mayors past and present. Happy faces indicated good guys, and frowns signaled bad guys. The new police chief went into the good guy column, but the old police chief was still around and apparently was a bad guy. Police aligned with both factions wore indistinguishable uniforms. Then there were the Afghan soldiers. On the one hand, the Afghan Militia Force was effective but couldn't be trusted. The Afghan National Army, on the other hand, was loyal but ineffective. The good news was that we would at least be able to recognize them by their American forest camouflage. That wasn't the case for the average thug.

"How do we know who's a bad guy?" I asked.

"They speak Arabic."

"How do we know whether they're speaking Arabic or Pashto?"

The briefer didn't have a response, and my confidence level shrank. Since every Afghan household had at least one gun, we couldn't assume that being armed meant someone was hostile. Nor could we expect locals to notify us of any danger. Passing along information of an ambush up the road would be a death sentence for the informant and his or her family.

Our enemies worked like the Mafia. They earned cash by running illegal roadblocks and extorting shop owners. They used that revenue to bribe police commanders, buy cheap weapons, and recruit young thugs. They taught them a few easy techniques, the most important being the hit-and-run ambush. They kept their organizations small and outsourced the riskiest missions. They'd pay farmers two hundred dollars for every rocket they pointed at the Americans from one of their fields. Stuck in a ten-year drought in a stagnant economy, it was hard to blame the farmers, though it would become easier after enduring rocket barrages.

Children had a record of giving good intelligence tips, but they had also been used by the Taliban to fire pen guns at passing soldiers on patrol. We suspected some kids were responsible for planting roadside bombs under bridges and on tree branches. These bombs, known euphemistically as Improvised Explosive Devices, or IEDs, were growing in complexity and destructiveness as insurgents in Iraq collaborated with their colleagues in

Afghanistan. Earlier that summer, I had received a letter from a classmate in Iraq. His report of children shooting at him and having to shoot back had made me shake my head when I read it. What would it be like to look at every kid as a possible threat? How would a child look through a gunsight?

TWO HOURS AFTER LANDING in Gardez and less than twenty-four hours after arriving in Afghanistan, I went on my first combat patrol. I sat in the backseat of the Humvee as we sped out past the guard post and gunned the engine to forty miles an hour. My brain was like cotton candy from the combination of sleeplessness, obscure Afghan names, and altitude.

That first patrol introduced me to dust. Layers of dust, settling in thick layers on every surface, horizontal and vertical. Inhaling dust, making it even harder to breathe whatever oxygen existed in the thin atmosphere. Dust stinging my eyes, as it swirled around our Humvee. Over the course of the deployment, I swallowed my own body weight in Afghan dust.

The sheer scale of the area we were attempting to secure was daunting. We drove for four hours and covered only half of our area of operations, a neat circle on the map twenty miles across. No census had been done in nearly thirty years, but Gardez's population was estimated at more than one hundred thousand. If the estimate was correct, then I had roughly one soldier for every three thousand Afghans.

Paktia's population was unusually dispersed. Families lived in multigenerational households spread among compounds dotting the entire zone we had to patrol. Humvees are tough trucks, but even NASA would have difficulty building a rover to maneuver in the Afghan countryside. A route that looked straight on the map turned out to be a roller coaster that whiplashed my head between a soldier's right knee in the gunner turret, the door handle, and the antitank bazooka suspended from the roof behind my head. I could almost hear the lug nuts and door hinges shaking loose with the bumps, rolls, and braking halts. There were more potholes than flat spaces. And that was a road. The other routes so neatly designated on the maps were more like recommendations: If someone were to build a road, we might recommend it go in this general direction. Thus it was possible to be both on the route and off the road. Nothing was marked, especially when we descended into the warren of dried riverbeds known as *wadis*. Piles of rocks marked either land mines or property boundaries. In either case, the rule was to steer away, even if that meant tipping the Humvee 45 degrees on a side to skirt along the edge of a wadi.

Downtown Gardez was India without the sacred cows. Fortunately for us, the driver from the 82nd was skilled. He knew where to drive without consulting the map and anticipated bumps from memory. He also sped up while crossing culverts to minimize the roadside bomb threats. Weaving through the city, the absence of stoplights caused no concern. He drove with the confidence of a New York cabbie and zigzagged through traffic effortlessly.

In the heart of Gardez, beneath the old city fortress, a solitary policeman stood in the center of the city's main rotary junction. He had a waxed handlebar mustache and wore a well-creased uniform damp with sweat at the armpits. His white gloves had already begun to split at the seams. As dust and trash swirled around his pedestal, he stood like a man trapped in the eye of a hurricane. His cheeks bellowed as he blew his silver whistle, and his arms gesticulated wildly like an epileptic mime. None of the drivers appeared to take notice.

I TURNED TWENTY-FIVE THE day before my men finally arrived three days later from Kandahar. My platoon's late arrival in Gardez meant we would have only forty-eight hours to do a relief-in-place with the 82nd Airborne. The object was for the veterans to pass on as much useful knowledge as possible so we wouldn't make the same mistakes. By the time the platoon arrived in Gardez, I had followed the 82nd's platoon leader everywhere except the bathroom, asking questions, hopping on patrols, and picking his brain for any scrap of information that might help our platoon.

Despite the plentiful food, my squad leaders were overjoyed to have left Kandahar. They had tried to make use of the delay to get their soldiers some shooting time on the rifle range at Kandahar. In an ironic twist of history, the range was at Tarnak Farms, the compound where President Clinton had hesitated to launch a strike at Osama Bin Laden when he was living there with his family. Every time a plane took off or landed at the airfield, the range had to stop shooting. Huber, the squad leader with a linebacker's proportions, was livid.

"Sir, seriously, the only way one of those planes was gonna get shot was if a soldier shot his rifle straight up into the air."

"Glad to be here then?" I asked.

"Is a frog's ass watertight?" Huber answered.

The relief-in-place went by far too fast. At the motor pool I read a long receipt listing four Humvees, several .50-caliber heavy machine guns (".50 cals") and automatic grenade launchers ("Mark-19s"), and an arsenal of ammunition large enough to stock a midwestern militia. Before signing the receipt and becoming financially responsible for over a million dollars' worth of equipment, I had the 82nd Airborne lieutenant show me each item. I had seen three of the Humvees but couldn't find the fourth one. "Have you seen this fourth Humvee listed on the receipt?"

"Oh, that's the good news." He smiled slyly at me. "It's not missing. Let me show you the garage."

We walked over to two large shipping containers. A faded green tarp was slung between them and secured with heavy logs. In the shaded area underneath sagged the missing Humvee. Its condition was only slightly better than the ghetto sled. The mechanic rattled off a laundry list of repairs and parts needed to return the truck to duty.

"If that's the good news, what's the bad news?" I asked.

"The backlog for parts is a mile long, and we're in line behind every broken Humvee in Iraq. We've been cannibalizing this Humvee to fix the other three when they break down. Better still, you have only one mechanic."

My mouth gaped. Three Humvees meant I could move only fifteen guys at a time. I couldn't very well take the ghetto sled into a gunfight.

The lieutenant must have anticipated my concern. "Don't worry," he said. "You can ask the reconstruction team to take one of the Hi-Luxes." He pointed across the motor pool at the fleet of unarmored Toyota pickup trucks splattered with mud. Compared to the Humvees, the Hi-Luxes looked as if they were made of cheap plastic.

"You could take one out with a BB gun," I said.

"Drive faster," he responded.

I PUT SERGEANT HOWARD "Chuck" Adams in charge of getting the men trained to fight from vehicles. Before joining the Army, Chuck had been in the Marine Corps. He met almost every stereotype I had of a Marine: monosyllabic, tough as boot leather, and exceptionally competent. He had taken the Marine Corps up on every school it offered, from sniper school to mountain warfare. Chuck looked like a bulldog—heavy jowls, thick skin, and compact muscles. He had two quirks. One, he could shoot eighteen holes on the golf course at par. Two, he refused to shower in a combat zone. It would take six weeks and another Marine's intervention to get him bathed.

Chuck was the only guy in our light infantry platoon who knew much about heavy weapons. The 10th Mountain was a "light" division, designed for rapid deployment from the United States to any given hot spot. The "heavy" divisions, such as the 3rd Infantry Division or the 1st Cavalry Division, would arrive later with the big guns. Consequently, our division had no tanks and very few Humvees. At Drum our training had focused almost exclusively on foot patrols and house-to-house urban combat. We never trained with Humvees; there simply weren't enough at Drum to spare. Only a few of my men had ever fired the .50 cal or Mark-19, the two heavy weapons we kept mounted on the rooftop Humvee turrets. They comprised most of our firepower in Afghanistan. Unfortunately, they weren't easy weapons. The manuals were several inches thick, and it took practice to handle the recoil. The smallest guys, trying to keep hold of the big guns in the Humvee turrets, looked as if they were wrestling rodeo bulls.

The Humvees themselves were strange beasts for men accustomed to walking at four miles an hour. Our newly designated drivers were awful at first; it was like watching my brother, Gary, learn how to drive. Everyone else in the truck had to suffer while they figured out how to maneuver through ten-foot-deep wadis. We choked on dust driving in circles, trying to get un-lost. Chuck had us run through "Rat Drills," like a combat version of a Chinese fire drill. Designate anyone in the truck as dead and then clamber through the Humvee to change seats while the Humvee keeps moving. I'm not sure we were more confident at the end of those drills. I still felt as though I were riding in a death trap.

We had doctrine for fighting on foot but little guidance for fighting in Humvees (much less pickup trucks). These were supposed to be utility trucks, ferrying rear supplies far behind enemy lines. But in Afghanistan there weren't any enemy lines, so we did what every infantryman in history has had to do in combat: We improvised. "Semper Gumby," as Chuck joked. Always Flexible. Problem: How do you put a machine gun on a Toyota? Solution: Strap it to the top of the cab with cargo ties. Problem: No armor. Solution: Drive faster.

22

Movement to Contact

A movement to contact is an offensive action that seeks to
gain or regain contact with the enemy. Usually, a unit moving to contact lacks detailed information about the enemy.
Upon making contact, a unit identifies the enemy strengths
and weaknesses as it develops the situation.

ARMY FIELD MANUAL (FM 7-8)

THE PRINCIPLE BEHIND NEIGHBORHOOD WATCH OR-
ganizations is that the best policeman is the one who is able to spot what
is out of the ordinary. In a country that is part arms bazaar, part drug depot,
and part third-world kleptocracy, everything was out of the ordinary. Gardez was as different from Watertown, New York, as Bangkok was from
Rhode Island. Even the best weapons won't help you kill your enemy if you
can't find him. Mao famously compared guerrillas to fish swimming in a
sea of people, able to sustain themselves by local cooperation or indifference. After a couple of weeks in Afghanistan, I couldn't agree less. If Mao
were right, finding the fish would have been easy. Any net could separate
fish from water. As another theorist pointed out, our adversaries were more
like fish swimming among other fish.

Captain Worthan instructed me to make our movements unpredictable,
never to take the same route at the same time or on the same day of the
week. We went on dozens of patrols every week—on foot, on wheels, in
the day, and at night. Despite saturating the city with patrols, the attempt
to impose our will on an uncooperative population we didn't understand
and an uncontrollable enemy we couldn't find was both frustrating and

futile. Reality was never more than an approximation, and our intelligence was seldom better than a probability. Fish among fish indeed.

THE FIRST TIME WE drove through downtown Gardez, men in their mid-twenties glared at us. They couldn't see our suspicious gazes because we shielded our eyes with wraparound sunglasses. One group held up their index fingers in a number one gesture. I held out my index finger. Yes, America is number one! After the patrol, my interpreter told me it was the Afghan way of giving us the bird.

On another patrol we stopped at a police station nicknamed the Tank Farm. A half-complete two-story building stood inside a low-perimeter wall. At each of the four corners was a rusting Soviet tank. Investigating the Afghan police, our partners, had become part of the weekly routine. Specialist Lucas "Red" White pointed out that the turrets were facing toward our base—again. A Native American from Washington State, he seemed to have an innate ability to sense when something wasn't right. He had joined the Army five days after September 11. Red was the platoon wiseass. On the predeployment form asking whether he had kids, Red had replied, "Not sure." I sent him and a couple of volunteers from the platoon to scurry through the tank hatches and check for tank rounds before heaving the turret around 180 degrees. One of the tanks had twenty-five rounds in it.

The next police outpost was even more disheartening. There was nothing around it for miles except the patch of gravel in front of it that we called a road. A four-foot-by-ten-foot hut bathed in full sun had a bunk bed sitting on the roof. It looked like a cell in a 1940s prison—metal springs and a two-inch mattress. Two rocket-propelled grenade rounds and a mortar shell were arranged in a symmetrical display beneath a makeshift flagpole. The Afghan flag hung limp on two wooden staves lashed together with old shoelaces.

The guard woke up with a nudge from my gloved hand. As he snapped to attention, his belt cinched around his waist. He was nearly as skinny as the improvised flagpole. He smiled under his blue baseball cap, handed me a "badge" with a flourish of pride, and reported that he was part of the new police force. Apart from the display of munitions, he had neither a rifle nor a launcher for the grenades.

Later in July we attempted a night patrol downtown. The plan was to approach the city by an indirect route through the fields. We drove around for several hours in the pitch-black, lost in the wadi system. I strained to see anything at all through the triple filter of night vision goggles, dirty windshield, and a vortex of dust. Lights began flashing from the fields above our wadi. The wadi got deeper and deeper, with the walls now fifteen feet high on both sides. Suddenly, my Humvee screeched to an abrupt halt, and my head whipped forward and then back again.

"What the hell?" I barked at my driver.

"Sir, every truck in front of us is braking."

The radio squelched, and Staff Sergeant Christopher McGurk asked me to move up to his lead truck. McGurk had arrived in the platoon in May to take one of my squads. He had ice-blue eyes, an American flag pillowcase, and an obsession with heavy metal music and Irish culture. A native of New Windsor, New York, McGurk had three brothers in the Army.

As I walked up to McGurk's murky green silhouette, he pointed out two tiny pyramids of stone on the floor of the wadi thirty yards ahead. My heart raced in time with my analysis. Flashing lights. Marker stones. High-walled cul-de-sac. One plus one plus one equals ambush.

"Let's go. Now. Turn around." I galloped back to my truck as each Humvee did a nearly simultaneous three-point turn. I was certain we were about to be ripped apart by an ambush from the high ground. As soon as the wadi got shallow enough, my driver gunned the truck up the bank and onto the high ground. Branches scraped along our doors, and Markam cried bloody murder from his saddle in the turret. Miraculously, our un-planned escape route took us right into the city. Huber's squad dismounted from the Hi-Lux, and I joined their foot patrol. There were no lights in town; the city generators had stopped working at 11 p.m. The only scent in the air was the heavy odor of hashish smoke. A few stray dogs picked through trash along the gutters. I sensed that we were being watched from the shadows, but we walked all the way to the traffic circle and back. We saw nothing.

Several nights passed before I sent McGurk's squad on a similar night patrol. We heard gunshots at the base, and the next thing I knew we were rushing in the dark to load every available man into Humvees and pickup trucks. The reports were patchy, and McGurk was out of breath on the radio. Several men had fired shots in his direction and then run through a wadi away from him. We flew through the gate and up onto the road toward town.

When we arrived, I questioned several policemen standing idle along the bridge crossing the wadi. They told me they had seen nothing unusual. "No gunshots?" I asked through the interpreter.

"Nothing," they responded.

I tried several different questions and got the same "see no evil, hear no evil" response each time. As my frustration grew, a pickup truck sped out of the wadi up toward the bridge where my men stopped it. I walked across to question the driver. He was dressed in a *kurta* pajama and vest, and the smell of cologne and sweat filled the cab. We questioned him for ten minutes, but he stuck to the story that he had just left a wedding. I let him go, unsatisfied. Fortunately, none of McGurk's men had been wounded in the hit-and-run exchange. When I returned to the base, I wrote my patrol report. Somewhere in Kandahar a staff captain would add another entry to his statistics, lending our patrols an air of precision to an inherently blind process. In Afghanistan our enemy was everywhere and nowhere.

Not every mission was as dramatic. I accompanied the reconstruction team on a mission once where we moved schoolbooks from an old Taliban warehouse to a local school. From floor to ceiling bundles of books were stacked. They spilled out of their burlap sacks across every flat surface in giant mounds. I waded across and picked up a neatly bound hardcover. I dusted off the front and unveiled the gorgeous Arabic calligraphy of the Koran. After placing it back on the pile, I saw a school workbook written in English. It was an English primer for elementary school students. On the back of the book was a list of mottos students should memorize, including the rousing anthem "Jihad is our path." I paged through the short glossary of a hundred words. It had far more military terms in it than one would expect for a grade school English book: bayonet, garrison, overrun, invade, capture. To explain the grammatical concept of a clause, the following example was used: "The mujahideen ran up the mountain, but he was not tired." The reading exercises featured constructions such as "Were you trained by your commander before you started armed jihad?" In case the student was unsure what training might be necessary, the reading exercises went on to remind him: "The battle wasn't fought before my brother oiled his gun. He could use light and heavy arms, even antiaircraft machine guns, too." And to emphasize why such struggle was necessary for Afghans, each student would read the categorical statement: "Wherever there are Russians, there is cruelty." I had read earlier that the Russians disguised mines as children's toys, but until I read these children's primers, I hadn't really absorbed the full measure of Afghanistan's misery. For nearly thirty years the country had been at war, and suffering was woven into the fabric of Afghan society.

The headmaster of the local school greeted us with a large smile. In a province where fewer than one in three adults could read, his work was heroic. In addition to the books, we deposited with him pencils, school backpacks, and a dozen soccer balls. I took a peek in the classroom. There were only a few seats in the room, no chalkboards, and no light except for the natural light flooding in from the oversized windows. The nattily dressed headmaster thanked us profusely and asked us to pose for a group photo. I obliged, but in the back of my head I wondered what good it was to recycle mujahideen propaganda.

The next generation of Afghans was the one we needed most for Afghanistan's long-term stability, but it was the hardest demographic of all. Walking through town on patrol, I often felt like the Pied Piper of Gardez, trailing children behind me in anticipation of more food, water, or candy. *How are you? Gimme water. How are you? Gimme food, mister.* We must have looked like alien invaders with our laser sights, reflective sun-glasses, and dangling antennas. They called us the "Helmeted Ones." I thought about gesturing with three fingers and addressing them in jest: "Greetings. We are from Planet America. We are here to help you." As I walked, the kids laughed and smiled and ran laps around the squad in hand-me-down pajamas and bare feet. Red gave one of the kids some sweets secreted away in his cargo pocket. The flock swarmed around him like a celebrity. Ten steps away stood their elders; their faces spelled indif-ference. I asked a few questions through my interpreter. Have you seen any bad men in the village lately? Have the police been through recently? The answer was always no, but I asked anyway, for the report I needed to fill out when I returned. What happened between ages eight and eighteen? It occurred to me that it would be the same if strange men with guns and sunglasses walked through my hometown: The strangers would be a curios-ity for the young and an intrusion for the old.

Years of training had shaped the way I interpreted my environment. Every door and crooked tree was a potential ambush. I peered at shadows in expectation of trouble and searched for cover that my men and I could use to protect us. Military officers plan for the worst and hope for the best. *Stay alert and stay alive.*

This attitude was well suited for a battlefield or training exercise. Gardez was neither. I wasn't prepared to walk through a village that was neither "friendly" nor "enemy." I wanted to take kids' pictures, not imagine them in suicide vests. This was the frustration of Gardez in microcosm: how to stay focused on protecting my men while simultaneously engaging the local population. One pundit called this "armed social work," evoking the image of Peace Corps volunteers with pistols. The real difficulty, however, was psychological: seeing every local as indeterminate, neither friend nor foe, but potentially both, at different times, in different circumstances. Lieuten-ant Colonel LaCamera's warning echoed in my head: Be polite. Be profes-sional. Be prepared to kill everyone you meet.

23

The Rockets' Red Glare

And the rockets' red glare, the bombs bursting in air
Gave proof through the night that our flag was still there.

FRANCIS SCOTT KEY

"THE SOUNDS OF SILENCE" WAS PLAYING WHEN A loud explosion boomed outside the gates. Neither McGurk nor I took alarm. We were watching *The Graduate* on DVD, anxiously anticipating Dustin Hoffman's seduction by Mrs. Robinson. The engineers at the base were always blowing up captured munitions without notifying us. I just figured that this was another one of their controlled detonations. But then there was a second and a third explosion, and they were louder, and closer. A siren began to wail from the compound. This was no controlled detonation. We were under a rocket attack.

McGurk and I bolted from the tent. He ran to the Humvees, where soldiers were already ripping the dust covers from the machine guns and starting engines. Sergeants Huber and McGurk moved quickly, having already prepared the vehicles that morning for on-call quick-reaction missions. I ran to the Tactical Operations Center to find out more.

As I ran across the gravel, another series of whining rockets screamed by the flanks of the base and exploded a hundred yards away from the perimeter. The rockets were getting closer with each volley. In the operations center I was able to hear the radio reports from the watchtowers. The rockets were being launched from the foothills to the east.

I sprinted back to the parking lot where the vehicles were lined up, ready to roll. "Drive toward the hills—fast." Speed was paramount if we were to have any chance of finding the rocket launchers before they escaped into the hills or blended back into the villages.

"Roger, sir."

It was a moonless night, and everything turned a tadpole green as I flicked on my night vision. We pulled out of the base and onto the blacktop airstrip. The convoy raced to the east along the road and pulled off onto a dirt track heading into the hills where we suspected the rockets had been launched. We reached the grid coordinate that the operations center relayed to us and scanned with our electronic eyes, looking for any silhouettes among the bushes and boulders.

Nothing. I arrayed the Humvees in a broad semicircle facing the mountains. We waited patiently for what seemed like hours but was actually minutes.

A number of silhouettes jogged across our horizon at two hundred yards.

"You. Stop!" yelled my interpreter. Metallic clicks on our rifles switched from safe to fire. The ghosts stopped, but only for a few seconds. Then they began to run again, straight toward the hills. Over the radio, McGurk called me.

"Permission to fire?"

"Engage."

The night erupted in cracking reports and rapid machine-gun fire. Tracers laced across the desert like a laser light show. I was momentarily mesmerized by the firepower that leaped from my platoon's weapons like an extension of my will. I began to work up a fire mission for the mortars at the base. I wanted each of the fleeing shadows eliminated by whatever means I had at my disposal.

As I called in the grid coordinates for a mortar strike, the executive officer in the operations center demanded a situation report. I relayed what I knew, but he wasn't satisfied. We weren't authorized to shoot unless we were certain those men presented an immediate threat. Since they hadn't shot at us, we weren't allowed to shoot them. *Shit.*

"Cease fire! Cease fire!" I stepped outside the vehicle and waved my left

hand in front of my face as a signal. The fire died down as abruptly as it had begun.

We sped in a wedge of vehicles toward the men we had seen. My heart was racing now. Had we killed them? Could we capture them? With my interpreter at my side, I walked from compound to compound, asking the same questions. Did you see where the rockets were fired? Do you know who fired the rockets? Did any strange men arrive in your village tonight? They had seen and heard nothing at all. Everything was normal—or so they said. In the end we had no choice but to turn around and return to base—empty-handed and exhausted.

We took stock the next morning. Fortunately, none of the seven rockets had landed inside the base. No one had been killed or wounded. Analysis of the rocket craters clearly pointed back at the village. I sat down with the squad leaders and talked through our actions. We all agreed that our marksmanship at night had been atrocious. How was it possible for us to miss a single target with all our guns blazing? This needed immediate attention. Alone later, I scrutinized my own performance. I was glad that I hadn't panicked when the rockets began landing. On the other hand, I had been too impulsive to shoot. I should have known better. There was a strong possibility that the men running from us were just ordinary Afghans. I would probably have run, too, if American Humvees were crashing through the brush toward me.

I was uneasy with the excitement I felt about shooting. Shouldn't I have felt remorse at aiming live rounds at other people? Where was the clinical detachment? This had been raw and unfiltered. Perhaps it was a release from the frustrations that had been mounting—the futility of our patrols, the homesickness, and the boredom. The roadside bombs that threatened our patrols left no one to retaliate against. For once we had someone in the crosshairs. Discovering this killer instinct unnerved me, challenging my sense of humanity. I could kill—and I might even like it. Only later would I realize this wasn't entirely true. At this point I had only pulled the trigger. I was yet to see the point of impact.

———

THAT FIRST TASTE OF combat coincided with the arrival of a new platoon sergeant. Sergeant First Class Vern Story walked straight out of a John Wayne movie and into our platoon. His face was chiseled granite—sharp and hard. He wore a high and tight haircut like a crown on his sunburned scalp. Veins snaked along his tattooed arms, as thick as Popeye's. I had come back from a patrol to find him chewing out one of the privates for a dirty weapon. At first I couldn't understand a word he was bellowing. He had an untraceable accent, part southern and part Texan. When he was angry, his commands took on a cadence and color that was iconic drill sergeant.

Story's first mission was fixing Chuck. Even after a month in Gardez, he still hadn't taken a shower. It was like a high school biology project I had done once where I placed a piece of bread in a Petri dish and watched the mold grow. Day by day Chuck's odor amplified. At first I asked the other sergeants to intervene, "Please make Chuck shower." No result. Then I threatened Chuck with the Uniformed Code of Military Justice: "I'm giving you a direct order. Shower or face the consequences." Again, no result. Worse still, Chuck never took his boots or helmet off. He lay on his cot every night in full combat gear. I began to get concerned about what might be happening inside his boots, but he wouldn't take them off for my investigation. Chuck didn't want to lose one second responding to a rocket or gunfight. I applauded the professional dedication but just couldn't take the smell anymore. Neither could his soldiers. I knew the time for action had come when the interpreter told me Chuck's body odor was repelling the local Afghans he was trying to question. I asked Story to get Chuck into the shower, fully clothed if necessary. The two shared a common Marine affinity. In low voices they talked in grunts.

"Ugg. Hooah hooah ugg shower."

"Ugg?"

"Shower hooah hooah ugg, semper fi ugg ugg."

Whatever Story had said, it worked. Chuck began taking regular showers, and order was restored. Story was exactly the type of platoon sergeant every lieutenant hopes for: honest, tough, and experienced. Within a week he had infused every soldier in the platoon with a new sense of urgency. He demanded high standards and enforced them with tyrannical vigilance. He was able to do so in part because he met the Gunny Oakes Ranger School standard; Story could "walk the talk." His fifteen years of experience included combat with the Marines in Kuwait during Desert Storm. For the last three years he had graded a thousand lieutenants as a lane walker at the Army's exercise center in Louisiana. He had every Army qualification from expert marksman to Ranger. And he could run harder and push more ground than anyone in the platoon.

I sat down with Story that first night, and we talked through my expectations of him and what he could expect from me. His professionalism was reassuring. He understood our roles and promised his loyalty and hard work if I would make the same promise to him. We shook hands. His were callused and rough—like my father's. At that point I had little idea how much the two of us would be tested or how strong our bond would become.

24

Combat Casual

I have not been at the front, I have been in front of it.

WILFRED OWEN, 1917

SOME NIGHTS I COULD ALMOST TASTE HOME. WITH my headphones on and eyes shut, I was driving a brand-new Corvette down a perfectly flat stretch of freeway at eighty miles an hour. Often, my fantasies were culinary flashbacks. I could just taste lobster and drawn butter from the seafood buffets I used to go to with my father at the Nordic Lodge. Then there were all those Oxford meals—venison in a juniper reduction, a late-night snack with Matt and Hayden at Hassan's Kebabs, or the mounds of fresh pasta I ate with Meena at Gino's by the bus station. It was possible to spend forty-five minutes dreaming just about the one-pound Ranger Burger at the Four Winds Restaurant near Fort Benning. I could barely fit my hands around it. Sipping on a nonalcoholic can of beer in Gardez, I would perform imaginary alchemy and turn it into a large frosted mug of Sam Adams.

Each of us found a way to escape from Afghanistan. Within hours of arrival at Gardez, our tents had been transformed. As I walked down the aisle, these alcoves provided me with glimpses of my soldiers' lives back home and their dreams for the future, often side by side. Wallet photos of girlfriends were sandwiched between pinups of *Maxim* models and *Playboy* centerfolds. Pictures of expensive Harley-Davidson motorcycles were next to photos of muscle cars they had tinkered with for years. Crucifixes and Saint Christopher medals balanced the shrines to breasts and chrome. We tacked up inspirational quotes and lucky four-leaf clovers. Next to my bed

I propped up a photo album of Meena, the obituary of John Hottell III that Colonel LoFaro had given me at West Point, and a bottle of mouthwash.

Sometimes the attempt to make Afghanistan more like home created bizarre juxtapositions. Satellite television beamed in sports at the wrong time of day. In October we would watch the Red Sox–Yankees playoffs at eight o'clock in the morning while downing scrambled eggs and Afghan naan bread. We also tried bringing our sports to Afghanistan. We rigged volleyball and Ping-Pong nets from military-issue nylon cord. We played football in body armor in order to build our stamina with the extra twenty pounds of weight. Running presented a particular problem because of snipers hidden in the two hills closest to the base, forcing us to run within the Hesco barriers. The laps were short enough that we had to alternate directions in order to keep our legs from developing asymmetrically. To spice up the exercise regime, I organized a volleyball tournament complete with a boom box and nonalcoholic beer. There wasn't a beach for a thousand miles, but we conjured one out of thin air. The constant verbal communication on the court built a valuable tactical habit. In combat, bump, set, and spike became distance, direction, and rate of fire.

Although many modern conveniences were available—hot food, a "gym," air-conditioning, satellite television—we had our share of minor privations. No one was going to mistake Gardez for Watertown, New York. Before we left Fort Drum, one comedian who had deployed to Afghanistan earlier posted instructions on how to prepare:

1. Renovate your bathroom. Hang a green plastic sheet from the middle of the bathtub and keep 4 inches of soapy, cold water on the floor. When you take showers, wear flip-flops and keep the lights off.
2. Keep a roll of toilet paper on your nightstand and bring it to the bathroom with you. And bring a gun and a flashlight as well.
3. Cut a hole in your vacuum bag and every morning run the vacuum through your house.

4. First thing in the morning, make everyone in your family brief what he or she did yesterday. At the end of the day, make everyone brief what he or she did during the day. Do this every day—seven days a week.

5. Go to the worst crime-infested place you can find wearing a flak jacket and Kevlar helmet. Set up shop in a tent in a vacant lot. Announce to the residents that you're there to help them.

WHEN I LEFT THE United States, I hadn't expected to communicate with friends and family. At best I thought I might get a letter off once a week. My expectations were wildly off the mark. Mail was regular in Gardez and arrived with almost every helicopter flying in from Kandahar. Meena sent tea and trail mix and a steady stream of Bollywood films to screen for my platoon. Charlie Hooker's five-year-old mailed a hand-drawn birthday card and a huge bag of beef jerky. Katie Larson bundled magazine articles. My sister Bridget sent her special brownies (they lasted exactly seven minutes). Every week I received a ten-day-old copy of the Sunday *New York Times* from the mother of Liz Young, my Oxford and West Point classmate. Packages also arrived from random charities. Mountains of PowerBars and Twizzlers towered in the tents. We acquired a curious collection of sanitary napkins (we were an all-male infantry unit). As the deployment wore on, we shared more and more of our loot, keeping just a few choice items for ourselves from every package.

There were odd restrictions. Meena received a sharp directive from Captain Worthan's wife not to send "any matter depicting nude or seminude persons, pornographic or sexual items, or non-authorized political materials." Meena found the warning hilarious and wrote to tell me about it: "Craig, I'm not sure which was more bizarre, the prohibition against swimsuit pinups or the juxtaposition of politics and pornography." (My men had no problem acquiring porn. It was ubiquitous.) Meena sent novels and history books, inscribing encouragements to continue challenging my mind. On slow days I could open a camp chair and escape Afghanistan through the books she sent. With an iPod and headphones, it was easy to close my eyes, drift back in time, and hear Hayden snapping his fingers along with the saxophone and clarinet of Dave Brubeck's "Take Five."

The same elaborate network of satellites and gadgetry that synchronized our GPS locators and allowed us to talk with jets thirty thousand feet above the deck also enabled soldiers to reach home with relative ease. Each of the tents in Gardez had an Ethernet cable, and many of my soldiers had brought laptops. Twice a day I checked my email and downloaded the digital photos my family sent me. We had a half-dozen satellite phones at our disposal. I got particular satisfaction from calling friends on weekends. One morning I called Bryan, who was working in San Francisco that summer.

"Bryan, what's up? It's Craig."

"Craig?" I could just make out his confusion above the loud music in the background. "Hold on a second." The bass line thumped *uuntz, uuntz, uuntz*. "Are you okay?"

"Yeah, I'm fine. Just thought I'd give you a ring on the satellite phone." Bryan's end of the line went quiet. "You still there?" I asked.

"I'm here. I'm just trying to wrap my head around getting a phone call in a club from a friend in Afghanistan."

"Reach out and touch somebody, right?"

COMMUNICATION WAS A TWO-WAY street, however, and I didn't always want to know what was going on outside of my corner of Afghanistan. In particular, I didn't want to deal with my parents' divorce, but it kept reaching out to me from the other side of the world. A few weeks after arriving in Afghanistan, I received a letter from my father. He asked the usual questions about how I was doing and what Afghanistan was like. He said nothing about the divorce or why he had walked out on our family in the first place. There wasn't a word of contrition in the letter. As I read it, I got angrier and angrier at the pedestrian tone of the letter, as if nothing had happened. The pain seared again as much as it had before I had left for Afghanistan.

My father couldn't have picked a worse time to desert my family, but I was helpless to do anything about it. I grabbed my notebook and wrote a short response to my father. I answered none of his questions but gave him an ultimatum instead: No communication would be possible without a full explanation and an apology. I folded the letter in thirds, stuck it in an envelope, and dropped it in the cardboard box that served as our mail bin. Then I tore up his letter and burned the scraps.

BEYOND AFGHANISTAN, THE NIGHTLY news brought us images and sounds from a newer battlefield—Iraq. I watched with shock as the first roadside bombs in Iraq rocked Baghdad's streets. Intelligence reports confirmed that daily attacks there dwarfed those in Afghanistan in scale, frequency, and geographic spread. I worried about Trent, the Parsons twins, and Major Nagl. They were busy enough (not the good kind of busy) that my messages didn't get replies for months. We were stretched thin in Afghanistan, both in terms of boots on the ground and resources. The growing insurgency in Iraq would stretch us even further.

VIPs began to visit Gardez with frustrating frequency. Gardez represented the new model of armed nation building. We had new schools and clinics open for inspection and a new unit of Afghan soldiers to showcase our handover of responsibilities to the Afghan government.

One night in September we got word that Secretary of Defense Donald Rumsfeld was arriving the next day. Our patrols were canceled, and we spent the day raking stones, sweeping tents, and hiding the "semi-nude" pictures on the wall. Sergeant Grenz followed the instruction a little too literally.

Scott Grenz, despite his chubby cheeks and unassuming demeanor, was a natural leader in the platoon, perhaps a result of his growing up as the oldest of five boys in rural Nevada. Grenz had two hobbies back home: motocross bike racing and hunting. He could shoot a beer can at three hundred yards with one eye closed and an empty six-pack by his side.

"He's fully clothed, sir," responded Grenz when I looked incredulously at his practical joke. He had replaced a *Penthouse* centerfold with a clothed pinup of Leonardo DiCaprio.

"Keep it up," I said, secretly hoping it might provoke a response from Secretary Rumsfeld.

"Another fucking drive-by visit," Markam chimed in. More accurately, they were "fly-by" visits; driving to Gardez was too dangerous (for them, not us). The routine was identical every time.

The delegation arrived by helicopter, an hour late as usual. The reconstruction team met them at the airfield (not with the ghetto sled, though) and escorted the mob of television cameramen and perfectly coiffed news correspondents toward the base. They wore "combat casual": khaki cargo pants, boots, and safari vests. And carried cameras, of course. Inside our dining hall they received a twenty-minute PowerPoint presentation. The commander, when asked, reported shortages of critical parts and requested a dedicated helicopter to get around the province. The VIPs nodded, and aides jotted notes on their dusty legal pads. As far as I could tell, these requests evaporated on the return flight from Kabul to Washington.

After a half hour, lunch was served. All morning the cooks had slaved in the kitchen to perfect culinary masterpieces. There was demi-glace for the steak and drawn butter for the lobster. This visit even merited a layer cake. I was always allowed to send three soldiers to join the lunch. With so many visits it was possible for nearly every soldier to rotate through the feasts, enduring dumb questions (Do you miss home? Is it *very* dangerous?) in exchange for good food. We never ate better than when politicians visited.

As the clock ticked on the two hours allocated for their tour of the front lines, the delegation got antsy. A lackey applied hairspray to a reporter's mussed hair and handed him a fresh bottle of Evian. After lunch came the photo op. A large American flag hung on the mud wall. I stood with two other soldiers while our executive officer read our promotion orders. By the authority of the president, I now had the double silver bars of a captain. Secretary Rumsfeld shook my hand. He was shorter than I had expected.

As the secretary's delegation returned to a waiting helicopter, his aide left behind a handful of enamel coins for me to distribute to my men (a military tradition to express gratitude or reward performance). During the visit, most of my men had sat in their sweltering Humvees, staring out from the perimeter at passing dust devils.

Despite the rosy picture painted for visiting delegations, reality wasn't a PowerPoint slide show. They didn't see that the Afghan soldiers they inspected weren't reliable enough to take on patrol or that they sold their uniforms and equipment on the black market because they weren't getting their paychecks from the government. They didn't drive through the streets and see the glaring eyes of current and future insurgents or the total absence of police to lock them up. There was certainly strategic value in having the media and American politicians see the good work the reconstruction team was doing in Gardez. With luck, they'd pen articles and return to Congress inspired to fight for reconstruction funding. And the focus on new schools and clinics would signal to Afghans that the American mission was as much about helping Afghans as it was about capturing and killing the Taliban. Yet I couldn't help but be frustrated with the necessary brevity of these visits and the disruption they caused at a tactical level. An hour on the ground just wasn't long enough to get any real sense of its contradictions, challenges, or opportunities.

After the helicopter lifted off, I handed out the coins. Grenz thumbed his and asked whether anyone had inspected the tents.

No. There wasn't time.

25

Hearts and Minds

And they will hammer their swords into plowshares and their spears into pruning hooks. Nation will not lift up sword against nation, and never again will they learn war.

ISAIAH 2:4

OPERATION DOOLITTLE. THAT IS WHAT THE HEAD of the reconstruction team dubbed our upcoming missions. With my troops providing security, the mission called for a small detachment of physicians and veterinarians to provide health care and vaccinations to the nomadic Kuchi tribes assembled near Gardez. We planned to set up a mobile clinic in a different location each day for five days.

We had done dozens of convoys before, but I still spent an hour talking the team through our standing procedures for responding to a roadside bomb or ambush. The speed at which each squad leader could rattle off the steps was a testament to their training. If we ever had to respond, I was confident they would act immediately and appropriately. Each squad leader briefed me on the routes and checkpoints as well as the primary and alternate radio frequencies we would use for communications. As for the clinic locations, we knew the various sites well after five weeks of patrolling Gardez. Developing a perimeter security plan was a simple matter of positioning our vehicles to cover every possible approach.

Our first destination was Dara, a tiny village along a famous mountain pass to our east. The Satakandow had a storied past. As the only pass over the Hindu Kush Mountains between the Afghan cities of Gardez and Khost, its strategic importance made it a valuable piece of real estate during the Soviet-Afghan war. When the Russians first tried to seize the pass, an entire battalion of Soviet motorized infantry was destroyed in an ambush, having fired from their personnel carriers until all their ammunition ran out. Mujahideen control of the pass continued to stymie the Russians until the winter of 1987–88, when more than two divisions of Soviet paratroopers and special forces fought a tooth-and-nail battle to relieve the siege of Khost. At great cost in Soviet lives, Operation Magistral was a success, but only temporarily. Soon after, the mujahideen regained control of the pass, and in April 1988 the Soviets began a phased withdrawal from Afghanistan. Even during our deployment, the pass remained dangerous for American forces. We slowly crawled up the serpentine bends of the road to an altitude of over nine thousand feet. Above us, silhouettes of soldiers and guns stood atop the ridges, vestiges of the combat scarecrows that the mujahideen had placed to spook the Russians.

We arrived safely at a half-completed, two-story school, and I began to set up our perimeter. I placed trucks facing down the road in each direction and another truck behind the school facing the hills. One squad of soldiers remained inside the waist-high courtyard of the school playground to search male patients one by one before the doctors saw them. There was a separate tent for women. In the field beside the school, two shelters were set up for the veterinarians and their boxes of vaccines. I hadn't realized until then that the Army even had veterinarians.

It was still early in the morning when we finished setting up for the day. As the sun rose higher behind the mountains, what looked like rivers of refugees streamed toward our makeshift clinic. Clouds of dust hovered above herds of sheep, goats, donkeys, and camels. As they got closer, their thundering hoofs and bellowing brays and snorts combined with shepherds' sharp commands to form a cacophonous din. The trucks began to report in over the radio: "I am surrounded by goats. What do you want me to do?" I walked over to McGurk, whose squad manned the gate into the courtyard. Outside the gate was a crowd of men jostling for position. Chuck was trying to shoo them into a line with gentle prods of a large stick he had found.

Since joining the Army, I had practiced dozens of ambushes and raids. At Fort Benning I had devised elaborate defensive perimeters with trip wire triggers, booby traps, and planned artillery targets. But I had never, not once, practiced a humanitarian mission like this. I was prepared to make a final stand if surrounded by communist hordes. I was not at all sure what to do when surrounded by a herd of goats or a mob of locals speaking an alien tongue.

Semper Gumby. Chuck quickly discovered that his curses were unintelligible to the tribesmen and found a better solution. He found the oldest man with the most elaborate turban, handed him the stick, and in a matter of minutes the situation was under control. The men soon lined up along the wall, sitting on their haunches in what looked like an incredibly uncomfortable but certainly unthreatening posture. The gunners on the Humvees took their hands off their heavy machine guns, pulled out their phrase books, and mimed a standing push-up to the shepherds while exhorting them to "move away, please." The result was like Moses parting the Red Sea.

As the hours passed, I moved among my Humvees, the gateway, and the makeshift clinic inside the school. The line of patients never dwindled. The half-dozen Afghan and American doctors worked without rest, conscious perhaps that they were the only medical hope for this underserved population. Unfortunately, they lacked all but the most basic medicines. Logistical delays meant that hundreds of doses of lifesaving vaccines were unavailable. All they had to give them was aspirin.

In the afternoon an elderly man arrived carrying his paralyzed wife on his back. He had walked nearly ten miles. There was little our doctors could do. Another young man came limping to the makeshift clinic, his lower leg lacerated with shrapnel. He had stepped on one of the thousands of land mines littering these mountains. During the 1980s, the Soviets had carpet-mined entire ridgelines to deny their use to the mujahideen. Many of the minefields remained unmarked, and only a fraction of the known mines had been removed. An Afghan medical student removed the visible shrapnel, applied an antibacterial cream, and bandaged the leg, giving careful instructions on how to keep the wound clean.

Outside, the field looked like the Washington County Fair that my father used to take me to when I was a kid. He would lift me up so I could pat the cows and brush the horses' manes. We wore identical work boots as we tramped through the fair, stopping every so often for Dell's frozen lemonade or a stuffed quahog. Twenty years and seven thousand miles later, I stood before hundreds of animals of every shape, size, and smell. Bobbing above the fray like bright buoys were the vibrant orange, yellow, and red head scarves of eight-year-old shepherdesses and the floppy boonie caps of soldiers. The veterinarians were dressed in khaki overalls and managed the pandemonium with ease, clearly in their element. I joined the assembly line for the task of shooting syringes of deworming medicine into the mouths of bleating sheep. As we counted sheep, a civil affairs soldier made a tick on his clipboard and branded each sheep with spray paint—u.s. The vets handled the larger animals: camels, donkeys, and horses. They set broken bones, shoed hooves, and bandaged wounds. I turned to see one vet with his arm up the ass of a cow as far as his bicep. Now that is love of country, I thought. While the doctors were able to treat only a couple of hundred people, the vets handled more than five thousand livestock. The Kuchi depended on their herds for sustenance, clothing, and shelter. The value of a dairy cow or camel was a family's life savings and insurance. In winning the hearts and minds of the tribes, Army vets were worth their weight in gold.

Later in the afternoon, I sent a small patrol out beyond our perimeter. About an hour into their patrol, I received a report on the platoon radio frequency: "Gator 1-6, this is Gator 1-1. You better come check this out."

"What you got?" I asked.

"It looks like a cache of ST-1's. We might want to blow them in place. It could be too dangerous to move them."

I had no idea what an ST-1 was but didn't want to relay my rookie ignorance. "I'll be right there. Send your location, over."

I walked the half mile to the grid coordinate they gave me and found Sergeant Huber, as serious as a caretaker. "Let me see."

Huber gestured with his arm at the ground ten feet away. I heard a snicker from Red, but when I turned back to the group, everyone was scanning his slice of the perimeter. I looked again where Huber had gestured but couldn't see anything other than a few rocks and fire ants.

"There are more caches like this farther up the hillside, sir."

"I'm not sure what you're talking about Huber. Where are those ST-1's?"

"Right there, sir, like I told you. A whole pile of S-T-O-N-E-S. We found some T-R-double E's as well."

Everyone burst out laughing. "Fuck," I said under my breath and hoofed it back to the compound. When I left the platoon, one of the gifts they gave me was a half-pound stone with ST-1 stenciled on its side.

The following days had the same pattern. On day two I watched our company executive officer, the senior lieutenant in the company, go for a ride on a pony, falling off a couple of times without a saddle and bridle to keep his balance and control. A hockey player from Boston, he was no equestrian. I asked an interpreter if I could mount one of the camels and pose for a photo. He found the ugliest camel and negotiated with its owner. With my helmet, body armor, and rifle slung over my back, I sat right on top of the single-humped camel reclining in front of me. The owner nudged me gently to slide farther back on the camel and to wrap my arms around the bulging hump. I did as instructed, and the camel stood to full height, thrusting me six feet off the ground. A crowd of children and adolescents began to gather around, laughing and pointing at the "helmeted one" sitting on a camel. I smiled as one of my guys took photos with my camera. This will be a good one for Meena, I thought. No danger here, just a petting zoo. I reached back with my left arm as if I were going to slap the camel's butt.

Bad idea. Thinking I really intended to ride the camel, the kids started striking the camel's butt with small sticks. Before I knew it, the camel was running off at a gallop with me holding on for dear life. Camels move a lot faster than you think. Behind me, a mob of kids and teenagers ran along laughing and continued to spur the camel on faster and faster. I tried to maintain my cool, conscious that America's reputation and my own was at stake. But how to stop a galloping camel? The camel knew how. While still running, it started snapping its head back toward me with teeth bared and its odious breath overpowering me. Again and again the head snapped back, now with its teeth biting. Are camels carnivores? I had no option but to dismount before being eaten. I attempted a Mary Lou Retton dismount but instead landed in a yard sale on the ground, helmet upside down, rifle in the dust, and my heart racing with adrenaline. The kids lifted me back up, placed my helmet on my head, and began cheering. The adolescents attempted to lift me to their shoulders for a glorious (or mocking) procession. Fifty yards away my soldiers were bent over laughing.

Our third day's mission took place at a compound used by the United Nations High Commission on Refugees. At lunch I discovered a dozen Afghan contractors in *kurta* pajamas playing volleyball on a dirt court. They were playing better volleyball than the varsity team at West Point. Every serve was blistering, and each volley was a perfect bump, set, and spike. Where did these guys learn to play? I yielded to the urge to join them for a few points, reliving my one season on the men's volleyball team in high school. Despite my poor play, they invited me to break with them for lunch. Anything was better than an MRE, I thought, and joined them.

Lunch featured a potato and chickpea curry with the standard mountain of naan bread and bottomless cups of green tea. I gorged myself and answered their questions—some in German, some in Urdu (in spoken form, nearly identical to Hindi), and some in broken English. Along with their unintelligible Pashto, there were four languages being spoken at once. I showed them the photo of Meena I kept as a bookmark.

"Meri patni hai," I told them, meaning "my wife." I didn't know how to say "fiancée."

The picture went around the circle. All agreed that she was *bohut khubsurat* (very pretty).

"Pakistani?"

"No. Indian," I corrected. "Tamil Nadu." That was where her parents had grown up.

"Children?"

"No," I said as their eyes shifted down in sympathy, "but soon, hopefully."

"In sh'allah." God willing. Before long we had moved past family questions to singing Bollywood anthems and then on to American celebrity gossip. I knew it was time to go when they asked me to sing Britney Spears songs. There are some things no self-respecting Army officer can do.

At the end of every mission we dispersed blankets, food, farming tools, and backpacks filled with school supplies. At first we handed the items out from the back of the truck. This was a dumb move, and my men had to intervene to prevent the truck from being overtaken by the desperate wave of tribesmen. We grew smarter with experience. By day three we had learned to sit the various tribal chiefs in a line by themselves. In front of each one we placed a small pile of humanitarian items. If one of the chiefs grabbed anything from the pile before we said so, we removed him from the distribution line. As the piles grew larger, we lined up our convoy to return to base. Hoarding and fighting were bound to happen, but we weren't staying behind to separate the Hatfields and McCoys. With engines ready, we bolted from the scene as soon as we gave the command to the khans to take their loot. In the rearview mirror, one man picked up his hoe and swung it at the head of another khan, knocking him out cold and taking his pile. There must be a better way, I thought to myself.

An Army photographer later provided me with copies of the photos he took during the mission. In one, an adolescent girl is sitting on her heels and staring at the camera, her bright pink dress standing in stark contrast to a strand of barbed wire and an olive drab tent. In another, a grandmother with deep wrinkles on a sunburned face holds a young boy in her arms. His eyes are sapphires glittering in the desert sun, but his empty stomach is distended from parasites.

These photos stand side by side in my office with pictures of the battlefields on which we fought and sacrificed. War is not only terror and exhilaration, courage and cowardice. It can also be the protection and comfort provided to the innocent. For a few days that is what we were able to do for regular Afghans caught in the cross fire of a war they never asked for. While I may never be able to point to a tangible result of our countless patrols and brushfire skirmishes, my soldiers will always be able to look back on that mission as a time when we put our weapons down and helped heal a broken country. It made me proud to be an American soldier.

26

Marking Time

Patience is bitter, but its fruit is sweet.

AFGHAN PROVERB

WHEN I TOLD MY MEN THAT WE WERE GOING ON A three-day mission to Ghazni, they were nearly as excited as I was. Three days away from the routine at Gardez was an appetizing proposition. Unfortunately, I had to leave half the platoon behind in Gardez to protect the base. Our mission was to escort a dozen members of the Gardez reconstruction team as they performed a reconnaissance of Ghazni. At the time there was no American presence in Ghazni Province, an enormous territory to our west that was home to nearly two million Afghans. Our goal was to find a location in Ghazni suitable for another provincial reconstruction team and perhaps a larger infantry battalion to patrol and extend the central government's influence.

The day before we departed, we learned of a vicious attack along the route we planned to travel. The Taliban had stopped four Afghan employees of a Danish relief organization, tied them up, and shot them. Their bodies had been left to rot in the sun. The attack underscored the difficulties of rebuilding Afghanistan. The communities that needed the most help were by definition the most remote and least secure. Humanitarian organizations, without armed protection, made tempting targets on lonely back roads. The easiest way to discredit the central government was to stall the delivery of government services to rural areas and reinforce the perception of violent instability. As we drove the fifty miles between Gardez and

Ghazni, I was keenly aware of our vulnerability even though we were better armed than our predecessors. Along one stretch we snaked downhill on forty-foot switchbacks with steep cliffs on either side leaning over us. If ambushed, we would have had zero mobility. Killing us would have been as easy as shooting fish in a barrel.

As the convoy rumbled into Ghazni's outskirts, her famous Towers of Victory stood in the distance. Built in the twelfth century, the pair of minarets were over a hundred feet tall and featured elaborate geometric designs along the raised brick surface. They looked like outsized grain silos. We soon turned onto the best road in Afghanistan, the centerpiece of the international reconstruction effort. Its renovation had cut the driving time in half between Kabul and Kandahar, spurring the recovering Afghan economy and providing thousands of jobs to construction workers along the route. It was a hard-won accomplishment, costing the lives of many brave Afghans and foreign construction managers who had been terrorized by insurgents eager to detour the ambitious project.

The new road had no potholes. There were even streetlights and sidewalks. It was as if we had moved from the horse-drawn nineteenth century to the automobile twentieth century. Finishing a daylong convoy with a victory lap on a real freeway was exhilarating. The presence of American Humvees must have been a surprise to the locals, given our conspicuous absence until now. As we drove, a group of three women walked along the sidewalk in long robes and veils. Markam became giddy in the gunner's turret. Then I saw why. The women had lifted their veils to look at us. Markam was sure they were flirting.

"That was full facial nudity, sir. Seriously."

We pulled into a modern compound with twenty-foot walls and guards posted on either side. We had arrived at our destination—the Governor's Guest House. We gaped open-jawed as we wandered on the premises.

My first requirement was relieving myself. I asked in Pashto where the toilet was, expecting to be pointed to a moderately odious outhouse. I received a response in the Queen's English: "You will find the toilet on the first floor, sir, next to the stairway landing. Would you like me to show you?"

I was led to an immaculate bathroom. Its temperature was 20 degrees cooler than outside. Richly painted tiles covered the floor and walls, and a modern toilet sat like a throne at the back of the room. There was a beautiful porcelain sink with hot and cold taps, and the fixtures were a freshly polished brass. This was the lap of luxury after two months of camp living. My standard for luxury had probably dropped, but by any comparison, the Guest House was a nice place to spend a couple of nights.

There was nothing to do for the rest of the day except relax and wait for dinner. I took out a book, planted myself in the center of the governor's rose garden, and read contentedly for several hours. I lifted my eyes from the book occasionally to enjoy the rose blooms, the melody of songbirds, and a curious miniature deer roving the grounds. At intervals, a servant brought out glasses of rosewater, lemonade, and green chai.

In the evening, servants led us to a long room with beautiful hand-woven carpets running down its length. European chairs lined the edges of the room, but we were encouraged to sit cross-legged on the rugs. Twenty-five of us perched eagerly in anticipation of the food. Servants sprang into action, delivering bushels of pilaf rice, steaming ladles of rich stew, and racks of lamb chops seasoned with mint and coriander. We ate ravenously, but the spread before us never diminished. Neither did our glasses. We consumed gallons of green tea and a delicious yogurt drink with a hint of cucumber.

One by one, each of us leaned back from the food and reclined on our elbows. Someone flipped on the television. and a special about Massoud was playing. Ahmad Shah Massoud, "the Lion of Panjshir," had been the most famous Afghan mujahideen leader, surviving countless attacks on his mountainous redoubts northeast of Kabul. Just two days before al-Qaeda stunned the world on 9/11, a suicide bomber linked to al-Qaeda killed Massoud. As the leader of Afghanistan's Northern Alliance and a folk hero on the scale of Che Guevara, many Afghans felt his assassination keenly.

Afghanistan's history, whether its ancient past at the crossroads of many empires, or its recent guerrilla and civil wars, illuminated the war we were fighting. We could expect skill and tenacity from warriors who had mountain fighting in their blood. Their capacity to endure environmental hardship was unbelievable. They had reserves of patience that had outlasted Alexander the Great, Genghis Khan, the British Empire, and the Soviet Union. And even though the United States wasn't interested in acquiring Afghanistan as an imperial territory, history forecast different challenges. The Afghans had always been able to unite in order to eject outsiders. But without the unifying prospect of invasion, Afghanistan had most often fractured into warring tribes and regions. Geography reinforced those divisions, separating communities between mountain peaks so that neighboring valleys often spoke mutually incomprehensible dialects. The practical reach of a central ruler was limited. Stability was the exception in Afghanistan, not the rule.

THE PROPOSED SITE FOR the new Ghazni reconstruction team was an uninspiring building outside the city. We drove there and provided security while the Gardez delegation examined the compound. Satisfied with the location, they determined that it was sufficiently far from the highway to reduce the risk of a car or truck bomb. Their caution was wise. Although these were rare tactics in Afghanistan in 2003, they would increase dramatically starting in 2006. Instead of returning immediately to the guesthouse, the reconstruction team decided to go on a shopping trip in central Ghazni.

"I don't think this is a good idea," I protested.

The team leader responded, brushing aside my safety concerns. I thought of my trip to India and Tim Strabbing's excursion to Kashmir. *Oh, come on, guys. Who would kidnap a Marine?*

We drove through streets that grew narrower and more crowded the closer we got to the central bazaar. We made a brief stop to get cash. I handed our interpreter two hundred U.S. dollars—the amount my men wished to exchange for Afghanis, the local currency. This represented three months' wages for the average Afghan. I decided to send a couple of guys with guns to watch his back as he made the transaction in a dark alley. The interpreter returned with an enormous bundle of Afghanis. All we were missing was a black briefcase. I divided the money among my solders in the amounts they had contributed. This involved much more math than I was comfortable with, especially while holding about eight thousand tattered bills.

Our next move was to place the vehicles at either end of the bazaar. I planned a rotation so that everyone would get a chance to buy a souvenir. When it was my turn, I brought Private Joshuah Howe along with me to the nearest stall selling fabric. Walking down the street, it was as if everyone was watching me with hidden daggers ready to strike. I knew I was being paranoid, and reasonably so. There was no cavalry to call if something happened; we would have to fight our way out of the busiest part of the city. I hurriedly picked out a few yards of pink and emerald silk to bring home for Bridget and Meena. I turned to see Howe eyeing a burqa.

Howe was my radio operator, my ears and mouth when we went into the field. Everywhere I went, Howe tagged along two steps behind with a twenty-pound radio strapped to his rucksack, usually humming Lynyrd Skynyrd or Ozzy Osbourne. Howe was the youngest private in the platoon, an eighteen-year-old from a small town in New Hampshire. He had joined the Army because he believed it was an obligation for every American male to serve. The maturity of his commitment contrasted with the baby fat clinging to his waist. Before we left Drum, I signed a pass for him to return home for his girlfriend's senior prom. They married shortly thereafter.

As we returned to the Humvee, Howe handed me the headset of the radio.

"What's up?" I asked the squad leader over the radio.

"Some fifteen-year-old just asked me how many Americans were in the bazaar."

"Did you tell him?"

"Of course not, sir."

"Anything else unusual?"

"The same white pickup truck has driven by us a few times."

I thought through the evidence as my pace picked up. We were being sized up for an attack, possibly involving a car bomb in a busy bazaar. I blasted a command across the radio to rally at the Humvees for a rapid withdrawal.

"Let's go, Howe. Shopping trip's over."

We ran through the bazaar with our cheap plastic shopping bags in one hand and weapons in the other and got back in the Humvees. My driver stepped on the gas, and we barreled through the streets back to the governor's house. I'll never know whether we escaped an attack or just bugged out unnecessarily.

BEFORE LEAVING GHAZNI, I had time to show my men the history they were shaping. From the governor's house, the ancient citadel of Ghazni loomed in the distance like the Parthenon in Athens. We drove up a steep dirt track through the ruins until we were nearly at the apex. There was a Soviet tank buried up to the top of its treads. We crawled in and around the tank, taking photos in the bright summer sun. I took out the Afghan history book I had brought along and glanced through my notes.

Ghazni was one of Afghanistan's most strategically important cities. Located along the main highway between Kabul and Kandahar, it had played a pivotal role in Afghan and Asian history. The earliest records of Ghazni noted that it was a Buddhist city in the seventh century. In the first of many sackings, it was conquered by Islamic Arabs and subsequently became the seat of the great Ghaznavid Empire. Under the leadership of Sultan Mahmud, the Ghaznavids became the scourge of central and southern Asia. They conquered territory stretching from Iraq and Iran through Afghanistan, Pakistan, and India, bringing with them a zealous, iconoclastic version of Islam. On dozens of raiding parties into India, Mahmud captured and brought back to Ghazni a celebrated treasure of gold and jewels. The treasure allowed Mahmud to build the citadel and sustained his successors. They were the ones responsible for the hundred-foot towers we had seen earlier. Unfortunately, Ghazni was razed by another tribe, the Ghorids, rebuilt, and razed again by Genghis Khan.

In modern history, Ghazni's fame derived from its role in the Anglo-Afghan wars in the nineteenth century. The impressive fortress on which we stood had blocked the British from advancing on the capital city of Kabul. Its tall ramparts and deep moat looked impregnable; a frontal assault would have been suicidal. Fortunately for the British, a captured Afghan revealed a weakly defended portal on the Kabul side of the citadel. Under cover of night, British sappers destroyed the gate with explosives, and the British fought a pitched battle inside the walls, eventually defeating the Afghan garrison. The hand-to-hand fight at night must have been a gory affair, soaking the dusty ground with blood.

After hearing about Ghazni's fall, the ruler of Afghanistan, Dost Mohammad, asked for surrender terms and later fled into the mountains. Thereafter, the British installed a puppet whose reign was short-lived. As soon as the British troops left Kabul, he was assassinated. Other weak rulers came and went, and civil war plagued Afghanistan through much of the twentieth century. The Soviet tank I stood on was a clear symbol of the tragedy that most living Afghans had endured. It was also, however, a point of Afghan pride. Barely an outline of the Soviet red star remained. I kicked it with my boot, and a few flecks of paint chipped off and settled in the surrounding dust. An echo reverberated inside the tank, hollow and impotent.

We made one last stop, at the tomb of Sultan Mahmud. It was an unpretentious building, cool and refreshing inside. The sarcophagus was carved of a solid block of Afghan marble. The walls featured stunning calligraphy chiseled in marble panels. It was a simple, beautiful tomb for a complicated and violent man.

As we drove away from the tomb, the twelfth-century towers shrunk behind us. The pair had survived countless invasions, insurrections, and earthquakes but still stood tall. Their endurance spoke to something in the Afghan character that was different from our own. Afghans say Americans have all the watches but *they* have all the time.

27

Out of the Frying Pan

Front Towards Enemy.

M18A1 CLAYMORE MINE INSTRUCTIONS

I WAS EAGER FOR OUR PLANNED MOVE TO THE BAT-talion headquarters at Orgun, a relatively safe location in the neighboring province. A change of scenery would be good for everyone in the platoon, including me. After dinner I made my way over to the operations center for our routine evening teleconference with Captain Worthan. With pen and paper in hand, I looked forward to more details about the move there.

In his typical Iowa deadpan, Worthan was abrupt: "Change of plans. We're heading to Shkin. Taking over from Charlie Company."

"When?"

"Two weeks. Practice ambushes. Work on marksmanship. Bring every bullet."

"Roger."

"When you get to Shkin, your platoon's getting another soldier, Private O'Neill. He's good."

"Roger, sir." O'Neill's name was familiar. He had been one of only a handful of soldiers in the company to earn the Expert Infantryman Badge during our training that winter. I put the handset down and turned to Story.

"I guess we won't be finishing that volleyball tournament," he joked.

"Guess not. I had better tell the men. Get 'em together in the tent in fifteen minutes."

"Roger, sir." Story walked out of the room and across the gravel to the chow hall.

I found a seat in the orchard and processed the new information. Captain Worthan's admonition to "bring every bullet" underlined the conditions at Shkin. The epicenter of insurgent violence in Afghanistan, Shkin's reputation was infamous. Just miles from the border with Pakistan, recent clashes had prompted the American military spokesman, Rodney Davis, to declare Shkin the "evilest place in Afghanistan."

My men crowded inside a large tent. I squeezed past Sergeant Huber's large frame and maneuvered to the center of the tent. I envied my soldiers' nonchalance as several skimmed three-month-old *Playboy* magazines. Up until now our combat activity had been restricted to chasing rocket launchers and patrolling uncertain roads. Although nerve-racking enough, we hadn't yet had a single instance of direct fire contact. This would surely change in Shkin.

I had planned to deliver a rousing speech to embolden my men. In my mind I had stitched together inspiring lines from Shakespeare's *Henry V* with gung ho slogans from *Apocalypse Now*. I imagined standing on an ammo crate with my arms on my hips and a cigar clamped loosely in the corner of my mouth. Instead, the inside of my mouth was like sawdust, and I panicked with the realization that somebody else's words wouldn't work. Where was my war face now?

"Can everyone hear?"

Nods of assent.

"Our company is going to relieve Charlie Company."

Barely audible mumbles.

"We're going to Shkin."

You could have heard a grenade pin fall on the floor. In the past month two snipers had been shot and killed in Shkin. A senior platoon sergeant had lost his leg. Another scout had been wounded seriously enough to return home to Fort Drum. The operations center had burned down after an unusually accurate barrage of rockets struck a munitions bunker. We were heading into the lion's den.

EVERYONE IN THE PLATOON digested the news differently. McGurk, my senior squad leader, approached the situation as seriously and professionally as every other mission, but with more urgency. He had friends in the New York City police and fire departments. For him this was an opportunity to do what they couldn't do—take the fight to al-Qaeda. On the other hand, I was ready to prescribe medications for Chuck, my hygienically challenged former Marine and second squad leader. He was more frenetic than ever, pinging me with endless questions about Shkin. My challenge for him and his squad was to ration that energy so there would be reserves when the luster of combat wore off. Grenz, in addition to being a crack shot, was stoic, intelligent, and mature. I could count on him. As a team leader in McGurk's squad, he would be on point for the platoon, at the front of our column. His sober expression belied his twenty-four years. I was sure Story would put O'Neill, the new guy, in Grenz's fire team.

I took my cue from Story. He didn't talk much about his experiences fighting through Kuwait with the Marines in Desert Storm, but his appetite for glory seemed tempered by whatever ghosts still followed him. After propping his boot up on the desk across from my cot and planting another plug of Redman chew in his cheek, he took the news in perfect stride, as if the forces of fate had already predetermined our move to Shkin.

"Worrying never solved nothing, sir."

How did he know I was worried?

"What we can do, you and I, we've got to improve our marksmanship. We've got to be able to beat these fuckers on their own terrain."

He struck the perfect balance between motivational bravado and professionalism. He was already focusing on the fine-tuning the platoon needed in the little time remaining. His composure certainly helped set an example for me as I obscured my fears behind a façade of confidence.

The younger privates had more diverse reactions. Some were genuinely excited. Red and Markam boasted about the damage they would do to al-Qaeda, talking trash as if they were heading into the state football championships rather than a hostile battlefield where soldiers their age had just been killed. Howe said nothing, focusing instead on making sure, as he did every night, that all our radios were loaded with the correct frequencies. I wondered how his new bride would react to the news. She had only just told Howe she was pregnant. Others retreated into their journals and letters, perhaps banishing their fears to paper rather than having their comrades witness their insecurity.

They were a motley crew, but they were *my* motley crew. Since starting with them in Fort Drum, we had spent eight months training and patrolling together. I knew my sergeants' strengths and weaknesses. I knew who would respond to open-ended missions with ingenuity and who needed more specific guidance. I understood which soldiers were ready to step up into leadership roles and which soldiers needed more seasoning. I knew their finances, their families, and their faiths. Most important, I knew how to balance those interpersonal dynamics and build a team that would, I hoped, follow me into a wall of fire without a moment's hesitation.

My part of the contract, the responsibility that came with the privilege of leadership, was never to spend their lives cheaply. I carried the weight of that responsibility on every patrol, yet unlike a rucksack or a Kevlar helmet, I could never slip it off when we came back inside the wire. It was there when I woke up at midnight to check how they were faring in their lonely guard towers. It was there when I walked through their tent that night and when I returned to my cot for a night of restless sleep, turning every hour on a narrow cot. *This* was the price of a salute.

28

Hit the Ground Running

If you're going through Hell, keep going.

WINSTON CHURCHILL

EARLY IN THE MORNING ON SEPTEMBER 26 WE BOARDED our Chinook helicopter. As its twin rotors washed hot air and dust over the platoon, we scurried across the tarmac. The rotor blades whirred yards above the tallest soldier. Nonetheless, we hunched over to avoid an imagined and entirely implausible decapitation. We labored to fit the extra ammunition that Captain Worthan had requested along with our heavy rucksacks. It had been more than two months since my last helicopter trip, and I looked forward to a similar scenic flight over eastern Afghanistan's stunning peaks.

Instead, the pilot flew a gut-wrenching roller-coaster ride a hundred feet off the deck. The great irony of helicopters is that they are safer flying close to the ground. To an insurgent on the ground aiming a rocket-propelled grenade (RPG), the low-flying helicopter presents a faster-moving and, hence, more difficult target. Our helicopter pilot, presumably knowledgeable about the Soviet experience with Stinger-toting mujahideen, hugged the corrugated terrain as closely as aeronautically possible. The technique is called "Nap of the Earth." It has absolutely nothing to do with sleeping.

My stomach dropped from my throat as we touched down at Shkin Firebase. Technically, Shkin was a Forward Operating Base. To the two hundred or so soldiers garrisoned there in 2003, it was a "firebase"—a term lifted from Vietnam. The word conjured up an outpost in hostile territory where soldiers returned from long, dangerous patrols and the night was punctuated with enemy artillery salvos and triggered perimeter flares. The dusty fort where we landed was *definitely* a firebase, as demonstrated by our evasive landing pattern and the proximity of Pakistan's jagged peaks only a stone's throw (or mortar's range) away from our landing zone.

WE HIT THE GROUND and immediately began running. It would be three days before I caught my breath. Captain Worthan was by the landing zone to meet us.

"We had a rocket attack this morning. I'm sending you on patrol in two hours to find the spotter who has been calling in corrections as the rounds land."

So much for small talk. As he escorted me around the firebase, Worthan filled me in on the current situation and the base defense plan. Intelligence indicated that the enemy's so-called Fall Offensive had begun in earnest and would last another ten days. Attacks against the firebase had accelerated, with rocket attacks every day for the past four days. Even more chilling was Worthan's report of an attack on the local police barracks. By the time he had arrived, all that was left were the grotesquely disfigured bodies that the Taliban had decapitated.

Major Nagl had shared only one war story with me at West Point. In the carnage of the first Gulf War, his tank platoon had discovered several dead Iraqi torture victims. Their bodies were striped in progressively darker bands of charred skin from feet to head. Each had been slowly dipped in vats of burning oil. Pure evil. That is how he had described it. He said that sight erased any residual guilt he had about destroying Iraqi tanks. Thinking of the headless corpses in the police station, I now understood what he meant.

Worthan pointed out our mortar positions and the squad there standing by for immediate reaction to incoming fire. Our flank to the south and west was a large gorge as deep as 150 feet in some places. Friendly Afghan militia stood guard along its cliffs in hardened bunkers and lookout towers. Back in his room, Captain Worthan pointed out our base's preplanned targets. If al-Qaeda tried to assault the firebase, our mortarmen would know exactly where to hit them. My task, as Worthan repeatedly emphasized, was to internalize the targets and the perimeter contours. In Shkin, just five miles from Pakistan, I had to know the base defense plan in my gut. If attacked, I would have to react like a boxer, moving my platoon without delay in the middle of the night, under fire. This combat knowledge had to be instinctual, impervious to cognitive fallibility under stress. I observed the small map board tied around Captain Worthan's neck and encased in Plexiglas—he didn't trust his memory either. I jotted down a note to have Howe construct a pair for Story and me.

After walking the perimeter with the commander, I returned to the motor pool, where Story had assembled the platoon for the afternoon patrol. He had already briefed the rest of the platoon on the layout of the firebase, the enemy situation, and the operating quirks of our Humvees. Howe had programmed the radios to the appropriate frequencies, and the trucks were loaded and lined up for departure. Story had already assigned O'Neill, the newest addition to the platoon, to McGurk's squad. He sat with the rest of the squad along the bed of the cargo Humvee, eager to start the mission.

"Welcome to Spearhead Platoon," I said and grabbed his hand. He looked me square in the eyes. They were an unforgettable hue of ice blue, just like my brother Gary's.

"Hooah, sir," O'Neill responded.

"Mount up," I shouted, and I smiled as my driver revved the engine.

"Gator Base, Gator Base. Gator 1-6 leaving the wire for probing patrol, time now."

This was it, our first sortie from the firebase's comforting safety out into Shkin's treacherous backyard. We rumbled through the gate, down into the wadi on the north flank of the firebase, and crawled up onto a trail whose dust compelled us to pull out our time-tested scarves and cover our mouths. My head was on a swivel, my eyes scanning the road for potential bombs.

My mouth was pasty and dry, but inside my shooting gloves, my hands were clammy with sweat. On this first patrol in Shkin, every bush hid an insurgent and every metallic click sounded to me like the initiation of an ambush. I pestered my squad leaders and the gunners to keep their ears and eyes peeled. They needed no encouragement.

"Bravo 0-1, over." Chuck called the checkpoint precisely as he passed it. Behind us, my gunners swiveled in their rooftop perches, shouting observations down to their team leaders in the cab. The radio crackled with information passed between vehicles.

"I've got dead space in the wadi to my left."

"Keep an eye on the compound on that cliff."

By the hundredth patrol in Gardez, they had become more concerned with anticipating bumps than ambushes. Shkin sharpened our focus, maybe too much. I imagined itchy trigger fingers lighting into a goatherd with the full force of an American infantry platoon.

Fortunately, no herd emerged, and our patrol continued for another two hours before we rolled back onto the base with no new intelligence, just frayed nerves and full magazines of ammunition. The most dangerous patrols are the first and the last—the first because you are so keyed up that you're likely to start an unprovoked fight, and the last because routine and habit have dulled your senses. For those of us who had arrived only hours before, it was a relief to have completed our virgin patrol without incident. By my estimate, we would have at least a hundred more.

MUCH LIKE OUR HOME in Gardez, the Shkin firebase centered on a traditional Afghan mud-walled compound leased from a local. Outside the compound was the airfield, the Afghan militia barracks, a few storage huts, and several guard shacks at the entry points in the wire. All included, the firebase was probably the size of five city blocks, although the central compound was only about one hundred yards across. The towers on each corner had been reinforced with sandbags, Plexiglas, and heavy machine guns.

Soldiers reached the inner sanctum through capacious metal gates that could accommodate the extra-wide Humvees. The doors had a typically garish Afghan floral design. Inside, a signpost was planted conspicuously in the dirt. Wooden arrows pointed toward towns I had never heard of: SWARTZ CREEK, MICHIGAN—11,176 KILOMETERS and MOULTRIE, GEORGIA—12,373 KILOMETERS. One arrow pointed straight down: HELL—0 KILOMETERS.

I lumbered through the compound, across the packed gravel, to the operations center. The nerve center of our military operations along the border hummed with sophisticated communications gear. Icons flashed on impressive panel displays. The equipment was eight centuries more advanced than its home in a squat mud-walled room. Imagine putting the NASA mission control center inside a cave.

After a quick debrief with Worthan, I walked by the base-within-a-base compound housing the resident "spooks"—what we termed the special operators in fatigue bottoms and North Face fleeces sporting REI glacial sunglasses and enviable tans. Outside, under an awning, were their souped-up Toyota Hi-Lux pickup trucks, complete with state-of-the-art communications gear and jury-rigged armored protection. Who they worked for, no one knew. If asked, they would respond "OGA"—Other Governmental Agency.

After showering, I found Story and the squad leaders and stood in a line snaking out from our chow hall, another windowless stone structure inside our compound. Dinner was nothing to write home about. There was a stew of mystery meat in the American food containers and a basket of naan bread and a tub of rice on the Afghan menu. Flashing back to Rob's comedy routine at Oxford, I wondered what he would make of this material. I mixed and matched, and joined my men in the dining room which doubled as the TV room. *Old School* was on again. I had seen it twenty times already. With fraternity antics as background noise, we rehashed the day's patrol, and I filled the squad leaders in on the base defense plan and the orientation patrol that Worthan wanted us to go on the next day.

Exhausted by a long day, I wrote a letter to Meena, spent an hour reviewing the latest intelligence reports, and asked the other platoon leaders about their experiences in Shkin to date. As they rattled off terrain features, I struggled to follow along on the small-scale Soviet-era map we were issued. The 1:100,000 scale squeezed a square mile of complicated terrain into a fingernail-sized map square. As I had found out on the first patrol, many ravines weren't even marked on the map.

WE SPENT THE NEXT morning running laps around the perimeter (in body armor, with weapons), inspecting and preparing the vehicles, and rehearsing imagined ambush scenarios. This was the meat-and-potatoes work of a platoon leader in combat: training, planning, and rehearsing—all so that we would be ready when the shit hit the fan. After devouring a big lunch, we were about to depart the firebase with another platoon for an orientation patrol when plans screeched to a halt.

A five-minute barrage of rockets impacted around the firebase. I scrambled to the operations center to see if anyone had picked up where they had come from. Reports from the towers zeroed in on Losano Ridge, barely a half mile into Afghanistan and right under the nose of Pakistani observation posts that dotted every mile along the rugged border. Our big guns, the 105-millimeter howitzer artillery pieces, fired back. As usual, the enemy was two steps ahead of us. By the time our fire missions had been calculated by the fire direction center and transmitted to the cannons, the rocketeers were long gone.

I breathed a sigh of relief when reports from around the firebase confirmed that no one had been hurt in the attack. During our analysis, we determined that the rockets had been progressively more accurate. In contrast, at Gardez the rocket attacks had been very erratic, and the launchers' sophistication involved little more than propping rockets up on stones. This attack was more like a fire mission that an American platoon leader might call, bracketing a target in successively smaller increments, zeroing in the artillery by indicating from a forward position whether rounds were short, long, wide right, or wide left. We concluded that there was probably an enemy forward observer directing the rocketeers from somewhere in the hills west of the firebase.

We scrapped the reconnaissance patrol, and Captain Worthan and I sketched a plan to ambush the enemy forward observer as he approached his observation post, probably in the early morning hours. That afternoon I sat with Story, Adams, and McGurk for three hours planning the ambush. Back and forth we debated each point of the plan, improving it with each iteration. Afterward, we rehearsed with the whole platoon and then got two precious hours of sleep.

THERE WERE MORE SHADOWS than soldiers as my men gathered for the mission. It was after midnight and shards of light from a sickle moon broke across their sharply angled noses and clamped lips. My mind flashed to the frigid mountains of northern Georgia, where as a Ranger student Gunny Oakes had taught me how to ambush Cortinians. Back then, before 9/11, I had never expected to apply those lessons. Now, patrolling new ridges in the night, I was glad I had recycled the Mountain phase. I had gotten twice the practice. One by one I inspected the patrol, following the checklist scorched in my memory by Ranger School.

Shiny metal. Cover it with black electrical tape.

Shake the canteens. Fill them to avoid sloshing water.

Ammunition magazines. Press the last bullets against the spring to see if they are full.

Batteries. Flick night vision devices on and off.

Weapons. Cleanliness. Laser-aiming devices. Safety switched on.

Radios. I can hear my squad leaders. They can hear me. Fresh batteries. Frequencies.

Body armor. Check for ceramic plates. Heavy but essential.

Medical. First aid pouches. Evacuation plan. Succession of command if I fall.

Extras. Smoke canisters. Flares, whistles. Infrared chemical light
sticks. Grenades.
The Plan. Checkpoints. Passwords. Timeline.

Two hands slapped my calf as I passed through the wire and whispered
through the handset. Story and the medic counted every soldier as they
passed and fanned out into a rehearsed wedge formation.

"1-6, this is 1-7. All up." Story confirmed that all were accounted for.

We skirted between and behind the small hills on the western flank of
the firebase. The moon was still low on the horizon as we moved through
the dark. The night vision device mounted on my helmet pressed against
my face. I warmed up quickly, and sweat moistened my T-shirt under the
body armor and small patrol pack. Apart from the periodic whispers of
Howe calling in checkpoints, the only sound was boot soles rolling across
gravel and sand.

We stopped short of our planned ambush location and formed a small
cigar-shaped perimeter. McGurk and Chuck met Story and me in the center of the perimeter. Our position was far enough away from the ambush
site to be out of earshot, but we still whispered to one another as we planned
a small reconnaissance of the objective. A few minutes later I crept forward
with McGurk, Chuck, Howe, and one of the snipers attached to our patrol.
After pinpointing the wadi we wanted to overwatch, we identified a hill to
our right where the snipers could gain a better vantage point with their
powerful scopes. I pointed out a large outcropping of stone where I would
position myself between my two squads. I determined the left and right
boundaries of the ambush, and McGurk recommended a position for the
machine-gun team.

Returning to the rest of the platoon, McGurk and Chuck quickly relayed the plan to their squads. They placed each man on the ambush line,
carefully spaced apart and concealed in the tiny ground wrinkles that
infantrymen know so well. My sniper team flashed an infrared signal to
identify their position to the platoon. I placed my smoke grenades and

flares next to me and called in to the operations center: "Gator 1-6 in position. Time 0340." And then we waited.

And waited.

And waited some more.

Warm sweat slowly cooled against my skin. By 5 a.m., I was shivering. Chuck, McGurk, and the snipers called in every thirty minutes to confirm that their men were still awake. The high desert air grew colder and colder as the night approached dawn. By 6 a.m. even New Hampshire native Howe remarked that it was "as cold as a witch's tit in a brass bra." As the sky slowly blossomed pink above the border mountains behind us, I lifted off my night vision goggles as the sun cast its first long shadows over our position.

I poised myself to initiate the ambush if necessary. Nerves steeled, I was ready for my first real ambush.

On a herd of goats.

Creeping across the wadi floor was a lone shepherd, at most seven years old, and thirty scraggly, mottled goats. I held my fire.

We waited another hour as the ground warmed, and then we patrolled the 150-foot-deep wadi adjacent to our base. The sun climbed higher, thawing us out as we walked. McGurk's squad picked its way down into the wadi single file. Chuck looked crestfallen as his squad passed my position. He was so eager to test his combat leadership that the familiar sequence of escalating anticipation and deflation was taking its toll.

"Chuck," I whispered, "stay focused."

We leapfrogged along the wadi, me on the high ground with Chuck's squad and the snipers, Story in the low ground with McGurk's squad and the machine-gun team. We would creep forward, establish an overwatch position, and then we'd cover McGurk as his squad cleared the low ground. After a quarter mile, steep terrain forced us into the wadi with McGurk. Fifteen-story walls on either side of the dry riverbed dwarfed us. Only an hour before, we had been in an ambush position above the wadi. Now, who was watching us?

After a nerve-racking hour snaking through the ravine, we finally stumbled through the gap in the concertina wire. Immediately, packs dropped, helmets clunked off the ground, and shorn scalps steamed as canteens emptied over my soldiers' heads. No sooner had we reached the compound, ready to sleep, than a telltale screech advertised another rocket explosion. "Goddam," I muttered under my breath as I donned my body armor and helmet and sprinted on weary legs to the operations center. Over the next couple of minutes, seven rockets burst harmlessly around the perimeter. We had been played.

In the last twenty-four hours we had survived two rocket attacks, conducted one Humvee patrol, and set an overnight ambush. Not a bad day's work on two hours' sleep. I urged my men to get some rest while they could before I collapsed fully clothed on top of my sleeping bag.

Five hours later I emerged to eat a hasty dinner and analyze the map with Story, McGurk, and Chuck. If we were going to fight, it would most likely take place on the jagged border to our east. The firebase had absorbed rocket attacks for six days straight, and each attack had originated from ridges on the Pakistani border. The next day Captain Worthan was sending another platoon to an over-watch position near the border to deter a rocket attack while our firebase was being resupplied by Chinook helicopters. Captain Worthan was giving our platoon a day to catch our breath. In the morning we would unload the helicopters. Other than that, our main responsibility was to keep our gear ready in case something happened to the other platoon. I looked forward to an easy day—reading mail, spending some down time with the guys, and developing a training agenda.

I couldn't have been more wrong.

29

The Unforgiving Minute

My limbs sink, my mouth is parched, my body trembles, the hair bristles on my flesh. The magic bow slips from my hand, my skin burns, I cannot stand still. My mind reels.

ARJUNA TO LORD KRISHNA,
The Bhagavad-Gita

PRIVATE HOWE RAN INTO THE GYM, PANTING BREATH-lessly. His report came between gulps of oxygen. "Second Platoon." Breath. "Under fire." Breath. "Losano Ridge." I sprinted to the operations center, ducked through a five-foot portal, and twisted past the lawn chairs in front of computer terminals. The room was abuzz with activity. Dry erase markers scribbled friendly and enemy positions in green and red. Large protractors plotted ranges for mortars and howitzers; target descriptions crackled over the radio. Hot coffee splattered my sleeve as I jostled for elbow room in the suddenly overcrowded cave.

Major Paul Wille, the battalion operations officer and the senior officer at Shkin, barked at specialists and privates who moved too slowly in response to his orders. A graduate of the Army's elite School for Advanced Military Studies, his grasp of military operations was impressive. He had developed much of the large Anaconda operation in 2002 as a division planner. In his spare time he read military history. Unfortunately for us, he reserved patience only for books. Every forty-five seconds he would emit a much-caricatured "Goddaaaaammit." His eyes glowered beneath the brow of his oversized head, crowned with a crewcut of red hair marred by gouges he had inflicted as his own barber. I always looked to

Major Wille's cheeks as an honest barometer of current conditions. At the moment their ruddy hue was a bad sign.

Captain Worthan grabbed my shoulder and updated me. "Second Platoon has been taking fire from Losano Ridge. They took a couple of casualties, but things are under control now. They've been hammering the ridge with artillery and mortars. You're going to clear the area where they think the fire is coming from to see if anyone survived our artillery barrage."

I tried in vain to follow my map as he spoke.

"Any questions?"

I didn't even know where to start.

STORY, MCGURK, AND CHUCK hustled the platoon from their video games and headphones. The motor pool where the Humvees lined up resembled a NASCAR pit stop. MRE boxes were chucked from trunks and replaced with additional ammo. Sergeants harangued privates who had forgotten kneepads or had emptied their canteens since the morning inspection. Drivers scurried between tires and surfaced from hoods with grease and oil smearing their faces. Howe was busy confirming radio frequencies and checking batteries. The heavy machine gunners in the Humvee turrets tightened the lashes securing their ammunition boxes.

I jumped in behind Chuck in the lead vehicle. I leaned out the window and counted two more armored Humvees and the flatbed Humvee, crammed with nearly a dozen soldiers from McGurk's squad. Captain Worthan's Humvee with its "antenna farm" of radio operators raced through the big compound gates and joined the middle of the convoy as we bucked and braced down a switchback slope into the wadi leading toward Shkin Bazaar.

The four miles to Shkin Bazaar took us over an hour to cover in our rugged trucks. A brisk walk would have been faster. It took almost another hour to move the last three miles to Second Platoon's position high on a plateau overlooking Losano Ridge and the Pakistani border. I fanned out my vehicles along the bluff and joined Captain Worthan looking for Thompson, Second Platoon's lieutenant. We found him kneeling behind the armored door of his Humvee. While pointing out suspected enemy positions, he was as calm as if he were pointing out gopher holes in his backyard.

I faced east over the bluff toward the border with Pakistan. I scanned the vista with fresh eyes, looking for landmarks that matched my map. The two-dimensional representation disappointed yet again. Not five feet in front of our position was a ten-story drop-off and a wadi the width of three football fields rising on the other side to Losano Ridge. Another wadi lay behind Losano Ridge, and beyond it the hills climbed steeply another two thousand feet to a jagged mountain range inside Pakistan. The map represented all of that with a few squiggly contour lines, hardly the topographic information necessary to move vehicles and dismounted troops through unfamiliar hostile terrain. Gee-whiz technology allowed me to put a bomb through a chimney if I wanted, but did little to get me to the objective in the first place. The map did indicate our altitude, though. On the bluff we stood at 7,100 feet, a mile and a half above sea level. Walking hills with fifty pounds of gear at that altitude, in hot weather, would have been a challenge even under peaceful circumstances.

I asked Thompson where the border with Pakistan was.

"Your guess is as good as mine. We're in Afghanistan now. Losano Ridge is in Afghanistan. Those observation posts up on the higher ridge behind Losano are in Pakistan. The border is somewhere in between."

In front of me, a track barely wide enough for a Humvee tripped down the side of the escarpment and continued up the spine of Losano Ridge. Thompson pointed out the smoldering ruins atop Losano Ridge where the enemy had launched its mortars at his platoon earlier that day. Losano Ridge, named after an American airman who was killed in action there only five months earlier, looked like a Louisville Slugger. To the south was the handle, the only point where vehicles could start the ascent north toward the thicker, higher part of the bat. The ridge ended abruptly after a mile on a bald knob of gravel one hundred yards across. Along the ridge's thick brow, a trail slalomed between boulders and four-foot scrub pines. I kicked a few loose pebbles across the withered grass and over the ledge.

Thompson, Worthan, and I hashed out a plan. My platoon would clear across the ridge to be sure there were no more fighters remaining on Losano. To minimize the risk to the convoy from a roadside bomb blast, I would space my Humvees one hundred feet apart as we drove along Losano's spine. To protect my flank I would send Story with McGurk and his squad through the wadi between Losano and the Pakistani border. I would move the Humvees along the ridge, set in position, and then cover the guys on foot as they moved parallel to us in the wadi. Six or eight leaps like that and we'd clear the ridge and the wadi. Captain Worthan's antenna farm and another squad would follow behind. We identified the bald spot at the end of Losano in the north as our best available medevac landing zone. Gunny Oakes at Ranger School had at least taught me not to forget that.

We needed to move quickly. I doubted that any enemy would have remained after the repeated artillery barrages and helicopter gun runs earlier that afternoon. We had four hours of daylight left to find out. By nightfall we were certain our adversaries would be back across the border, where Pakistan appeared to grant tacit sanctuary.

HUMVEES BARRELED PAST AT forty miles an hour, jostling the turret gunners like rag dolls. I jabbed Chuck's shoulder and squeezed the top of Markam's boot as I yelled up the turret: "Hang on up there!" Through the haze of dust behind us I counted four more Humvees. I recalled the motivational videos that West Point screened before lectures. To the thunder of AC/DC's "Big Guns," a host of Abrams tanks had crested sand dunes and fired salvo after salvo from their turrets. A thousand cadets cheered. A column of Humvees had just a fraction of a tank's firepower, but I felt as if I were living inside a video reel.

As we drove toward Losano Ridge, Thompson called in a mortar mission over the company radio frequency, requesting a smoke round where he had seen movement to the east. The smoke would help the Apache attack helicopters circling above us identify the suspected area before flying in to check things out. A plume of gray smoke preceded the sound of impact by a fraction of a second.

As often happens with artillery and mortar fire, the round landed far from where Thompson had intended. When Captain Worthan learned that the round had wounded three enemy fighters he ordered the mortars to repeat the mission and to "fire for effect." The technical command understated what was about to happen. Every mortar tube fired several bass drum volleys of high-explosive ammunition on identical trajectories. *Whooomp. Whooomp. Whooomp.* The concussions reverberated in my chest. An indeterminate hill between Losano Ridge and Pakistan erupted as nearly a dozen mortar rounds fell in a tight cluster over the next couple of minutes. Whereas the first mortar round had been luck, these rounds were dead-on, literally.

While the concussive explosions reverberated across the hills, the Apache helicopters approached in tandem for a closer view, drawing fire from below. Buzzing above me like a giant dragonfly, the lead helicopter rolled off to the south with amazing dexterity. The trail helicopter, sharing the call sign "Widow-Maker," opened fire with its chain gun and splintering 2.75-inch rockets.

"Fuuuucccccckkkk yeaaaaaahhhh!" Markam shared his delight at the rippling explosions, no doubt shaking his fist in the rattling turret above me.

The helicopters circled in again for the kill, but their prey was already dead. Our mortars had killed a half-dozen enemy fighters and destroyed their own 82-millimeter mortar system. It looked as though we had just destroyed the enemy that my platoon was looking for along Losano Ridge and in the wadi. I smiled from ear to ear. Mission accomplished.

Nevertheless, over the radio Captain Worthan ordered us to complete the sweep as planned. McGurk's squad, augmented with a three-man machine-gun team and Story, tumbled out of the flatbed Humvee, brushed off a quarter inch of dust, and moved down into the wadi on the far side of Losano Ridge. I tapped knuckled fists with Story and wished him luck.

By the time my Humvees reached the northern limit of Losano Ridge and parked in a semicircle facing Pakistan, it was already dusk. Captain Worthan's party was making its way back up the slope to our position. All eyes were focused on McGurk's squad as they finished their wadi sweep. Once they covered another football field of terrain, they would hike up the steep flank, join us on top, and pile into the Humvees. We would all then return to the base for a shower and hot chow. They began clearing the last set of ruins below, looking like ants eating a graham cracker. Markam handed me the binoculars and I took a closer look. McGurk knelt in the center of the compound. I grabbed my radio handset.

"What you got?"

McGurk was always precise. "Fresh footprints, probably Converse. Some candy wrappers, looks like Snickers. And what looks like recently burned wood."

"Where do the footprints lead?"

"Toward the right, away from this hill to my front and toward the Pak observation post. The footprint trail might be a trap. I'm going to send Grenz's fire team up the hill in front of us instead."

Grenz's fire team of four advanced in a wedge up the small hill. There were three distinct rises, each with a short drop-off before rising to the next, slightly higher rise. As Grenz crested the last rise, a burst of gunfire snapped the silence.

Grenz surprised three Taliban who were crouched underneath a scrub pine fifteen feet in front of him. One gripped a double-handled detonator. Grenz leveled his rifle and shot all three—killing one and seriously wounding the others. From where I stood I couldn't tell any of that, of course. All I observed were the consequences: We had hit a wasp's nest with a baseball bat.

Suddenly, the entire border flashed like camera bulbs at a concert. A cacophony of fire from heavy machine guns, rifles, antiaircraft guns, and rocket-propelled grenades signified a coordinated ambush. Behind me, Captain Worthan and the antenna farm bounded down the slope toward McGurk.

What do we do now, sir?

This was the minute all of my training had prepared me for. As rounds whipsawed past me and spit up gravel, I had to decide whether to follow Worthan down the hill into the ambush or to stand my ground and coordinate the Humvees' heavy machine-gun fire. By doctrine I needed to be wherever I could best influence the fight. *But where was that?*

As I stood, a trio of bullets ricocheted off the adjacent Humvee. I pivoted back toward the Humvee. I would make my stand on Losano Ridge. That decision, made in seconds, would later replay in my head a thousand times.

"I can't see anything!" I bellowed at Chuck. "Where's McGurk's squad?"

"Right between us and those muzzle flashes." Buzzing small-arms fire interrupted Chuck's reply.

"Get the Mark-19s on the flashes. Cease fire with the .50 cals. I don't want any low rounds to hit our guys." I had to shout just to be heard above the din.

Chuck coordinated his gunners' fire over the vehicle radio, stepped out of the Humvee, and motioned with his hands where he wanted the two grenade launchers to split the target area. The reassuring *thumpity-thump-thump* of the Mark-19s was quickly followed by the detonation of their 40-millimeter grenades landing eight hundred yards away.

I hefted the Humvee door open and took three long strides to a small tree. I had to get in a better position to see down into the wadi and identify where the incoming fire was originating. Howe followed with the radio on his back. Kneeling down, I grabbed the handset. The first words I heard sent an icy chill down my spine.

"We've got a KIA. O'Neill's KIA."

No way. My knuckles turned white strangling the handset. *No fucking way.* McGurk repeated the status report. I stared at the radio in disbelief. *This isn't happening.* Small-caliber rounds dented the Humvees around me, but it was strangely silent, as if someone had pressed the mute button.

O'Neill had been with the platoon only a few days. We'd shared only a handshake, and yet now I was responsible for his death. All I could remember were those eyes—glacial blue, like my brother's. *There's no way O'Neill's dead.* This wasn't a game or an exercise or a movie; these were real soldiers with real blood and real families waiting back home. *What had I done wrong? Who's next? McGurk? Story? Me?*

Bullets snapped through the air, but the muzzle flashes were harder to isolate. I had my gunners lob dozens of grenades at the spark of every enemy muzzle they saw. Still, the distinct hammering of enemy machine guns and the cracks of sniper fire remained. My men in the wadi were firing everything they had. Although I had a rifle, I couldn't pick out targets that wouldn't risk hitting my own men below me. The only weapon of any use was the radio. It became my eyes and ears as well as my voice. I pieced together what had happened to O'Neill from the radio traffic among Grenz, McGurk, Story, and Worthan.

Grenz had moved under withering fire, recovered O'Neill's exposed body, and moved him to a sheltered position down the slope. O'Neill had been shot three times below the body armor, shearing a main artery. A medic and McGurk dressed the wound in vain, but O'Neill had already hemorrhaged too much blood. That is when McGurk had reported him KIA.

"I need a litter team down here ASAP!" screamed Story over the radio. He wanted to move O'Neill back up the hill for evacuation by medevac helicopter. If we got him to the doctors fast enough, maybe it wouldn't be too late.

Behind me, the whine of worn-out brakes made me turn my head around quickly. Chuck maneuvered his Humvees to positions offering better fields of fire. His long experience with heavy weapons in the Marine Corps was proving valuable. Below, Grenz dodged RPGs to get hold of a radio and started marking enemy positions with smoke rounds from his grenade launcher. A shower of hot brass casings tumbled like quarters off the side of a nearby Humvee as Markam fired five-second bursts of the .50 cal at Grenz's marks. Markam was a master—timing the length of his bursts to balance firepower and accuracy. The rounds ripped along the border, shattering trees into showers of thick splinters. Even at a range of a mile and a half, a .50-caliber bullet hit with the force of a .44 Magnum at point-blank range.

Story was back on the radio, angry. "I need that litter team! Where are they?"

Running at a crouch between Humvees, I grabbed every soldier on the hill who wasn't firing a heavy machine gun or driving. I sent three down the steep slope toward the sheltered position where O'Neill had been moved. They skidded down the slope like their boots were on fire. Rounds kicked up dirt around them as they slalomed to avoid enemy fire.

LaCamera used to say, "No one pays to watch a one-ball juggler." Well, if combat was a circus, I was in the center ring juggling a dozen flaming torches, piecing together fragments from three radio frequencies, coordinating a half-dozen weapons systems, and dodging the rounds ricocheting off Humvee doors and furrowing the dirt near my position. It was loud and chaotic, and I wanted to piss in my boots, which was exactly how LoFaro had described combat to me in Normandy five years before. And just as he said it would, the sense of confusion dissipated as I gained my bearings. Confidence replaced dread. Eventually, incoming fire slowed. For the second time that afternoon the battle looked as if it were over. It seemed as though we had been fighting for hours, but when I glanced at my watch, I realized fewer than twenty minutes had elapsed since Grenz triggered the enemy ambush.

The familiar buzz of helicopter rotors grew louder as the silhouettes of two Apaches skimmed in our direction. They banked in tandem toward the suspected targets, and the border lit up in sparks of enemy muzzle fire. I crouched near a shrub on the edge of Losano Ridge with Chuck and Howe as the Apaches fired their chain guns. A host of smoke and sparks blasted toward our position from the east.

"RPG! Get down!" Chuck screamed while diving to the ground.

Howe and I dove in unison as a whistle introduced a loud thud in the gravel ten feet away from us. The explosion was muffled.

"You all right, Howe? Chuck?"

"I'm good. You, sir?" Howe responded with a startled look on his face as though he had seen his own ghost. Chuck was dirtier than normal but otherwise unscathed.

"Yeah, I'm fine." I ran my hand over my uniform to be sure.

I smiled at our luck. I thought Chuck had been mistaken in his identification. The whistle sounded a lot more like a mortar round than a rocket-propelled grenade. Whatever it was, it had exploded into the earth, showering us with harmless dirt instead of jagged hot shrapnel. Meanwhile, explosions continued to perforate the ground near my men below.

Chuck interjected, "Sir, those rounds are being fired from the Pak OP."

"Are you positive?"

Damn. Plumes of smoke trailed from the Pakistani observation post as grenades screamed toward McGurk below. Action steadied my nerves. I raised the radio handset to my mouth and called the artillery battery. I read off the grid coordinates—two letters and eight numbers—enough to level our ally's observation post. I understood now what it meant to kill or be killed.

Minutes later the first tree-shredding explosion missed the observation post by two hundred yards. I quickly called in a correction over the radio.

"*Cease fire! Cease fire!*" Captain Worthan's voice was distinct and loud over the radio.

My frustration was barely veiled as I explained what I had just seen with my own eyes.

"I know. You gotta trust me on this."

"Roger," I muttered indignantly.

I bit my lip to prevent my rage from finding insubordinate expression over the radio and began moving between Humvees, helping to identify targets with tracer fire from my rifle. One of the Apaches broke from the tandem back toward the north to find and escort the medevac helicopter to our position. As the Apache banked above us, I could see the holes where enemy fire had riddled its fuselage like a colander.

Meanwhile, Captain Worthan ordered the mortars to fire burning white phosphorous rounds on an area where Grenz had identified movement to the east. The initial round landed a hundred yards away from the intended target, but nevertheless wounded another three enemy fighters. For the second time in one day, errant mortars had been lucky. Chance, apparently, worked both ways. Three repeat missions silenced the enemy position, killing another seven, including a senior al-Qaeda commander in the Shkin area.

The subsequent lull in enemy fire allowed the casualty evacuation team to make faster progress up the steep slope. Four men moved O'Neill the length of five football fields in order to reach the top of Losano. One of the privates who had carried O'Neill up the hill approached me. His uniform was stained with blood. A grimace accented by the pallor of his cheeks had replaced his grin. He looked as if he had aged twenty years when he looked down at me.

"I am leaving after my contract is up."

He delivered his verdict straight-faced, without a trace of cynicism. His resignation struck me between the shoulder blades. My men were no longer bulletproof. Neither was I.

I marked the landing zone for the helicopter with smoke grenades and talked the pilot toward our position. As the helicopter flared to land, the rotors pulsed hot air over the entire ridge, enveloping us in a storm of dust. Just as it set its skids on the ground, a half-dozen rocket-propelled grenades whined through the air. The medevac pulled off hastily as the third firefight of the day erupted from a two-mile arc along the border. *Could this get any worse?*

There was so much lead coming our way that it was hard to tell where the fire wasn't coming from. Five Humvees churned in unison, unloading a small arsenal of munitions at what we believed were at least thirty enemy positions. Every round fired from the border had our address. The temptation of knocking an American helicopter out of the sky must have been irresistible. Fortunately, the helicopter was able to pull off without suffering severe damage from the surface-to-air attack, although it hadn't been on the ground long enough to get O'Neill.

The combined fire of my Humvees allowed the medevac to remain in a holding pattern to the west. The Apaches began lighting up the area, strafing the border with rockets, Hellfire missiles, and machine-gun fire. Dozens of enemy fighters fled toward Pakistan, only to be mowed down like stalks of grass by the Apaches.

"I've got two A-10s inbound in thirty seconds!" Worthan was practically cheering over the radio as the Air Force jets approached.

The A-10 is the infantryman's best friend in the Air Force. Designed specifically to support ground troops under fire, the twin-engine jet can carry an assortment of five-hundred-pound and two-thousand-pound bombs. Its seven-barrel Gatling gun fires nearly four thousand rounds per minute of powerful 30-millimeter ammunition large enough to slice tree trunks in half.

There was so much dust and smoke to the east that no one on the ground could properly identify targets for the jets. This was Clausewitz's "fog of war," all right. In a stroke of brilliance, Worthan improvised, turning over control of the A-10s to the Apache pilots, who presumably had a better view of the target area. The coordinated dance of the helicopters and jets was beautiful to watch. The Apaches dodged heavy ground fire, marked their targets, and exited stage right so that the A-10s had a clear line of fire. The ground shuddered as smoke puffs lined the entire ridge. The sound of the Gatling guns reached our ears a half second later. Unlike our machine guns, the seven-barrel Gatling guns spun so fast that you couldn't make out the sound of individual rounds. It sounded like a wood chipper grinding thick logs. In an eight-second burst of fire, the pair of A-10s unloaded one thousand rounds on the ridge. The earth boiled with explosions. Two passes silenced every gun aimed at us.

Dusk had fallen before the attack on the medevac helicopter had taken place, and it was rapidly growing dark. We still needed to get O'Neill to the field hospital fifty miles away, although, by now it was far too late. The helicopter returned without resistance this time. Less than a minute after touching down, the medevac lifted off with O'Neill and sped to the north, escorted by the two Apaches. As the helicopters disappeared in the distance,

I regretted that I hadn't seen O'Neill's face before he left. He was gone, and I would never be able to apologize.

We wanted to get off the ridge before dark and had half an hour to consolidate all the troops on Losano Ridge before driving back to the fire-base. As McGurk's squad moved back up the ridge, Grenz found his way to the dead fighter who had held the detonation device in his hand. He looked to see what it was connected to. He led his team, now one man down, toward the Humvees, following a wire only superficially buried. Upon reaching the top of Losano Ridge, he traced the wire to an antitank mine buried five feet away from my Humvee.

Holy shit. The realization suddenly hit me. McGurk's squad hadn't been the object of the initial ambush earlier in the afternoon—our vehicles were the target. A mine designed to destroy a Soviet tank would have lifted our up-armored Humvee off the ground and killed all five soldiers inside. In fact, when we later returned to Losano Ridge, we found not one but *five* antitank mines, daisy-chained together so that one initiator could blow five Humvees to little chunks of scrap metal. Captain Worthan surmised that the ambush they had planned was even more complex. Perhaps, he said, the plan had been to force an American casualty in the wadi and then trigger all five mines on top of Losano Ridge as the medevac helicopter arrived in a spectacular, deadly explosion. In any case, Grenz's quick thinking had saved us all.

NIGHT FELL. WE LOADED up the Humvees and made slow progress down Losano Ridge and back toward the base. An hour later our fleet of vehicles pulled into the motor pool as if we had completed any other routine mission. Drivers backed the Humvees into their parking spaces so they would be ready to go at a moment's notice. Soldiers began shuffling back into the compound. Amid otherwise subdued voices rang one command: "Alpha Company. Fall in around me."

Soldiers hurried back to the motor pool. Covered in blood and dust, the company clustered together in front of First Sergeant Woodworth, the senior sergeant in Alpha Company. He began the company roll call.

"Adams, Howard."

"Present."

"Grenz, Allen Scott."

"Present."

He continued in the same even tone through the first half of the alphabet, including McGurk and Mullaney in the M section.

"O'Neill."

No answer.

"Evan W. O'Neill."

A long pause without an answer.

"Private First Class Evan W. O'Neill. Second Squad, First Platoon, Alpha Company."

A minute later Story responded according to custom.

"Private O'Neill is no longer with us."

Tears welled in my eyes. There were few dry eyes around the company, although all strained to hold the tears back until safe in their sleeping bags. I should have tempered my grief with some satisfaction from the mission. Headquarters estimated that we had killed more than sixty al-Qaeda and Taliban fighters. The platoon had fought its first sustained firefight with impressive skill on unfamiliar terrain. My men had run into walls of lead and repelled multiple ambushes. Right now, none of that mattered. With my head hung low, I stumbled back to my cot. I tossed my helmet onto a pile of clothes in the corner and draped my webbed vest on a hook in the wall. My bones ached from exhaustion as I unlaced my left boot. I reached to unlace the other boot, but my fingers wouldn't obey, making it impossible to undo the tight knot of nylon cord. I shivered slowly.

I slipped my journal from under my pillow and opened to a fresh page. Tears fell as I wrote, smudging my confession. *I lost a soldier today. I barely knew him, but I was responsible for him.* His parents had entrusted me with his life, and I failed.

No excuse, sir.

Taps

There will be time, there will be time,
To prepare a face to meet the faces that you meet
There will be time to murder and create,
And time for all the works and days of hands
That lift and drop a question on your plate;
Time for you and time for me,
And time yet for a hundred indecisions,
And for a hundred visions and revisions.

T. S. ELIOT, "The Love Song of J. Alfred Prufrock"

I AWOKE THE NEXT DAY IN THE LATE MORNING. FOR a minute, I believed my memory of Losano Ridge had been a nightmare—imagined, reversible. My body told me otherwise. I was exhausted even after twelve hours of uninterrupted sleep, and my muscles ached fiercely. I still had my right boot on, and my journal was open to a tear-smudged page.

I took a long shower. Alone in the bathhouse, I washed away the crust of dust and sweat caking my scalp, changed into a fresh set of fatigues, and shaved. As I looked in the mirror, I forced a serious, unshaken composure. Be the tough leader. That's what I had been taught at West Point, in the Shakespeare verses we memorized. "Yet, in reason, no man should possess him with any appearance of fear, lest he, by showing it, should dishearten the army." I laced my boots up tightly and bloused my pant cuffs around the top. Okay, I said to myself, time to face the platoon. No tears.

As I walked across the compound from the chow hall, I caught my breath. Against the mud wall of a building were two boots, a rifle bayoneted into the ground, and a wide-brimmed camouflage hat with the distinctive chevron and rocker of Private First Class Evan William O'Neill. O'Neill's dog tags hung from the trigger well of the rifle, a morbid wind chime in the breeze. I clutched my own tags beneath my shirt and shut my eyes.

Someone had left a folding chair in front. I sat down, propped my elbows on my knees, and gripped my ears as I sunk my head and sobbed. I closed my eyes and said the Our Father. But where was my father now? Who was going to tell me I had done my duty? What would he have done in *my* boots? He never answered my letter. Did he even care anymore what happened to me? Would he be there, like O'Neill's father, to accept my casket?

"Sir," said McGurk, standing behind me.

No tears, I reminded myself, and put my sunglasses on. "I was just on my way to your hooch. I'll walk with you."

We ducked into the low-lit room. Grenz was leaning back against the wall, staring at nothing at all. I wanted to find something inspirational to say. If I could say it, maybe I could believe it myself. There were no words. I wasn't a coach at halftime in a losing game. This dejection was so much more complete. Everyone, including me, wanted to end the game; it wasn't fun anymore. We had all lost that cocky sense of invincibility. I said nothing and sat down on a cot. It was better to be with my men than alone. We grieved together silently. Under our helmets and armor, we were still men.

Later that afternoon a helicopter arrived with a chaplain and a pair of psychiatrists from division headquarters. Story and I were asked to join McGurk's squad and the team that had carried O'Neill to the helicopter. I was skeptical of the shrinks. What did they know about what we had just been through? The psychiatrists introduced themselves to the group and explained their backgrounds. Both had been in combat themselves. They reassured us that they didn't think we were crazy. They asked me to reconstruct the day's events.

There was so much I couldn't retrieve from my memory. McGurk interrupted to recall what had happened beyond my blurry vision in the wadi below. Grenz argued with McGurk although they had been barely twenty feet apart for most of the fight. Story sat as silent as a stone, clearly perturbed to be there at all. After an hour and a half of debate and discussion, I was more confused than before. What were facts to me conflicted with the certainty of others' recollections. Distances and directions were jumbled. The sequence was out of order. Time was elastic: Some experienced events happening in a blink, whereas others experienced a sense of excruciating slow motion. The only thing that was clear was that none of us had been in the same battle.

At some point the tone of the discussion changed. Slowly, McGurk's men expressed their anger, frustration, and fear.

"Why were we being shot at from the Pakistani observation post?"

"Why couldn't we shoot back?"

"I was scared at first," said one soldier, "when I couldn't tell where we were being shot from."

Heads nodded in agreement. I was surprised. I assumed I was the only one who had been terrified.

The litter team talked about how hard it was to move O'Neill up the hill, how someone had to hold on to his bloody uniform in order to keep him from sliding off the litter. McGurk blamed himself for not being able to stop the bleeding. Grenz was angry because he had left O'Neill on an exposed flank. He thought he had let his guard down toward the end of the sweep. According to Grenz, before O'Neill went unconscious from his wounds, his last words were a question: "Is everybody else okay?"

Everyone had tearstains on their cheeks, including Story and me. So much for no tears. On this day what my men needed most was compassion. Our session ended with the shuffle of boots outside announcing dinner. The psychiatrists asked me to stay. "Keep them talking," they reminded me. "You are each other's strongest support system."

They were right. Who else were they going to share their fears with? Yet I thought to myself, "Who am *I* going to talk to?" Leadership was a damned lonely place. Talking about fear just wasn't something leaders did, especially with the men they were trying to lead. Who would want to follow a petrified jumpmaster out of an aircraft? Who would want a guide who was himself lost? But I had to talk to someone or I was going to fold. There was too much to keep inside.

The counseling session left me deeply conflicted. On one hand, the tears and anger of my men troubled me. They hurt badly. They were shaken hard by O'Neill's death and the conclusion that his loss meant they had failed in their first test of combat. No matter how many dozen enemy we killed, the only statistic that mattered in their calculations and mine was the one KIA on our side. I weighed their combined sufferings on one scale with nothing to counterbalance it. I wondered whether I would be able to pull the team together for the missions left on our docket.

On the other hand, knowing that my men shared my self-doubt, fear, and anxiety about our remaining weeks at Shkin made it less isolating. They cried, too. And I was relieved in a way to know that they saw how hard O'Neill's death had hit me. They knew I cared. I hoped they knew how far I would go to protect them, even as they comprehended the limits of that protection.

THE NEXT DAY, CHAIRS formed neat rows in front of Evan's display. I had a seat next to the podium, facing the crowd. There was no chatter, not even the usual greetings between soldiers. I read the memorial pamphlet over and over again, but my eyes kept returning to the photo of O'Neill in full battle gear. It was recent. I bowed my head so that my red eyes were less obvious. I wiped them with my sleeve, making it look as if I was mopping a runny nose.

I stood and read from the Gospel of John: "Greater love has no man than this, to lay down his life for his friends." I tried to read more but couldn't. I choked up but bit my lower lip hard and sat down without shedding a tear. First Sergeant Woodworth repeated the roll call. One by one we stood to attention. At "O'Neill. Evan W. O'Neill," I swallowed hard. We turned to face seven soldiers standing above us on the western parapet. *Crack. Crack. Crack.* They fired three volleys in perfect unison. They were the first shots anyone had heard in two days. At the first note of taps, two hundred hands snapped, edging sharp salutes. A tear rolled down my face. With the final unsung verse, "God is nigh," I walked out of the compound.

31

Hallowed Ground

We made our way along that lonely plain like men who seek
the right path they have lost, counting each step a loss till it
is found.

DANTE, *Purgatorio*

UNFORTUNATELY, THERE IS NO PAUSE BUTTON IN
combat. The company spent the day after O'Neill's memorial service rehearsing for the return to Losano Ridge. The officers in the company
agreed that we had telegraphed our punches too often, alerting our prey by
long and loud vehicle approaches. Yet we couldn't think our way out of the
box. The futility of finding al-Qaeda by trial and error was by now clear to
almost everyone. It was like throwing darts in a dark room. Sometimes we
hit the bull's-eye, but we didn't deserve to. Without helicopters, without
real roads, there was simply no way to act quickly and covertly in response
to intelligence of short shelf life. Captain Worthan wasn't satisfied with our
cynicism. "We're going to be the hunters, not the hunted." Together we
planned an audacious night infiltration near Losano Ridge for the following evening. By sending several platoons along different routes, we hoped
to mask our combat power and trap fighters who might have returned after
licking their wounds.

AT 3 A.M. OUR CONVOY proceeded with blacked-out lights down the
one paved road in Shkin, toward the border. We dismounted a few hundred
yards south of the border control post and stayed kneeling beside the trucks

as the other two platoons disappeared from the range of our night vision goggles. To my left, Captain Worthan towered above a retinue of radio operators, watching his company evaporate into the mist.

Captain Worthan's fighting spirit was genuine. He must have had an inexhaustible reservoir of energy to keep pushing. In his command of Alpha Company, his earnestness to pursue our adversaries was genuine. My men and I were weary. We didn't want to hunt *or* be hunted; we wanted to go home. We began to weigh survival more heavily than the mission. It was like the end of Ranger School, counting down the days, anxious not to risk graduation by twisting an ankle in a midnight ambush. I was unenthusiastic and afraid.

We walked in a wide wedge through waist-high grass down into Losano Ridge's moon shadow. I flipped up my night vision to watch my men in the moonlight. They moved as one body, in perfect synchronization, parting the tall grass with unbelievable grace. I smiled and tightened my chin strap across the stubble on my jaw.

Despite the nervous anticipation, the mission was uneventful. No Taliban popped out of hidden caves. No caches of rockets were discovered. Each member of the platoon marched on that ground with an eye cast back four days to his actions on Losano. I matched the ground truth with my incomplete recollections, searching for the distant ridges from which we had been fired upon, correcting distances and directions in my head. I found the tailfin of a Chinese mortar where I had thought an RPG had impacted near Chuck, Howe, and me. I stared at the Pakistani observation post where the round had originated and shoved the rusting metal into my cargo pocket to take home. I assumed the Pakistanis were watching me, so I flipped them a middle-finger salute.

On the small hill between Losano Ridge and the border, Grenz showed me the tree where he had shot the three men with the detonator. He noted the Snapple bottle on the ground, no doubt stolen from our firebase by a local worker and sold to the local Taliban cell. Another one of my soldiers pointed out half a torso and part of a foot. Flies buzzed about the dried blood. As he retrieved a camera to take a photo, I pulled his arm down.

"We don't photograph dead bodies." He looked at me incredulously and then moved downhill.

This—5.56 millimeters—was how a bullet plowed through a human torso. I had never seen a dead body up close. There were other bodies like this in the hills, bodies shredded by machine-gun fire and artillery I directed. I suddenly felt heavy, as if the pull of gravity was stronger where I stood. Back at West Point, where I had taken my first shots at plastic "Ivan" targets, they always bounced back up. These bodies weren't bouncing back. Neither would we.

I looked up from the scraps of tissue in the dirt. Around the knoll were trees scarred black from grenade blasts and impaled with shards of metal. White phosphorous had stripped their foliage. As a cadet I had read a poem by a French World War I veteran. He asked how much fire it took "to roast a human corpse." Now I knew.

Before we concluded the mission, we detonated the remaining mines on Losano Ridge. Even from a half mile away, the explosion was impressive— five new craters deep enough for foxholes. I hoped we would never have to use them. The explosion was a fitting cap to a mission whose value lay largely in vanquishing our ghosts.

The mission restored a degree of confidence after our shared tragedy. We were able to confront danger again without cringing. We were back in the fight. I recognized a difference in my men and in me. Where before our conviction grew out of enthusiasm and a measure of naïveté, our resolve now originated elsewhere.

Veterans often call their first taste of combat a "baptism." Unlike the religious sacrament, we were cleansed not of sin but of innocence. We no longer had the ability to pretend we were on a stage acting out a drama with blank rounds and fake wounds. O'Neill forever eliminated our ability to wish away terror and uncertainty. Real blood doesn't always stop. O'Neill wasn't going to come back on the next helicopter. The battalion commander wasn't going to call an end to the training exercise and gently critique our technique. This wasn't a video game, a training scenario, or a scene from *Platoon*. Our return to Losano Ridge made this painfully obvious.

One must learn to endure what one cannot avoid. Lacking the superficial enthusiasm of the apprentice, I developed a deeper resolve. I accepted that our missions would be dangerous and that our planning and training could shape but never eliminate the risk. I shuddered, thinking I would likely lose another soldier. But the road home ran through the Valley of Death. We would have to face fear on every patrol, stare it in the eye, and continue the mission. I owed my men resolve, and they owed it to one another. It simply did not matter whether I was scared.

Fuck self-pity, the Ranger instructor had said. *This isn't about you.*

32

Fight Club

When the blast of war blows in our ears, then imitate the action of the tiger: stiffen the sinews, conjure up the blood, disguise fair nature with hard-favored rage.

SHAKESPEARE, *Henry V*

THE SHADOWS LENGTHENED AS AUTUMN CREPT UP on our forgotten corner of Afghanistan. The frenzied pace of our first week at Shkin had slowed. Whether the vigilance of our patrols was abating or our foes were retreating remained uncertain. The mercury dropped with more measurable conviction, hovering above freezing soon after the sun set in the hills to our west. The days were crisp and clear, our visibility restricted only by the occasional squall of dust dancing across the barren valley toward Pakistan.

Unlike the dog days of August in our closing weeks at Gardez, this quiet was pregnant with apprehension. I no longer needed to admonish my men against complacency; their alertness was by now an acquired survival trait. No one wanted to jeopardize his safe return home with a misplaced step. As we moved through beautiful cedar glens along the border, heads continued to swivel, expecting a violent interruption. There was no returning to our illusions, no gleeful anticipation of combat action.

The simmering tensions at the border flared regularly. On one mission we explored an unfamiliar streambed along the border north of Shkin. An accidental trespass across the border prompted a half-dozen Pakistanis who were manning the border post to mount RPGs on their shoulders and point them menacingly at our vehicles. Fortunately, our reversed course satisfied our allies, and I counted myself lucky to have avoided a more consequential incident.

I waged my own battles with the chain of command. The senior officer at Shkin, Major Paul Wille, egged me on continuously. At nearly every meal Major Wille asked whether I wanted wine with my food, playing on my Oxford background. The other officers laughed. Most of the time in the Army, having studied at Oxford earned me either unsolicited compliments or complete indifference, but Oxford wasn't always a badge of honor in the military. Ever since the commander at Benning dubbed me "Professor Mullaney," I had had to fight the perception that I couldn't be both a scholar and a warrior. At the beginning of my officer training, it had probably been for the better, forcing me to work extra hard at every military and physical test to insulate myself against unwarranted criticism. Given Wille's advanced military history studies, I was surprised by his attitudes and didn't know how to read him. Was he just busting my chops, or did he actually resent my education? In any case, I decided not to defend myself. After a few months in Afghanistan, I no longer needed to prove my bona fides.

On one mission where he accompanied my platoon, Major Wille chided me at every unfolding mishap. When a Humvee cracked an axle and forced us to tow it back twenty miles to base, he compared us to a dog returning home with its tail between its legs. He second-guessed my decisions in front of my men, making it even more difficult for me to command their respect. The animosity was personal, or at least that is how I perceived it. My bookishness either threatened or disgusted him.

Soon after the mission with the cracked axle, we received our first mail since arriving at Shkin. A package arrived from Amazon. I ripped it open to discover an expensive set of language tapes I had ordered. While I walked with the tapes across the compound, Major Wille stopped me. "What are those?"

"Hindi tapes, sir."

"You know, Mullaney, you should focus on being a better platoon leader, not screw around with languages. If you lose another soldier, you're only going to blame yourself for not doing more to prepare."

I walked away without rising to the bait. My skin grew hot. I could have killed him with my bare hands. How could he imply that O'Neill had died because I had failed to prepare? I wasn't ready for this criticism. It stung because several times a day, every day since the attack, I had been asking myself what I had done wrong. Moreover, I was angry at the implicit accusation that preparing my mind was unconnected to becoming a better leader. At that moment Major Wille became a lightning rod for my dissatisfaction with those few officers I had come across in my brief career who disdained the value of formal education. Our profession so clearly depended on judgment and clearheaded analysis. I hated having to defend my time at Oxford, euphemizing my academic experience as being "stationed in England." I wanted to be judged on my performance as a leader, not on the weight I could bench-press.

Still, I hated to consider that Major Wille might be right. Maybe I wasn't sufficiently focused on the fight at hand. Combat has the effect of crystallizing the value of one's choices. Time spent studying a language was time not committed directly to honing my tactical knowledge. Maybe Wille was pointing out that there was something more beneficial that I could have been doing with my time. He was right, but I also had to hold on to myself by lying down with headphones and closing my eyes for just twenty minutes a day. In the midst of so much chaos and fear and unrelenting pressure, the certainty of language, with its rules and rhythms, helped me stay sane.

I RETURNED TO MY rack to read through the accumulated letters from Meena. There were six or seven, all dated on the back of the envelope so I could read them in the correct order. It was tempting to jump to the last letter, but I also relished the excitement of finishing a letter and having the satisfaction of immediately reading the next installment. Our letters were always slightly out of phase with each other, like left and right speakers playing the same song two seconds apart. As a result, it took two weeks to figure out how Meena had taken the news about our recent spate of fighting along the border. After all, it contrasted so strongly with my days vaccinating camels in Gardez.

Meena at the time was alone in Lancaster, Pennsylvania, doing a medical school rotation, staying in a hospital dorm room, and eating all her meals in the hospital cafeteria. Captain Worthan's wife had sent an email to soldiers' spouses and loved ones after Losano Ridge, telling everyone that serious fighting had taken place at the border and family members of the wounded and dead would be notified by telephone. Meena looked at her cell phone and saw that a voicemail message was in her mailbox. With a lump in her throat, she listened to a message from my sister asking for an Indian recipe. I wondered if every call was like that for her now, wondering which one would make her heart stop. I considered how difficult it must have been for her to know I was in danger without having any power to help. I doubted whether I could have stood in her shoes had our roles been reversed. I finally got a chance to call Meena when the satellite phone was fixed.

"How are you doing?" I asked.

"How am *I* doing?" repeated Meena. "With what?"

"With the firefight and everything?"

"I heard it was another company."

"No," I corrected her, "it was us."

"Are you sure?"

"Yeah, I'm sure. It was my platoon. One of my men was killed."

"Oh." Meena gulped. "Are you okay?"

"They had us talk to some counselors. I'm doing all right, I think."

"Can you tell me more about the fight? What happened?"

I told her in eight-minute bursts as the satellites went in and out of reception. Meena didn't ask any hard questions, but she listened. I could only imagine how hard it was for her to listen to that without closing her ears to the reality I would likely face again.

"I love you," Meena said as we closed our conversation. "Stay safe."

"I love you, too."

I couldn't stay safe, though. Our letters after O'Neill's death began to reflect that. More and more I worried about Meena. It was as if I had another platoon to protect. The risks I faced extended to her as well. I couldn't protect my platoon and Meena simultaneously. Staying safe meant staying home. For now I had to focus on my mission even though doing so kept me anything but safe.

Most days at Shkin I wanted to ignore home. I had heard nothing from my father since the letter I had written him in July. I asked my mother whether my father had asked about me. *Was he worried about me?* I wanted my mother to say yes. Like a game of hide-and-seek, I didn't want to be found, but I wanted to know he was looking. He hadn't asked, wrote my mother.

I was empty. There were no tears left to cry.

AT ONE OF OUR regular nightly planning sessions, Captain Worthan announced an unusual schedule for the following day. It was his birthday, and he wanted to celebrate at Shkin. Secretly, he had planned an entire day of festivities, including sports, a feast of fresh spit-roasted meat, and bon-fire skits.

My men were ecstatic, particularly at the proclamation that we could wear civilian clothes all day. Soon after, duffel bags were eviscerated in the hunt for baseball caps, jeans, and sweatshirts. We had been told to pack one set of civilian clothes before deploying. Until now I had kept mine buried beneath the third extra pair of boots. I had assumed I would go through the boots before I ever wore civilian clothes in Afghanistan.

The day dawned bright with promise. Breakfast tasted better. I pulled on a favorite pair of jeans and a T-shirt and joined McGurk and Grenz outside our building. Donning sunglasses, we reclined in unison in nylon folding chairs, soaking up the sun. Twenty yards away, several soldiers played dominoes to the rhythm of Cuban music. Our austere camp life only heightened the pleasure of what few luxuries came our way. The music was fresher, the sun warmer, and the sky more blue. I sipped one of the nonalcoholic beers that Captain Worthan had unveiled. Twenty more and I might even have a buzz.

After a preciously lazy morning tanning and reading, I joined the increasingly loud throng of soldiers gathering outside the compound wall. Men climbed up on the turrets of Humvees. Some were perched on the compound parapet. I wiggled in to see what was going on.

In the center of a cheering ring, two soldiers pummeled each other with boxing gloves. The taller soldier had six inches of reach on his opponent, but the shorter grunt was giving him a run for his money. At each blow the crowd reverberated with cheers. With no helmets or mouth guards, this was only one step above bare-fisted street brawling. Third Platoon's sergeant refereed with a light touch, just as eager as the crowd for the blood that splattered as the two pugilists smashed each other's noses. Eventually, he called the fight a draw, although the company clearly supported the tenacity of the underdog.

Captain Worthan and the company executive officer battled next. The men cheered wildly as the former rugby player and former hockey star traded powerful, methodical punches. Captain Worthan looked ridiculous in the outfit he had chosen for his birthday—an olive drab Afghan *kurta* pajama. The fight ended abruptly with a roundhouse from Worthan. The lieutenant's body lifted off the gravel as his jaw rotated away, trailing a fountain of blood. His body twisted as he fell flat on his face. The company medic rushed to help him up, and the ring of spectators roared with approval as he cracked a bloody smile. He wiped the blood off his face with a brown towel, and the referee raised Worthan's arm in triumph. A second roar erupted when he put the other arm over his lieutenant's neck.

"Who wants to challenge?" prompted the referee in an echo of the popular film *Fight Club*. He dismissed a few call-outs as egregiously lopsided.

From my right, Major Wille bellowed out a challenge: "Does Mullaney want to fight?" He turned to me with a smirk from ear to ear. The crowd fed off his bravado, sensing a less than cordial intent in the challenge. When Wille wasn't in the command center, he was in the gym or reading glossy muscle magazines. Testosterone radiated around him. He was a meat-eating, knuckle-dragging gladiator, and the company was frothing with anticipation at the clash.

This was an opportunity I couldn't miss. "Let's go."

My men elbowed in to better viewing positions on the edge of the ring. I walked into the center, conscious only of the twenty-five pairs of eyes that mattered to me at that moment. I imagined myself representing my platoon's honor, their unelected representative in the ring. I stripped my shirt off and held my arms out for the gloves. They were stained with dried blood.

I anticipated being battered by Major Wille. He had forty pounds of muscle and four inches of reach on me. Nor did my record give me confidence. Every boxing match I had had, from Plebe year through Ranger School, had been ugly. My record of 0–6 spoke for itself.

My platoon probably wasn't expecting much of a performance. Most were familiar with the infamous bout when a sergeant in the platoon had nearly decapitated me on the day I took command.

Worthan approached with something in his hand. As he came closer, he folded a piece of cardboard into a T shape and shoved it into my mouth as an improvised mouth guard. This was a bad omen. The referee, who towered over Major Wille and me, instructed us to touch gloves with arms outstretched and commenced the battle with a sharp "Fight!"

We danced around each other for thirty seconds, reconnoitering for weaknesses. I jabbed first, stinging Wille on the nose and evoking a snorting chuckle. I stepped away as he missed with an unguided roundhouse. I stepped back in with two quick jabs, exactly as I had been taught as a Plebe. I was enjoying this.

Wille was a brawler rather than a boxer. He kept his hands low and swung wildly from the hips, telegraphing his hooks. If he landed one, it would hurt, but I could take advantage of my painful Plebe boxing lessons to wear him down slowly. I landed three punches for every glancing blow I ducked. My mind blocked out the sound of the crowd, but I recognized the pumping fists of my men with each of my strikes. As the round wore on, I absorbed a series of crushing blows to my right temple. My head swam, and Wille blurred in front of me. He hit the left side of my head with the force of a sledgehammer, and I lost my balance. My knee hit the gravel, and the referee separated us. I stood back up. The cheer of the crowd made my heart race faster. I jabbed twice with my right and crossed with my left, hitting Wille square on the nose. I wanted to pounce on the blood dribbling down his upper lip, but the referee called the round.

I lumbered over to my corner, where the company medic tilted my head back and swabbed my face with cotton balls. I was surprised to see blood when I glanced at his hands. Blood was splattered over my bare chest and on my jeans. I wasn't sure whether it was Wille's or mine. McGurk grabbed my cheeks and centered my attention on him.

"Watch his roundhouses."

I nodded and dribbled spit at the same time.

"Keep pounding his left eye. You might be able to open a small cut there on his eyebrow."

"Uh-huh," I acknowledged. I quickly turned to look toward Wille. He was breathing heavily, with much more difficulty than I was. Adrenaline was pulsing through my body; I was doing well.

The referee called us back to the center. Wille looked much less cocky now. I had the psychological advantage. As we broke, I tried to keep moving around the ring to tire him out faster. He plodded slowly after me, but without much enthusiasm. I let him catch up. He swung blindly with his left, leaving his left eye exposed. I jabbed once with my left, coiled my right arm, cocked my hips, and unleashed a vicious right cross. I saw Wille wince a split second before my arm went limp. A bolt of pain rippled through my upper body, and I immediately recognized that I had dislocated my right shoulder, the same injury that had nearly eliminated me from Ranger School. I pulled my left glove up in front of my face and tried unsuccessfully to will my right arm back to the horizontal. The referee blew his whistle to break the fight, and I pulled away, bending over like a jackknife.

"Do you want to keep fighting?" asked the referee.

I remembered all the times Aram had helped me relocate my shoulder during our wrestling days at West Point. I thought of the overtime when he had urged me to throw the headlock to win the match. I didn't want to keep fighting; I had to. *I fight, therefore I am.*

"Just hold my glove against your shoulder." I pushed against the referee's resistance and popped my shoulder back into its socket. "I'm not done yet."

Wille was bent over, wheezing with exhaustion. He was startled to see me lift my gloves back up into a ready position and move toward him on the attack. We finished the round with a decreasing frequency of punches as we both tired. I jabbed ineffectually with my left glove and held my right up as a face guard. The second and final round ended with us bloody and battered. The company applauded loudly, but my right shoulder seared with pain. Captain Worthan helped remove my gloves and then manipulated Major Wille and me into a pose. Unprompted, Wille draped his arm over my shoulder and smiled as another lieutenant snapped a Polaroid photo.

I hobbled to my bunk and lay down. It was as if my brain had been inflated with a pump until it bulged against the inside of my skull. The pounding of my heart had been replaced by the pounding of my head. My shoulder throbbed and my back ached. I closed my eyes and swallowed a painkiller. The medicine was just starting to take effect when I looked up to see Major Wille staring down at me. He was smaller now.

"That was a tough fight," he said.

"Yes, sir," I replied.

"You were pretty intense. I haven't seen that before. Where'd it come from?"

"It's part of who I am." I didn't have time to explain my father's focus and intensity.

"Are you that intense when you go outside the wire?" he asked, dropping the condescending tone I was accustomed to.

"I think so." I paused. "But it's different. Out there it's like boxing with a blindfold."

"Craig," he began, using my first name for the first time, "you're smart and you're tough." He laughed as he gestured at his swollen left eye. "You have to combine the two. You don't have much longer as a platoon leader. Make it count."

"Yes, sir. Thank you, sir." I tried not to show him what the compliment meant to me—a reconciliation of heart and head, of physical and intellectual that I had been trying to achieve my whole life. In my mind I had been boxing my father.

STORY WOKE ME AT DUSK. "Come on, sir. It's chow time. You earned it."

My headache had subsided, but my rib cage ached and my muscles radiated pain. My mouth was cottony from dehydration. I chugged a nonalcoholic beer and emptied a canteen. Outside the chow hall, the entire company was standing in line.

"What's the occasion?" I asked Story. Food here wasn't usually in such high demand.

"You forgettin', sir? Get hit too hard?" Story guffawed.

"No, seriously, what's for dinner?" I asked again.

"Beef. Red meat, fresh from the butcher." Story grinned, and I recalled Worthan's scheme. He had bought a whole cow from a local villager. A few of the boys from Texas had been slow-roasting hunks of beef all day. I savored each juicy bite of my medium-rare rib eye steak. I melted a thick slab of butter on top of a baked potato and devoured a mountain of baked beans as the sun ducked below the high western wall of the compound.

In the middle of the compound, soldiers erected an enormous stack of pallets, doused them with fuel, and sparked a raging inferno. The company gathered by the bonfire, waddling like dusty penguins with the added ballast of all-you-can-eat steak. My platoon congregated together, deploying camp chairs to recline by the fire. I returned to our hooch and dug out the cigars a friend had sent in the last mail drop. I opened the box and buried my nose beneath the lid, inhaling deeply. The scent of cloves was powerful and enticing.

By the fire I distributed the cigars like ammunition. There were enough cigars for everyone in the platoon who wanted to smoke. Grenz opened his Zippo lighter and lit my cigar. The smoke burned my lungs.

After the company sang "Happy Birthday" to Captain Worthan, squads of actors took turns performing skits, often mocking another platoon. We roared with laughter disproportionate to the comedy. It was so good to laugh. Three months had elapsed of our tour in Afghanistan. We had gone through so much pain together that laughter became a rarity. Captain Worthan beamed underneath his black watch cap.

Some of the privates in my platoon got up to do a skit. Grenz smirked mischievously. They reenacted a training exercise at Gardez when my Humvee had hit an enormous pothole and I had dropped my rifle out of the vehicle. They poked fun at the indifference I had feigned afterward when I asked to drive back to "check the targets." I hadn't realized that everyone knew.

Their gentle ribbing made me glow. I was one of them. For the first time since Losano Ridge, the platoon cohered. The laughter had finally balanced the tears. We were a family again. As we smoked our cigars down to smoldering nubs, the fire dimmed to orange cinders. Flicking my cigar into the dust, I ground the ashes under my boot and walked through the night with my sergeants. I went to bed light-headed, unsure whether it was the tobacco or something else entirely.

33

Redemption

For this is your duty, to act well the part that is given to you.

EPICTETUS

I LAY STARING AT A FLY DANCING ACROSS THE CEIL-
ing. It zipped down to settle on my chest, making no imprint on my dusty
uniform blouse. Restless, the fly dive-bombed my left ear, and I swiped at
it aimlessly. I was awake before my men again and unable to recall the
nightmare that left me even colder than the October mountain air.

Our remaining days at Shkin were drawing short. In a couple of weeks
another company would take our place, and we would winter at battalion
headquarters in Orgun. Our patrols over the past two weeks had been unnervingly uneventful. The much-heralded Taliban fall offensive had shifted
to other provinces after the fight on Losano Ridge.

At dawn, as the cooks began clattering in the field kitchen, I quietly
laced up my sneakers and slipped out to the compound perimeter for a run.
Through the razor wire I could see an endless band of morning mist hovering above the hard ground. The mountains to the east fractured with shards
of rose and amber as the sun rose from Pakistan and settled on Afghanistan.
The moment evaporated as quickly as the fog, another platoon's trucks
kicking up whirlwinds of dust as they exited the firebase for a morning
patrol. My platoon remained at the base as a quick reaction force. Things
had been quiet, and I hoped, against reason, that today would preserve the
streak.

Afghanistan forever cured me of liking surprises. Continuing a pattern that had begun with the first rocket attack at Gardez, silence was punctured abruptly by emergency. An hour after breakfast, Captain Worthan found me and briefed me on a developing situation. The thick-muscled, bearded special operators who occupied a compound on our base had been ambushed thirty miles south while patrolling with their Afghan militia at Khand Narai Pass, the next mountain pass south of Shkin. They had been exploring one of the infamous "ratlines," a route over the Hindu Kush preferred by insurgents, between an al-Qaeda stronghold in Wana, Pakistan, and Kandahar, Afghanistan. One operator was already dead, and several Afghans were seriously wounded. Via satellite transmission, they requested our help in repelling the Taliban assault, securing a perimeter, and evacuating the wounded.

It took at least thirty minutes to line up the convoy of a half-dozen Humvees. Worthan's unarmored flatbed rolled up last, filled to capacity with the usual farm of antennas. In addition to his radio operators, I noticed that Worthan was bringing our field surgeon, an Air Force team that could direct Air Force jets against ground targets, and Sergeant Major Watson, the Mogadishu veteran. I briefed the bare bones of a plan to Story, Chuck, and McGurk, and I barreled out of the gate in the lead truck. Time was precious.

Sitting in front of me, next to the driver, was "Chris," our guide. I had seen him around the base with the other special operators from the OGA—Other Governmental Agency. I doubted his real name was Chris. The pseudonyms regularly used by the operators added to their mystique, of course. Everyone on base watched these guys with admiration. They had custom-made rifles, custom-made vehicles, and custom-made physiques straight off the pages of *Men's Health*. They swaggered around base with well-deserved confidence, long hair, and cool gadgets. They had satellite television and, it was rumored, a secret stash of beer.

At a signal from Worthan, we ripped downhill into the wadi and south toward the Khand Narai Pass. Chris rolled down the bulletproof glass on the Humvee and suspended his arm against the door frame. His long blond hair swept back from a tanned, wind-burned complexion. Ray-Ban sunglasses rested on a stubby nose. A plain white T-shirt poked out from beneath his body armor. Although he exuded nonchalance, I also sensed that Chris knew exactly where we were, where we were going, and what he would do when we arrived.

"How long do you think it will take us to get there?" I asked.

"Probably three or four hours with a convoy this size," Chris responded. "As the crow flies, it's thirty miles. As the Humvee drives, it's a lot longer. The map is misleading. The terrain gets really ugly up ahead. We're going to have to do a lot of tacking and jibing." Chris turned and pointed on the map to a glacial valley we would have to descend between two ridges. "It gets pretty hairy here where we enter the gorge. With so many vehicles, it's going to take time."

Sometimes it is better not to know what you're heading into. Three hours was a long time to contemplate driving into a firefight. The expectation of enemy contact was both exhilarating and terrifying. My heart pounded even hours away from the objective. I anticipated the lethal force I would be able to deliver with our Humvee-mounted machine guns and mortars and the leverage of Air Force jets and Apache helicopters. Power coiled up inside me. My confidence soared as I reflected on the training we had done over the last few weeks. We were ready. There was nothing like commanding a well-trained, experienced rifle platoon. That confidence pulsed through my veins.

Nevertheless, I doubted whether *I* was ready. *What do we do now, sir?* Would my answer today be better than on Losano Ridge? Unfortunately, the convoy wasn't going to pause while each of us conversed with our personal gods. We pushed south, marching toward the guns.

THE SUN HAD CLIMBED steeply since my morning jog. An hour into our drive, we pulled to a stop before a pair of enormous boulders straddling the goat trail we had been following south toward Khand Narai Pass. Chris popped his door and walked briskly to the front of our vehicle.

"Why'd we stop?" I rushed to catch up with Chris.

As I approached, he motioned with a sweep of both arms, "Voilá!"

Beneath us, the skirt of the gorge plunged a hundred yards before shallowing into a dusty U-shaped valley edged on either side with fierce eight-thousand-foot peaks. Far below, a sinuous wadi traced through the valley. I informed the convoy of the changing terrain, emphasizing the need to keep distance between the vehicles as we followed gravel switchbacks to the valley floor. I was keenly aware that our route would leave us surrounded on three sides by high ground. I assumed the worst, that our adversaries would have anticipated our route and planted mines or an ambush.

"Watch the high ground," I radioed to the rest of the convoy. A half-dozen machine-gun barrels pivoted toward the ridges.

The convoy inched slowly down the escarpment and through the sandy wadi. Our progress was frustratingly slow at six miles an hour. If we had had enough transport helicopters, we would have been at the objective by now. At this pace I wondered whether there would be a fight left to join. An hour later we came abreast of a hard-packed dirt road leading due east through the Khand Narai Pass toward Wana, Pakistan. This was where the operators had been patrolling for al-Qaeda. Finally, we picked up their radio signal, and John, the leader of the ambushed patrol, coached the convoy toward his position.

The pace accelerated quickly. The convoy pulled up next to the punctured hull of a white Toyota Hi-Lux pickup. The windshield was a spider web of cracked glass. Like BB pellets through cheap plastic, I thought. One of the operators had been shot dead in the truck during the initial ambush.

I got out of the Humvee with Chris and crouched in the lee of the Toyota with Worthan and Story. John, the OGA patrol leader, pointed out his Afghan militia grouped in twos in a 360-degree perimeter around our position. Forty-foot-tall knobs of dry dirt embraced the curvy truck track on both sides. Small trees sprouted randomly from their crests. Firing had ceased an hour or so before our arrival, and John didn't anticipate any more trouble. Apparently, an A-10 strafing run had already cut down al-Qaeda's reinforcements. Before we returned to Shkin, John wanted Chris to sweep

east a hundred yards with a squad of my men while I drove south with the
gun trucks to retrieve a fatally wounded enemy fighter.

I took Chris's front seat in the Humvee. Chris joined Story, Howe,
McGurk's squad, and our medic. They disappeared over the hill as I drove
south along the gravel road. We didn't have to drive far before we reached
the al-Qaeda fighter, groaning as he bled into the dust. He was a more
complete version of the severed torso we had found after our fight on Losano Ridge. This time I didn't have the same impulse to retch. We pulled
up short. I didn't make it two steps before a loud gunshot cracked the air.
I immediately reached for the radio handset. There was heavy traffic on the
radio, but it was broken and hard to decipher. I recognized Story's voice
and a wave of goose bumps erupted on my arms.

"Contact, front. I repeat, contact front. . . ."

"Fuck," I muttered. "Let's move!"

We ripped the gravel out of the road moving back to our original position in the saddle of the hills. "Stop here!" I ordered and bounded toward
the antenna farm three-quarters of the way up the hill that Chris and
McGurk had disappeared over. The climb was steeper than it looked from
below, and the ground stung my hands as I tried to get a purchase. I had to
get a situation report from Worthan; Story's garbled radio transmissions
were worthless. Worthan pointed three hundred yards down the other side
of the hill, where I could just make out bobbing helmets popping above the
network of narrow four-foot-deep wadis crisscrossed like stitches on a
wound. At least one sniper was harassing my squad below, and Story was
demanding—between bursts of fire—a medic and a radio. Howe and the
medic were with him, weren't they? Worthan thought he had heard a casualty
report from Story, but it was hard to make out. I figured Story was using
his platoon walkie-talkie, a weak signal baffled by the occluding terrain.

I ran back toward my truck, tripping frequently and just barely managing to stay vertical. I yelled to the company medic, panting as I reached the
bottom: "Get your aid bag. Let's go." I tried to catch my breath as I waited
the agonizing seconds for him to grab his medical backpack. We started up
the hill again at a slow gallop. The medic kept falling behind.

Bits of Story's transmissions were coming through on the platoon walkie-talkie. "KIA." Killed in action. How many I couldn't hear. My mind raced through the possibilities. Who was hit? I was desperate to know. I had to assume it was one of my guys. "WIA." Wounded in action. Was this a correction to his original transmission or an additional casualty? Why wasn't Howe transmitting the messages for Story? Was Howe hurt? I gripped my rifle even tighter and prayed it wasn't Howe.

"Hurry up!" I yelled at the medic as he crawled up the hill on all fours.

"I'm trying, sir."

I ran back downhill twenty yards and yanked the aid bag from the medic. Indignant, I threw it on my back and continued the climb.

"Stay on my ass. There's at least one casualty down there, and I'm going to need you."

I clambered the last few yards to Captain Worthan and an OGA operator grabbed my shoulder.

"I'm coming with you. I'm a medic."

His confidence was invigorating. "Stay low," he whispered as if someone might hear us above the typewriter crackle of gunfire.

Together, the three of us plunged over the crest of the hill and lurched down at breakneck speed toward the lattice of trenches three hundred yards below us. My legs had never moved that fast. I was a bullet train, unstoppable. I had no fear.

A machine gun ripped bullets through my silence. I hoped it was ours. It wasn't. *Fuck.* Puffs of dust erupted in the tracks we had made moving downhill. Another burst of adrenaline propelled me faster. My left boot struck a rock. I somersaulted through the air ass-over-helmet and landed with a thud in a four-foot-deep, six-foot-wide natural trench. We moved hunched over through the lattice of trenches. Up ahead I saw two camouflaged uniforms crouched by a boulder. I crossed myself in gratitude as I recognized Howe and the platoon medic.

"Where's Story?"

"Up ahead."

"You're coming with us. I need the radio, Howe. And Doc, there's a couple of casualties. Stay in the back until I link up with Story."

We continued moving through the gulch with our knuckles nearly dragging across the gravel. The shooting increased in frequency and amplitude, just inches over our heads. We turned a bend. There was Story, his back to the trench wall, peeking furtively over the top. Grenz was farthest away, popping off rifle shots between grenade rounds. Sergeant Major Watson was helping him spot targets. McGurk was hunched over on his knees, his back toward me, his rifle lying across his boots. He looked like a Catholic at confession. Slowly, McGurk turned his face to look at me. I followed his eyes to a body prostrate in the dust.

It was Chris. His white T-shirt was shredded and red, deepening in color toward the center of his chest where his blood spurted in irregular bursts. McGurk's stained hands tried to stop the bleeding. My mouth agape, I stared at Chris. He was so pale. I took off my gloves and touched his face. Beneath the stubble, his cheeks were cool, but the blood on his chest was still warm. With two fingers I touched his carotid artery. His pulse was faint.

Story dragged another body down from the front of the wadi—one of our Afghan militiamen. Our medics went to work on him while the OGA medic assisted McGurk with Chris. Their attempts to resuscitate him were becoming increasingly futile; Chris had already lost too much blood. Under my fingers, his pulse disappeared.

Story shoved a radio headset into my chest. "Sir."

Pause.

"Sir."

More forcefully this time.

"*Sir!*"

I turned to look straight at Story.

"Your fight."

I snapped out of my trance, turned away from Chris, and gained my bearings. Story showed me where the enemy shots were coming from, a hundred yards away and uphill. The shots I heard earlier were directed at Chris as he bravely attempted to take out the sniper by himself. Unbelievable. Story had run behind, trying to give him some backup, but was too late. Chris had already been shot. Story exposed himself to withering fire in order to pull Chris to safety. He warned me not to maneuver any closer. My machine-gun team was keeping the sniper's head down, but he was well protected in another trenchlike wadi. I reached Captain Worthan on Howe's radio and relayed our status. I reported Chris as wounded, though I knew he was already dead.

My actions were instinctual, intuitive. A pair of Apache helicopters hovered at a safe distance away from us, primed for the kill now that someone with a radio could direct them onto a target. Hours of training were instantly validated. The harassing recitations of Plebe knowledge. The high-speed free-fall skydives. The night patrols in Ranger School. It was like switching to autopilot.

I identified our position with a bright strip of orange nylon I had kept in my cargo pocket for that very purpose, and directed the Apaches onto the position Story had shown me. They swept in directly overhead, firing 2.75-inch rockets and splintering rocks and tree branches. I had my machine gunner fire tracers into the enemy position and asked the helicopter pilots to finish off our adversary. I was energized by the power I commanded through the radio. It was like an incantation, like casting a spell, like summoning a demon. At a word I could unleash a hail of rocket shards on the fighter who had shot Chris. Vengeance commingled with professional satisfaction.

The fourth gun run was less accurate. Several rockets landed less than thirty feet away from the lip of the trench, scouring Grenz's and McGurk's arms with shrapnel. *Damn.* So much for "minimum safe distance." I called the helicopters off into a holding pattern. I needed to move our casualties through the wadi and back to the landing zone. Two litter teams comprised of my men and Afghan militia finally arrived. McGurk coordinated his fire teams to cover our withdrawal.

I grabbed part of the litter and helped move Chris, but the Afghans ahead of us were moving too slowly. We had hundreds of yards to go, and the terrain was uneven. All shared a look of terror and purpose. I urged the Afghans on in Hindi, *"Chale, chale,"* drawing one suddenly important phrase, "Let's go," from the many hours of language tapes and Bollywood films. Sweat glistened on every brow in the afternoon heat, and my grip was slippery. My forearms ached from the weight. We removed equipment from the litters to speed our movement, yet it still took an hour to reach the helicopter landing zone. Story alerted me once everyone was accounted for.

"All up, sir."

I moved with two of the gun trucks to a position overlooking where I had just been. My two Mark-19s opened up after a burst of fire erupted from where our enemy, amazingly, had survived. A malfunction. A second malfunction. Both guns fell silent. Chuck leaped out with a Leatherman tool and repaired the guns as rounds impacted around the trucks. A bullet grazed his arm while he fixed the grenade launcher, but Chuck didn't skip a beat. Captain Worthan and I coordinated the coup de grace, using the Mark-19s to mark the target while an A-10 jet eviscerated whatever resistance remained. The Apache helicopters assessed the battle damage from overhead, counting three dead.

My heart rate eased as Story organized the convoy for the return. Daylight faded as we began our movement north toward Shkin. As we entered the maw of the valley, the temperature dropped. The high peaks to our west blocked the setting sun, and their silhouettes cast jagged shadows high on the opposite ridge. A chill ran up my spine.

I sat in the front seat of the lead vehicle, conscious that I had replaced Chris as guide. Ninety minutes into our journey, as the sun dropped fast, a pickup truck broke down in the wadi. While we waited patiently for the amateur mechanics to fix it, our escort helicopters warned us of a possible enemy ambush ahead. Captain Worthan decided to sacrifice the Toyota. The Afghans hastily salvaged the stereo and communications equipment, and we left the truck behind and continued moving, slower now without daylight. I turned one last time to look at the distinctive notch of Khand

Narai Pass. An Apache launched a Hellfire missile at the truck we left behind. It vaporized in the dusk, adding another rusting carapace to Afghanistan's graveyard of military vehicles.

The ambush never materialized. Perhaps they were deterred by the pair of Apache helicopters that stuck with us despite their dangerously low fuel levels. They barely limped back on fumes to the fuel depot at Orgun.

Chris's face kept flashing in my head, a split screen between life and death. Chris full of life, laughing, and then suddenly pasty white skin and violent red blood. Chris hadn't "fallen." Chris wasn't "KIA." I didn't "lose" Chris like a watch or a wallet. He drowned in his own blood. There were no euphemisms.

If a guy like Chris could bleed to death, what chance did I stand? Suddenly, and for the first time, I felt vulnerable. The adrenaline that had sustained me began to wear off. My legs ached as though I had run a marathon, and my uniform chafed against my skinned knees. I tried to focus on my map, but it blurred and my head pounded with pain. My helmet seemed to weigh a hundred pounds. As it grew colder, I wrapped my scarf tightly around my neck. In the dark, under my night vision goggles, I stared in silence at a world turned sickly green.

34

Last Patrols

A rational army would run away.

MONTESQUIEU

CAPTAIN WORTHAN HANDED ME A LETTER HE HAD received from O'Neill's father. As I unfolded the letter, a photo fell onto my lap. Stripped of the camouflage, he reminded me again of my brother—same age, same smile, same blue eyes. I teared up as I read. Mike O'Neill was so proud of his son's sacrifices. He had himself been a paratrooper in Vietnam. He knew that Evan would be happy to have earned the same pair of Purple Heart and Bronze Star medals. He wrote that Evan had always wanted to be a soldier, that he had hoped to go to West Point and Ranger School one day. Evan had said that the proudest moment of his life was when his father had pinned his Airborne wings on his chest. It made me think of my father pinning on my Ranger tab three years before.

When Evan's body arrived at Logan Airport in Boston, Mr. O'Neill, his fellow firefighters from North Andover, and a group of veterans were there to join him on the final convoy home. At the wake, a line stretched for nearly half a mile outside the funeral home. Nearly every policeman, firefighter, and veteran from the county came in uniform to salute O'Neill and honor his sacrifice for the community. Mr. O'Neill then described where they had buried his son, at the closest cemetery to his fire station. What a long journey home from Losano Ridge, I thought. One day I hoped to find his grave and render my final salute. Mr. O'Neill signed off his letter with our battalion's motto, a fitting elegy for his son's sacrifice: "To the Top!"

I wept where my men wouldn't see me. Converging waves of pride and sorrow swept over me. I wondered how my own father would react if I were killed. How would he find out? Would he be as proud as Evan's father? O'Neill had left a fiancée behind. It was too hard to imagine her grief. When I tried, all I could think of was Meena. I wanted to write Mr. O'Neill but couldn't muster the courage.

OUR NERVES FRAYED AS October closed. We were at our peak as a combat platoon. Squads had cohered into tight fighting units. Marksmanship was better than ever. We knew the terrain and were confident in our ability. Yet every morning and night as I walked past O'Neill's equipment hanging by the door of our room, I was reminded that each mission pushed our luck. Often in Afghanistan the scariest mission was just moving from point A to point B. Our routes were predictable, and it was only a matter of time before another ambush or roadside bomb snared us.

Our days at Shkin dwindled. On one patrol we detained five young men. They had been driving three vans stripped of passenger benches and loaded with suspicious packages of soap detergent and drums of kerosene, two ingredients for an explosive fuel bomb. After three days of questioning at the base, we had no choice but to release them with compensation for the windows we had smashed to open the doors. They all stuck to the story that they were distributing fuel and soap to gas stations in the province. Later that spring a succession of car bombs in Kabul made me wonder whether we had released the perpetrators.

One day a farmer approached the base to inform the commander that he had found a rocket pointing toward the firebase. Captain Worthan asked him to point to the location on the map. He had never seen a map before and was unable to make heads or tails of it. My platoon drove with the farmer toward Losano Ridge and asked him to lead us to the rocket. The farmer meandered through the hills, with us trailing behind. I worried that we were being drawn into a trap.

His hands shook as we drew closer to a menacing Pakistani border post. I kept glancing at my GPS to make sure we weren't trespassing on sovereign

Pakistani territory. I didn't want a repeat of the encounter with our ally's observation post and its trigger-happy tribesmen. A hundred yards from the border post, the farmer showed us a four-foot rocket propped up on a rock under a bush. It was connected to what looked like a Nintendo video game cartridge and a kitchen timer. It was good to find the rocket before the rocket found us, but its proximity to the border post highlighted the tenuousness of our relationship across the border. What else was happening right under their noses? We destroyed the rocket in place with C4 explosives and returned home. Could we ever win as long as Pakistan offered implicit sanctuary to the Taliban and al-Qaeda? Would another platoon still be patrolling Losano Ridge five years after we left?

The first platoon of our replacements at Shkin arrived in early November. While coaching them through orientation patrols, we realized how familiar we had become with the small two-hundred-square-mile box we crisscrossed on foot and on trucks. Our learning curve had been steep and perilous. I hoped that theirs would be less so. Our adversaries were watching us. Every time units played musical chairs in Afghanistan, we became vulnerable again. Every time the music stopped, another unit would start over learning the physical and cultural terrain. The lack of continuity certainly frustrated relationships with local khans. Trust was hard-won in this part of the world, and we were treating Afghan leaders like contestants in a round of speed dating. All the same, our combat power was degrading. Two months of nearly continual fighting had beaten us down. Soon we would start making more mistakes.

When the battalion commander flew out to observe our handover, he pulled me aside. In light of our company's upcoming move from the front lines at Shkin to the headquarters at Orgun, he told me I would become his adjutant. The position had been unfilled for months, and a mountain of pay issues, unfinished medal proposals, and promotion orders frustrated morale across the battalion and needed urgent attention. Now that I was a captain, he had no choice but to move me to the staff and replace me with a lieutenant. I was crestfallen. I wanted to stay a platoon leader as long as possible.

Four years at West Point and a year of training had all been focused on being a platoon leader. It was all for this: the ten months with Spearhead Platoon, the training, the tears, the laughter, the camaraderie. My last day with my men was November 11, 2003: Veteran's Day. After more than a hundred days in combat, I had finally earned their salutes.

I had no illusions that my departure would affect the platoon's performance. A platoon moves through time without regard for the officers who come and go. Back when I had first trained my men at Fort Drum, Captain Worthan told me that my objective as a leader was to ultimately make myself dispensable. I had; and now it was someone else's turn.

As I waited for the Chinook to take me to Orgun, Story assembled the platoon to bid me farewell. I had learned since my first introduction in January not to bore them with a long speech. This time I recited only a few well-worn verses I had memorized years ago as a Plebe studying Shakespeare. For the first time the words seemed appropriate to recite outside a classroom.

"We few, we happy few, we band of brothers." What brothers, I thought, as I looked in their eyes. Although most heroism in combat goes unseen or unrewarded, I was proud of the medals my men had earned. For his poise and courage on Losano Ridge, Grenz had won the Silver Star, the Army's third highest award for heroism, as did Captain Worthan for his command of the fight. McGurk and Story had won two Bronze Stars each and a pair of Purple Hearts between them. Among the younger soldiers were shared more than a dozen Army Commendation Medals with "V" devices for valor. I stood in the company of heroes. I mangled the rest of Henry V's speech and spoke from my heart, "Thanks for the privilege of letting me fight with you."

Story helped me carry my bags to the Chinook. Before the crew chief raised the ramp, Story tugged on my arm from outside. "You done good, sir. You done good." He saluted and ran away from the bird. I smiled. It was the highest compliment I have ever been paid.

The helicopter engine hummed to life. I hadn't realized how exhausted I was—not only physically but also emotionally. The tension of continual alertness had worn me down; the eagerness I had brought with me to Afghanistan was gone.

The rotors whirled slowly, moving faster and faster until the individual blades blurred. We lifted off the ground with a jerk. The border receded above the open ramp door. From five hundred feet, Losano Ridge was small. I could barely see the bald patch where we had airlifted O'Neill. I blinked and couldn't find it again. Only the jagged edge of the mountains remained. Even the firebase had disappeared. Below the helicopter, the sun cast a shadow racing over parched ground.

35

Phantom Limb

Perception of painful and non-painful phantom sensations that occur following the complete or partial loss of a limb. The majority of individuals with an amputated extremity will experience the impression that the limb is still present, and in many cases, painful.

INTERNATIONAL CLASSIFICATION OF DISEASES

ORGUN WAS A CROSS BETWEEN A SIBERIAN PRISON and a training center for lunar landings. The base's triangular perimeter jutted out toward imposing mountain ridges on every side. Apart from the camouflaged roofs of the base, there were precious few signs of life in the mile-high basin. From the air, the barren fields formed a checkerboard stretching into the foothills. There had once been a thriving city in Orgun, but the Russians had leveled it in retaliation against marauding mujahideen. Orgun's population was only now returning from refugee camps across the border.

We landed on a football field thickly carpeted in rock to keep the dust down. I dropped my bags and looked for my new boss, Major Wille.

"Hey, Mullaney." Wille always growled, even when he was being friendly. "I have a laundry list of things for you to get started on. Got a notebook?"

He proceeded to outline my responsibilities. An adjutant is a hybrid animal: part accountant, part human resources manager, and part ghostwriter. An adjutant is not a warrior. This became clear as I filled up two pages in my notebook with administrative tasks. My first responsibility every morning would be to brief the commander on what amounted to an attendance roster. This involved updating one single PowerPoint slide. I was also supposed to make sure everyone got their mail and their pay on time. This sounded only marginally more interesting. Most important, Major Wille instructed, I would be in charge of making sure that soldiers in the battalion received the awards they deserved.

"Where do I put my gear?" I asked.

"Gallo will help you."

Andrew Gallo was the logistics officer for the battalion, and we knew each other from West Point. Gallo was built like a tank and had a gruff New York City accent to go with it. Next to his cot was a bookcase stacked with protein supplements. "Getting big is the only consolation for being a staff officer. You'll see." I took an empty cot along the wall across from Gallo and threw my duffel bag underneath. I tacked up a photo of Meena and my family, and then Gallo showed me the gym.

The floor was a cement slab stacked with dozens of benches, squat racks, and leg presses. Above the dumbbells, stenciled red letters spelled out: THE ENEMY TRAINED TO KILL YOU TODAY. WHAT DID YOU DO? Beside it was Rommel's quote: THE MORE YOU SWEAT IN PEACE, THE LESS YOU BLEED IN COMBAT. Apart from these slogans, there was little connection between my new role and the war outside the wire.

Our schedule was numbing in its consistency. Every morning each member of the staff briefed the battalion commander. The slides read like scripts from a weather broadcast: "Today, winds will be from the northwest at 10–15 knots with a 30 percent chance of rockets." Within a week I had memorized the other officers' slides. I would scribble in my notebook while Gallo repeated the same update on vehicle repairs that he had given 150 days in a row.

The battalion commander sat next to Major Wille, his executive officer, at the opposite end of the table, tapping his pen like a metronome while we briefed. He never swore, but his face would turn a scarlet red and his long arms seemed to reach across the table to extract your pulsing heart. "What do you mean we've got four broken Humvees and no parts?" he would say, his voice rising with each syllable. Half in jest, one of the staff officers donned body armor one morning.

After the meetings, Major Wille dressed our wounds: "Don't worry, guys. You're doing great. No one ever joined the Army to be a staff puke. I know it sucks. But you're making this battalion run. You're in an infantry unit—you have to love the suck." He was right about the last part. Misery, even as a staff officer, was in an infantryman's job description. Later I overheard Wille defending us behind the closed door of the colonel's office.

Since the boxing match, my opinion of Wille had changed. He recognized that the biggest problem for Afghans in our province was their failing farms, not the Taliban. Although agriculture was absent from the infantry field manual, "Farmer Paul" Wille improvised. He spent dozens of hours online figuring out which fertilizer and seeds to buy. Then he tasked our engineer with designing cheap modular greenhouses that we could teach Afghans to build. Wille even managed to get money from Kandahar to purchase tractors. Maybe he wasn't the meathead I had pegged him to be. And since our boxing match, Wille had cut me slack for my bookishness. As long as I delivered the reports he needed, he didn't say another word about the language tapes.

I had a strange "office." My desk consisted of a few two-by-fours and a piece of plywood. The stone wall in front of me featured bullet holes and powder burns from its old days hosting a Soviet brigade. Above me was a wafer-thin tin roof that rattled like a snare drum on the rare days when it rained. I fought a daily battle to keep the sand and dust from destroying my laptop. I waged war against spreadsheets of personnel numbers and edited stack after stack of award citations.

I was hermetically sealed in the headquarters, watching the war unfold on a projector screen, with patrols reduced to geometric shapes on maps. I paid attention to Alpha Company's rectangles and chafed at being so far removed from my men. The only weapon I would use from now on was a red pen.

I was sitting at my computer one afternoon when rockets impacted a hundred yards away. I put on my Kevlar helmet and body armor and continued typing. There was nothing else to do. The rocket either landed in our headquarters and I burned to death, or it landed somewhere else and I wrote the report. Under no circumstance would I find myself hurtling out the gate in a Humvee on the chase. One such rocket attack had interrupted Gallo's lifting session. He threw a helmet and vest on and reclined on a folding chair in his shorts, waiting it out.

Major Wille walked in, took one look at Gallo, and grinned. "Well, aren't you cool, sitting there in your shorts with your balls hanging out." We were still laughing when the next rocket hit.

Later, long after I had returned from Afghanistan, I would bring my history students to see *Journey's End*, a British play written by a World War I veteran. After a barrage of artillery fire, one officer inquired of another about the damage. His typically British response—"There's nothing worse than dirt in your tea"—had me bent over laughing. The rest of the audience was silent, and I shrank into my velvet seat.

THE FIRST SNOWS BEGAN to fall in the middle of November. Orgun grew more desolate by the day. The snow muffled the sound of our boots crunching paths between barracks, headquarters, and the latrine. Like an ice-fishing hut, the outhouse stood by itself with silvery stalactites dripping from its eaves.

I was busy one morning typing a report when a frenzy of radio reports echoed from the operations center down the hall. My ears perked up when I heard the call signs of Shkin firebase.

"IED . . . cargo Humvee . . . small-arms fire . . . grid . . ."

I knew the six-digit grid by heart: Losano Ridge. I stood up and walked into the operations center. A million thoughts raced through my mind.

Were my guys patrolling today? Who would have been in the cargo Humvee? McGurk?

"Two wounded . . . one litter, urgent . . . one ambulatory, shrapnel . . . "

The radio rattled off their battle roster numbers, a letter-number combination that uniquely identified members of the battalion. I wrote down the numbers, but my hand was shaking violently. I moved to my computer to match the numbers to names. As the adjutant, I was responsible for sending casualty reports up the chain of command.

Please don't be my platoon. Please don't be my platoon. I scanned down seven hundred rows of numbers and names. *It wasn't Chuck. It wasn't Grenz. It wasn't Howe or McGurk.* Each name I crossed off in my head eased the tension. Finally, I had my answer. *It was Story.* He was the "ambulatory, shrapnel"—wounded but walking.

The details of the attack paralyzed me. My platoon was with Bravo Company, conducting an orientation patrol along Losano Ridge. Story kept telling Bravo Company to stay off the roads, but the terrain kept pushing the convoy back onto old tracks. Suddenly, a powerful blast lifted the six-thousand-pound Humvee off the ground and hurled it thirty feet away. The Humvee had nothing but ad hoc sandbags to deflect the blast of the roadside bomb. Pieces of metal burned Story's face in the bed of the Humvee, but he was okay. Just a few more scars for an ugly face, he would probably say. The "litter, urgent" description belied the severity of the second wounded soldier. Shrapnel had ripped through the thin metal floor of the cab and mangled his leg. Despite his own injury, Story got the badly wounded soldier on the medevac. Later, the doctors had to amputate his leg. Given the power of the explosion, he was lucky to have escaped alive.

My stomach was a figure-eight knot. That could have been me. That *should* have been me. I traveled that route three times a week. The wounded soldier, a squad leader, had sat in *my* seat. Like the mortar that should have killed me on Losano Ridge, the roadside bomb explosion made me angry at fate's razor-sharp distinctions. I had felt lucky before. Now I felt guilty: Not being with my men cost another soldier his leg. It wasn't fair. Life wasn't supposed to work this way.

I also had a vicarious pride in my men. Despite being thrown from the Humvee, despite the chaos that followed, they had instinctively returned fire. They were my men, and they were good. Yet I wasn't there with them. I should have been leading that fight instead of sitting at a desk.

I passed the casualty notification to Kandahar. As I did, I kept seeing Evan's body on the stretcher. I watched Chris bleed out in front of me. Over and over and over again. I couldn't take the sterility of the operations center anymore, the calm recitation of grid coordinates and medevac arrival estimates. It was all incredibly disjointed and alien. I walked outside and stared at the snow.

STORY AND MCGURK BURST into my office on Thanksgiving morning. The platoon had just arrived from Shkin. Story had a fresh scar on his face from the shrapnel.

"You look even uglier now."

"You ain't so pretty yourself, sir."

We thumped one another's backs with closed fists.

"You should have seen the guys the other day," said McGurk. "They just responded instinctively, as if they'd been in dozens of ambushes."

"I wish I could've."

Story left to get the men settled in their new barracks, and McGurk caught me up on the platoon. By his description, it seemed as if I had been gone a year. I hadn't realized how much I missed them. Compared to being a platoon leader, being an adjutant was a lonely post. We all shared a table at the Thanksgiving dinner. Gallo had coordinated the delivery of turkeys, cranberry sauce, pumpkin pie, and even Starbucks Frappuccinos. Major Wille had negotiated with local butchers for a half-dozen freshly slaughtered lambs. Around us, the chow hall was bedecked with paper turkeys and gaudy cornucopias. Every table had a bottle of sparkling cider. I looked around at my men. I knew each one of them would walk through fire to save my life, and I knew I would do the same for them. No matter the distance and the deprivation, celebrating Thanksgiving with my men was one of the best holidays I could recall.

Still, despite the camaraderie, being away from home during the holidays was difficult. I wasn't there when my family needed me most. I missed our stupid family traditions: watching *The Sound of Music* (we had the sing-along version) and gorging myself with my mother's cookies. I wondered what the new house looked like. Did my mother still put up two trees to accommodate all the ornaments she had collected over thirty years? I remembered my father, sitting in the recliner in his flannels, drinking his coffee black, watching us open presents on Christmas morning, and then frying bacon and eggs for all of us to eat. I missed him. Who would take on that responsibility now that he was gone?

Gallo and I made do with what we had. We put up a two-foot plastic Christmas tree in our room, decorated it with tinfoil from the mess hall, and stuck a cardboard star on top. We watched the end-of-season Army-Navy football game at 1 a.m., cursing as Navy ran up the score against Army. I tried in vain to spot my brother's head in the crowd. In the distance, crackling gunfire reminded us how much had changed since West Point, which in retrospect seemed carefree, quaint, and utterly disconnected from the war we were waging. Did Gary know how much he hadn't learned yet?

We each received a special present on Christmas morning. I helped the commander arrange for the Army Chief of Staff to present the Combat Infantryman's Badge to every soldier in the battalion. Established during World War II, the CIB (or "C. I. Been There," as it was sometimes called) was designed to recognize the courage demonstrated by infantry grunts in active combat. Since then, it had become an emblem on uniforms separating the combat-tested from the combat virgins. After the presentation, Red found me and dragged me over for a picture with the whole platoon. "Come on, sir. You got your CIB with us. You oughta be in our photo."

THE LAST MONTHS IN Afghanistan crawled. Snow fell in pelts six inches thick. Blizzards blocked the airfield for weeks, and without helicopters, we had no mail. We watched the same pirated DVDs over and over again as treatment for acute cabin fever. The snowdrifts stopped the rocket attacks, but they also stopped our Humvees from pushing out from the firebase into the surrounding hills and villages. Snowball fights replaced gunfights. In a stroke of comic brilliance, one enterprising soldier built a snowman and draped a captured ammo vest and AK-47 over its shoulders. It was the only Taliban anyone saw for months. The new enemy was boredom.

Concentrating became increasingly difficult. I filled in crossword puzzles compulsively; I doodled in meetings; and, often, I just sat on my cot and stared at the wall. I began to have more nightmares about the firefights. I fingered a piece of rocket shrapnel incessantly. I jumped every time one of our cannons fired, and I wasn't the only one. There was always some soldier in the barracks who would yell "outgoing" to differentiate it from an "incoming" rocket. I began to wonder about the transition to normal life. *Was I the same person? Was I going to go crazy? Was I already gone?* Many of my former soldiers were already taking antidepressants. Others probably needed to but were reluctant to ask for help. One day two of them got into a fistfight over a guard rotation. The smaller guy was beaten within an inch of his life. I told Meena about the fight in the platoon but tossed it off as typical barracks antics. "It's just stress," I said. "I'm sure everything will be normal once we're back."

"This isn't just stress, Craig. Given what you all have gone through, you probably need therapy."

"They'll screen us before we get back. Don't worry about it," I said but without much confidence. At what point would I forget what "normal" was? Had I already?

Our replacements began to arrive in March, just as the snowdrifts began melting. The lightning bolts on the shoulder patches of the 25th Infantry Division were beautiful to our eyes. They made our return home close enough to touch. Over two weeks, the proportion of 10th Mountain Division soldiers in Orgun dwindled rapidly. A core group, including Gallo and me, remained to coach our replacements. On my last morning in Orgun, I gathered my bags by the airfield. The air shuddered as the Chinooks touched down. A sergeant ticked my name off the manifest as I passed him with my bags. I threw them to the crew chief on board and took my seat, placing my rifle between my legs. I waved at no one in particular as the helicopter pulled off the ground.

36

Purgatory

Go with this man . . . ; take care to bathe his face till every
trace of filth has disappeared, for it would not be fitting that
he go with vision clouded by the mists of Hell.

DANTE, *Purgatorio*

KANDAHAR TASTED LIKE SAWDUST. MY TONGUE WAS
like sandpaper despite gulping water in half-gallon increments. It was only
April, yet the temperatures were already soaring above the three-digit mark.
It was like having a hair dryer blown in my face. Two hundred of us were
trying to escape the midday heat inside a temporary hangar. It was as big
as a football field and lined from end zone to end zone with cots caked in
silt. Soldiers were splayed out on their cots, trying to increase surface area
to decrease the discomfort of the heat. A few soldiers tossed a football back
and forth.

Sweat dripped onto my dog-eared copy of *The Red Badge of Courage*.
Stephen Crane had written his masterpiece about a young soldier in the
Civil War without ever stepping on a battlefield. As a high school student,
I had wondered with a groan why I had to read it. The Civil War was an-
cient history. What was courage to a fifteen-year-old? It made no sense at
that age, but it made sense now.

Henry Fleming, the main character of the book, is a young soldier in the
Union Army. He isn't sure how he will stand up in battle. He postures along
with the others, cloaking his fears in bombast. In his first test under fire, he
runs. When next pressed into battle, Henry rises to the challenge, carrying

the colors forward under withering fire. He redeems his shame. In both fights, fear is a constant. It is Henry's will to face that fear that changes.

I tore through the book, scribbling in the margins. Henry's meditations on courage intrigued me now that I had observed courage firsthand. If, as some of Henry's fellow soldiers contended, courage was an immutable characteristic, then you either had it or you didn't; you were a hero or a coward. That wasn't what I had observed, though. In combat, men were all heroes *and* cowards, at the same time and in varying degrees.

All my training had been one pressure cooker: Plebe hazing, jumping out of planes, wrestling, Ranger patrols, even travel. West Point taught us in boxing that fatigue makes cowards of men. Pain is weakness leaving the body. Perhaps courage was more like a muscle than an innate character trait. Maybe courage was a capacity for chaos and danger that increased with exposure. Maybe the fight at Losano Ridge, with its pressure and pain, had prepared me for the next battle. Maybe combat was both the ultimate test of courage and its classroom.

KANDAHAR WAS JUST AS strange after nine months on the frontier as it had been when we first arrived in Afghanistan. I was used to certain rhythms and rituals: bringing my rifle with me to the shower, shaving in cold water, and lying on my cot listening to language tapes like a meditation mantra that took me away from it all. I had spent the last five months in Orgun trapped inside a five-acre base. I knew the numbers of steps between my room and the outhouse (thirty-seven), the time every night when our artillery would fire blindly into the hills (two o'clock), and what Major Wille wanted in his coffee (nothing). Waking up in Kandahar was like a prisoner's first day out of jail. There was no mission for us, no daily schedule. Now we were just waiting for a Freedom Bird to take us home; it could be tomorrow or two weeks. We could eat as much as we wanted, whenever we wanted. American contractors even provided hot showers with individual stalls. This was luxury.

The first night there, after the temperature dropped to a bearable 90 degrees, I went for a walk with Gallo. Kandahar Airfield—or "Kaf," as everyone here called it—housed thousands of soldiers, the majority of whom had never left the base; their only contact with Afghanistan was a weekly bazaar in a wired enclosure near the perimeter. This was the Army of the twenty-first century: For every "trigger puller" in the field, there were at least five soldiers supporting him with food, ammo, and intelligence. Distances on base were long enough that you had to watch out for John Deere tractors ferrying people around at thirty miles an hour. Soon after the sun set, overhead lights came on everywhere. It was like the dawning of the first day in Genesis.

The electric sunshine made our jaws drop when we saw it. For 278 days I had navigated a path to the bathroom by a red-lens flashlight. Gallo echoed what I was thinking: "You've got to be kidding me. It's like Disneyland here." In front of us was a boardwalk surrounding two beach volleyball courts straight out of a pro tournament in San Diego. Gallo fumed, "That's where all the lumber's gone that I requested for our guard posts. A fucking boardwalk!"

Apparently this was the social hub of Kaf. A line snaked a hundred yards from the Green Beans café, which was selling iced chai soy lattes. The base exchange next door sold flat-screen televisions. This week they were on sale. Every season of *The Sopranos* was available; no need to miss a single episode. Around the boardwalk thronged crowds of male and female soldiers. I overheard one conversation reminiscent of bachelor parties in Vegas: "What happens in Kaf stays in Kaf." A look in the base store validated my hunch: It was stocked with fifteen varieties of condoms. Every soldier was on the prowl. They preened in tight-fitting T-shirts that showed off the muscles they had had nine months to sculpt in the Kandahar gym. I saw the gym the next day with its thirty-foot climbing wall and Nautilus machines. An attendant handed out towels. Aerobics began at 8 p.m.

Meanwhile, our battalion had spent nine months on the border.

The only women we saw wore burqas. Our muscles were atrophied from months of long patrols, interrupted sleep, and insipid food. We were skeletal, and our loose-fitting uniforms stank with layer upon layer of sweat and dust. It was impossible not to resent the standard of living our counterparts had enjoyed while we were downrange. We expected a level of deference our less bloodied comrades were loath to grant.

KANDAHAR HADN'T CHANGED, BUT we had. When we had first arrived in the country, we were wide-eyed and eager. Each of us, whether we articulated it or not, was looking for action. We had trained for months and waited for weeks to get to Afghanistan, keen for adventure and a test of our training. We had imagined heroic battles against al-Qaeda. Maybe someone would get hurt, but not us.

We were more seasoned now. We had paid in the dearest currency for the Combat Infantryman Badges we wore. Twenty thousand Americans in Afghanistan with fewer than a hundred casualties—the odds of death had once seemed remote—until the odds bit us in the ass. In our minds, *it won't be us* became *it might be us,* and, finally, inevitably, *it will be us.* We wore our weariness on our wrists with silver bracelets engraved with the names of the casualties we had sustained. To us, "Never forget" was a needless admonition. We never would.

It is possible for war to change nothing except its participants. We had no scoreboard to measure our success on the battlefield. We were never really sure whether we were winning. But *we* had been transformed. Together we had laughed and screamed, and bled and cried. We found ourselves among the crowds, recognizing one another by the shape of a silhouette, the peculiarity of a gait, the unique contours of an accent.

In the Catholic catechism, Purgatory is a place sinners go to have their sins purged before entering Heaven. Kandahar was a type of Purgatory for soldiers leaving Afghanistan. We turned in our live ammunition and washed the war off our gear. We began to observe the inane strictures of life in a peacetime garrison. We began saluting one another again, and sergeants taught privates all the things they had forgotten about drill and ceremony.

Forward, *march*. Dum-dum-DUM-DUM-DUM.

The farther you are from the front lines, the better you march.

III

Veteran

I felt like I was doing something wrong, walking along, staring at people who could not stare back.

DANTE, *Purgatorio*

37

Dislocated

No man ever steps in the same river twice, for it's not the same river and he's not the same man.

HERACLITUS

WE TOUCHED DOWN ON THE AIRFIELD, AND I OPENED my window shade. Snow melted slowly on the side of the runway. Grass punched through cracks in the pavement. I made my way to the stairs. An overcast sky hung above a drab terminal. Outside there was no marching band and no crowd of waving family members. We filed off the plane and rolled our boots across the asphalt. We were home.

A bus deposited us at the barracks, and I stood in line with the rest of Alpha Company as a sergeant opened the arms room. One by one each of us turned in his rifle, reading the serial numbers we had memorized months before. I handed over my weapon, and the sergeant carefully returned it to a slot in the metal rack. Within an hour our entire arsenal was placed back under lock and key—shotguns, machine guns, rifles. There they would wait.

I walked fifteen feet to my office and opened it up. I grabbed the towel hanging in my locker and shuffled to the shower. This was the same routine I had followed after every field problem at Drum. Turn in weapons. Wash off the grime. Change. Go home. The normalcy was disconcerting. I changed into the sneakers, jeans, and T-shirt I had last worn for Worthan's birthday bonfire. The clothes fit loose on my frame, as if they belonged to someone else.

I walked over to the battalion headquarters, where my new office was. I found Major Wille. "Sir, I turned in my rifle. What do I do now?"

"Go home."

"Just go home?"

"Sure. I'll see you tomorrow morning at formation."

I hoisted my rucksack over my left shoulder and walked out the front door. I didn't get three steps outside before I was ambushed by my mother, my sister Kelsey, and Meena. They smothered me in hugs and kisses. I didn't want to let go of Meena as we embraced. We walked to the car, and I sat in the backseat with Meena. As my mother drove back to my apartment at sixty miles an hour, it seemed as if we were racing at twice that speed. From habit, I swung my head continually and scanned the darkness at the verge of the road. I held Meena's hand in mine the entire way.

Waking up the next morning, I instinctively reached with my legs to where I had always placed my shower shoes next to the cot. Instead, my feet touched the hardwood floor. It was rough and cold. I felt like Rip Van Winkle, as if I were waking up after a nine-month sleep to find that the world had continued to turn on its axis while I had stood still. I rubbed my eyes and opened the shade. A car drove past, its headlights illuminating a street deserted at 5 a.m.

I had one last military duty before being released for the weekend. The battalion massed in the parking lot in our least wrinkled uniforms. To the drumbeat of the 10th Mountain Division band, we marched into the gym and stood at parade rest before our assembled families. Seats in the front row had been reserved for photographers and reporters. After recitations of the 10th Mountain Division song and the national anthem, we were officially released. The photographers were probably disappointed. Since everyone had already reunited with their families the night before, the staged version in the gym lacked authenticity.

Visiting my brother, Gary, was my first priority. I drove south to West Point and met him outside Grant Hall. He stood taller than before. I wasn't sure whether it was the extra inches he claimed or his posture. Wearing his uniform, Gary looked as though someone had welded steel rebar to his spine. Chest out and shoulders back, he smiled and saluted. His shoulders were broader, but he still had the dimples in his cheeks that undercut any attempt to look tough.

I saw O'Neill when I looked at Gary. Same age. Same smile. Same blue eyes. I deflected Gary's questions with one-word answers.

"What was it like?"

"Long."

"Are you glad to be back?"

"Yes."

"How do you feel?"

"Tired."

Gary stopped asking questions, and we began talking about West Point. As he recounted the travails of Plebe year, I laughed with him. He told me how he would shake so violently when the upper class worked him up that his nickname became "Shakes" Mullaney. While proud of seeing Gary in cadet gray, I was ambivalent about his choice. I wasn't sure I wanted him to move from the parade field to the battlefield. I didn't want to lose him as I had lost Evan.

I next visited Charlie and Lisa Hooker in New Jersey, the family who had provided me an escape from West Point, guided my wardrobe selection for the Rhodes interview, and helped me find an engagement ring for Meena. Charlie had taught me more about leadership over cigars and fine scotch than any other mentor at the academy. Coming back from Afghanistan, I was eager to share stories with him. I began to flip through my photos when Charlie got up and opened a drawer containing a handful of old photographs. The vegetation looked remarkably similar to where we had fought along the border. I asked Charlie where the photos were from. I knew he couldn't tell me; he never told me any of the places where he had served with his Special Forces team.

Charlie was more of a father than a mentor, and my real father's absence only made me more eager to be seen by Charlie as a real warrior. I handed him a tiny bottle of sand from Losano Ridge. He placed it next to his collection of sands from Iwo Jima and Saipan, battlefields where his father had fought—a place of honor. He gave me a bear hug long enough for me to regain my composure, and soon after, we left for dinner.

I ate an entire chateaubriand steak by myself and washed it down with half a bottle of red wine. As the waitress arrived to clear our plates, Lisa stated proudly that I had just returned from Afghanistan.

"Is that so?" said the waitress.

"Yes, ma'am."

"Well, welcome home."

"Thank you, ma'am."

"What was it like?"

"It's just good to be home," I said. I wasn't ready with a small-talk re-sponse to a question that asked so much.

"Well, at least you weren't in Iraq." She paused. "Afghanistan mustn't be too dangerous these days."

I squeezed the leg of the table. It was a good thing she had taken my steak knife. She meant well, I'm sure. There was no reason for her to know much about Afghanistan's violence. There was scant broadcast coverage of Afghanistan, and Iraq was getting more deadly by the day. I smiled meekly. She had already turned down the hall.

Over the next year I heard the waitress's reaction countless times. Most Americans had no idea we were still fighting in Afghanistan. After 9/11, they had been told to "go shopping." And they did. Apart from the less than 0.5 percent of Americans in uniform, most people continued with their daily commutes, picked up the dry cleaning, and mowed the lawn. What if, instead, Americans had been asked to sacrifice? Would I have patrolled with unarmored pickup trucks? Someone else fought the war "over there." When the war intruded on the nightly news, it was easy to change the channel.

But I couldn't. I scoured the back pages of the newspaper to find anything about Afghanistan. Descriptions of fighting were vague and incomplete; even the journalists had abandoned that front. Yet, as our deployment faded, the units that replaced us faced more and more cross-border attacks and roadside bombs. The casualty rate worsened; Afghanistan was unraveling.

After visiting Charlie, I drove to see Bryan at Yale Law School. That weekend we went to a cocktail party at another student's apartment. The apartment was cramped with twentysomethings in business casual elbowing for drinks in the kitchen. Nibbling on canapés, I floated from group to group. They talked about obscure legal doctrines, celebrity romances, and law school gossip. If they talked at all about the war, it was the war in Iraq. "It's awful, isn't it?" was the most common banality. I had never felt so acutely conscious of standing apart from my civilian peers. Only two years before, at Oxford, I had gone to dozens of cocktail parties just like this. The scene was the same, but my perspective had changed.

In one discussion a student commented, "Believe me, I support the troops. I just don't support the war." I wondered exactly *how* he supported the troops. He must have seen the doubt in my eyes because he followed up quickly that he "would sign up to serve." He paused and then added the caveat, "If I could guarantee a challenging assignment." Was he serious? At West Point we'd learned that responsibility preceded privilege. I had forgotten how odd that sentiment appeared outside the military.

AT FORT DRUM I returned to the rhythms and routines of garrison life. The psychologists had told us before we left Orgun that the transition would be difficult for everyone. The shrinks were right. Homecoming wasn't all smiles. There were still battles to fight.

The first night I spent alone in my apartment was the hardest. I cooked pasta and sat down at my table. My fork and knife scratched unnervingly across the plate. I got up and turned on the stereo. Afterward, I sat on the couch and stared at a blank television. I had never bothered to attach the antenna. Bored, I pulled my cell phone out of my pocket and called Meena in Philadelphia. She didn't pick up; she was probably working late at the hospital. I called Story. He was playing with his kids and couldn't talk. I called a few of the other sergeants and got the same response. I got up and made myself a vodka tonic. I drank it quickly and made another. In Afghanistan, I had yearned for privacy. Now it was suffocating me.

The nights alone started to include stronger drinks. As I flipped through photos, I relived both the highlights and the tragedies, but especially the tragedies. Eventually, as the night got long and I thought about Evan and Chris, I drank faster. One night, while speaking on the telephone with my mother, she told me that my father had been having an affair.

"Before he left?"

"Yeah."

"How long?"

"Maybe a couple of years."

If that was the case, the father who visited me in Oxford had already abandoned us. The dishonesty removed whatever remaining respect I had for him. I drank half a bottle of Jack Daniel's and passed out on the couch. I woke up to Meena's bedtime call. She knew I wasn't well but was helpless to do anything from three hundred miles away in Philadelphia. Every night she would ask what was wrong, but I wouldn't respond. I was uncommunicative and half drunk most of the time. Part of me worried about the genes I shared with my father. How would this bode for our marriage? Was infidelity in my DNA? What would her parents say about my parents' divorce? In the middle of the night I woke up in a cold sweat and stared into the black. I didn't know what was wrong. I wasn't the me I was before.

I TOOK LEAVE IN June to spend a week with Meena in Italy. I needed to get away, and we needed time together. It was taking longer than I had hoped for our relationship to thaw out. Our embraces were awkward, and the rhythms of our conversations were out of sync. I was distant even when we were close.

We stayed on a farm near Orvieto, a hilltop city near Rome. Over quiet dinners and long drives through the hills, Meena and I began to reconnect. One day we went for a long walk in the Sibylline Mountains. We sat on a grassy slope in the sunshine. Below us, a carpet of wildflowers bloomed in purple, red, and yellow. One road crossed the valley in a ribbon of black. On either side of the road, the lentil fields were just coming to life. Above us, faint traces of snow trickled down the ridges like white frosting. Meena reached for my hand, and my fingers slid into hers like familiar grooves. I told her everything. When I stopped, she held me in her arms as I sobbed.

Over the course of the week, I began to smile. I laughed with Meena as I related my camel-riding adventure and my soldiers' antics. I had been wrong about our relationship. It wasn't *us* that had to thaw out; it was *me*.

WHILE WE WERE IN Italy, I received an email from the battalion commander. My request for a reassignment closer to Meena had been approved.

"Meena, come read this."

She peered over my shoulder at the screen. "What's the 'Old Guard'? Is this good news?"

"Meena, this means I'm moving to Washington."

She nearly strangled me in my seat she was so happy. The Old Guard was the Army's elite ceremonial unit, stationed outside Arlington Cemetery in Washington. More important for us, the Old Guard was close to Baltimore, where Meena hoped to continue her training as a surgeon. Marching in parades wasn't what I had imagined doing after Afghanistan, but it was the one way I could continue to serve in the Army and be with Meena. Soon after receiving the news of my assignment, we set a wedding date for the following May, just four years after I had first told Meena I loved her.

EVERY WEEK AT THE Old Guard offered something exciting—from the arrival of a foreign head of state to planning the evacuation of important bureaucrats in the event of a terrorist attack. When I suited up in my uniform and unsheathed my saber, it was always electrifying. What an incredible honor to represent the Army to the world. Unfortunately, many of the missions were more somber. Every week, and sometimes more often, we sent a detachment of soldiers to Dover, Delaware, to recover dead soldiers.

Inevitably, we buried our own: soldiers from the Old Guard who had returned to the line. The first thing I did every morning at the office was to scan the *Washington Post*'s list of American casualties. It was the part of the day I hated the most, but I had a strange compulsion to look. When would I see a West Point classmate or one of my soldiers? I both wanted and didn't want to know at the same time. Scanning those pages was a form of penance, the only connection I had to the war. I was desperate not to forget them, and I was desperate not to forget my own experiences. I willed myself to record every shard of memory I could recall from the deployment. It helped me close the distance.

While I struggled to remember certain meaningful details, other memories ambushed me with disturbing frequency. A police helicopter buzzing overhead triggered thoughts of the fight on Losano Ridge. Cannon fire from the salute battery during ceremonies made me jump every time, because they reminded me of incoming rockets. Another veteran got into the practice of yelling "Outgoing!" to calm my nerves. "Don't worry, Mullaney," he said, "you'll get used to it. We were all like that when we got back." Lunch conversation with the other junior officers inevitably worked its way toward Iraq and Afghanistan. We would swap tales of near misses, unbelievable heroics, and botched missions. In retrospect, those bull sessions were an important mechanism for processing our experiences—of turning fear, tragedy, and insecurity into stories, just as every band of warriors has done, from the Greeks at Troy to the Americans at Normandy.

A month before our wedding, I walked with Meena through Arlington Cemetery. I had walked through it countless times yet continued to be struck silent by the serried ranks of granite crosses—three hundred thousand of them. When we reached the bottom of the hill, we stopped to walk through the Faces of the Fallen exhibit. In a long, cold hall were over a thousand artists' portraits of each service member killed in Iraq and Afghanistan. I walked slowly down the hall, conscious of Meena standing beside me. There were watercolor paintings, pencil portraits, silhouettes, and etchings. I knew we were going to be late for lunch, but I wanted to say a prayer for each one. I had to. Meena's grip on my hand tightened when we reached O'Neill's portrait. It was beautiful. I paused longer and said a prayer for his family. One day I hoped I could tell them his story, but I wasn't ready yet.

"Are you okay?" asked Meena.

"No," I said.

Meena kissed my cheek, and we walked outside, through the graveyard, together.

38

Vows

Your heart I take in mine. Whatever is in your heart shall be in mine, whatever is in mine shall be in yours. Our hearts shall be one, our minds shall be one. May God make us one.

PANIGRAHANA VOW

I MARRIED THE SAME WOMAN TWICE. ACCORDING TO a Hindu astrologer's precise calculation, my wedding to Meena had to occur between 9:00 and 9:30 a.m. on a Friday morning in May. The second wedding the next day required no astrological seal of approval but instead required, since I was marrying a non-Catholic, an awkwardly worded "dispensation of cult." Father Matt, the priest who had first met Meena in Rome, did the paperwork.

The rituals of a South Indian wedding evolved over five thousand years and are rich in symbolism. The wedding altar, or *mandap*, was a raised dais covered in rich carpet with a backdrop curtain of gold fabric and mirrored sequins. Two small stools were arranged facing our guests, and in front of them stood mounds of bananas, oranges, and coconuts that the Hindu priest would use during the ceremony. At the center of the *mandap* was a fire representing God's presence. Our priest, swaddled in white robes and with his hair pulled back in a knot, sat across from us on the *mandap*. His forehead bore three distinct white stripes, marking him as a Brahmin devotee of Shiva. My immediate family and I wore traditional Indian clothing that Meena's parents had generously given us as gifts the day before.

There was much ringing of bells and Sanskrit chanting as the priest blessed the altar, and Meena's parents tied a turmeric-powdered thread around her wrist to ward off evil. We moved outside for the next portion of the ceremony. As I stood opposite Meena, exchanging garlands of flowers, the woman in front of me took my breath away. When Meena's grandparents had performed this rite at their own marriage, it was the first time after their betrothal that they had seen each other. As I looked at Meena, I had the same sense that I was seeing her for the first time. She was unrecognizable from the girl in an oversized backpack I had met five years before. Wrapped in a royal purple sari of gold-embroidered silk, Meena was resplendent. Gold amulets suspended from a part in her hair. A dozen bangles on her arms clinked and glinted in the light. At the priest's instructions, I clasped Meena's right hand in mine, her fingers pointed upward in the shape of a lotus blossom meant to signify the blossoming relationship between us. Her hands had rich patterns of henna, traced into flowers and vines. Her anklets tinkled as we walked toward an ornamental swing meant to symbolize life's ups and downs. We sat on the plush seat facing our family and friends while female relatives fed us milk, honey, and fruit.

After moving back to the *mandap* inside, the priest tied a thread around my own wrist, and I stood next to Meena and her father. Meena held out her hands, and the priest placed an orange in them. He then placed Meena's hands on top of her father's open palms. As Meena's mother poured water over the orange, the priest rang his bell loudly and moved Meena's hands into mine, a symbolic giving away of the bride.

"Repeat after me," said the priest, who then continued in Sanskrit.

I parroted back exactly what he said but had no idea what I was saying. Meena's aunt, narrating the wedding for our guests, translated:

"Craig says, 'God has given you to me to be the mistress of my household. . . .'"

I couldn't keep a straight face and burst out laughing. "That'll be the day," I said, forgetting that the priest had placed a microphone on me. Meena erupted in laughter along with the rest of our friends.

The priest blessed a heavy gold necklace, the equivalent of a Western wedding ring, and passed it among the elders to sanctify. I placed the necklace around Meena's neck, and my sisters tied three knots in it. Indian oboes soared and drums beat loudly. Our guests showered us with flower petals and turmeric-coated rice, clapping along with the rhythm of the drums. "Welcome to the family," Meena's mother said, beaming, as her father vigorously shook my hand, grinning again as he had when we first met.

Meena and I then took turns leading each other around the holy fire, pledging loyalty in the pursuit of righteousness, desire, prosperity, and unity. The priest placed Meena's foot on a heavy grindstone, and I knelt beside her. Above her toes, a floral bouquet in henna rose underneath the hem of her sari and disappeared under jeweled anklets. As I slipped two silver rings on her second toe, we pledged in Sanskrit to be as steadfast as the stone. While remaining on my knees, holding her foot in one hand and her hand in the other, I moved her foot seven steps, symbolizing our first steps together on our journey as a married couple. With each step we recited our vows, among them a promise to nurture each other's beliefs and dreams, to find fulfillment in our work, to alleviate the suffering of others, and to live a life full of joy and laughter. Each time I placed Meena's heel on the floor, her anklets jingled with a metallic laughter only the two of us could hear.

After a prayer to the star Arundhati, symbol of eternal love and devotion, our marriage received its final blessing from the priest. Meena's grandmother, five feet of wit and energy, shouted out to a chorus of laughs: "You may now kiss the bride!"

THE FOLLOWING DAY WE completed the twin weddings with a traditional military Catholic ceremony. I walked in with my mother on my arm and stood near Father Matt as our flower girls spread a carpet of rose petals along the aisle. I wore my Old Guard dress uniform, complete with medals, ornamental belt, and saber.

Among the guests before me were several in military uniforms—Trent Moore, Liz Young, Lieutenant Colonel Nagl, my brother, Gary, in his cadet summer whites, Tim Strabbing in the high-collared dress blues of the Marine Corps, and Staff Sergeant McGurk. Most of the military invitees couldn't make it. My old roommate Bill Parsons and wrestling partner Aram Donigian were overseas. So, too, was Captain Worthan and half of my old platoon. At the last minute, Story called to tell me he couldn't come. A Fort Drum soldier had been killed in Iraq, and Story had to coordinate the notification of his parents. The rest of the platoon had scattered to other units or left no trace behind when they finished their service. I had lost touch with mentors such as Yingling and LoFaro at West Point, Gunny Oakes from Ranger School, and Colonel LaCamera from Fort Drum. I wished I could thank them for what they had taught me.

The doors swung open, and I followed the eyes of my guests toward Meena. I have never seen her so beautiful. Meena's slender curves were swathed in red silk embroidered in gold. Her smile was incandescent even in the bright light of the conservatory. As she stepped to the beat of the song I had chosen, the first one she had taught me to sing in Hindi, I recalled the thousand things I loved about her: the crook in her smile and the curve of her hip, the smell of mustard seeds frying in her skillet, how she never noticed when I was holding a chair out for her to sit, the fact that she could take a bullet out of a neck but couldn't figure out how to take a cork out of a wine bottle. I wiped a tear from my eye with my white glove, knowing no one would see me as they, as transfixed as I was, watched Meena gliding down the flower-strewn carpet, one parent on each arm.

One by one our friends and family read passages from the Bible and from the Bengali poet Rabindranath Tagore: "Only from the marriage of two forces does music arise in the world." As if to prove Tagore's point, our friend Katie Larson, the classmate who stood with me before Lincoln College's gate, sang a beautiful folk song accompanied by the soaring chords of another close friend's viola. I squeezed Meena's hand, grateful for the friendships that had sustained us and helped us grow.

When it was Father Matt's turn to give the homily, he made a crack at the obsessive planning I had done for the wedding.

"Does anyone know what time it is?" he asked. "Because according to the schedule I got from Craig, I'm supposed to speak from 11:28 until 11:38. I'll know if I'm in trouble if he draws his saber."

Our wedding party laughed, having spent the previous night rehearsing every detail in the thirty-page plan I had written. "You've gotta be kidding me," Matt and Hayden had exclaimed when I told them they were going to have to be dressed for photos by 7 a.m. I stared back. "Okay, okay. We'll be there." Father Matt finished his homily with a reference to Victor Hugo: "To love another person is to see the face of God." Our love for each other, he said, was a gift of grace. Looking at the glow on Meena's face, I felt blessed. At Father Matt's command, we stood and faced each other. Bryan, my best man, and Meena's sister handed him the rings to bless. Repeating after Father Matt, I slipped the ring on Meena's finger "in the name of the Father, and of the Son, and of the Holy Spirit."

"I now present to you Captain Craig Mullaney and Doctor Meena Se-shamani. You may kiss the bride." I kissed Meena to the cheers of a hundred guests. After four years the lines I had drawn on that yellow legal pad at Oxford finally intersected. As we walked arm in arm to the sounds of Beethoven's Ninth Symphony, I could barely contain the joy bursting in my heart.

At the reception we entered through an arch of sabers. Just as we were about to pass through the final pair, Tim Strabbing and Andrew Gallo lowered their sabers to block our path.

"The price of passage is a kiss," demanded Gallo.

I leaned over and kissed Meena. The sabers raised, and we took another step. As we cleared the arch, Trent took his saber and hit Meena's butt. "Welcome to the Army, ma'am!"

39

Teaching War

You may not be interested in war, but war is interested in you.

LEON TROTSKY

I WAS AN ARMY OF ONE. NINE MONTHS AFTER AR-riving at the Old Guard, I had yet another set of orders, this time to the Naval Academy in Annapolis, Maryland. Tim Strabbing, my Marine friend from Oxford, had recommended that I fill an opening there to teach history. I submitted an application but never expected that the Army would let me teach at Navy. Annapolis was "The Dark Side." The irony of an Army officer teaching at a naval academy was lost on no one, including my department chair, who, in a twisted practical joke, assigned me to teach naval history. I had never even been on a Navy ship; to me, *bow* was a verb and *stern* an adjective, not nouns representing the front and back of a ship.

The Naval Academy was as strange a culture as any I had explored before. Although we were firmly onshore, everything had a nautical designation. Thus, I worked on the third "deck" of the building, washed my hands in the "head" to the left of the "ladder," and nailed my Army memorabilia into the "bulkhead" of my office. When students came by, they knocked on my "hatch" and said, "Sir, permission to come aboard, sir." Before leaving they asked to "shove off." The first time I heard the expression, I thought an eighteen-year-old was insulting me.

When I started at Annapolis, I expected a fever pitch of interest in the war. When I had visited Gary at West Point, almost all of his professors were recently returned combat veterans. His summer training exercises had intentionally mimicked Iraqi forward operating bases. In their new Army camouflage uniforms, cadets looked primed to fight. In 2005, the Naval Academy felt extraordinarily remote. One day, walking out of the office in my uniform, a civilian professor asked whether it was Warrior Day. "Yeah, sure," I replied, unclear what he was referring to. Wasn't every day Warrior Day? The next day a colleague told me that Warrior Day was the one day every other week when midshipmen and officers wore their service's combat uniforms: flight suits for the pilots, overalls for the submariners, and camouflage for the Marines—as if the uniform made the warrior rather than the other way around.

When I began teaching, I avoided the tactics of naval warfare and led my students through a history of American foreign policy. We discussed the Navy's role in foreign relations, from its intervention in the first war on terrorism against the Barbary pirates to the naval blockade that arguably kept the Cold War cold during the Cuban Missile Crisis. I blended the teaching styles I had observed at Oxford and West Point. I rarely delivered a lecture, for instance, leaving it to them, not me, to learn. I would help them up the mountain, but I wasn't going to carry them on my back. Breaking my class into small groups at the beginning of the semester, I posed questions that each group researched and shared with the rest of the class. I demanded that they challenge one another and work together.

History isn't about memorizing dates; it's about investigation, interpretation, and imagination. I wanted them to challenge conventional wisdom and to think for themselves, to take intellectual risks, not just physical ones. Question the answers, I repeated every class. Reevaluate your conclusions when the evidence changes. I asked them to evaluate President Harry Truman's decision to drop the atomic bombs, but made them debate from the position they disagreed with. We studied World War I in depth, not because I wanted to shock them with the horrors of the trenches, but because I wanted them to see how rational statesmen had blundered into a war no one wanted.

We probed the necessity and the limits of reason. We watched Robert McNamara's chilling confessions in *The Fog of War*. Years after his controversial tenure as secretary of defense during the 1960s, McNamara pointed out with regret how much faith he and his colleagues had put in their ability to calibrate and control the situation in Vietnam. According to McNamara, most variables in war, especially at the strategic level, are out of our control or unknowable. As Donald Rumsfeld stated so poetically, "There are *known knowns*. These are things we know that we know. There are *known unknowns*. That is to say, there are things that we know we don't know. But there are also *unknown unknowns*. There are things we don't know we don't know." Strategy isn't a mathematical equation, I told the midshipmen; there is not always a "correct" answer. History, more than any other subject, showed how often the "best and the brightest" got it wrong. Beware the unknown unknowns.

My teaching was motivated in part by knowledge that one of my students might eventually command an aircraft carrier, a nuclear-armed submarine, or a Marine regiment. I wanted that future officer to weigh decisions with a supple mind and to be comfortable with nuance and uncertainty. I was conscious, however, that I was holding back from my students. At the end of one class, a student pointed out that I always evaded questions about my service in Afghanistan. "How come you never talk about it, sir?"

"We have a lot to cover," I said. It was a bad excuse, and I knew it. It was easier to discuss grand strategy. I didn't want to tell my story. I saw in each face a younger version of me. I knew they would question, at least in their own minds, the decisions I had made. I wasn't ready to stand trial.

At the end of October, on the two-year anniversary of the fight at Khand Narai Pass, where Chris had died, I decided to speak. If I wanted them to be better than I was, I had a responsibility to share my mistakes and what I had learned. I arrived in class with a crate of maps, photos, a jagged piece of rocket shrapnel, and the tail end of the mortar that should have killed me. I motioned to the class to pull their desks in tighter. I sat on my desk, propped my boots on the seat of a chair, and started to tell my story. They listened as I related the battle on Losano Ridge in clinical terms: movement to contact, suppressive fire, and medical evacuation. In telling the story, I reconstructed events from a dozen perspectives, rendering to the battle a clarity that distorted the reality as I had experienced it: chaos, noise, fear, exhilaration. I asked if I could start again. Of course, they answered. This time I tried to put them under my helmet, seeing and hearing and touching the battle. They sat still, rapt with attention. I finished with O'Neill's memorial service. A couple of midshipmen averted watery eyes, and I was surprised that I was not in tears myself. I found that telling the story was more of a relief than a trial.

"What do you think, sir, that you would have done differently?"

A hundred thoughts went through my head before I punted the personal question and talked about the larger strategy.

"The best thing we could have done for Afghanistan was to get out of our Humvees and drink more green chai. We should have focused less on finding the enemy, and more on finding our friends." Getting the strategy right hadn't been my responsibility. My mission had been to fight well and bring my men home, and although we had fought well, I had failed to bring every soldier back. The unsettling truth was that I still had no idea what I had done wrong on Losano Ridge. Was there anything I could have done differently to save O'Neill's life? I still didn't know, and I expected I never would.

The midshipmen wanted to believe that they could "get it right," that they would be able to eliminate risk by understanding and manipulating all the variables to their advantage. As a cadet, I had believed the same thing. I could coldly analyze any tactical problem and seize the objective. It was part of the Ranger Creed I had shouted a thousand times—cold, wet, and/or miserable. *Fight on to the Ranger objective and complete the mission, though I be the lone survivor.* I had to believe that. The alternative— that I would not be in complete control, that the enemy had a say, that there was no such thing as "minimum safe distance," that I might succumb to fear or indecision—would have been paralyzing. Successfully leading in combat required faith in the perfectibility of my men and myself. Everything about training at a military academy emphasizes that imperative to control and banish chaos, from the manipulation of sails to master the wind, to the daily battle against dust on their mirrors. I wasn't ready to tell the midshipmen that they could "get it right" and still lose.

A skinny Plebe raised his hand.

"Were you ready?"

I looked down at the shrapnel.

"I was as ready as I could be," I replied.

There were some lessons they would learn only by experience. No classroom or field exercise would ever fully simulate how difficult it can be to keep your wits about you while your men are wounded or dying. The only fact you might know is that someone is just as desperate to kill you as you are to stay alive by killing him. How do you teach a future officer what to say to his men after he has failed to protect them? How do you explain resolve? How do you teach courage?

ONE AFTERNOON THE SKINNY Plebe who had asked whether I was prepared stopped by my office. "Permission to come aboard."

"Ahoy," I said with a grin, "come aboard."

"I wanted to show you something, sir, before I left for the summer."

He lifted his forearm to chest level and turned his wrist. He was wearing a silver bracelet with a name etched on it. I had seen only a few midshipmen wearing these bracelets, personalized reminders of Americans killed or missing in action.

"I had it engraved with your soldier's name, sir. See"—he turned it upright—"PFC EVAN W. O'NEILL KIA 29 SEP 03."

I kept looking at the bracelet, identical to the one on my wrist.

"I don't know anyone who's over there, and I wanted something to remind me of what I'm here for. After your story, I looked up your soldier. I figured you'd want to know."

"This means a lot to me. Thank you."

"Permission to shove off."

"Permission granted."

I shut the door behind him, sat down, and stared at the photo of my platoon mounted above my desk. We had taken it at first light on a cold morning wearing watch caps and long underwear. By this time our cotton fatigues had the stiffness of canvas. My men perched on top of the Humvees: Chuck on the left, thick-jowled and stern; Grenz wrapped in a brown scarf, his grenade launcher slid open as if he were about to load a round. There were McGurk and Story, Markam and Red and Howe. All of us in sepia except one. O'Neill's face was missing from the lineup. He had been killed before we had a chance to take a photo including him. For all its tragedy, that platoon on my wall made it all worthwhile. I fought for them. My men.

My students had many challenges before them, and I hoped I taught them something they would remember. Unlike professors at civilian universities, instructors at a military academy must work under the haunting imperative that what we fail to teach our students could kill them or those they lead. My contribution in the classroom was one small part of that mission. I hoped I taught them to be better thinkers. I hoped I taught them enough intellectual humility to question their own answers. I hoped I taught them resolve and courage and even a little compassion. But I also share the curse of every teacher: I will never know whether I succeeded.

40

Echoes

The challenge of education is not to prepare a person for success, but to prepare him for failure.

ADMIRAL JAMES STOCKDALE

THE DEEPER THE CAVERN, THE FARTHER THE ECHO travels. I was in frigid water up to my chest in a Guatemalan cave. My brother, Gary, and I had spelunked for several hours already, pausing at intervals to admire the stalagmites, scramble up waterfalls, or search for a passageway through the inky black. Two miles into the cave system, our echoes seemed no closer to finding its deepest recesses. They kept bouncing back and forth, back and forth.

It was freezing cold, even in our wetsuits and boots. Our guide was barefoot as he forged ahead holding a single wax candle to light his way. I turned my helmet, and its beam spotlit Gary, about to plunge from an ad hoc diving board into a pool of unknown depth. I wanted to yell at him not to jump, but I restrained the impulse. He was fearless in the way only twenty-year-olds can be. Everything I did, he had to take one step further. He wanted to prove something. Maybe to me or maybe to himself.

Our expedition to Guatemala on Gary's spring break his junior year was my attempt to build our relationship. I wanted to impart a little of what I had learned traveling the globe: how to safeguard your passport, where to grease the bureaucracy with baksheesh, what to bring on a camping expedition. That was the limit of the advice I gave Gary. It had been two years since I had returned from Afghanistan, but I still hadn't talked about it with him. The lessons I wanted to share stayed between my ears. I could tell my students, but not my own brother. Partly, I wanted to believe Gary wouldn't face the same trials. I hoped beyond reason that Iraq would quiet down. But, in fact, things there were getting worse. My friends were deploying yet again. Gallo was commanding an airborne company. Bill Parsons was about to take command of a Stryker company. Liz Young, who had taken the same path I had to Oxford, was gearing up for her second deployment to Iraq. How could I watch them go to war, how could I watch my own brother go to war, while I sat on the sidelines?

There was a more important reservation, however, that made me most hesitant to talk with Gary. I had failed to bring every man in my platoon home safely. What would Gary think of my leadership at Losano Ridge? Was that failure redeemable?

Doubt made me consider my father, present in my life largely by his conspicuous absence. When my car's fuel gauge dipped below a quarter tank, I heard my father chiding me. When I listened to country music, I remembered seeing Kenny Rogers with him—my first concert. When the plumbing in my house clogged, I wanted to ask him what to do. I shaved and saw his beard. He was and wasn't there. He was a shadow, always lurking behind me. I wondered whether I shared his cowardice in the face of duty. Was it a genetic marker like the dark eyes I had inherited? Would his fate be mine? And what about Gary? Didn't he evaluate me through the prism of our father? If he saw my flaws, wouldn't I be just as phony as the father we condemned? For that reason it was Gary's respect that I, the older brother, so desperately needed. But that desperation was conflicted. My fear that he wouldn't understand tempered the obligation I felt to teach him what I tried to teach my students. Fear outweighed duty, and I kept my confessions to myself.

ALTHOUGH I NEEDED GARY'S respect, I also needed a ghost's forgiveness. It was time to visit O'Neill. I bought a train ticket to Boston, and a friend drove me to the cemetery in North Andover, just outside the city. American flags fluttered off the highway overpasses, most tattered and faded with age. We exited from the freeway onto quiet roads shaded by oaks and bordered by stone walls and old houses. We passed the village green with its white-steepled church and the fire station where Mr. O'Neill served. Just down the road were the gates to the cemetery.

It was the week before Christmas, and the barren trees made the twilight seem darker than it really was. I stepped out of the car and shivered in my overcoat. The first snow had fallen, and my dress shoes were entirely unsuitable. I walked across the hilly cemetery searching for O'Neill. In the letter he had written to the battalion, Mr. O'Neill said they buried his son at the highest point in the cemetery, like the hill where he had made his final patrol. I crunched through the snow and stopped in front of a simple gravestone.

EVAN WILLIAM
O'NEILL

PFC US ARMY
AFGHANISTAN
APR 16 1984
SEP 29 2003
BSM W/V KIA
PURPLE HEART
CO A 1 BN 87 INF
10 MOUNTAIN DIV
PARATROOPER

Surrounding the grave were two American flags, a stone angel, a Christmas wreath, and a little wooden Uncle Sam. I stood by the gravestone, but my mind returned to Losano Ridge: McGurk's voice over the radio telling me O'Neill was dead. The medevac, riddled with bullet holes, carrying his lifeless body off that damned hill. Those eyes.

Bowing my head, I asked Evan to forgive me. But then for the first time I realized that something had changed. Somewhere between Annapolis and

Andover, I had finally forgiven myself. As soldiers we were well trained, in peak physical condition, and focused on our mission. But we weren't immortal, and we weren't in control. I did my best; I fought well. So did Evan. Yet there was nothing any of us could have done to save him. The enemy had his vote.

I thought of the obituary by John Alexander Hottell III: *We all have but one death to spend.* I lifted my head and made the sign of the cross. In the name of the Father, and of the Son, and of the Holy Spirit. Evan spent his death well. He died a warrior. Amen.

A YEAR AFTER I visited Evan's grave, I had to visit another. In November I lost a second soldier from my old platoon. Sergeant Lucas "Red" White had been killed by a roadside bomb in Baghdad just two weeks shy of returning home. When Story called me with the news, I drank a glass of twelve-year-old scotch in Red's honor, remembering his antics as I swirled the glass. The ice melted slowly into the liquor. His sixth sense had failed him at last.

The morning of the funeral, I ironed my uniform and shaved. On my wrist I wore O'Neill's bracelet. It was scratched, and his full name was getting harder and harder to read. Later, I thought, I would have to order one for Red. Outside, the sky was overcast and the air cold. Winter was approaching. I drove along Route 50 from Annapolis to Arlington Cemetery. I had buried others in Arlington, but never one of my own.

Outside the cemetery administration building, we lined up our cars to go to the grave site. Markam, now a college ROTC student, caught my eye. "One last convoy, huh, sir?"

"One last convoy, Markam."

Red's wife sat in the first row, burrowed in a warm coat against the chill. Red's parents and grandparents were there as well. I stood to the side with Markam and two of my other soldiers. As the Old Guard honor guard approached, the metal taps on their heels rattled on the cold pavement.

The funeral was short. In crisp, quick movements, the honor guard folded the American flag that had been draped over Red's casket. "On behalf of a grateful nation," began the officer as he handed the folded triangle of blue and white stars to Red's wife. She was stronger than we were. My men and I, we cried.

After the ceremony, the four of us lingered by the grave to pay our last respects. I raised my hand in a salute, joining my stiff fingers in a knife-edge against the wind. As I walked back to the convoy, I swiveled my head at my men walking behind me in a file. Our rucksacks were missing, but the weight remained.

Glancing at the granite slabs we passed, I noticed for the first time that each bore the byline of Iraq or Afghanistan. Every grave in the section was fresh. I shut the car door and pulled away from the curb. As our convoy departed, another followed behind. Another was probably behind that one. I opened the windows for some fresh air. In the distance, synchronized rifle volleys and faint bugle notes echoed across the cemetery—back and forth, back and forth.

41

The Distance Run

To strive, to seek, to find, and not to yield.

TENNYSON, *Ulysses*

A WEEK BEFORE MY BROTHER'S GRADUATION FROM West Point, I spent an afternoon at home combing through a half-dozen duffel bags stuffed with military gear that had accumulated like barnacles on a ship. I dumped the bags on the storage room floor—green and black items clumped together as the detritus of an Army career. There were yards and yards of nylon cord, a rusty entrenchment tool, a lot of knives I didn't remember buying, a first aid pouch, suspenders, a stormproof whistle. I sorted the mess into the things I would keep, the things I would throw away, and the things I would give to Gary.

My progress was slow. I smiled at the vinyl map case that had kept my maps dry in Florida's swamps. I put it in the bag for my brother, knowing he could use the help in his land navigation exercises. There was a small flashlight with a red lens that I had used to read in the field and a favorite insulated shirt I had worn on cold nights at Drum. They might make Gary more comfortable, I thought as I placed them in the duffel. I picked out brass insignia and name tags thinking that he could never have too many. As I continued packing, the only gear remaining was from Afghanistan.

Seven empty magazines rattled on the concrete. They still had the green tape and loops I had rigged to help me change magazines faster. There was the panel of bright nylon I had used to signal helicopters. I folded it and put it in the bag. Next, I lifted the boots I had worn in Shkin. The boot-laces were fraying. One had snapped. There was a stain of blood on the heel. I sat down on the floor and held the boots in my lap. Gary could use the magazines, but the boots were beyond repair. I continued sorting. A stack of T-shirts had my last name and blood type stenciled in big block letters. Holding a folded shirt in both hands, my eyes fixed on the black B+.

We shared the same blood type.

Gary didn't need a blood type, I wanted to tell myself. He was just going on another field exercise. Blank ammunition. Plastic targets. Notional casualties, notional blood. I sat there for what must have been an hour, the realization finally sinking in that Gary would likely face the same trials I did. He, too, would have his courage and conviction tested. He might lose soldiers under his command, have to watch them die in his arms. He might even be wounded or killed himself. Up to now what had I taught him that would help him with those challenges? Very little, I had to admit. Part of preserving an eleven-year-old kid brother in my mind meant avoiding those discussions. As I sat on that cold concrete floor, I realized I owed it to Gary to share whatever I had learned, even if in doing so I exposed my record to his judgment.

THE PAVEMENT SHIMMERED WITH heat as my car shifted gears climbing over Storm King Mountain toward West Point. A thousand feet below, enveloped by the wide ribbon of the Hudson River, West Point looked as enduring as the mountain sliding beneath my wheels. Its granite ramparts surrounded the perfect emerald expanse of the Plain. The bright summer sun glinted off the cadets' bayonets as they circumscribed the parade field. As I coasted downhill on Highway 9W, West Point's inner sanctum disappeared from view. I turned off the highway and drove along the golf course and past the private security guards at Washington Gate. I knew the route by heart. It was the same tree-lined avenue I had first marched along as my class finished Beast. In the four years that followed, I wore an imperceptible groove in its sidewalks, marching, walking, or running.

West Point looked the same as it had seven years before, but its agelessness made it easy to forget how much time had slipped down the Hudson. When I began, Gary had just turned eleven. I have a photo of the two of us standing next to each other. He's wearing my dress gray uniform and smiling as he makes an earnest attempt to stand at attention. I later learned that after I graduated he kept that dress gray on a hanger by his bed. Thinking of his height and breadth now, I laughed. He would probably split the seams of his "big" brother's uniform. It was hard to believe that Gary was about to become an officer. Both he and the world had changed. We had been at war for nearly six years. His class had entered West Point three months after the Iraq invasion. His challenge would be even tougher than mine. I couldn't help but consider the remarkable symmetry of our paths: He was set to join a cavalry squadron in Iraq just as I was set to leave the service. We were soldiers passing in the night, conducting our own two-person relief-in-place.

Gary's graduation followed a script that hadn't changed since I had endured it. A procession of parades, awards ceremonies, dinners, and inspections culminated in a grand ceremony at the football stadium. After the euphoric hat toss, Gary rushed to change out of his cadet gray and into his officer green. We waited for Gary at a monument overlooking the river. Two hundred yards across the parade field was the room I had once shared with Bill Parsons. We spent countless hours looking out the window, wondering about the challenges we would face as lieutenants. Neither of us could have predicted the course our careers took. Just a week before, he sent me a chilling email from Iraq. His twin brother had nearly died when a roadside bomb destroyed his Stryker vehicle. He crawled out of the hatch seconds before it went up in flames. The three of us had run together preparing for marathons. Now, Bill's brother had to fight to walk again. While I wanted to concentrate my prayers on his recovery, all I could think about was Gary. Would I ever have the strength to relay bad news if it involved my brother? I couldn't bear the possibility, yet I had to.

At the monument Gary and nine of his friends, all newly minted second lieutenants, stood at attention in front of us wearing dress uniforms devoid of all decorations except their name tags and branch insignia. The switch from gray to green added five years to their faces. Gary's height placed him in the back row, and he looked straight ahead, conscious for perhaps the first time in his life that a dimpled smile wouldn't be appropriate. As his company officer read the oath of commissioning, I stepped up with my mother and my sister Bridget to pin gold bars on his epaulettes and beret. A round of applause erupted from the gathered friends and family. I stood in front of Gary and saluted him.

There was so much I wanted to say to him that I wasn't sure where to start. I wanted him to know that the greatest privilege I had ever had was leading men in combat. He was going to be tested over and over again in ways he could never predict or simulate in training. There were going to be times when he would be afraid, but I wanted him to know that courage had more to do with facing that fear than forgetting it. His men would expect him to share their risks and to stand with them in the storm. But they would also expect him to set a course, decide, act, and lead. He couldn't afford to doubt himself. The only way to never make a decision he would regret would be to never make any decisions at all.

Finally, I wanted to tell him that doing everything right might still entail heart-wrenching consequences. Gary would have his own unforgiving minutes, I feared, but what mattered was that he fill those minutes with "sixty seconds' worth of distance run." And just as important were all the hours of demanding preparation *before* the unforgiving minute: the education and training, the running and marching, the deliberate planning married to decisive action. His men expected no more than everything he had; they deserved no less. Yet the only way Gary would be able to measure success would be to look in the mirror.

But even as these thoughts ran through my head, I realized how little I could convey in a few phrases. The rest Gary would have to learn for himself. As we hugged, I whispered in his ear: "Take care of your men."

It was all I could think to say.

A READING LIST

Reading has been an essential component of this soldier's education. With that in mind, I offer the following partial list of works organized loosely by subject.

Afghanistan

Afghanistan by Stephen Tanner

The Bear Went Over the Mountain by Les Grau

Ghost Wars by Steve Coll

The Great Game by Peter Hopkirk

The Kite Runner by Khaled Hosseini

Not a Good Day to Die by Sean Naylor

The Places in Between by Rory Stewart

The Punishment of Virtue by Sarah Chayes

Soldiers of God by Robert Kaplan

Taliban by Ahmed Rashid

Three Cups of Tea by Greg Mortenson

History

American Diplomacy by George Kennan

An Autobiography by Mahatma Gandhi

The Best and the Brightest by David Halberstam

Eichmann in Jerusalem by Hannah Arendt

History of the Peloponnesian War by Thucydides

In Retrospect by Robert McNamara

"A Problem from Hell" by Samantha Power

Thinking in Time by Richard E. Neustadt and Ernst R. May

The True Believer by Eric Hoffer

War of the World by Niall Ferguson

What Is History? by E. H. Carr

Literature

All the King's Men by Robert Penn Warren

A Man for All Seasons by Robert Bolt

Atlas Shrugged by Ayn Rand

Beowulf, translation by Seamus Heaney

Blood Meridian by Cormac McCarthy

Breakfast at Tiffany's by Truman Capote

The Brothers Karamazov by Fyodor Dostoevsky

Catch-22 by Joseph Heller

A Clockwork Orange by Anthony Burgess

Crime and Punishment by Fyodor Dostoevsky

Darkness at Noon by Arthur Koestler

The Divine Comedy by Dante

A Doll's House by Henrik Ibsen

Dreams from My Father by Barack Obama

The Educated Imagination by Northrop Frye

An Experiment in Criticism by C. S. Lewis

Fathers and Sons by Ivan Turgenev

The Great Gatsby by F. Scott Fitzgerald

Heart of Darkness by Joseph Conrad

Henry V by William Shakespeare

The Importance of Being Earnest by Oscar Wilde

Innocents Abroad by Mark Twain

Journey's End by R. C. Sherriff

Midnight's Children by Salman Rushdie

A Moveable Feast by Ernest Hemingway

The Nick Adams Stories by Ernest Hemingway

Nineteen Eighty-Four by George Orwell

On the Road by Jack Kerouac

A Passage to India by E. M. Forster

The Power of One by Bryce Courtenay

Pride and Prejudice by Jane Austen

Pygmalion by George Bernard Shaw

The Quiet American by Graham Greene

A Room with a View by E. M. Forster

A Suitable Boy by Vikram Seth

A Time for Gifts by Patrick Leigh Fermor

The Trial by Franz Kafka

Vision Quest by Terry Davis

Military Affairs

"28 Articles" by David Kilcullen

All Quiet on the Western Front by Erich Maria Remarque

The Army and Vietnam by Andrew Krepinevich

Band of Brothers by Stephen Ambrose

Black Hawk Down by Mark Bowden

The Campaigns of Napoleon by David Chandler

Counterinsurgency Warfare by David Galula

Destroyer Captain by James Stavridis

FM 3-24: Counterinsurgency Field Manual

The Face of Battle by John Keegan

Fiasco by Tom Ricks

The Forgotten Soldier by Guy Sajer

Gates of Fire by Steven Pressfield

Going to the Wars by Max Hastings

Goodbye, Darkness by William Manchester

Good-Bye to All That by Robert Graves

The Great War and Modern Memory by Paul Fussell

The Last Ridge by McKay Jenkins

Learning to Eat Soup with a Knife by John Nagl

The Memoirs of Field Marshal Montgomery

Men Against Fire by S.L.A. Marshall

One Bullet Away by Nathaniel Fick

On Killing by David Grossman

On the Origins of War by Donald Kagan

On War by Carl von Clausewitz

Ordinary Men by Christopher Browning

Platoon Leader by James McDonough

The Red Badge of Courage by Stephen Crane

A Rumor of War by Philip Caputo

Scribbling the Cat by Alexandra Fuller

Seven Pillars of Wisdom by T. E. Lawrence

"Shooting an Elephant" by George Orwell

The Sling and the Stone by T. X. Hammes

The Soldier and the State by Samuel Huntington

Storm of Steel by Ernst Jünger

The Things They Carried by Tim O'Brien

This Man's Army by Andrew Exum

Under Fire by Henri Barbusse

The Village by Bing West

We Were Soldiers Once . . . and Young by Harold Moore and Joseph Galloway

With the Old Breed by E. B. Sledge

Wooden Crosses by Raymond Dorgelès

Oxford

Looking for Class by Bruce Feiler

Oxford by Jan Morris

Brideshead Revisited by Evelyn Waugh

Philosophy

The Book of Job

Candide by Voltaire

Émile by Jean-Jacques Rousseau

The Enchiridion by Epictetus

Essays by Michel de Montaigne

Just and Unjust Wars by Michael Walzer

Madness and Civilization by Michel Foucault

Meditations by Marcus Aurelius

The Myth of Sisyphus by Albert Camus
Night Flight by Antoine de
 Saint-Exupéry
The Prince by Niccolo Machiavelli
The Stranger by Albert Camus
"The Wall" by Jean-Paul Sartre

Poetry
Caligrammes by Guillaume Apollinaire
T. S. Eliot
Robert Frost
"If" by Rudyard Kipling
Opened Ground by Seamus Heaney

Wilfred Owen
Jelaluddin Rumi
"Ulysses" by Alfred Lord Tennyson

West Point
Absolutely American by David Lipsky
Duty First by Ed Ruggero
"Duty, Honor, Country" by Douglas
 MacArthur
The Long Gray Line by Rick Atkinson
Soldier's Heart by Elizabeth Samet
"A Soldier's Obituary" by John Alexander
 Hottell III

AUTHOR'S NOTE

There is only the fight to recover what has been lost
And found and lost again and again: and now under
    conditions
That seem unpropitious. But perhaps neither gain nor
    loss.
For us there is only the trying. The rest is not our
    business.

T. S. ELIOT, "Four Quartets"

This is a true story. Considering the scope of time it covers, by necessity I had to rely on more than my memory in writing this book. To that end I was fortunate in having journal entries, letters, emails, and photographs to supplement my recollections. For the Afghanistan portion of the book I also had the benefit of patrol reports, maps, and radio logs. Additionally, I interviewed many of my soldiers and colleagues and asked them to read early drafts and to correct any inaccuracies. Finally, my research brought me back to many of the settings in the book, helping to bring focus to more hazy recollections. Where my memory conflicted with another, more objective source, I based my account on the latter. By necessity, the dialogue is an approximation of conversations that I can't recall verbatim. This book contains no composite characters or scenes, and the sequence of events is chronological except where indicated otherwise in the text. I apologize in advance for inaccuracies; none are intentional.

I am often asked why I wrote this book. At first it began as an attempt to hold on to memories I felt were slipping away from me. I hoped that by putting those experiences on paper, particularly the more painful memories from Afghanistan, I could finish the war I had brought back home with me. In early 2006 a friend approached me with the idea of publishing what I had written. I was ambivalent about whether my story would be of any interest to someone else, but I changed my mind when I recognized that the book might be helpful to readers. If I could tell the story well, it might help America better understand its military, might inspire some to serve, and most to appreciate, and might shed some light on operations in Afghanistan that seem to have been largely forgotten by the American public. I could either continue complaining that people lacked understanding about military service or I could do something to bridge that gap. Finally, as I watched my brother and my students inch closer to graduation and inevitable combat deployments, I felt compelled to pass on what I had learned. It is said that a fool learns from his own mistakes and a wise man from others'. I hope my mistakes make future leaders, in the military and elsewhere, a little bit wiser.

I owe the Army far more than it has extracted from me—for teaching and training me at West Point, for the opportunity to study and travel abroad, for the chance to lead and learn from incredible soldiers and officers, for the privilege of teaching, and for making me a better man and husband. I hope this book settles some of that debt, but I know my duty will never be complete. Ultimately, I wasn't strong enough to continue serving in uniform and to meet the duties I had to my family. My battles will no longer be fought in boots and camouflage, but I hope still to serve this country I love that has given me so much.

TO THE DEGREE THAT this book approaches the goals I set for it, I owe gratitude to countless mentors, colleagues, and family members. Although many are named in the book, brevity kept me from including others whose stories are intertwined with mine. Among those to whom I am most indebted are all the members of Spearhead Platoon, Alpha Company, 1st Battalion, 87th Infantry, and the nameless pilots and logisticians who helped bring most of us home. This book is written in memory of those in our ranks who made the ultimate sacrifice.

At West Point, thanks go to my classmates in the Class of 2000 and the many mentors who were role models of selfless service and professional dedication, particularly John Bender, Robert Doughty, James Gentile, Mike and Brenda George, Liz Halford, the Hooker family, Pat Hoy, Inga Kohn, Tom Kolditz, Chris Kolenda, Ken Lavin, Guy LoFaro, Mia Manzulli, Mike Meese, Rich Morales, Bill Ostlund, John Nagl, Andre Napoli, Jay Parker, Jeremy Quimby, Jack Reed, Elizabeth Samet, the Salomone and Silveira families, Don Snider, Colonel Wells, Father Wood, Scott Wheeler, and Paul Yingling.

At Oxford, I am indebted most of all to the Rhodes Trust for the opportunity of a lifetime and the invigorating challenge to "fight the world's fight." Bob and Sheila made moving to England less difficult than it could have been without their help. Lincoln College provided a wonderful home for my studies and a fascinating assortment of colleagues from all over the world. Thanks to my rowing and lacrosse teammates for teaching me the Queen's English and enduring my endless questions. I am grateful to Avner Offer for nudging my curiosity and honing my historical analysis and to my colleagues at Oxford for their friendship. To Ian, June, Victoria, and Elizabeth—thank you for the space to work, your company, and the endless cups of tea.

In the Army I am forever grateful to the Ranger School instructors who lived the Ranger Creed, especially Master Gunnery Sergeant Keith Oakes. I was proud to serve briefly with the soldiers of 2nd Battalion, 75th Ranger Regiment. Adam Rocke, Todd Brown, and Mike Perry took me in and made me a better platoon leader. Thank you. At the Old Guard, Colonel Charles Taylor, Darren Wilson, Ara Megerdichian, Glen Helberg, Carrie Wibben, and Kevin Jefferson helped me meet the regiment's high standards and were incredibly supportive in helping me transition from Afghanistan.

At Annapolis I had the pleasure of joining an incredible faculty. In particular I am grateful to Dave Bonfili, Dave Peeler, and Mike Halbig for finding me a home in the History Department and to the faculty volunteers in the UKSP who worked selflessly to help midshipmen.

My deepest gratitude lies with those who read early drafts and critiqued, encouraged, and arm-twisted me toward completion: Claude Berube, Barret Bradstreet, Todd Breyfogle, Leland Burns, Temple Cone, Brandon Dammerman, Mira and Alex Debs, Lauren Eisenberg, Chelsea Elander, Sean and Jen Fahey, Tim Feist, John Freymann, Jen Gaudiani, Chris and Ulcca Hansen, Joe Hess, Mike Howard, Marcus Jones, Katie Larson, Bryan Leach, Bill McBride, Trent Moore, Rich Morales, Chris Nelson, Marilyn Nelson, Jim Poisson, Jeff Robinson, Niels Rosenquist, Animesh Sabnis, Jason Sanders, Tim Strabbing, Luke Tillman, Brian VanDeMark, Dorothy Van Duyne, Susi Varga, Anna Wheeler, Ryan Worthan, Rob Yablon, and Paul Yingling. I am especially grateful to Nathaniel Fick for his support from beginning to end and to Tom Ricks for his advocacy and advice.

I was lucky in finding an outstanding agent and friend in E. J. McCarthy. Without him this book never would have left my laptop. Jane Fleming and the rest of the crew at Penguin Press have been nothing short of incredible, from editing through production. They taught me that some questions are worth asking even if they can't be answered.

My family couldn't have been more supportive of this endeavor, from reading drafts to finding pictures and letters, thereby opening up their personal lives to public scrutiny. To Kelsey for always smiling, to Bridget for leadership, and to Gary for keeping me honest: I'm proud to be your brother. To my uncle and grandparents, thank you for believing in me. To my in-laws, I am grateful for your love and encouragement. Most important, to my mother, thank you for giving me the courage to write.

And, finally, I thank Meena, my wife, editor in chief, and best friend, who gave me unwavering support and love. My words fall short, but Rumi's poetry comes closer:

In your light I learn how to love.
In your beauty, how to make poems.
You dance inside my chest,
where no one sees you,
but sometimes I do,
and that sight becomes this art.

AN APPEAL

Many people want to "Support the Troops," but are unsure what to do besides expressing symbolic support. There are a number of exceptional nonprofit organizations that help military families, veterans, and our wounded warriors. A portion of the proceeds from this book will be donated to the following organizations. If you can spare your time or make a tax-deductible contribution, please consider contacting these organizations to see how you can help.

Fisher House Foundation (www.fisherhouse.org)

Because members of the military and their families are stationed worldwide and must often travel great distances for specialized medical care, Fisher House Foundation donates "comfort homes," built on the grounds of major military and VA medical centers. These homes enable family members to be close to a loved one at the most stressful times—during the hospitalization for an unexpected illness, disease, or injury. There is at least one Fisher House at every major military medical center to assist families in need and to ensure that they are provided with the comforts of home in a supportive environment. Annually, the Fisher House program serves more than ten thousand families, and has made available nearly 2.5 million days of lodging to family members since the program originated in 1990. By law, there is no charge for any family to stay at a Fisher House operated by the Department of Veterans Affairs; and Fisher House Foundation uses donations to reimburse the individual Fisher Houses operated by the Army, Navy, and Air Force. No family pays to stay at any Fisher House!

Disabled American Veterans Charitable Service Trust
(www.dav.org)

The DAV Charitable Service Trust supports physical and psychological rehabilitation programs, meets the special needs of veterans with specific disabilities—such as amputation and blindness—and aids and shelters homeless veterans. The Trust accepts gifts through workplace giving campaigns, including the Combined Federal Campaign and United Way, employee matching gift programs, and similar special giving arrangements, and provides a variety of direct services for America's disabled veterans.

The Veterans Northeast Outreach Center
(www.northeastveterans.org)

Headquartered in Evan O'Neill's hometown, the Outreach Center provides support and advocacy to the over thirty-six thousand veterans in the region who are eligible for care. It provides a continuum of care to veterans and their families, from the very basic food and shelter needs to advocacy, information, referral, career, and education services.